Aggregression and Sufferings

Indians and Southern History

AGGRESSION AND SUFFERINGS

SETTLER VIOLENCE, NATIVE RESISTANCE, AND THE COALESCENCE OF THE OLD SOUTH

F. EVAN NOOE

The University of Alabama Press
Tuscaloosa

The University of Alabama Press
Tuscaloosa, Alabama 35487-0380
uapress.ua.edu

Typeface: Adobe Caslon Pro

Cover image: The Georgia Militia under General Floyd, attacking the Creek Indians at Autosee, ca. 1825; The Historic New Orleans Collection, The William C. Cook War of 1812 in the South Collection

Cover design: Sandy Turner Jr.

Cataloging-in-Publication data is available from the Library of Congress.

ISBN: 978-0-8173-2174-1 (cloth)
ISBN: 978-0-8173-6113-6 (paper)
E-ISBN: 978-0-8173-9473-8

Contents

Figures

Foreword

After waging war on Indigenous people and dispossessing them of their lands, how did white southerners then reframe their actions to make themselves appear the victims of ruthless Native aggression? How did white settlers and their communities come to think of themselves as victims of colonial violence rather than the perpetrators of it? These are the questions that Evan Nooe addresses in his engaging exploration of settler memory in the early nineteenth-century South.

Nooe focuses upon the recurring acts of violence that white southerners committed against their Indigenous neighbors. As Native southerners responded to these threats in kind if not in number, white settler history coalesced around a set of public and private narratives through which they portrayed their own violence as the defensive acts of helpless victims. White southerners, Nooe explains, weaponized the resistance of Native southerners to craft a regional identity justifying the forced expulsion and dehumanization of Indigenous people. In doing so they created a settler narrative that turned the tumultuous history of the region upside down.

Aggression and Sufferings asks us to rethink the origins of violence in the South, the enduring legacies of settler memory, and the ways that Indigenous people have shaped the history of the South on both local and regional levels. We are thrilled to include it as the newest volume in the "Indians and Southern History" series.

ANDREW K. FRANK

ANGELA PULLEY HUDSON

KRISTOFER RAY

Acknowledgments

The completion of this project would not be possible without the support and encouragement of dozens of individuals and several organizations. For their willingness to offer a helping hand, often compensated with nothing more than a simple “thank you,” I again humbly say thank you for making this book possible.

I have been fortunate to receive guidance from talented mentors that I have both sought out and lucked in to meeting by happenstance. Throughout the course of this project, Robbie Ethridge has provided invaluable critiques, suggestions, and limitless encouragement on the value of the work. I have lost track of the number of chapters and drafts she has been willing to comment on for me. There are few people in this world as well versed in the dynamic history of the Native South as she, and I am fortunate to benefit from her brilliance. Likewise, Ted Ownby and Charles R. Wilson proved enthusiastic critics and supporters willing to take on topics that at times stretched their own expertise on the American South but always offered insightful contributions to help maintain the work’s regional relevance. I am also grateful to the late John Neff for introducing me to the field of memory studies. Everything in this book connected to memory in the South started with conversations I had with him many years ago. While I can no longer thank him personally, I’d like to thank his family who shared him with us and to let them know his kindness and intellect still resonate with those who knew him. I am also indebted to Paul C. Anderson and Rod Andrew Jr. for helping crystallize the genesis of this project and its potential at the earliest stages. Furthermore, Rod has been generous with his time and support, insights on overlapping topics, and even sharing complementary research since my time at Clemson University. Additionally, I must thank Clarissa W. Confer for her passion and inspirational teaching on both the American South and Native American history. Her enthusiasm for the subject matter helped set the trajectory that resulted in this book.

Finding my way to the Indians and Southern History series with the University of Alabama Press has been a serendipitous experience with gratifying results. I was fortunate to be approached by both Andrew Frank and Claire

Lewis Evans, unbeknownst to each other, about my work and its suitability for the press. I could not imagine a better assemblage of professionals to help guide my book into its final form. The topical, chronological, and geographic scope of my project seems to merge at the center of a scholarly Venn diagram between the expertise of series editors Andrew Frank, Angela Pulley Hudson, and Kristofer Ray. They immediately grasped the project's goals and its importance to the history of the American South. Each offered vital and instructive critiques on how to make it better. Throughout the process Andrew has been a steadfast and welcoming mentor. It has been a true pleasure discussing the book, work, and life with him over phone and Zoom calls. I am grateful for this professional opportunity creating space to get to know Andrew and his family. As acquisitions editor Claire has been the model of professionalism. She has been everything a first-time author could hope for in seeing a manuscript through to print. I thank the two manuscript readers, Robert M. Owens and Gregory D. Smithers, for lending their time and expertise to evaluate the project. They each excelled at identifying areas that would benefit from improvement and providing instructive critiques on how to practically implement or address the revisions.

I am also thankful for the direction and support provided by several institutions that offered financial assistance and their staff that provided guidance on locating materials. This project is made possible thanks to financial support from the Clemson University Department of History, the University of Mississippi, Austin Peay State University, the UNC Charlotte American Studies Program, the Louisiana State University Libraries, the Institute of Southern Studies at the University of South Carolina, and a RISE grant from the Office of the Vice President for Research at the University of South Carolina. I am thankful for the talented librarians and archivists I had the pleasure of meeting throughout my research. In particular, I thank Jim Cusick at the University of Florida PK Younge Library, Jennie Amy and Ben DiBiase (though both since moved on) at the Florida Historical Society Library, Graham Duncan at the South Caroliniana Library, Jennifer P. Wiggins at Auburn University Special Collections, and Carol Mahler at the DeSoto County Historical Society. I am also grateful for assistance with reproductions and permissions for the images used in this book provided by Allison Hudgins at the Georgia Archives, Todd Hoppock and Edward Blessings with the University of South Carolina Libraries, and Kevin Harrell and Jennifer Navaree both at the Historic New Orleans Collection. I am also grateful to Sarah Mattics, Kathryn H. Braund, and the University of Alabama Press for permission to reprint the map of the Creek Nation following the Treaty of Fort Jackson. I would also like to thank the staffs at the Alabama Department of Archives and History, Clemson University Libraries,

South Carolina Department of Archives and History, the South Carolina Historical Society, the Georgia Archives, the University of Florida Libraries, the State Archives of Florida, the Louisiana State University Hill Memorial Library, and the Tennessee State Library and Archives. Finally, segments of this book were previously published as "Common Justice: Vengeance and Retribution in Creek Country," *Ethnohistory* (2015), and as "Zealous in the Cause: Indian Violence, the Second Seminole War, and the Formation of a Southern Identity," *Native South* (2011).

This project has also benefited from a generous cohort of scholars and several professional organizations which have provided opportunities to further refine portions of this book. I thank Kathryn H. Braund for providing feedback on parts of this project and ancillary pieces. She has given her time and shared her expertise without hesitation. Her encouragement has been especially inspiring. Additionally, this project is better thanks to the forums provided by the American Society for Ethnohistory, the Southern Historical Association, the Florida Historical Society, the Society for the Early American Republic, the Allen Morris Forum on the Native South sponsored by the Department of History at Florida State University, and the W. Brent Burgin speaker series at the University of South Carolina Lancaster Native American Studies Center. I thank Boyd Cothran, David Dinwoodie, Jeff Fortney, Matthew Jennings, Wayne E. Lee, Greg O'Brien, Alaina Roberts, Kristofer Ray, Christina Snyder, and Greg Waselkov for providing thoughtful feedback on the developmental work that went into this book.

I am also fortunate to have the support of an enthusiastic and encouraging group of scholars and administrators at my professional home at the University of South Carolina Lancaster. I am grateful for the interest and encouragement on this project offered by Walter Collins III, Todd Lekan, David Roberts, Stephen Criswell, Dick Van Hall, Chris Judge, Brittany Taylor-Driggers, Ashley Lowrimore, Suzanne Penuel, Ernest Jenkins, and Tracey Mobley Chavous. The community at USC Lancaster and the Native American Studies Center is one that I am proud to be a part of as I complete this project.

It is challenging to quantify the value of a sympathetic ear while navigating the challenges of research, writing, and publishing. As a result, I am fortunate to enjoy the privilege of getting to know a special group of colleagues who have offered and continue to offer their encouragement and friendship. For their willingness to listen, earnestness in offering advice, and ability to commiserate, I thank Matthew Bailey, Denise Bossy, Bill Boyd, Kari Case, Amy Fluker, Lisa Tendrich Frank, Daniel Grafton, Amanda M. Hartman, Juneisy Hawkins, Joshua Haynes, Jason Herbert, Natalie Inman, Lucas Kelley, Tony Klein, Eric Lager, Jennifer McCutchen, Maureen Meyers, Jamie Mize, Stacy Moore, Amanda Nagel, Steve Noll, Deirdre Cooper Owens,

Steven Peach, Otis Pickett, Deninne Pritchett, Christine Rizzi, Kristalyn Shefveland, Sheila Skemp, Minoa Uffelman, and Jeffrey Washburn. I must also thank my former colleagues at Charlotte for their collegiality and encouragement. Special thanks go to Paula Eckard, Jeffrey Leak, Krystion Obie Nelson, Jolanna Erickson, Mark West, Ashli Stokes, Karen Cox, Janaka Lewis, Peter Ferdinando, Carol Alexander-Higham, and Dan Dupre.

The most invaluable source of support and encouragement has been found with my family. My parents, Franklin W. Nooe and Sue Line, have unquestionably supported my professional pursuits and aspirations. As a family, they (perhaps unknowingly) fostered an inquisitive consideration of the past with childhood vacations and day trips to historic sites such as the Castillo de San Marcos, the Bulow Plantation Ruins, Old Fort Harrod, and the National Museum of America History. When I started work on this book, I never imagined having two children of my own when it was finally complete. I suspect I will frequently retell how Cora and Walt each napped as infants in my office into the late hours of the night while I pondered over nineteenth-century documents and proofread revisions. Most importantly, they reminded me (whether I wanted to be reminded or not) that the best parts of life take place away from work. I must also thank my mother-in-law, Pamela Srinivas, for her assistance and excitement to see an author in the family. Finally, there is no way to sufficiently describe the importance of Meena's support over the duration of this project. Meena has been an unflinching champion of my abilities and the potential of this book. She has literally and figuratively been by my side through research trips, conferences, and the writing process. This book would not be possible without her.

Abbreviations

ADAH	Alabama Department of Archives and History; Montgomery, Alabama.
ASPFR	*American State Papers, Class 1: Foreign Relations.* Washington, DC: Gales and Seaton, 1833–1998. 6 volumes.
ASPIA	American State Papers, Class 2: Indian Affairs. Washington, DC Gales and Seaton, 1832–34. 2 volumes.
ASPMA	American State Papers, Class 5: Military Affairs. Washington, DC: Gales and Seaton, 1832–61. 7 volumes.
AUL	Special Collections and Archives at Auburn University Libraries; Auburn, Alabama.
CRNC	*The Colonial Records of North Carolina.* Edited by William L. Saunders, 10 volumes. Raleigh: Josephus Daniels, Printer to the State, 1886–90.
CRSGA	*The Colonial Records of the State of Georgia.* Edited by Allen D. Candler, Kenneth Coleman, and Milton Ready. 28 volumes. Atlanta: Franklin, 1904–16.
CUSC	Clemson University Libraries, Special Collections, Clemson, South Carolina.
CW-BH	Benjamin Hawkins, *A Sketch of the Creek Country*, in *Collected Works of Benjamin Hawkins, 1796–1810*, ed. and intro. by H. Thomas Foster II. Tuscaloosa: University of Alabama Press, 2003.
EAIS, 30257	*Message from the President of the United States, Transmitting a Report of the Secretary of War, Relative to Murders Committed by the Indians, in the State of Tennessee* (Washington, DC: Roger C. Weightman, 1812), 16–18, *Early American Imprint Series, 1801–1819*, series no. 30257.
FHS	Florida Historical Society, Cocoa Beach, Florida.
FSUSC	Florida State University, Special Collections Archives and Manuscripts, Tallahassee, Florida.

GHS:BH	*Collections of the Georgia Historical Society: Letters of Benjamin Hawkins, 1796–1806*. Volume 9. Savannah: Savannah Morning News Print, 1916.
GHS:HL	*Collections of the Georgia Historical Society: The Letters of Honorable James Habersham, 1756–1775*. Volume 6. Savannah: Savannah Morning News Print, 1904.
LJWBH	C. L. Grant, *Letters, Journals and Writings of Benjamin Hawkins*, 2 volumes. Savannah: Beehive Press, 1980.
LSU-LLMVC	Louisiana State University, Hill Memorial Library, Louisiana and Lower Mississippi Valley Collection, Baton Rouge, Louisiana.
OLB-WC	*The Official Letter Books of W. C. C. Claiborne, 1800–1816*, edited by Dunbar Rowland. Jackson: Mississippi State Department of Archives and History, 1917.
PWD-RRC	*Papers of the War Department, 1784–1800*, Roy Rosenzweig Center for History and New Media, George Mason University, https://wardepartmentpapers.org.
SCDAH	South Carolina Department of Archives and History, Columbia, South Carolina.
SCHS	South Carolina Historical Society, Charleston, South Carolina.
SLAF	State Library and Archives of Florida, Tallahassee, Florida.
SNAD	Southeastern Native American Documents, 1730–1842, Digital Library of Georgia. http://dlg.galileo.usg.edu/.
TCC	Telamon Cruger Smith Cuyler collection, 1754–1941.
TPUS	*Territorial Papers of the United States*, edited by Clarence E. Carter. Washington, DC: Government Printing Office.
TSLA	Tennessee State Library and Archives, Nashville, Tennessee.
UF-PKY	University of Florida, P. K. Yonge Library of Florida History, George A. Smathers Libraries, Gainesville, Florida.
UGA-H	University of Georgia, Hargrett Rare Book and Manuscript Library, Athens, Georgia.
USC-SCL	University of South Carolina, South Caroliniana Library, Columbia, South Carolina.

Aggression and Sufferings

Introduction

In 1773 Anthony and Elizabeth Hampton settled on contested land along the Tyger River Valley in the recently organized Ninety-Six District of modern-day Upstate South Carolina. Joined by their adult children and grandchildren, the Hamptons' homestead facilitated the extension of South Carolina's colonial reach, pushing the northwestern fringes of the colony's claims deeper into Indigenous territory. While it's unlikely the Hamptons saw themselves as a menacing spearhead of colonialism, the family contributed to a multiplying threat of Native land loss and physical violence. The Hamptons' Tyger River settlement was part of a broader swell of white families pressing against and into Native territory. For generations the Cherokee and their Indigenous neighbors faced waves of aggressive colonial incursions that included slave raids, epidemic diseases, and militant expeditions into Native land. Since the end of the French and Indian War in 1763, British colonial officials sought to pacify settler aggression along the Cherokee-South Carolina border and assist in safeguarding the integrity of Native space. Much to the aggravation of westward-looking colonials, the British Crown attempted to contain settler expansion with the Proclamation of 1763. The royal declaration prohibited settler migration and colonial land sales west of the Appalachian Mountains, and through 1775 the British colonial government prioritized a policy of separation between white and Native peoples.

By 1766 Cherokee representatives and South Carolina colonial officials established a mutually agreed-upon boundary dividing white and Native space delineated by natural features and humanmade markers. When the Hamptons arrived in the Tyger River Valley, the uninhabited site they discovered was not a product of preordained grace but the result of an agreement between the Cherokee and South Carolina to refrain from American colonists settling along what contemporaries referred to as the "Indian Boundary."[1] The Hamptons' encroachment, whether done out of ignorance or opportunity, directly challenged Cherokee territorial security and disregarded imperial guarantees of protection for Native communities. The Hamptons' act of colonial aggression in 1773 precipitated the suffering they soon endured in 1776 when the Cherokee launched a war to defend their people and lands against colonial expansion. Ultimately, the Cherokee were unsuccessful. In the aftermath of conflict, white southerners such as the Hamptons prospered from the violent acquisition of Native land and the selective memorialization of their role as founding settlers. The Hamptons quickly reframed the memory of Native resistance along the Indian Boundary from settlers threatening Native safety and sovereignty to peaceful white victims brutalized by duplicitous Native neighbors. As the Hamptons prospered across generations, first as backcountry merchants to wealthy slaveholders and then influential politicians, they perpetuated a family lore that erased their role as aggressive invaders and portrayed themselves as suffering victims of Native violence.

Originally from Virginia, family patriarch Anthony Hampton was on the rise in the late eighteenth-century South. Born in 1715, Anthony descended from English colonists who arrived in Virginia not long after the founding of Jamestown. While his ancestors received generous land grants from the colony upon their emigration, by the time of his birth, the more than two thousand acres of colonial headrights enjoyed by his forebears had been either sold off or diluted through multiple inheritances. As a young man in the late 1730s, Anthony was farming on rented land in Prince William County, Virginia, with seemingly few prospects of personal wealth or community prestige. Not long after the death of his father in 1748, Anthony and his family, eventually including seven sons and two daughters, began a series of migrations that took advantage of colonial expansion and Native dispossession. The Hamptons headed to the western edges of the North Carolina colony, and by 1754 Anthony was able to purchase a three-hundred-acre tract of land along the Dan River in Rowan County near the Virginia border.[2] As a newly organized county in 1753, Rowan was vast and ill defined. The county's northern border followed the Virginia line, but its western reaches according to North Carolina's colonial government remained unspecified.[3] Over the next few decades, the Hamptons accumulated wealth through land speculation and local influence through county governance. When the French and Indian War hit settlers in North Carolina, the Hampton men served in the colonial militia. Alongside fifty mounted militia, Anthony rode in monthly patrols through the Dan and Yadkin River Valleys as far west as the foothills of the Appalachian Mountains to guard against Cherokee attacks.[4] For their service the colony offered militia men western land grants.

At least two of Anthony's sons, Preston and John, took advantage of the opportunity, claiming a total of five hundred acres that eventually became reorganized as part of the South Carolina colony. Despite the administrative adjustment, South Carolina honored the North Carolina grants, and Preston, John, and their brother Edward Hampton, who had preceded his siblings' relocation, acquired more property working as land surveyors and government officials on land that just a few years prior belonged to the Cherokee. One of the most prosperous endeavors for the Hampton men in South Carolina was thanks to Preston leading the family's involvement in the Indian trade. Under various company names, the Hampton brothers, including Preston, John, Henry, Richard, and Wade, prospered working in the South's deerskin trade, developing economic ties with the Lower Towns of the Cherokee at Keowee northwest of present-day Clemson, South Carolina.[5] With his sons' successes, Anthony Hampton sold off his North Carolina holdings to join his boys.

Whereas he had left Virginia decades earlier with little wealth or notoriety, Anthony and Elizabeth's venture into South Carolina benefited from capitalizing on the violent dispossession of Native Americans across the Carolinas. He acquired wealth through speculation of formerly Native lands, and social notoriety (and additional land) through militia service ranging against the Cherokee. His prosperity afforded him the opportunity to set up his sons' future ventures as they encroached on Cherokee borders and benefited from an increasingly one-sided Indian trade, thanks to the expulsion of the French as a colonial competitor to the English after 1763. While Anthony was well positioned financially to legally purchase a land title in South Carolina, historians have been unable to locate a colonial land grant for his homestead in South Carolina's Tyger River Valley, where he and his family settled. Most likely Anthony never applied for a grant due to the dubious legality of his homestead's location. At the time, the South Carolina colonial government established a buffer zone along the Cherokee border in which white settlers were prohibited from taking up residence. Anthony, likely following the lead of his sons, ignored the colonial decree and built his home within the buffer zone just one mile from Cherokee territory.[6]

The Hampton family's relocation coincided with a larger migration taking place by peoples of English and Scotch-Irish ancestry moving away from established settlements in the Virginia and Carolina colonies to lands with ambiguous and contested legal claims. The fringes of the South Carolina colony appealed to families such as the Hamptons in the early 1770s as a destination that lacked a clearly established American political or social order.[7] In 1767 the Charleston newspaper the *South Carolina and American General Gazette* reported that the Tyger River Valley was effectively devoid of any settlers.[8] The area remained sparsely populated into the early 1770s. This vacant land was, of course, not a coincidence but the result of a promise by the colonial government to provide the Cherokee protection from white settlement. Until the summer of 1772, the western border between North and South Carolina remained ambiguous. Catawba and Cherokee towns held considerable influence in the area through trade and politics. White families of limited and middling means without ties to the politically and economically entrenched families of Virginia or the Carolinas, such as the Hamptons at the time, imagined the uncertainty of destinations like colonial South Carolina's Ninety-Six District offering new opportunities in a fluid space. But such possibilities for encroaching settlers also came with the risk that Native peoples would justly defend their territory.

On the cusp of the American Revolution, growing instability shattered the settlers' short-lived calm in the Ninety-Six District. Cherokee from the Lower Towns aggrieved by colonial abuses, encroachment on Native land, and settlers' militarization of the border struck against white settlements along the Indian Boundary in the summer of 1776. Cherokee detachments made their way to the Tyger River Valley and raided the Hampton homestead, killing Anthony, Elizabeth, their son Preston, and their one-year-old grandchild. The raid against the Hamptons was not an isolated engagement or the result of an interpersonal grievance. The attack was part of a larger Cherokee war strategy to purge American settlers from squatting and encroaching on Native territory across Georgia and the Carolina colonies in the summer of 1776.[9] News of the Cherokee uprising spread quickly throughout the southern colonies. British officials looked upon the events with mixed feelings. The Cherokee campaign had the potential to complement the British Crown's effort to subdue the growing colonial insurgency in the South, but it also provoked settlers' ire about the British inciting Native Americans against colonists. Cherokee strategy aiming at exposed settlements meant that many of the early raids targeted colonial households and sparked fear and rage among colonists independent of their feelings about the concurrent American Revolution just getting under way.[10]

After learning about the destruction of the Hampton homestead, surviving members of the Hampton family rushed to join the revolutionary cause to exact retribution for their slain kinsmen. Henry, Edward, and Wade Hampton I, sons of Anthony and Elizabeth who were absent from the family homestead at the time of the Cherokee attack, swiftly enlisted in the South Carolina militia. Rather than address British efforts to subdue the initial salvos of the American Revolution in South Carolina, the militia's priority was to stamp out the Cherokee uprising. By the end of July 1776 six hundred South Carolina militia men, including Henry Hampton, signed on to join Col. Andrew Williamson's campaign against the Cherokee. Through the month of August, Williamson's army, supported by twenty Catawba scouts and five hundred Continental soldiers, tore through the Cherokee Lower Towns in modern-day Upstate South Carolina. The militias systematically rooted out the overmatched Cherokee raiding parties and razed Cherokee settlements, leveling homes, torching cornfields, and driving off Native livestock.[11] During the campaign, in an act of personal vengeance, Henry Hampton reportedly "killed with his own hand an Indian warrior, who had on his brother Preston's coat, which was immediately recognized as the one in which his brother was murdered."[12] While the Cherokee enjoyed initial success in the summer of 1776, white settlers from Virginia to Georgia banded together in mutual support to repel Cherokee advances and exact a harsh retribution through the heart of the Cherokee's Lower Towns. One Cherokee leader known as Turtle at Home recollected afterward, "Their numbers were much superior to any body of Warriors we could raise."[13] The cooperative effort on behalf of the southern colonies forced the Cherokee to terms in which the Patriot governments seized substantial land cessions across modern-day North Carolina, Tennessee, South Carolina, and Georgia. For the Cherokee people, it was the last war they ever fought against the colonials east of the Mississippi River.

Despite the Cherokee's commitment to peaceable relations with the United States after the American Revolution and the forced removal of several thousand Cherokee west of the Mississippi by the close of the 1830s, the memory of the 1776 Cherokee War resonated among white South Carolinians for generations. Within the Hampton family, the memory of the Cherokee attack against the Tyger River settlement became a traumatic spectacle and defining point of origin for the family in South Carolina.[14] As described by and perpetuated among surviving members of the family, the Cherokee raid was salaciously violent. Elizabeth and James Harrison, daughter and son-in-law of Anthony and Elizabeth Hampton, reported witnessing the violent deaths of their father, mother, brother, and infant child while concealed in nearby brush. Based on their retelling, the Cherokee warriors initially approached the Hampton homestead in a friendly manner, "as some of the Indians were known to both Preston Hampton and his father." Having no expectation of hostilities, according to family lore, Anthony Hampton met the Cherokee men "cordially," yet as he was "in the act of shaking hands" with a Cherokee man who approached the house, another Cherokee fired on Preston. At the sound of the gun shot, Anthony Hampton became the next target as, according to family memory, "the very hand which Mr. Hampton had, but a moment before grasped in friendship, now sent a tomahawk into his skull." The Cherokee raiders then killed Anthony's wife, Elizabeth Hampton, in a similar fashion, striking her in the head with a tomahawk. As retold by the Hamptons, the unnamed infant son of Elizabeth and James suffered the most jarring death. According to the Hamptons' account, a Cherokee warrior grabbed the small child, dashing him against the wall of the house, "which it spattered with its blood and brains." Among the violence, nine-year-old John

Bynum, grandson of Anthony Hampton, was taken captive by the Cherokee. Before leaving the settlement, the Cherokee set fire to the Hamptons' homestead. The attack's aftermath left a scene, as remembered by the Hampton family, produced by "fiendish malignity," with the "mangled bodies . . . lying scattered to and fro in the yard."[15]

Over the next sixty-five years, the Hampton family passed their oral history of victimization and revenge from one family member to the next. In conversation with Alfred Huger of Charleston around 1819, Wade Hampton I, Anthony's son, recalled his experience fighting against the Cherokee. Wade reminisced how "the Indians killed his parents and that he and his brothers vowed they would revenge their deaths." As veterans of the South Carolina militia, Hampton boasted to Huger that "each [brother] killed an Indian," adding, "We all kept our word, and a little more."[16] The family's thirst for vengeance imprinted upon the memories of those who witnessed the Hamptons' retaliation. In reminiscences taken from "descendants of the men who fought" alongside the Hampton brothers in 1776, subsequent generations were knowledgeable of the carnage the Williamson campaign wrought upon the Cherokee. In one incident near modern-day Franklin, North Carolina, Edward Hampton and thirty regulars blocked the escape attempt of a Cherokee party. According to the memory of militiamen at the fight, Hampton fought with a "zeal to punish the Indians" in retaliation for his family who "had been cruelly butchered." As the Cherokee attempted to flee, Edward Hampton, according to the memory of descendants who fought alongside him, "proceeded to the slaughter of as many Cherokees as he could."[17]

A parallel episode of personal vengeance occurred among the North Carolinians marching into Cherokee territory. In 1835 William Lenoir reminisced that he witnessed North Carolina militiaman John Roberson execute a Cherokee prisoner during the 1776 campaign because "the Indians had killed his father, or some of his relatives." While the general in charge wanted Roberson tried for a breach "of the rules of war," Lenoir recollected that the troops thought "seeing Roberson punished seemed rather disgusting." In accordance with the wishes of the men, Roberson was released, and the North Carolina militia continued its campaign of destruction against the Cherokee towns. Any disciplinary action was dismissed.[18]

Eventually, the Hamptons' memories of the Cherokee raid passed to the first generation of descendants that was not directly involved in the events of the Tyger River raid. In 1843 Wade Hampton II, Anthony and Elizabeth's grandson, recollected how his father Wade Hampton I and his uncles were zealous in the cause to exact revenge against the Cherokee for the Tyger River raid. He authored a family history for the *Charleston Mercury*, canonizing the family's memories of the summer of 1776. He described his father and uncles as "thirsting for vengeance" when they learned of the Cherokee attack. Wade Hampton II then went on to regale readers with the heroic accolades of the Hampton brothers defeating the Cherokee and British during the American Revolution.[19]

Alongside the Hampton family's rising prominence in South Carolina, their memory of the Tyger River Valley garnered widespread public interest and notoriety. In the early 1830s, Revolutionary War chronicler and future South Carolina governor Benjamin F. Perry collected oral histories on the war from residents still living in northwestern South Carolina. In 1834 and 1835, the Greenville newspaper the *Mountaineer* published Perry's "Revolutionary Incidents" as a series offering readers local reminiscences on the American Revolution.[20] One of Perry's most prominent and reprinted pieces was the 1776 Cherokee attack on the Hampton homestead, which popularly became known as "The Hampton Massacre."[21] The family history connected with South Carolina readers across the state and saw widespread republication and adaptation over more than the next century. In 1843 the *Charleston Mercury* newspaper and William Gilmore Simms's literary magazine *The Magnolia* separately printed lengthy retellings of the Cherokee attack on the Hamptons, as written by Perry.[22] In 1847 Perry authored an expanded chronicle of the American Revolution in South Carolina for the *Southern Quarterly Review* as a compilation of his earlier works, which again featured the Cherokee attack on the Hampton homestead. Before long, other chroniclers retold accounts of the Hampton Massacre, relying on Perry's original amalgamation of oral histories sourced from residents of the Upstate. In 1851 the twenty-seventh mayor of Charleston, Joseph Johnson, heavily relied on Perry's oral histories to retell the Hampton family's tragedy in his regional history of the American Revolution.[23]

In South Carolina's Upstate, the site of the Cherokee raid against the Hampton family become sacred ground as a public memorial to white victimization and Native violence that erased preceding acts of settler aggression against Indigenous people. While it is unclear whether the Hamptons ever reoccupied the Tyger River homestead for any significant amount of time after the American Revolution, by 1830 a man named Roddy Smith took over the property. When Smith arrived on the banks of the Tyger River, a neighbor welcomed him to the area by providing a tour of the Hampton family cemetery on his newly acquired property. As Smith cultivated the land over the next several decades, he preserved the 1776 gravesites of Anthony, Elizabeth, Preston, and the unnamed infant as they were when he purchased the land.

According to one visitor's account, Smith had kept his promise to act as an informal caretaker to the community's local heritage site. The visitor,

William S. Morrison, noted the Hampton burial site was plainly visible as an oasis among acres of plowed farmland, having "the appearance of an old grave yard" where "trees mark the graves."[24] Additionally, travelers moving along the roadway adjacent to the Hampton site publicly reported on the property as a physical testimonial on the landscape to settler victimization and Native aggression. One 1851 account published in newspapers in Greenville and Charleston reported how travelers on the road near the Spartanburg County Court House "passed near by where occurred in the Revolutionary war a bloody massacre." The former Hampton homestead now functioned as a notable roadside attraction where, as recounted in the South Carolina papers, "the bodies of General Wade Hampton's father, mother, and brothers lie buried . . . on the waters of Tyger river" marking how the family was "most treacherously murdered by the Cherokee Indians."[25] By the 1850s the Hampton Massacre was no longer a single family's oral history or local folklore. From South Carolina's Upstate down to the Lowcountry, Cherokee resistance to settler expansion in 1776 provided white South Carolinians a unifying point of coalescence and memorialized the origins of the state in Native violence and settler sufferings.

In the American South, settler violence and Indigenous resistance generated reciprocating processes of coalescence, facilitating the unification of white southerners. Through personal experiences and community memories, settlers and their descendants looked to their aggression against and suffering at the hands of Native Americans as generating an exclusionary regional identity built upon the violent dispossession of the Native South. As with the events and memory of the 1776 Cherokee attack on the Hampton homestead, chronicler John Haywood encapsulated this foundational sentiment among the white citizenry of Tennessee in 1823, writing "such was the irreconcilable hatred which the Indians and whites had contracted for each other, by a long continued course of aggression and sufferings, that it was almost as impossible for the government of the United States to restrain some of their citizens from acts of enmity, as it was for the Indian chiefs to restrain and keep within bounds, all those who were of their nations."[26] While Haywood limited his historical treatment to within the developing borders of Tennessee, much of the white South could characterize their personal and inherited experiences in the region as defined by a "long continued course of aggression and sufferings" between whites and Native Americans. While white southerners rarely acknowledged their own misdeeds or responsibility in the violence that came to define much of the antebellum period, individuals, families, states, and ultimately the region could look back upon the South's past through Haywood's perspective. White southerners falsely imagined the conquest of the region as justifiable retribution in response to Native resistance to colonialism. In doing so, aggression endured by and inflicted upon Native Americans alongside the contemporary and memorialized sufferings of white communities offered white settlers in the South an opportunity to coalesce in the process of the region's ethnic cleansing.

Traditionally, the concept of coalescence is a multifaceted anthropological model utilized to examine the transformation of Indigenous communities from precontact chiefdoms to Native tribes, confederacies, and nations in response to colonialism. The processes of coalescence and the reorganization of Indigenous peoples into coalescent societies vary significantly based on precontact cultural norms of Indigenous communities, the actions of colonizers, and the distinct historical interactions forged through Native and colonial exchanges. Scholars have identified numerous permutations of coalescence as a malleable model without constraining parameters. As anthropologist Charles R. Cobb states, coalescence "is a layered and multidimensional phenomenon that was practiced in a variety of ways and had numerous manifestations."[27] Indigenous peoples from the American Plains to Polynesia navigated a host of transformative circumstances as a result of colonialism that reinforced and created new bonds among culturally similar peoples.[28] At times, this meant Native-settler competition facilitated the centralization of disparate Indigenous groups with ethnically compatible traits, and in other instances Native people retained their decentralized settlements but reinforced reciprocal and kin bonds between distant towns.[29] In examinations of the Native South, anthropologists emphasize the distinct historic circumstances of Indigenous peoples of the seventeenth and eighteenth centuries fostering coalescence from remnant or refugee groups under the pressures of demographic collapse. A constellation of factors contributed to the shattering of precontact Mississippian societies across the South. These included the expansion of European settlements, the devastating impact of Old World diseases, accelerated warfare and violence, displacement, engagement with a global economy, and the transformation of captivity and slave raiding. Native southerners such as the Cherokee, Catawba, Creek, Seminole, and Yamasee forged new bonds or reinforced loose ties to navigate the circumstances wrought by colonialism.[30] From the contact era through the nineteenth century, coalescence represented the varied processes encompassing the social and physical amalgamation of disparate peoples with similar experiences coming together prioritizing reciprocity and cooperation for their mutual benefit.[31]

Coalescence as an encapsulating framework for the processes unifying the white South serves to emphasize the centrality of settler violence, Native resistance, memory, and place in the transformation of the Native South to the Old South. The coalescence of Indigenous peoples in the American South elicited reciprocal responses among white southerners from disparate ethnic backgrounds, classes, colonies, and later, states. While the white South never culminated in a coalescent society as a single integrated polity, the processes of Indigenous coalescence forged and sustained bonds between white settlers and their descendants in the US South. As once suggested by historian C. Vann Woodward, "the collective experience of the Southern people," in this case white settlers and their descendants, gave rise to a self-conscious place-based and racially restrictive identity for the region's white inhabitants.[32] In comparison to Indigenous coalescence, white southerners likewise navigated dynamic colonizing circumstances pertaining to migrations, imperial competition, accelerated warfare and violence, engagement with a global economy, and the codification of race-based chattel slavery. While settler societies noticeably expanded their borders and prospered at the expense of Indigenous peoples over the same period, white communities in the South came to ascribe a collective understanding of a place-based identity and demonstrated a mutually reciprocal "community of interests" likewise muting cultural divergences and binding an aggregate of similar individuals together.[33] The geographically anchored identity based in the settler conquest of the American South influenced how white Americans in the region saw themselves, their own history, and their place in the expanding United States during the long nineteenth century. White Americans living in the region came to identify with their physical location as the southern landscape came to embody a dynamic process in which their experiences, struggles, and memories endowed the region with qualitative substance.[34] Even when at times incorrectly professing their experiences as unique, white Americans living in the South constructed a conception of themselves and their region as distinct within the nation in response to Indigenous coalescence and various expressions of settler colonial violence.[35]

The adaptation and application of coalescence as a process to investigate the unification of the white South centers on the generative role of violence. While historians have previously put forth framing terms of southern "separatism" and "consolidation," none have attempted to grapple with the centrality of settler-colonial violence as a unifying factor for the white South.[36] As settler violence contributed to the coalescence of Native communities, Native resistance facilitated the coalescence of white southerners. Across North America violence played a common and critically transformative role in the processes of coalescence. As a strategic response, Indigenous peoples adapted to the violence of settler expansion with cascading consequences reaching far beyond the purview of settler documentation. Scholars of Native American history have pointed to a multitude of ways violence transformed Indigenous demographics, economics, and landscapes, resulting in the organization of new groups and identities.[37] In one example from the American South, violence played a formative role in Creek coalescence in modern-day Georgia and Alabama and became a critical part of their origin mythology. According to inherited oral histories, violence against supernatural and competing Indigenous peoples contributed to the coalescence of Creek towns and defined Creek connections to the Southeast.[38] Throughout the eighteenth century, Creek town leaders found themselves constantly facing common challenges stemming from settler expansion, thus forging shared experiences and mutual interests.[39] For generations historians of the white South have pointed to the significant and unifying role of violence among southerners as a common cultural trait.[40] Historian Bertram Wyatt-Brown put forth an influential unifying framework to understand white southerners' proclivity for violent delights as a product of "primal honor" in the antebellum South that articulated shared parameters and manifestations of acceptable behavior.[41] As an explanation of the white South's shared customs of violence, Wyatt-Brown pointed to inherited traditions of ancient European origin derived from prehistoric Indo-European peoples and their honor-related norms.[42] Others have put forth more local circumstances shaping the white South's unifying culture of violence, such as the weather, slavery, paternalism, class status, family and gender expectations, and Scotch-Irish ancestry.[43]

Yet, in considerations on regionalism, white solidarity, and violence, historians have largely removed Native Americans from the South's past. Historians such as Wyatt-Brown drew little attention to the influence of white violence against Native peoples in the South despite its ubiquity through the mid-nineteenth century. Instead, historical investigations into southern sectionalism have prioritized evaluating the South in opposition or comparison to the North, focusing on Black enslavement with a deterministic eye to disunion and civil war. The reception and longevity of such arguments "set the standard" for Southern history as scholars framed the antebellum South as those states that joined the Confederacy and supported a proslavery republic.[44] While still the predominant framework for southern regionalism, such an approach has not been without long-standing criticism.[45] As early as 1926, Frederick Jackson Turner stated, "Sectionalism in American history has been so commonly conceived of by historians as the struggle between North and South over slavery that the much more complicated sectionalism . . . has been neglected."[46]

A notable exception is found in John Hope Franklin's 1956 *The Militant South, 1800–1861*. In broad strokes Franklin considered the "phases of life that won for the antebellum South the reputation of being a land of violence."[47] Principally, Franklin's work fell in line with regional assessments of the South prioritizing slavery as a determining factor.[48] In a tangential consideration of frontier life in the antebellum South, Franklin alluded to the potential consequences of "the proximity of Indian tribes to Southern settlements." In an aside, Franklin considers how the threat of Indian depredations remained a persistent concern in the South "from the beginning of the [nineteenth] century down to the Civil War."[49] Despite broaching the opportunity to integrate Native history into the region, Franklin later suggested that "Native Americans played only a limited role" in the history of the South.[50] Distraught by such a characterization, Tiya Miles critiqued Franklin's cumulative work as effectively writing "Native people out of the South, ignoring the many Native nations that occupy the region and have contributed to shaping its history."[51] Since the late twentieth century, numerous scholars of Native American history have made similar objections to the state of southern history as a whole.[52] The utility of coalescence as an adapted framework to understand the unification of the white South not only serves to address the importance of settler colonial violence but also aims to intertwine Native and southern history. Adapting a traditionally anthropological model utilized almost exclusively by ethnohistorians to consider the white South addresses both the diversity of an interconnected region and the potential utility of transdisciplinary methodologies. Even with the flagging coercive strength of Native southerners through the early nineteenth century, Native Americans left an indelible mark on the region by predisposing settlers toward a shared place-based sense of community. White southerners looked to one another for mutual aid, constructed shared histories, defended one another from criticism by Northern reformers, and collectively chided federal Indian policies.

In inquiries outside the South, historians have grappled with the importance of Native Americans and settler colonial violence in forging an American consciousness and identity. Several of these important works focus on how American settlers ordered new communities as white colonists and their descendants encroached on Native space and violently displaced Native people. Historians Reginald Horsman, Jill Lepore, Fred Anderson, Patrick Griffin, and Peter Silver have examined the role of Native Americans and colonizing violence in codifying an American identity and even contributing to American independence.[53] For example, violence between colonists and Native Americans in the colonial Mid-Atlantic facilitated the unification of a wide-reaching white identity. As Peter Silver articulates, violence between Native Americans and settlers generated a political discourse characterized by a "horror-filled rhetoric of [settler] victimization" among colonists defining an "anti-Indian sublime" in which anyone who did not see the danger posed by Native Americans as acting against the best interests of a new group identity, more frequently referred to as "the white people."[54] The amalgamation of diverse colonists formed a homogeneous collective identity in opposition to an "other" represented by hostile Native Americans. As Silver explains for the Mid-Atlantic, "members of some groups came to suddenly see new kinships with one another."[55] Individual colonists who previously conceived of themselves as Irish, German, or English saw more in common with each other in opposition to their Indigenous neighbors.

In the American South, aggression against and suffering at the hands of Native Americans contributed to the coalescence of a white regional identity generated by the historic experiences of the South, the memorialization of settler victimization, and Native erasure over the long nineteenth century. As John Hope Franklin addressed in *The Militant South*, the persistence of Native communities in the region after the American Revolution "aroused grave apprehensions regarding the safety of the settlers," whereas the Mid-Atlantic and New England no longer faced such fears.[56] Though Franklin contends that Indian violence was primarily the concern of settlers on the frontier, white southerners in New Orleans, Charleston, and Savannah took notice of Native violence due to regionally connected networks and travel, the dissemination of salacious violence reported in personal letters and newspapers, paranoia, and their own community memories of Native-settler conflict. Culturally, white southerners embraced a militarist ethic grounded in shared bonds of honor and militant opposition to Native southerners.[57] Although some historians have discounted the cultural relevance of the white South's nineteenth-century martial tradition, regionally distinct traits offered white southerners the chance to embrace and perpetuate Southern militarism.[58] As proponents of the South's martial distinctiveness have pointed out, militia service, military education, and the maintenance of chattel slavery fostered a shared martial tradition across the region.[59] Colonizing violence against Native southerners through the mid-nineteenth century gave white southerners yet another forum to exhibit their civic militarism and bond in the shared experience of regional conquest. Throughout the antebellum period, white southerners never discounted the racialized bond with their national counterparts. Instead, white southerners across socioeconomic classes and states increasingly prioritized a regional identity, seeing themselves as interconnected within the nation and navigating place-bound circumstances.[60]

As white southerners supported each other in the conquest of the Native South, the region's martial ethos gave opportunity to further facilitate coalescence through an ethic of reciprocity among a wide range of collaborators.[61] White planters, merchants, middling and poor farming families, craftsmen, and squatters with a vested interest in the acquisition of Native land showed few qualms about the violent manner in which the processes took place and enthusiastically provided material and moral support to their fellow white southerners. Local, state, and national politicians in and from the South advanced and championed the violent seizure of Native land. Wealthy planters funded militia campaigns against Native communities. Poor settlers welcomed the potential of improved security. Merchants and craftsmen provided supplies and offered their services free of charge to assist in the dispossession of Native people. In times of open violence, a wide range of professionals volunteered to subjugate Indigenous peoples. Politicians, lawyers, newspaper editors, planters, and farmers made up the ranks of militia collaboratively razing Native towns. On the home front, white women in the South were often at the center of civic celebrations lauding the cause of conquest. Southern women supported volunteer soldiers preparing for war and organized to raise funds for militias. Perhaps most critically, white women in the South served as crucial conduits of family memories that personalized the region's ethnic cleansing as justifiable retribution for lost kin.

Directly and indirectly facilitating the violent dispossession of Native southerners provided the white South a culturally unifying experience across the region and through the memory of generations. For settlers and their descendants, collective experiences contributed to the coalescing of the white South and facilitated colonizing claims of ownership and nativism to the land grounded in a regionally bound sense of place.[62] While white southerners still conceived of their white non-southern counterparts as racially similar, they increasingly differentiated themselves by a sectional affiliation and prioritized a regionally bound, place-based identity so firmly that they referred to their southern countrymen as kin and upheld reciprocal martial obligations in the event of Native resistance to conquest.

ORGANIZATION

Aggression and Sufferings takes a chronological approach to consider the factors that contributed to the coalescence of a regionally bound white identity in the South as a product of violence between white and Native southerners. As articulated by John Haywood in 1823, "aggression" and "sufferings" both by and against white southerners involving Native Americans and the memory of those experiences, broadly categorize the framework of factors contributing to the coalescence of the white South. Throughout the antebellum period, violence between Native Americans and colonizers occurred across the South, ranging from interpersonal violence to state-sanctioned total war in a local, statewide, and regional capacity. White men participated in volunteer militias that patrolled and campaigned against Native communities. While militias often operated locally within their own counties or state borders, major conflicts against the Creek and Seminole prompted volunteers to travel thousands of miles beyond their point of enlistment to combat an enemy that posed no direct threat to their homes. As evidenced by such conflicts, southern states and territories often relied on one another to assail Native communities and collectively celebrated the honor and sacrifices of neighboring white southerners.

In another contributing factor, southern states and territories' reliance on one another provided a vehicle to criticize the federal government. In the wake of Indian resistance, white communities pointed to the federal government's lack of action as endangering white southerners. Towns, counties, territories, and states in the South lambasted the federal government as apathetic and negligent to the general safety of white communities for failing to take decisive military action or preemptively removing Native people. Likewise, the management of Indian affairs proved to be a frequent point of political conflict between southern states and the federal government. Tension mounted as northern states, often led by nascent abolitionists, attempted to derail Indian Removal and openly chastised white southerners' violent treatment of Native Americans. For the white South, Native Americans, the federal government, and white northerners increasingly came to represent oppositional others that were seen as impediments to the security, prosperity, and collective interests of white southerners.

Additionally, community memory played an indispensable role in binding the white South over an expanding region and throughout time. Concurrently and in the wake of the white conquest of the American South, settlers memorialized the experiences of their contemporaries and ancestors as celebrated conquerors of formidable savages and innocent victims of Native atrocities. White families in the South regaled their relations with tales of conquest and revenge against Native southerners to justify the violence against Indigenous peoples and establish their own indigenizing origins. White southerners proceeded to remake and retell the settler violence of Native expulsion almost as soon as the events took place. Newspapers spread sensationalized retellings of Native violence against white southerners and family memories romanticized the dispossession of the Native South. White communities across the region celebrated their militia's participation in campaigns of Native expulsion as justified by one-sided historic grievances concerning their white ancestors. Obituaries and burials of deceased settlers and soldiers provided future generations of white southerners a reminder of loss while rarely acknowledging the annihilation of Native communities. Historical chronicles by white southerners, often sourced from oral histories, provided a self-confirming account of white innocence and Native aggression. The monumentation of the southern landscape provided contemporary and future generations public testimonials to the suffering of white settlers and the vilification of long-expelled Indigenous inhabitants. Each reiteration offered white southerners and their descendants renewed claims to a constructed historical truth. Over time the various interpretations of the past created a self-referencing nexus with the same inherent biases to reassure white southerners' sense of victimhood and erase settler atrocities against Native peoples.[63] Through memory and reconstructing the landscape of the region, white southerners embraced a unifying image of the past as triumphant victims in the conquest of the South.

In considering the exhibition of violence between white and Native southerners, *Aggression and Sufferings* emphasizes the importance of an interconnected continuum ranging from personal acts of aggression to state-sanctioned wars of extermination. While consideration of the South's major Indians Wars recognizes the presence of Native Americans in the South, focusing on episodic US military intervention obfuscates the continuity of violence and does not adequately account for what is often amalgamated into "irregular" warfare. For instance, American military history frequently overlooks lesser-known Indian conflicts or those fought alongside wars with European powers such as the Oconee War or the Cherokee War of 1776. While the 1813 Creek War was a prominent event in Creek history and well known among scholars of American Indian history, the conflict still struggles to move out of the shadow of the War of 1812.[64] Notably, major treatments on the First Seminole War also project a misleading teleological compartmentalization of a conflict that eschews precise parameters. The sequential labeling of the First Seminole War establishes its relevance as a precursor to the more volatile conflict taking place when the Florida Indians opposed removal between 1835 and 1842. When focusing on a regional rather than state perspective and forgoing the deterministic downstreaming of Seminole coalescence, the 1818 American invasion of Florida is better understood as a continuation of the 1813 Creek War and expression of settler expansion.

Moving away from compartmentalizing Indian Wars also allows for emphasizing the importance of individual white southerners as active engines of colonial violence and Native dispossession. Local and interpersonal conflict between settlers and Native southerners gave white southerners cause for justifying and expanding violence against Indigenous peoples. Settler communities took on the shape of militarized outposts to claim disputed lands and intimidate Native neighbors. Native resistance to the expansion of white households gave settlers cause for indiscriminate reprisals. The manner, casualties, and justification for such reprisals were often beyond reproach within white communities in the South, regardless of mitigating circumstances or appeals by Native southerners. The self-ascribed victimhood of white southerners came to be a forceful political tool in the dispossession of Native southerners.[65]

Geographically, this work prioritizes events in the places that become Tennessee, Florida, Georgia, South Carolina, and Alabama. While by no means a comprehensive accounting of the region, the events and experiences under examination resonated widely throughout the American South. Local violence quickly garnered regional and even national attention. Newspapers in North Carolina and Kentucky kept a keen eye on Native-settler violence in Florida, Georgia, and the Mississippi Territory. Militia volunteers from Louisiana and South Carolina traveled hundreds of miles to assist white southerners they had never met in states they had never visited yet conceptualized the white victims of Native resistance as family within a region-based fictive-kin network.[66] Southern politicians aggressively advocated for federal policies and state prerogative over Indian affairs and championed Indian relocation by invoking the memory of local grievances against Native Americans and federal negligence. Promoting and embellishing their martial conquest, white southerners baptized themselves in the blood of their southern conquest attempting to relegate Native Americans to the past and claiming white nativism through an exclusionary identity of southerner intertwining whiteness and region.

Chapter 1 considers how divergent systems of violence and justice between Native Americans and white settlers functioned in the South. Operating within racially bound communities by the end of the eighteenth century, the practice of blood revenge among Native Americans and honor among white settlers generally satisfied the expectations of Native and white participants independently. As the American South increasingly became an intertwined space between Indigenous and white communities, conflicting standards on how to equitably resolve interpersonal violence threatened to erode the way honor and blood revenge operated as a restraining force on violence. Increasingly, nationalist authority in coalescing Indigenous communities displaced clan and town authority to resolve violent conflict. Complicating the transformation of Indigenous communities in the South, colonists, and later US agents, sought to displace clan and town obligations in favor of individual accountability as the preferred way Native southerners satisfied white demands for justice.

Chapter 2 investigates the contemporary and historically interconnected consequences of a series of settler deaths in the years preceding the 1813 Creek War. The deaths connect to both the past and future of the early nineteenth-century South. As white southerners moved into and through Native space, Creek men, eventually calling themselves "Red Sticks," expressed displeasure with unfettered white encroachment and responded with violence. The deaths of white settlers in Creek country, Tennessee, and at the Cache River along Kentucky's border reveal the value of violence to both white and Native southerners. Each episode connected to immediate grievances by Native southerners against white colonialism and white southerners looked upon the incidents as confirmation of Native savagery. The events resonated throughout the South by word-of-mouth, newspapers, personal letters, and government documents and became intertwined with the memorialization of white victimization. In the aftermath white southerners valorized the deaths of the early settlers and vilified Native southerners collectively.

The following chapter considers the white South's effort to combat the Red Sticks in the 1813 Creek War. For years, white Southerners had been advocating for an invasion of Creek country to subdue the Creeks and seize their land. The Creek civil war and Red Stick assault on Fort Mims gave white advocates of Creek annihilation all the justification necessary. Southern militia men and southern states and territories mobilized to act with minimal assistance from the federal government. With the US preoccupied with the simultaneous War of 1812, soldiers from Tennessee, Georgia, the Mississippi Territory, and the Carolinas rushed to the battlefields in Creek country. Throughout the conflict, southern militias and state governors coordinated and collaborated to invade and dismantle Creek country. In the years following the conflict, chroniclers of the white South's past memorialized the 1813 Creek War as a regional conflict. They championed the efforts of white southern militia men and chastised the federal government's indifference toward the defense of the southern frontier.

Chapter 4 explores the events from the August 1814 Treaty of Fort Jackson through the US acquisition of Florida to evaluate the implications of persistent low-level white-Native conflict. While previous interpretations of the Creek War end with Andrew Jackson and the Battle of Horseshoe Bend, violent conflict continued between white and Native southerners. After the Treaty of Fort Jackson, Native southerners in northern Florida conducted border raids and sought out international allegiances attempting to thwart white expansion and settlement along the Spanish border. White families along the border derided the federal government for failing to subdue the Creeks and demanded action. Eventually, an American army composed mostly of white southern volunteers invaded Spanish Florida under the guise of national security. For some volunteers, the ambiguously lawful invasion of Florida represented a chance at personal retribution for grievances about their ancestors. The invasion by federal soldiers, state militias, and US-allied Indian forces helped leverage the acquisition of Florida from

Spain and the relocation of the majority of Florida's Native peoples to a reservation within the new US territory. After the 1818 Invasion of Florida, white families across southern Georgia and Alabama praised the success as critical to their security and prosperity and memorialized the event as the beginnings of their own community's history.

Chapter 5 examines how the Florida Indians' resistance to their expulsion from the South sparked a unifying call to arms from white communities across the region. While major Native violence played out in Florida, white southerners as far away as Louisiana and Missouri headed to the peninsula determined to subdue and expel the Florida Indians. In public meetings across the South, local organizers rallied civic support for their "suffering brethren" in Florida. Southern states pledged men, money, and munitions to quell a "savage" foe that allegedly continued to terrorize the region. As southern men promoted themselves as protectors, they publicly lambasted the federal government for extending a "criminal kindness" to the Indians and failing to provide for the safety of white southerners. As white communities cheered militia musters, the war provoked an exhibition of martial enthusiasm, invoked calls for southern cooperation, and perpetuated racialized depictions of Native Americans in the minds of white southerners. The shared experience, cooperative action, and martial zeal of white volunteers from southern states facilitated the unification of white communities across the region.

Indigenous opposition to dispossession in Florida provided white southerners the opportunity to embrace and perpetuate a notion of Native violence against settlers as a hallmark of the region's past. Chapter 6 explores how white southerners constructed, propagated, and perpetuated harrowing tales of colonizers as innocent victims in the violent expulsion of the South's Native peoples. Constructing a regional memory of white victimization took many forms, including contemporary news reporting on Native violence, the private and public adulation of the dead, monumentation of the southern landscape, intergenerational family reminiscences, and printed chronicles of the region's past. The various mediums came to function as self-referencing loops reaffirming assumptions of Native aggression and white sufferings. Across the region and across generations, white southerners and their descendants shared accounts of white suffering that fostered a vicarious traumatization, whereas contemporaries and descendants came to internalize the violence against their compatriots and ancestors as their own. Personal correspondence on the loss of family members in Florida connected white southerners with people and places across the region. Distant communities memorialized the sacrifices of volunteers and consecrated the landscape to honor the deceased. Volunteers of the 1836 campaigns to expel the Florida Indians crafted historical chronicles describing the peninsula's Indigenous peoples as immutably violent toward settlers. Mid-nineteenth-century chroniclers selectively connected the victimization of Florida settlers in 1835 with colonial precedents glorifying their Spanish predecessors, presenting the conflict as a renewed Yamasee War, and celebrating white forefathers who combatted Native peoples during the American Revolution. Reports from Florida on the deaths of settlers and violence against settler families spread across the region, facilitating the contemporary and historical memory of white victimization. Collectively, these totems of settler memory produced a mythology of settler innocence and Native aggression that went largely unchallenged among white southerners into the late twentieth century. Settlers deployed this mythology to justify anti-Indian violence and Native dispossession of ancestral lands, and to construct historic origins stories for their nascent communities across the South. Combined with written historical chronicles, remembrances of white-Native violence transcended generations, defined families, and forged connections between white communities across the physical and temporal dimensions of the nineteenth-century South.

The final chapter addresses the memory of settler violence and sectionalism in the post-Removal South through the twentieth century. The campaigns to expel Native Americans across decades and selective memories of victimization offered white southerners a point of commonality. Settler families and their descendants were often at the center of crafting and perpetuating memories of white victimization and Native aggression in the conquest of the American South. In the sectional crisis of 1861, the memory of land secured through blood and loss gave cause for a generation of white southerners to defend their conquest. In the post–Civil War ruin, white southerners looked back upon their antebellum past as Indian fighters to find a conciliatory point of pride when reckoning with Confederate defeat. While white southerners may have been defeated by the Union, they could console themselves as descended from victors of earlier Indian wars. In the post-Reconstruction South, the legacy of inherited suffering and conquest continued to bind the white South. Southern politicians such as Wade Hampton III leveraged the memory of his backcountry ancestors to unify white South Carolinians under Redeemer Home Rule. Into the twentieth century, Confederate memorial associations likewise invoked reminiscences of Native resistance as acts of aggression to define the landscape through monumentation and memory.

A brief epilogue considers how southerners continue to make and remake memories of Native dispossession in the modern South. The section provides a comparison of how white southerners have glorified the conquest of the American South by erasing acts of violence against Indigenous peoples and how Native southerners remember the violence and trauma of the region's ethnic cleansing. An investigation into the monumentation of the modern South demonstrates the contrasting and conflicting memories of the past for settler and Native communities in Alabama. As white southerners dismiss the historic violence inflicted upon the region's Indigenous peoples, Native southerners express through family memories and commemorative architecture the trauma they have endured and their permanence in the American South.

1

"Endeavors to Put the Guilty to Death"

Systems of Violence in the American South

In the antebellum American South, a duel was not a hasty or haphazard affair. White men looking to properly partake in the ritual adhered to a complex set of procedures involving preliminary correspondences, a public airing of grievances, precise scheduling and location selection, attention to attendees, agreed upon weapons, and firing sequence. In 1838 South Carolina governor John Lyde Wilson even produced a reference text outlining proper dueling etiquette for those involved in the performance. As a manifestation of culturally sanctioned violence, the duel was far more than simply an attempt to murder or maim an opponent. White men in the South held the ritual in high regard as a method to defend personal honor, reinforce patron loyalty, affirm their class status, and publicly perform gendered obligations.[1]

Dueling embodied explicit manifestations of the white South's culture of violence regarding common expectations on the expression, execution, and purpose of violent exchanges. The violence served a purpose. The community of participants and observers held a consensus on the permissible extent of violent behavior and acceptable measures for interpersonal conflict resolution. Despite the prevalence of duels in the South and the popular memory of these ritualistic stand-offs, the South's elite white men were not the sole arbiters of the region's cultures of violence. Even within white communities, socioeconomic class status influenced the varying standards of acceptable violent behavior.[2] In addition, the South was home to a multitude of ethnicities and three major racial groups organized around white, Black, and Native identities typically describing Americans of European ancestry, African Americans, and Indigenous Americans, respectively.[3] Just as white southerners established acceptable parameters of violent behavior, Native American communities in the South had common expectations of culturally sanctioned violence embodied in the shared practice of blood revenge. Among many Indigenous groups of the eighteenth-century Eastern Woodlands, blood revenge functioned as a locally rooted system to facilitate equitable justice between groups delineated by matrilineal clan kinship. However, the practice of blood revenge was potentially at odds with settler expectations of individual accountability regarding violence and justice. Frequently, the involvement of white Americans, either as victims of Native violence or as advocates of abolishing blood revenge, precipitated reconsideration by Native southerners on defining acceptable standards for violence that crossed racial lines. As culturally divergent expectations operated in the same geographical space, exchanges of violence between white southerners and Native Americans had transformative ramifications on the region and its inhabitants.

During the eighteenth century, diverging parameters of violence and reprisal challenged the restraining forces implicit in corresponding cultures of violence. Homicide proved to be particularly challenging for Native and white communities to reconcile in the context of honor and blood revenge crossing racial lines. Up to the American Revolution, colonial officials frequently relied on the persuasive influence of Native leaders among individual towns and clans to placate colonists' calls for justice in the aftermath of a killing. Working within the framework of blood revenge, Native leaders and clans navigated and, at times, modified their own culture of violence to assuage the expectations of colonials who insisted on individual accountability. In the years after the American Revolution, white communities became increasingly resistant to negotiated settlements. In the final decade of the eighteenth century, a surge of violence between whites and Native Americans along Creek borders in modern-day Georgia and Tennessee threatened to throw the region into war. In 1797 settler accounts of the murder of John Gentry in Tennessee and Isaac Brown in Georgia by southern Indians characterized white communities as victims of Native aggression. Despite substantial grievances by Native Americans precipitating the attacks, white settlers leveraged their victimization to advocate for extensive reprisals against Creek towns. White communities not only vilified Native Americans as unrepentant savages but also lambasted the federal government for prioritizing the interests of Native communities and emasculating the survivors of Indian attacks. While an all-out Indian war was avoided, white communities in Georgia and Tennessee saw common interests in each other's experiences as both Native Americans and the federal government came to embody an oppositional other impeding the interests and jeopardizing the safety of white settlers. Settler memoires of white victimization at the end of the eighteenth century lingered for decades. Local family folklore perpetuated settler memories of Indian violence and predisposed future generations of white southerners to consider their own violent acts against their Native neighbors as justifiable vengeance in defense of their ancestors.[4]

Colonial Accountability

Blood revenge was a deeply rooted tradition among Native Americans in the antebellum South. The Cherokee newspaper the *Cherokee Phoenix* once reported that blood revenge, likely predating European colonization, "originated from time immemorial" and was "universal with the North American Indians."[5] As a clan-based judicial process, blood revenge operated as an intragroup mechanism to provide an aggrieved family satisfaction in the event a Native American of the same tribe or nation killed another member but of a different clan. In addition the law of retaliation functioned as an intergroup system shaping Native American responses to grievances accountable to nontribal members.[6] Combined, blood revenge and the associated law of retaliation operated as a system of conflict resolution and restraint to manage disputes involving homicide within a matrilineal clan framework to satisfy debts of life and death. In a matrilineal system, individuals inherited their clan affiliation from their mother, and the matrilineal line of ancestry emphasized women as progenitors of the clan. Therefore, violence against an individual was both personal and an assault against the victim's matrilineal family. To obtain satisfaction, the victimized clan had an obligation to retaliate to avenge any potential imbalance resulting from the death of a clan member.[7]

Within Native American communities, blood revenge restrained violent conflict, but English, Spanish, and French colonization of the American South beginning in the sixteenth and seventeenth centuries introduced diverging cultures of violence. Intermingling communities of Natives, settlers, and eventually enslaved Africans confronted "New Worlds" as colonialism reshaped the American South.[8] Throughout the eighteenth century, elements of blood revenge conflicted with colonizers' expectations of justice and retribution. First, blood revenge was predicated upon clan-based equity, not necessarily intent. Losing a clan member, either intentionally or accidentally, created an imbalance and necessitated retribution against the individual or community deemed responsible.[9] Second, matrilineal clan identity could supersede individual accountability. Though the specific perpetrator was typically the individual punished, another individual of the same clan could act as a substitute.[10] Finally, blood revenge, and the law of retaliation, was locally rooted, offering the potential for flexibility directed by clans and towns to determine the appropriate course of restorative justice.[11] By the early 1700s, French and English colonial governments faced challenges reconciling a Native emphasis on clan obligation in opposition to European expectations of individual accountability. Trade agreements between the Creeks and British sought to require Creek leaders to procure punishment of any who committed crimes against British citizens. South Carolina and Georgia colonial governments likewise emphasized individual accountability regarding violent exchanges. However, the colonies struggled to secure compliance even when explicit terms were written into agreements with Native towns and nations.[12]

During the 1720s British colonial officials witnessed firsthand the importance of local authority and clan-regulated retribution among the Creeks as rival towns and clan leaders challenged one another for influence in the English trade. For several years British settlers and merchants operating out of Charles Town, South Carolina, aligned themselves with Brims, who was the leader of the Lower Creek town of Coweta located along the Chattahoochee River. Brims was likely able to gain influence among the Creeks through individual acumen and vital family connections. In the early eighteenth century, Brims was able to facilitate a policy of neutrality in relation to the three colonial powers occupying the American South. As a result Brims and Coweta held considerable sway over the movement of English goods through the Lower Creek towns and facilitated a prosperous five-year span of uninterrupted trade. In recognition of his importance and influence among the Creeks, the British would regularly refer to Brims as Emperor.[13]

Despite his favor among colonial powers, Brims faced internal rivals. Colonial violence and warfare offered opportunities to undermine his position, especially with the English. To curry favor with the British, Cusabo, from the rival town of Cusseta, exploited British displeasure with Brims regarding Creek attacks against English settlers and Brims's unwillingness to assist in raids against the Yamasee, who were friendly with Coweta. In March 1723 Cusabo led Cusseta warriors against the Yamasee and managed to displace Brims from his position with the British.[14] While Brims may have considered executing Cusabo for undermining his position and killing allied Yamasee Indians, historian Steven C. Hahn suggests expectations of clan-based retaliation likely dissuaded such an order. Though clan reprisals limited additional violence and helped maintain stability, the British trader Tobias Fitch chastised the Creeks for allowing what he characterized as internal discord and treason. Fitch lamented that for such actions in his country, a man "would be torn to pieces by mad horses." What Fitch largely overlooked at the time was the consensus approach to Creek unity and a lack of centralized institutions regulating Creek policies across largely autonomous towns.[15]

In the French colonial South, government officials struggled to implement European standards of justice unilaterally and often had to make do with compromises when Native-settler hostilities broke out. In French Louisiana, the colony's founding governor, Jean-Baptiste Bienville, accepted Indigenous methods of justice when the Natchez executed six men for the deaths of five French colonials. Although not all of the executed Natchez men were directly responsible for the Frenchmen's deaths, historian George Edward Milne points out that even though uncomfortable with the execution of innocent men, Bienville saw the implementation of "native justice" as a method to terminate bubbling interethnic hostilities.[16] In investigating an episode of Choctaw vengeance and retribution around 1746, ethnohistorian Patricia Galloway found that the French encountered a difficult situation when a faction of Choctaw Indians led by Red Shoe murdered three Frenchmen. Even though the Choctaw accepted Governor Pierre de Rigaud's demands of retribution for the deaths, the Choctaw "expected the French, as the injured party, to carry out the killings." The Choctaw feared that if they acted as executioner, it would invite retaliation against them even if working on behalf of the French; thus, as Galloway suggests, "there would be an unending train of vengeance set loose."[17]

To maintain a prosperous relationship with the British, Creek towns adapted practices of blood revenge when beneficial to resolve disputes between settlers and Indians.[18] In 1752 the British insisted on the punishment of Acorn Whistler for suspected crimes against a band of English-allied Cherokee. However, Acorn Whistler was connected to both an influential Creek clan and a leader of the town Little Okfuskee. Initially the Creeks refused to act, anticipating retribution from Acorn Whistler's kinsmen. The British eventually found satisfaction when Chigelly and Malatchi of Coweta convinced Acorn Whistler's nephew to carry out the execution. As Acorn Whistler's kinsman, his nephew could act within his clan's matrilineal prerogative without fear of retaliation.[19] In assessing the murder of clan relations, the British Indian trader Thomas Nairne observed that "if a man kills his brother . . . there is no punishment inflicted," as the clan would be forced to suffer again if vengeance was taken against the perpetrator. Therefore, with Acorn Whistler's nephew acting as executioner, the family would not owe a debt to another clan or nation.[20] Although the nephew was safe from retaliation, historian Joshua Piker notes Chigelly and Malatchi were potential targets of retribution for orchestrating the execution. Possibly under a secretive order from Malatchi, Acorn Whistler's nephew was executed, and Acorn Whistler's son accepted gifts to circumvent obligations of revenge.[21]

During the early 1770s, the British seemed no closer to reconciling methods of administering justice within Native borders. The influx of Scotch-Irish immigrants encroaching on Creek land in the western part of the southern colonies exacerbated tension between Natives and settlers. In one instance, when British colonists came upon a pair of Creeks suspected as horse thieves in 1771 near Queensborough, they killed one man and assaulted the other.[22] The Georgia Colonial Assembly issued a denunciation of the colonists' actions and assured the Creeks that they would "bring the offenders to Justice."[23] As proxy for absentee governor James Wright, the head of the Colonial Assembly, James Habersham, emphasized the importance of a centralized authority as the proper means to resolve the dispute. Habersham made it clear that "any people within the Government . . . know that they should have applied to me to Obtain redress."[24] Habersham's words provided notice to independent-minded colonists of the government's prerogative to manage affairs of justice as well as reassured the victimized Creek family. While the Georgia Assembly prioritized the importance of centralized judicial procedure, satisfaction for the murder was not automatically a concern of the Creeks as a nation.[25] Initially, the young warriors of the Creek town of Okfuskee demanded retribution, but the deceased Creek's uncle interceded. In assessing a metaphorical balance sheet, the uncle decided the death effectively settled "an Old debt," simultaneously encouraging peace, restraining further violence, and preserving balance. The uncle's personal influence and familial prerogative held significant weight in deciding the course of action. The family, according to the uncle's recollections, owed the "white people" satisfaction for two Englishmen killed in 1770. He professed "it was Just, that one should die for another" to provide satisfaction even if the latter victim was innocent.[26] Conversely, Habersham imprisoned the unnamed colonist involved in Georgia intent on punishing the specific offender.[27] Consequently, the man had to fear reprisals by the colony of Georgia but not the Creeks.

With the incident close to settled, a murder in December again demonstrated the disparities between Creek and Georgian expectations of violent conflict resolution. When visiting the town of Okfuskee in Creek territory, Indian trader and plantation owner George Galphin learned that a Creek named Sugley killed John Cary near Queensborough.[28] On behalf of the Georgia Assembly, Galphin implored the Creeks to "have [Sugley] killed immediately" or risk involving the "whole nation in Trouble." Habersham reiterated that the execution of Sugley was "the best and only proof" to the English the Creeks desired peace with the settlers.[29] Whereas the Creeks displayed flexibility through local negotiations to settle a blood debt, the Georgia colonial government made uncompromising demands on the Creeks as a nation. Galphin and Habersham were willing to acknowledge the murder of John Cary as the act of an unruly individual, but the Creeks would endure the consequences collectively if Sugley escaped punishment. Despite the demands imposed upon the Creeks as a nation, the town and clan continued to play a significant role. The principal headmen of the Upper Creeks met with Sugley's family to select a kinsman to act as executioner in similar fashion to the Acorn Whistler affair. By March of 1772, kinsmen of the "same family of the murderer" carried out the deed, appeasing English demands and heading off any potential reprisal by an aggrieved clan.[30]

The murders of the Okfuskee Creek and Cary reveal the colonial imposition of a nationalistic culpability upon the Creeks collectively but also Native persistence of clan and town autonomy.[31] When settling the murder of the Okfuskee Creek in October 1771, family and town exercised their influence to limit violence and declared matters even. In expecting retribution for Cary's death, Georgia reinforced the collective responsibility of all Creeks and made non-negotiable demands. If the Creeks did not obtain satisfaction in the manner the colony saw fit, Georgia threatened to castigate all Creeks. In assessing both Creek procedures and Georgia's inability to impose order on colonists, Habersham lamented that "this is certainly not Government," seeing only lawlessness in the decentralized management of justice.[32] The principles of blood revenge afforded Creeks the ability to maintain clan and town autonomy and to accommodate demands made by external communities. In contrast, Georgia and colonial authorities held to expectations of individual accountability and punishment.

Civilizing Violence

As a result of the American Revolution, European empires saw their influence waning in the South. Still, the United States government and the newly forged states were unable to unilaterally impose their judicial expectations upon Native communities. Instead, the federal government began a social and economic initiative known as the "civilization plan" to gain influence within Indigenous communities. The sweeping initiative encouraged a reorientation of Indian societies, bequeathing American advancements in exchange for land.[33] Historian Theda Perdue characterizes the program as an ethnocentrically modeled endeavor to mold Native Americans envisioned as "savages" into "rational, republican, agricultural, literate, entrepreneurial, patriarchal, and Christian" men and women.[34] A key architect of the civilization plan was secretary of war Henry Knox, who set up the program in 1789 as a federally institutionalized effort to assure US expansion while limiting violence between settlers and Native Americans.[35] Knox's program first sought to assert the federal government as the exclusive authority over Native affairs and to exclude state governments and individual citizens from conducting land deals and treaties.[36] The second part of the civilization program aimed to reorient Native society in the image of American settlers and assimilate Indian peoples into the United States. Both aspects had mixed results, with states continuing to challenge federal authority and Native peoples selectively participating in advantageous aspects but declining others.[37]

In the American South, Benjamin Hawkins oversaw the implementation of the civilization program as the superintendent of the southern Indians starting in 1796. Originally from North Carolina, Hawkins served alongside George Washington in the American Revolution as an aide, and as a North Carolina senator from 1789 to 1795, and was involved in US negotiations in the South with the Choctaw, Creek, and Cherokee. Upon his assignment as superintendent, Hawkins took up residence among the Creeks in modern-day western Georgia. At his homestead, Hawkins established an exhibition farm to demonstrate American farming techniques and cotton cultivation to the southern Indians. Though an appointed federal official, his tenure spanned four presidential administrations, and Hawkins provided a stabilizing hand in the region working to balance federal objectives, Native rights, and white settler expansion.

Shortly after Hawkins's arrival in Creek country, he found himself immersed in the complexities of colonial violence, mediating between Native Americans, white communities, and the federal government. Intermittent violence between whites and Natives marked the 1790s as settlers encroached on Creek land and pilfered Indian property and resources. In separate retaliatory incidents in January 1797, Indians killed Isaac Brown near the Oconee River in Georgia, and John Gentry near Nashville, Tennessee. With fears of an Indian war sweeping the region, the deaths of Brown and Gentry facilitated the recognition of common interests between settlers in Georgia and Tennessee, while the federal government and Native communities came to embody an oppositional other blamed for endangering white settlers. As an advocate of restraining violence, Hawkins coordinated with Creek leadership, emphasizing the importance of individual accountability and the suppression of blood revenge to administer justice, much like his French and British predecessors. Through the process of administering justice for slain settlers, white communities leveraged a collective victimization to advocate for reprisals against Creek towns and rebuked the federal government for failing to provide adequate protection.

The circumstances of Gentry's and Brown's deaths are confined to the purview of settler perspectives. Neither seems to have left behind a written record of his own making, and historians are left with what others said about them, rather than accounts in their own voice. The minimal documentation on John Gentry comes from just a few newspapers reporting on him by name, and federal agents, specifically Benjamin Hawkins, investigating the circumstances of his death in Tennessee. The historical record regarding Isaac Brown is comparably more robust but still confined to the circumstances and memory of his death in Georgia. The documentation on Isaac Brown comes from newspapers describing his death, and a result of his surviving widow, Mary Brown, attempting to secure remuneration and state assistance to alleviate her destitute position. The resulting documentation on Gentry and Brown reveal just a glimpse of who these men were, as each seemed to live in relative obscurity as members of the lower class on the social and geographical margins of white society in the South. It was likely not until their victimization at the hands of Native Americans that these men became singularly valuable to white communities. While Brown's widow certainly had a vested interest in settling the circumstances of her husband's death to assure her and her children's well-being, white communities in Georgia and Tennessee leveraged the murders to rally support for expanding violence against the Creeks and to stoke dissent toward the federal government. Based on the surviving documentation, Brown's and Gentry's deaths likely mattered more than their lives to white settler communities.

According to the limited record left behind on John Gentry, he appears to have been involved in the fur trade and resided in Middle Tennessee. He was likely either a resident of Nashville or living in the recently established white settlement along the Cumberland River. Most of the information about John Gentry comes from Nashville residents writing to a local newspaper about his death. According to one account, on or about January 31, Gentry was hunting with two other men when Creeks ambushed them somewhere "on our frontiers." The most likely location is suggested by a corresponding letter from Nashville describing how "Indians killed a man and his horse on the waters of the Harpeth" located west of the city.[38] The available sources indicate that raiders likely killed Gentry and shot his horse in an opening salvo of gunfire. Gentry's two compatriots fled the scene uninjured but suffered "the loss of their horses and other property, which they had along with them."[39] While both published letters labeled the assailants only as "Indians," Benjamin Hawkins shortly afterward identified the men responsible as Creeks from the Upper Towns.[40] Even with Hawkins's efforts at a quick resolution, the news of Gentry's death spread fast and wide, appearing in multiple newspapers as far away as Vermont.[41]

In a similar manner, news of the raid on the Brown homestead in Georgia spread first through personal correspondence before eventually making its way into the press. According to one account in a Philadelphia newspaper, the attack on the Brown homestead involved "a party of Indians consisting of ten, crossed the Oconee, two miles from the Long Bluff and fired on Mr. Isaac Brown and his wife." The Philadelphia newspaper reported that "Mr. Brown was killed on the spot, and Mrs. Brown wounded."[42] In Georgia, however, newspapers took a more extensive accounting of events presenting the violence against the family as a salacious spectacle. Papers in Augusta and Savannah detailed how "a party of Indians, about 10 in number, attacked the house of a man, by the name of Brown." The papers explained that in the raid

Figure 1. Settler-Native standoff. Engraving by William Croome portraying white fears of Native attacks against settler households and families. From John Frost, *Pictorial Life of Andrew Jackson*. Hartford, CT: Belknap and Hamersley, 1847.

"Brown was killed [by] the second shot, his wife fastened the door, the savages rushed up and attempted to force it" open. Mary Brown, according to the paper, held off the intruders as "she seized her deceased husband's gun, which happened to be loaded, and fired on them, on which they retired to the swamp." An unnamed "negro," presumably an enslaved African owned or leased by the Browns, made an escape to a neighbor soliciting assistance. A company of men led by Colonel Lawson arrived at the Brown homestead and persuaded the "unfortunate widow and her children," as reported in the paper, to "leave behind the corpse of her murdered husband" and seek shelter. After securing the survivors, Lawson and a larger contingent of men returned to bury Isaac Brown but "found the Indians had been there, cut off the head from the body and carried it with them, and set fire to the house."[43] As reported, the deaths of settlers such as John Gentry and Isaac Brown confronted readers with the violent deaths and mutilation of common citizens, portraying Native neighbors as capable of malicious deeds against white communities.

Despite the presentation of men such as Gentry and the Brown family as victims of wanton Native aggression, the attacks were not random or without cause. Both incidents demonstrated the jeopardy white southerners placed themselves in when encroaching on Native land, and the utility of violence to communicate Indigenous displeasure. In Georgia the Brown family challenged Creek Indians when they attempted to establish a homestead and cattle ranch on the west side of the Oconee River in an area known as Long Bluff near Washington County. The Browns' attempted settlement at Long Bluff was part of at least two decades of contested land claims among the Creeks, Georgia, and the federal government. In the 1780s the state of Georgia asserted its right to the land after an illegal deal with a minority faction of Creeks. Historian Claudio Saunt described the transaction as Georgia using "strong arm tactics to intimidate and coerce several Creek leaders" and sidestepping the will of the Creek people. The transaction did not go unchallenged. By 1790 Creek leader Alexander McGillivray facilitated negotiations between the Creeks and US federal government to overturn Georgia's purchase.[44] As negotiations continued through the first half of the decade, Long Bluff remained a contentious settlement site with intermittent violence, as Creek Indians claimed it as Native land in opposition to white settlers from Georgia.[45] In 1796 the Treaty of Colerain confirmed Native ownership and promised to establish a boundary with guarantees of federal enforcement. Despite assurances, the state of Georgia and the US federal government failed to sufficiently keep white settlers in check.[46] The actions of expansion-minded settlers and the lack of follow-through on behalf of the federal government led to the "displeasure of young [Creek] warriors" due to white occupation and destruction of Native hunting territory.[47]

Similarly in Tennessee the death of Gentry took place on contested land along the Cumberland River southwest of Nashville. Throughout the 1790s the area remained Creek territory primarily utilized as hunting grounds but frequently became a place of violent resistance to settler encroachment.[48] In 1792 petitioners from the Cumberland settlement reported that "they have much to Dread from the Indians" and implied the potential for a general war claiming the "Recent murders and ravages Committed by them on our Frontiers, too evidently proves their Intentions on this quarter."[49] Upon hearing of the violence, Indian agent James Seagrove reported to the secretary of war, writing, "Creeks have been killing some white people." After hearing directly from the Creeks, Seagrove deduced the attacks were specifically targeting whites that "belong to a settlement south of Cumberland river," and he noted the lands were never sold or ceded by the Indians to the federal government or the state of Tennessee. Despite the Creeks repeatedly ordering the settlers off the land, they refused to leave, thus resulting in the implementation of violence to expel the invaders.[50] In addition to trespassing on Creek land, men like John Gentry represented a challenge to the economic interests of the Creeks. Though waning in the later part of the 1790s, the deerskin trade offered a valuable livelihood for young Creek men. For much of the eighteenth century, selling deerskins proved a lucrative endeavor, especially for Creek men without significant social standing in their town. White hunters, such as Gentry, trespassing on Native land and harvesting resources claimed by the Creeks, undermined the economic security of Creek hunters and the clans they supported through the trade.

When connected, the violence against Gentry in Tennessee and Brown in Georgia fits into a broader picture of Native Americans in the South attempting to secure their borders against white incursion and avenge prior grievances. In an examination of the late eighteenth-century Creek-Georgia frontier, historian Joshua Haynes contextualizes Creek tactics against white settlers from Georgia "as the deliberate policy of a coalescing, indigenous nation."[51] Intermittent and disparate attacks against Georgia settlers fit into a broader strategy of the Creeks patrolling their borders against white trespassers.[52] Likewise along the Creek-Tennessee border, Creeks employed a similar strategy to obtain retributive justice and maintain territorial security. Through much of 1797, conflict between Georgians and Creeks mirrored violence between Native Americans and settlers in Tennessee. In January a resident of Danville, Kentucky, reported the roads between Knoxville and the Cumberland proved a frequent site of violence. In one instance Indians plundered three loaded wagons. In another two white men killed a pair of Indians who were out hunting. There were even misinformed rumors that month that Indians had killed the legendary frontiersman Daniel Boone and his family.[53] From January through April, newspapers reported additional violence between whites and Native Americans in western Virginia, North Carolina, and multiple sites in Tennessee, including at Powell's Valley, on the Pigeon River, at Sharpe's station near Knoxville, on the Kentucky Road, and again on the Cumberland settlement southwest of Nashville.[54]

Refuting the justification for Native attacks against settlers and the Creeks' strategy of limited violence, white communities in southern states leveraged their position as victims to sound alarms of an impending Indian war, denounce the federal government for failing to adequately protect settler communities, and champion the individual rights of settlers to avenge Indian attacks. After the turmoil of the dispersed Indian raids in Georgia and Tennessee during early 1797, white communities in southern states collectively fed their own paranoia of a general Indian uprising. Likely in reaction to the attacks on the Cumberland settlers, a Nashville resident reported on February 1, "neither do I know what will be the consequence—but we have reason to fear the worst." Just five days later, another Nashville letter prophesied more dire circumstances, indicating "inhabitants in this country think that a war must inevitably be the consequence, provided [the Indians] commit any further depredations."[55] In Danville, Kentucky, a settler feared, "Our peace with the Indians is likely to be of short duration. The Indians and White People have already been killing one another."[56] To the east a North Carolina paper expressed a similar sentiment, reporting, "Strong apprehensions are entertained," by residents of the Cumberland settlement, "of a war with the Southern Indians."[57] By the summer of 1797, Tennessee governor John Sevier sent a pair of letters to the Cherokee warning against their potential to facilitate a war against white settlers. Sevier indicated that while war "would be disagreeable to the white people," there would be "dangerous consequences" for the Cherokee.[58] Sevier elaborated that Tennessee expected the Cherokee to assist in quelling any potential violence and reject messengers, presumably from the Creeks, "requesting or encouraging your people to make war." Sevier alluded to the "many poor women and children that Always Suffers in consequence of such events," suggesting retaliatory violence against Cherokee clans and families.[59]

Alongside settlers foisting the blame for violence on Indians, Georgians and Tennesseans took the opportunity to criticize the federal government for prioritizing the security of Native Americans and failing to provide adequate protection for white communities. As characterized by historian David Nichols, in the late 1790s the federal government often "sided with the Creeks, both because they believed Indians had a right to keep their lands and because a disaffected and well-armed Creek confederacy seemed a greater threat than disgruntled Georgians."[60] From Tennessee, an article in the *Knoxville Gazette* criticized the federal government for what it saw as preferential treatment toward Native Americans. The article implied the federal government's position was that "the Indians . . . should be protected and not the whites" in response to recent violence. In 1797 some white Tennesseans even attempted to rally against the federal government when the US Army expelled white settlers from Cherokee land along the Holston boundary.[61] Likewise, newspapers in Savannah and Augusta incited white Georgians by portraying the federal government as demonstrating an indifference to their sufferings. Laced with mocking sarcasm, one response to the death of Isaac Brown gave "thanks to our glorious federal laws, which prevent the widow and fatherless, from receiving any pecuniary compensation, for their little (tho' to them) great losses." The article continued, "Should the pursuers come up with the savages, and take vengeance for the blood of their fellow citizens, butchered in the arms of his helpless family—will it be deemed an unwarranted breach of Federal law?"[62]

Shortly after the public criticism, tensions almost boiled over between white Georgians and federal soldiers. At the end of April, a company of federal dragoons arrested four men "who had crossed the Oconee into the Indian territories, for the purpose of hunting, contrary to the laws of the United States." On the road to imprison the men in the federal garrison near Milledgeville, "a considerable number of the inhabitants of Hancock county, collected in arms, with a determination to liberate them." The armed standoff was averted only at the "interposition and particular request of the prisoners." The arrested men apparently felt confident they would not be confined long, as the Georgia governor was writing to federal judges on their behalf.[63] Such an adversarial position between Georgians and the federal garrison was not without precedent. In 1793 federal Indian agent James Seagrove communicated to Governor Telfair that spies were constantly monitoring his movements, and local militias patrolling around the federal outpost, and he personally received "threats of the most insolent kind." As Seagrove described, the primary point of contention from local Georgians was his effort to maintain peace between the Georgians and the Creeks or, as he described, his opposition to the settlers' "darling object, an Indian war."[64]

With Seagrove's observation in mind, it becomes clear that restraining violence was not a universal objective. In the immediate aftermath of several assaults and thefts against settlers, white men gathered in small companies and patrols to exact their own retaliatory justice. After the raid on the Brown homestead in Georgia, upward of thirty men crossed the Oconee into Creek territory to pursue the assailants but failed to catch up with those responsible.[65] In response to a Creek raid in April on Cumberland settlers that left eight dead, a party of white men tracked and killed "seven or eight" Indians in retaliation.[66] However, each incursion by whites into Native territory to obtain personal justice was prohibited by federal law. In private letters and through the press, Tennesseans and Georgians called out the federal government for impinging upon their honor-bound obligations as men to protect their community and obtain vengeance. In response to the raid against the Brown homestead, an article appearing in Savannah and Augusta papers directly denounced the federal government for impeding the honor-bound passions of men seeking their personal form of retribution. The unnamed author queried, "Can it be supposed that men tamely and quietly submit to see their dearest friends and relations murdered in their view and resist the impulse of nature, so far as to acquiesce in the horrid scene, by a tacit obedience to our unnatural law."[67] In 1791 similar circumstances necessitated the secretary of war, Henry Knox, to write Georgia governor Edward Telfair to advise against allowing militia companies to avenge the murder of James Rorie, as his death was on account of settling a debt owed to the Cusseta.[68] In response to the events of 1797, Tennesseans similarly made overtures of taking matters into their own hands if the federal government did not promptly obtain satisfaction for the deaths of white settlers. Tennessee governor John Sevier made it clear to the secretary of war that he expected "decisive steps" against what he considered the "savage cruelty" of the southern Indians.[69]

In response to the outrage from Tennessee and Georgia over the violence between whites and Native Americans in 1797, the federal government pressured the Creeks through Hawkins to provide satisfaction for the recent deaths. Hawkins implored the Creeks that the perpetrators "must be punished to prevent the whole nation" from being held responsible.[70] By November Creek leaders identified the towns of the accused but initially left the request unfulfilled. High Head Jim of Tookaubatche proclaimed that the nation had decided to execute the Yuchi Indian responsible for Brown's death, but the perpetrator had fled. The Creeks considered executing one of the perpetrator's family "but were restrained" by the request to hold the individual accountable rather than the clan. Though it took almost a year for the Creeks to apprehend and execute the men blamed for the deaths of Gentry and Brown, the collaboration between Hawkins and High Head Jim helped to persuade the Creeks that settlers in Georgia and Tennessee would not be satisfied by executing a substitute.[71] Settling the affair in such a manner demonstrated the continued flexibility in blood revenge and the law of retaliation to arrive at an agreeable solution for those parties desiring restitution. The Creeks' decision to modify traditional standards of justice in carrying out the executions demonstrated the potential adaptability of the Creek's culture of violence when negotiated at a local level. High Head Jim's conscious modification of his approach when attempting to carry out the execution demonstrated the adaptability within Creek practices.[72]

For white communities in the South, Georgians and Tennesseans were momentarily satisfied with the course of justice, largely due to the Creeks' willingness to modify their culture of violence and collaboration between federal agents. While white men of the era such as Hawkins conceptualized blood revenge as something that Native groups like the Creek or Cherokee needed to rein in, white settlers in the South regularly adhered to a similar sense of kin-based identity and familial relationships as justification for violence. Obligations to relations and community were defining elements of the frequently all-consuming adherence to honor. The necessity to maintain community-based markers of status could motivate white communities in the South to vilify an entire race in the wake of Indian attacks, conduct both legal and extralegal campaigns against Native communities, and disregard federal mandates at gunpoint. As contests continued over land and proper procedures of justice into the nineteenth century, white communities in the South found common cause against the Indigenous inhabitants of the region in their honor-bound pursuit of what they considered justice.

At the close of the eighteenth century, violence between settlers and Native Americans in the South calmed but did not stop. As federal Indian agent James Seagrove alluded to in 1793, many settlers actively incited violence with an eye to provoking their "darling . . . Indian war."[73] The motives of individuals in Georgia and Tennessee likely varied, but the all-too-common outcome of escalating conflict between whites and Native Americans was Indigenous land loss. States regularly demanded land cessions in the treaties that sought to abate violence regardless of who started the conflict. To protect against settler incursions and secure Indigenous borders, the Native communities in the region sought to solidify national institutions and allegiances among towns of ethnically similar peoples to protect life and property. For the Creek, the recently constituted National Council operated as a permanent fixture meeting at least annually to manage issues pertaining to land claims, federal annuities, Creek debts, and settler access through Creek land. In May 1798 the council selected a speaker and executive spokesman "to deliver the voice of the nation." According to Hawkins, decisions made by the National Council in concordance with the speaker were "called the will of the nation."[74] One task taken up by the National Council was passing laws defining acceptable parameters of violence.[75] The council formed a police force and asserted jurisdiction to enforce the "Laws of the Creeks" pertaining to punishing criminals.[76] Despite the strides, coalescence was not uniform or linear. Hawkins recorded doubts on the initial influence of the National Council, and council chiefs expressed trouble maintaining compliance.[77] In 1806 the murder of the National Council's speaker by two Creeks from Cusseta demonstrated the challenges of coalescence within Creek country.[78]

The coalescence of Indigenous communities like the Creeks likewise facilitated a recognition of common experiences among white settlers living along Native borders. Native tribes and nations offered regional markers for the United States and white settlers. As the federal government attempted to impede settler incursion onto Native land at the end of the eighteenth century, the delineation between Native and white space fostered an oppositional recognition of regional distinctiveness. In the US Congress, legislation regarding military appropriations in 1797 and trade laws with Native Americans in 1799 were forced to account for the distinctive circumstances of Native-settler borders in the South. The violence of 1797 shaped the House of Representatives' discussion on the Military Establishment bill that proposed a significant expansion to the US Army during a national time of peace. Advocates for the bill emphasized the need to fund armed companies and fortifications for the defense of the country's western border. In congressional debate, southern communities living in proximity to Native borders found a temporary ally in New York's John Williams. Williams articulated a sharp dichotomy on the bill between "those who came from parts of the Union where there was no danger from Indians" and settlers in close proximity to Native communities. Williams chastised the bill's detractors as "opposing measures intended to secure their fellow-citizens who were exposed to danger." In Williams's advocacy for the bill, he professed a need for military garrisons due to Indians' inability to preserve "a lasting peace." His position appears to be colored by his own prior fears living on an exposed border in New York where "no post [fortification] was kept up between them, so that they were always open to incursions."[79] While treaties with Indians in New York during 1796 and 1797 helped secure the state for settler expansion, anxious memories of vulnerability seemed to instill compassion on behalf of Tennessee and Georgia. As a result of one of President George Washington's two vetoes in office, Congress was unable to pass the 1797 Military Establishment bill, and Williams eventually conceded that the "demands lately made for the protection of the frontiers of Georgia and Tennessee" proved too expensive.[80]

Instead of providing additional protection, two years later Congress attempted to limit violence by regulating settler access to Native land through updated legislation on "trade and intercourse with the Indian tribes" in 1799. The recent violence between settlers and Native Americans in Tennessee and Georgia resulted in special consideration for the new package of federal legislation. As part of the updated law, Congress specified the prohibition of settlers trespassing on Native land explicitly in the South. According to section three of the legal code, any person trespassing on Indian country "south of the river Ohio" could be subject to a fine up to fifty dollars and three months' imprisonment.[81] No such provision existed in prior versions of the law or put similar penalties on settlers trespassing on Indian lands elsewhere. The specification recognized the distinctive circumstances and challenges in mediating peaceable relations between white and Native communities in the South.

In addition to delineating the borders of a southern landscape, the violence of settler expansion lingered in settler memories and shaped the perception of future generations. The survivors of Indian raids and their relations functioned as living memorials to settler victimization and rarely acknowledged their own agency in the violence brought upon them. For white communities in both Tennessee and Georgia, the deaths of neither

Gentry nor Brown were conceptualized as isolated incidents of their own time. In Tennessee, Governor John Sevier responded to the death of John Gentry and attacks against the Cumberland settlers by directly invoking the memory of Native aggression during prior conflicts. Writing to the secretary of war James McHenry, Sevier suggested the Indians and the settlers were inherently at odds, and he identified a "line of conduct . . . obtained from history" as evidence of insurmountable incompatibility. Specifically, Sevier invoked the memory of how "the Indian tribes generally joined the [French]" during the French and Indian War, and "Americans felt the weight of their savage ferocity." Additionally, Sevier recounted that during the American Revolution the Indians "uniformly turned round in opposition to the Americans and French," again to the jeopardy of white settlers. Through a selective consideration of the past and Native motives, Sevier concluded, "I am not induced to believe [the Indians] ever had, or will have any good will towards us."[82]

In Georgia the survivors of the Brown raid crafted memories of settler victimization by perpetuating one-sided remembrances of their circumstances. As a result of Isaac Brown's death, his widow Mary and five children were left destitute. To ameliorate their hardship, Mary was awarded compensation from the federal government of 185 dollars and received an unspecified amount from Georgia after petitioning the state for assistance.[83] While Isaac Brown's killer was brought to justice in 1798, and Mary received financial compensation, his death and the violence surrounding it were neither forgotten nor forgiven by the Brown family. After the 1797 raid, Mary Brown and her children became living memorials to Isaac's murder and progenitors of settler victimization to future generations. The Brown family stayed in southern Georgia at least through the early part of the nineteenth century as Mary scraped out a living for herself and her children. Throughout this time Mary cultivated remembrances of loss and victimization within her family through the memorialization of her husband Isaac Brown's innocence. When hostilities broke out between the US and Indians in Florida in 1818, the memories of wounds past broke open. Mary Brown called upon her son, also named Isaac Brown, to use the Indian war of his own time as an opportunity to avenge the death of his father. Mary's son volunteered to join the Georgia militia to fight alongside Andrew Jackson in what escalated into an American invasion of Spanish Florida. As Isaac marched off to war against the Indians, his mother pleaded, "Isaac, my son, the Indians killed your father, and may kill you, but I had rather hear of your being killed than to hear that my son had acted the coward."[84]

In Bertram Wyatt-Brown's seminal work *Southern Honor*, he noted the importance of "honor as immortalizing valor, particularly in the character of revenge against familial and community enemies." Through Mary's invocation of her slain husband, she venerated his memory and called upon the next generation to stand against a familiar enemy. By invoking the death of her husband, Mary Brown perpetuated what Wyatt-Brown identified as part of the "rituals of family remembrance" assuring continuity and the preeminence of the patriarch's legacy.[85] Mary's call for her son to obtain retribution in 1818 connected the violence of 1797 across generations. Mary's son joined the fight against the Florida Indians in 1818, and his mother fulfilled her role as a leading matriarch calling for blood retribution in a quest to avenge the death of slain kin. Although the US government oversaw the campaign that eventually became known as the First Seminole War, volunteers such as the younger Isaac Brown held deeply personal motives rooted in asserting claims to honor, defending their places of native birth, and seeking out a sense of kin-bound personal vengeance. Even when violence calmed, the importance of blood and honor to white communities in the American South meant that suffering endured was not easily forgotten.

2

"Baptized in the Blood"

Settler Death and Consecrating Native Dispossession

In a series of reminiscences written to acquaintances in 1858, Thomas S. Woodward took stock of his life living and fighting in the South. Born in Georgia in the 1790s, Woodward claimed descent from English veterans of the French and Indian War, and South Carolina ancestors who he proclaimed were "among the first companies, if not the first" from the colony to fight for American independence.[1] Woodward spent his younger years as a militia volunteer with Georgia and later Alabama. During his service he joined campaigns against the Spanish, Creek, and Florida Indians, assisting in the expansion of US territory through the first half of the nineteenth century. When reflecting on the 1813 Creek War, Woodward recalled with certainty what provoked the conflict and precipitated his participation as a Georgia militia volunteer. "As probably as anything," Woodward wrote from his perspective in 1858, "that an occurrence in Macon county caused the Creek Indian war of 1813-'14. It was the murder of Arthur Lott, in 1812 by some . . . Indians."[2] Woodward's assertion condescended at least a half century of turmoil, grievances, and negotiations into a singular event of white victimization. The violence that tore apart the Creek Confederacy in 1813 and eventually became a war of American conquest had deep and complicated causes that historians up through the twenty-first century are still attempting to fully unravel.[3] Yet, looking back from 1858, Woodward saw the death of a single white settler as the impetus for the conflict, and the resulting war justified as a campaign in defense of white southerners and their families. Had the Creek not allowed the murder of Arthur Lott, in Woodward's estimation, the US would have never invaded the Creek homeland, seized twenty-two million acres, forced hundreds of Creeks to flee US territory, and left an unknown number of Native men, women, and children dead across modern-day western Georgia and central Alabama.

While thoroughly reductive, Thomas S. Woodward's 1858 perspective on the 1813 Creek War alludes to the white southern experience and memory of the years preceding the conflict. In 1812 and 1813, a series of murders in and along the borders of Creek territory demonstrated the contemporary and historically interconnected consequences of settler expansion across the Mississippi Territory. Creek killings of white settlers, such as Arthur Lott, resonated throughout the South. Word-of-mouth networks, newspapers, personal letters, and government reports retold the sufferings of white settlers ambushed by Native southerners. News of settler deaths on Native land portrayed a dire situation in which the federal government was doing little to protect white southerners against an unpredictable and terrorizing foe. Those far removed from the scenes of violence came to hear of settler deaths through one-sided accounts offering simplified portrayals reducing white southerners to innocents and Native southerners to violent aggressors. Violence against individuals provided conveniently encapsulated and personally relatable points of reference to galvanize white fear and outrage. The creation of white victimhood through the deaths of settlers fueled calls for a war of extermination and offered shallow, though effective, justification for Native dispossession based on selective accountings of Native-settler conflict. While the deaths of the settlers covered in this chapter occurred between 1812 and 1813, they speak to both the past and future of the early nineteenth-century South. Each episode connected to immediate grievances of Native southerners against white colonialism, and white southerners looked upon the incidents as confirmation of an immutable Native savagery. Such incidents, however, were products of long-standing animosities generated from settler pressure on and exploitation of Native communities.

As Woodward's reminiscences on the conflict suggest, the settler memory of victimization served to indigenize white southerners in Native lands. Death and suffering gave white settlers and their descendants an opportunity to consecrate the land in their shared memory of the South as conquered space fertilized with the blood of white southerners. Settler interpretations of prior Native aggression and settler sufferings provided a means to mourn but also celebrate martyrs and new foundings for white communities. The physical remnants and shared memories of settler victimization offered recently established white settlements a historic origin and justified dominion. Shallow graves, informal cemeteries, and roadside burials operated in tandem with remembered sites of violence to memorialize a white landscape in southern spaces. White settlers traveling through Native land and their descendant communities memorialized their sacrificial founders and used their deaths to give legitimacy to the dispossession of Native Americans. After the conclusion of the 1813 Creek War, white southerners and their descendants chronicled the region's past and memorialized the slain early settlers as a glorified vanguard of martyrs securing the region for future white prosperity.

TRAVELERS

In 1803 the United States acquired the Louisiana Territory from France, adding more than 800,000 square miles to the country at a cost of fifteen million dollars. Known as the Louisiana Purchase, the transaction secured colonial claims to the Mississippi River Valley and stretched as far west as the Rocky Mountains. In the American South, white southerners now had unfettered access to the entire length of the Mississippi River and improved commercial stability, thanks to control over New Orleans. White Americans quickly flocked west to take advantage of new land claims and commercial opportunities. Native southerners, such as the Creek, now faced navigating the constraints of US states and territories along most of their borders. The removal of the French from Louisiana left Native southerners with only the Spanish in Florida as an accessible trading partner and political ally to counter the US.[4] Creating additional challenges for the Creek, enterprising settlers were not the only travelers through Creek country. White families, enslaved Black southerners, and whole communities from the eastern states moved westward as well. Though the Creek and the US government facilitated settler migration to western territories, many white travelers routinely stopped short of their destination, squatting and settling on Native land. Settler encroachment and demands for increased access to and through Creek territory provoked Native opposition. As federal and state governments failed to address Creek grievances, a rising faction of Creeks, eventually known as the "Red Sticks," acted against American invaders on their own terms. White travelers and homesteads provided vulnerable targets for Creeks willing to protect their homeland against settler encroachment through violent resistance.[5] Beginning in early 1812, a series of Creek attacks against settlers moving through Creek land over a two-year period alarmed white southerners across the region. As Native southerners resisted colonialism, white southerners cried innocence when caught in the nexus of settler-colonial violence.

In the spring of 1812, Thomas Meredith Sr. left South Carolina heading for the southwestern corner of the Mississippi Territory. Traveling with his extended family, Meredith was part of the crush of settlers moving west to take advantage of new opportunities resulting from American control over New Orleans and the Mississippi River. On March 26 Meredith's party stopped along the Federal Road to cross Kettoma Creek approximately 150 miles west of Indian agent Benjamin Hawkins's residence. While preparing to ferry the waterway, a Creek named Maumouth attacked and killed Meredith Sr.[6] Accounts of Meredith's death initially relied on testimonials from Sam Moniac, a wealthy Creek who operated a tavern along the roadway, and Thomas Meredith, the son of the slain traveler.[7] According to the younger

Meredith's account, his father's death was a consequence of drunken Native violence and settler innocence. Meredith reported that as his father and another unnamed "old man" waited to cross the river, Maumouth and others attacked their party unprovoked. Meredith described that "they fell on [Meredith Sr.] without interruption and killed him dead, . . . and sorely wounded the other with knives and sticks so much that" they feared the second man would not survive. Meredith reported that Maumouth appeared intoxicated and that his father had not engaged with Maumouth as the caravan was in the process of crossing the creek.[8] From the younger Meredith's perspective, his party of settlers was a benign element in Creek country exercising their right to partake in the nation's preordained colonization of the continent.

Rather than being a random act of violence, the death of Thomas Meredith Sr. intersects with a host of provocations facing the Creek in the early nineteenth century. As historian Angela Pulley Hudson has pointed out, the presence of white families traveling in Native territory was cause for concern. Hudson explains that Creek opposition "was a clear recognition that these migrants were not mere travelers passing through; they meant to stay."[9] Though Meredith expressed intentions to settle in Amite County, far from the major Creek towns, a traveling party encompassing women, children, and slaves threatened permanent settlement. Additionally, the Meredith party's decision to ford the river on their own undercut the collection of tolls that Creeks were promised by the American government. Since an 1805 treaty, the Creek had arranged to have proprietary rights to the construction of toll bridges and the operation of ferries within their borders.[10] In 1811, a year before Meredith's murder, Margaret Ervin Austill recounted the tension produced when her traveling party refused to use Native infrastructure. Austill's party of Georgians decided to hastily devise their own bridge across a rain-swollen creek and forgo paying Native tolls. Austill observed the decision "gave the Indians great anger, and they threatened us with death."[11] While Austill's party proceeded without incident, her observation demonstrates a long-standing dispute over how white travelers would move through Native land. Finally, Meredith's assault at a river crossing is culturally consistent with historic assessments of Creek raiding traditions. Small Indian war parties regularly exploited geographical borders such as rivers, swamps, and mountain ridges when engaging targets.[12] Waiting until just two elderly men were alone on the riverbank provided an advantageous opportunity. While a potentially impulsive murder, the death of Thomas Meredith Sr. demonstrates a host of contemporary grievances by Creek Indians beyond the immediate interaction.

As details of Thomas Meredith Sr.'s death spread, white settlers moving across Creek land and in neighboring states grew anxious. Hawkins and the

Creek National Council stepped in to dictate measures of redress for Meredith's death and assuage settlers' fears. Writing Georgia governor David B. Mitchell, Hawkins reassured that he "required of the Chiefs . . . to cause justice to be done without delay."[13] Hawkins's communique provided a calming voice about the safety of white travelers and reassurances of retributive justice. Still, Meredith's death occurred just a few months after Creek leaders had cautioned Hawkins as to the "difficulty and embarrassment they should experience in protecting persons and property thro' their land."[14] Beyond Creek borders white southerners saw Meredith's death as confirmation that the Creek as a nation were incapable of their own domestic oversight. In the post-Removal South, white southerners codified the memory of the murder as an assault perpetrated by untrustworthy Creeks against innocent whites. In 1851 planter and lawyer Albert J. Pickett's *The History of Alabama and Incidentally of Georgia and Mississippi* described the murder of Meredith as just one in a series of depredations against white southerners. Pickett used the incident to demonstrate the perceived disingenuous nature of Creek promises of peace. While specifically invoking the memory of Meredith's death, Pickett wrote that even though "Chiefs, friendly to the United States" made assurances of justice, it did not stop "the commission of other murders."[15] Published and read in the post-Removal South, Pickett's mid-nineteenth-century account of Alabama's past offered colonizers a history that contributed to the white South's reassurance of violence against Native southerners as retributive justice.

Before the Creek National Council could resolve the Meredith murder, two additional incidents threatened to escalate US-Creek violence in the South. In May 1812 the death of Arthur Lott paralleled Meredith's murder in several respects. Arthur was traveling westward from Georgia with his extended family across Creek land. According to information collected by Hawkins's assistant Alexander Cornells and a passing traveler, Tallasee Creeks ambushed Lott with an intent to rob the caravan.[16] Through a conversation with Arthur Lott's son William, Moravian missionary Johann Christian Burckard documented William's characterization of events, writing, "The assassin had fired three shots. One which missed was intended for another elderly man traveling with that party, all of whom were from Georgia."[17] Burckard continued, "Fortunately, the timely arrival of one of the sons of the slain man (they had gone in search of a cow left behind the night before, and now happened to be in the company of a mounted postman) caused the flight of the criminal."[18] In concordance with the Meredith murder, Lott's death coincides with a backlog of grievances by aggrieved Creeks against white travelers. While the travelers were potentially just an opportunistic target of Creek frustrations, the Lott family was directly involved in the expansion of the white South and violent dispossession of Native southerners. In 1858 Thomas S. Woodward may have pointed to Arthur Lott's murder as the cause of the 1813 Creek War, but the life of Arthur Lott and men like him fueled the tension generating such a monumental conflict.

The Lotts had been a family at the forefront of southern settler-colonialism since at least the mid-1780s. A 1787 petition places Arthur and William Lott, along with at least four other Lott men, in Burke County, Georgia.[19] Settled along the lower western corner of the county near Washington County, the Lotts lived in a precarious position on the edge of disputed territory. In Burke County accounts from March and August 1782 attest to the opposition settlers faced from Native southerners and robberies by rogue thieves. The residents requested the Georgia governor provide aid against Indian raids, and supplies to stave off food shortages.[20] Three years later state land surveyors revealed that the county was not much better off. Surveyors looking to divide lots near the confluence of the Rocky Comfort Creek and Ogeechee River described "Several Poor but Honest Families Settled on the Lowery Survey." The surveyor described the community as comprised of "the first Settler[s]" to the area and had "Stood as a wall against the insults that might be Expected from the Savages." For their fortitude the survey team recommended the white squatters be permitted to remain on the "Barren Sand Hills" they had made their homesteads.[21] In 1787 the Lotts and their community of settlers were still fending off Native opposition.[22] The late 1780s witnessed an uptick in raids by Creek warriors attempting to defend their rights over land between the Oconee and Ogeechee Rivers against encroaching white southerners.[23] By the end of the decade, Georgians began seeking out opportunities to retaliate in force. The short-lived conflict known as the Oconee War, primarily fought between white Georgians and Creek raiding parties from the Lower Towns, sparked the panic of white southerners as far as Savannah. The City of Savannah even drafted local enslaved Blacks to construct defensive works for fear of Indian attacks.[24]

Back in Burke County, the Lotts and other settlers were likewise devising ways to secure their own safety. Settlers responded to fear of imminent raids by nearby Indians and nearly daily panics by attempting to improve upon an outpost known as "Wood's Fort."[25] Such fortifications were common among settler communities and contributed to a militarized pattern of settlement by white Georgians pushing against Native borders. Nineteenth-century Georgia politician Absalom H. Chappell, likely hearing stories from his grandfather, described the installation and importance of such forts during the late 1780s as characteristic of settlement construction over the decade. Chappell described settlers at the forefront of militarizing their homesteads and characterized such settlements as "semi-military colonies."[26] He wrote "by their own voluntary labor the people of each neighborhood, when numerous enough, built what was dignified as a fort, a strong wooden stockade or block-house, entrenched, loop-holed, and surmounted with lookouts at the angles."[27] The residents relied upon the fort for protection, and such measures helped, according to Chappell, to assuage the "perpetual peril" that white Georgians felt under the fear of looming Indian raids.[28] Similar outposts were spread out along the Oconee River. According to Spanish sources, Georgian settlers had built at least seventeen fortifications across six counties.[29]

The fear of Native violence defined the day-to-day lives of settlers in outposts such as Wood's Fort, and their experiences were not easily forgotten. Chappell noted that women and children made permanent residence within the fort's walls. Men spent their days "scouring the country, and tilling, with their slaves, . . . at night betaking themselves to the stronghold for the society and protection of their families, as well as their own safety."[30] When Georgia congressman Wilson Lumpkin advocated for passage of the Indian Removal Act in May 1830, he invoked the memory of such fortifications as one of few guards against the violence expected of Native Americans. Lumpkin proclaimed that "amongst [his] earliest recollections are the walls of an old fort, which gave protection to the women and children from the tomahawk and scalping knife of the Indians."[31] As a child Wilson and his family arrived in Oglethorpe County with the first white settlers along Long Creek in the 1780s. In a sketch of his early life for the benefit of his children, Lumpkin recalled that the settlement "encountered all the difficulties and dangers of settling a wilderness." He and his family, Lumpkin continued, were "exposed . . . to frequent depredations from hostile and savage Indian neighbors." As he conveyed to his progeny, Native opposition to their encroachment required his parents to collaborate "with their frontier neighbors to erect, and live within the enclosed walls of a rough, but strong built fort, for several of the first years of their sojourn in Georgia."[32] For Lumpkin, memories of a childhood in a frontier outpost demonized Native southerners for protecting their land. Rather than acknowledge his family's active role in Indigenous displacement, Lumpkin conveyed to his children that his terror-filled childhood provided justification for the expulsion of Native southerners.

In addition to improving Wood's Fort, Burke County residents petitioned the governor in 1787 to deploy fifty men and horses to provide for their protection. The settlers wanted a company to occupy a "large space of uninhabited and unguarded land, lying between us and the Indians."[33] The result would have planted a formidable fighting force in disputed space between southern Burke County and the Lower Creek towns. The placement of soldiers would enhance the de facto territorial claims over the disputed range in favor of white Georgians. Governor Mathews responded by calling upon county militias. He ordered three thousand men into the field and potentially another "fifteen hundred more, should the first [call to arms] not be adequate." Mathews likely echoed the sentiment of many white Georgians when he stated that "the State never can have a secure and lasting peace with that perfidious [Creek] nation, until they have severely felt the effect of war."[34] In times of such anxiety, men of fighting age, like Arthur and William Lott of Burke County, were deployed as the volunteers filling the ranks of the militia companies taking the "effect of war" to the Creek.[35]

The violence perpetuated by settlers such as the Lott family fed conflicts like the Oconee War and scarred the collective consciousness of survivors. The conflict often took on a personal tone involving raids against vulnerable towns and households, blurring lines between battlefield and home front. In an October 1787 raid, a Creek party crossed the Tugaloo River into South Carolina and killed a white family. One settler account described how "a small party of Indians" attacked a white homestead and "killed a man, woman, and child & wounded a child of about three months old, which appeared to be done by the Ball which killed the mother."[36] Such "Horrors of war" as characterized by one South Carolinian, provided ample fodder for white southerners to memorialize the origins of their communities and valorize the deaths of white settlers as honorable sacrifices.[37] Writing at the end of the nineteenth century, Chappell characterized such deaths as leaving the early history of Georgia as "baptized in the blood of men, women and children."[38]

Native southerners nevertheless had a plethora of examples to memorialize the traumatic violence inflicted upon them at the hands of white southerners as well. In an account to the governor of South Carolina, Creek leader Alexander McGillivray characterized settler-Creek conflict as inhumane, with shades of genocidal sentiment perpetrated by southern militias. McGillivray wrote that "whenever hostilities commence between Savages and an equally ferocious set of white people circumstances of barbarity often occur shocking to the human heart." He articulated that the Georgian militias, populated by men like the Lotts, "warred with an exterminating spirit" against the Creek. McGillivray recounted how a party of Georgia militia men "killed an Ofkuskee man and woman whom they flayed when partially alive." In a separate incident, Georgians "fell upon a camp of Tallassees out hunting of whom they killed eleven men, women, and chldren." Georgians then mutilated the bodies. McGillivray described a particularly gruesome scene where "the pregnant women were ripped open, the men's privates cut off and put in the women's mouths with other monstrosities of the like nature." Georgians also raided a party of Cusseta Creeks with similar barbarism. McGillivray concluded the Cusseta were "treacherously murdered, the bodies of whom were so mangled that they couldn't be known by Relations."[39] Though Native southerners were more often than not the victims of violence on a grander scale, white southerners crafted false equivalencies of victimization to justify their actions as heroic origin tales veiled in themes of retribution, progress, and inevitability.

Though it is difficult to say for certain that Arthur Lott and his kinsmen were intentionally targeted by Creek men in 1812, the Creek certainly had reason to despise the family. Going back to the 1780s, the Lotts had an active role as settlers encroaching on Native space. The family contributed to the militarization of white-Native borders through the construction of fortifications. The family contributed to Georgia's deployment of militia companies against the Creek. Finally, while historical evidence cannot identify all able-bodied men who fought in the Oconee War, Arthur Lott would have been of fighting age to serve in the Georgia militia. Whether it was an assault of opportunity or a premediated revenge slaying, the murder of Arthur Lott and attack on two of his sons is emblematic of the animosity and violence between Native and white southerners over the preceding thirty years.

Homesteads

Settler homesteads encroaching on Native borders and territory risked entering a long-standing and complicated ledger of violence that could tilt against them before they realized they were in danger. Without legal title to the land, white squatters were beyond the protection of county militias. While some settlers struck deals to live on Native land, many did not and proved to be vulnerable targets for Native reprisals. In mid-May 1812, Native southerners from Upper Creek towns attacked two settler families at the Crawley homestead along the Duck River west of modern-day Nashville.[40] According to survivor Martha Crawley, a party of eleven Indians charged the house in the early morning. The women and children of both families had been left with a young man named Hays while Jesse Manley and Martha's husband, Captain Crawley, were away purchasing provisions. Martha Crawley attempted to barricade the door; however, she was unable to impede the assailants. Overpowered, Martha became pinned between the back side of the door and the wall. The intruders turned to the visiting neighbors, Mrs. Manley and her week-old infant. The attackers killed the infant and shot Mrs. Manley.[41] The Creek men then killed Manley's two other children, two of Martha's children, and finally Hays. The only survivors were Martha Crawley and another unnamed child. The Creek men took Martha as a prisoner, sacked the homestead, and fled for a camp on the Black Warrior River in present-day northern Alabama.[42] In the raid's aftermath, the Creek assailants left a scene of death and destruction. Widower Jesse Manley reported he found the homestead destroyed and the bodies of the dead exposed where they fell.[43] The exhibition of violence and the imminent retelling by settlers effectively terrorized white southerners who quickly learned of the ordeal and demanded revenge.

In the aftermath of the Duck River raid, many white southerners exhibited no pretense of restraint and even advocated for the extermination of the Creek people.[44] Mississippi territorial governor David Holmes requested that the secretary of war provide federal soldiers for defense against "unfriendly" Creeks threatening white settlements between the Tombigbee and Alabama Rivers.[45] Commander of the Mississippi Territorial Militia Ferdinand L. Claiborne advocated for decisive and punitive measures against the Creek. In a letter to a territorial settler, Claiborne believed the conduct of the Creek had for some time past merited that "they should suffer severely of their temerity . . . to teach them by force of Arms their <u>entire dependence</u>, and the sooner the better for the interest of this section of the Union."[46]

Tennesseans were some of the most vocal in calling for vengeance and linked the deaths to the preceding string of raids against white settlers and travelers. Jesse Manley, the widower of the Duck River raid, indicated that he desired to "raise a party to take satisfaction for the injury he had sustained."[47] Tennessee governor Willie Blount characterized the response of the general populace, stating that "the spirit of the people in this state is so roused by the conduct of those Creek Indians who recently massacred some of our citizens . . . that they probably cannot be restrained."[48] The Tennessee House of Representatives conferred its support for reprisals by giving the governor the authority "to order out a sufficient force to exterminate the Creek nation."[49] The Tennessee press fomented settler rage and described a state bursting to bring a genocidal war against the Creek people. Often reaching a national audience through reprinted columns, Tennessee newspapers spoke to the intersecting motives of Tennesseans eager for reprisals and financial rewards through the elimination of their Native neighbors. The *Nashville Clarion* laid out the opportunistic confluence of settlers' desires to satisfy a need for vengeance and hasten Native expulsion. An editorial espoused how a war with the Creek presaged settler dominion over the South and appealed to a sentiment of settler victimization. The column stated, "Fortunately the crimes of [the Creek] have supplied pretext for the dismemberment of their country. An expedition will soon have to move against them to extract a terrible vengeance for the blood they have spilt among us and the republic must indemnify itself for the expenses of this movement, by appropriating to itself and dividing among the conquerors the better part of that and which is so useless to them, and which will be so valuable to us."[50] The columnist saw the present circumstances as "a favorable moment of accomplishing a part of this great design," with the potential to seize Creek lands, strengthen American control along the Gulf Coast, and even take control of the Floridas.[51] Within the context of the parallel War of 1812, the *Tennessee Herald* championed Tennessee's "forty thousand men, brave, robust and burning with impatience," eager to be called into action in the protection of the southern frontier against the "scalping knife and the tomahawk of the Indians."[52]

White Tennesseans also sought to affirm the current generation as conquerors on par with their colonial era forefathers of the state. In the press, public declarations to arms directly invoked the legacy of Tennesseans' Revolutionary War ties and settler conquest. One newspaper lauded the precedent of defeating the British and Native Americans: "There are still living among us many of those veterans whose courage triumphed over the British discipline at the battle of King's mountain; and of the early settlers of this country hardly one can be found who has not acquired the reputation of a soldier in the wars with the Indians."[53] Just four months earlier, Nashville's *Clarion* echoed similar sentiments. An editorial challenged white southerners to reprise the role of Tennessee's white founders by "act[ing] as your forefathers, and at the point of the bayonet subdue or extirpate the savage foe."[54] The culmination of such desires, one Tennessee columnist contextualized, appealed to the ethnic cleansing of the region, proposing a future that "looks forward to the moment when all the southern indians shall be pushed across the Mississippi: when the delightful countries now occupied by them shall be covered with a numerous and industrious population."[55] Though white Tennesseans may mourn the loss of a few settler families, their deaths offered a potential catalyst for the providence of settler expansion across the South.

One of the most vitriolic calls for retaliation against the Creek came from the commander general of the Tennessee militia, future president Andrew Jackson. Similar to his settler compatriots, Jackson's aggression toward Native southerners leveraged the vilification of Indigenous resistance to white expansion within appeals to additional land acquisition. Jackson covetously looked south to Creek country, eyeing vital river routes and rich soils. Native resistance to white expansion provided an opportunity, as Jackson championed, to "consolidate it [Creek country] as part of our Union."[56] In personal letters throughout 1812, Jackson invoked the Duck River raid as a justification for the destruction of the Creek people, describing his desire for retaliation in apocalyptic terms. Writing the Tennessee governor, Jackson proposed he would "penetrate the creek Towns, . . . and think [himself] Justifiable, in laying waste their villages, burning their houses, and killing their warriors and leading into Captivity their wives and children."[57] In a message to the Chickasaw, Jackson reiterated his intentions against the Creek and signaled that any who opposed the US would likely meet a similar fate. Jackson threatened that if the Creeks did not turn over the Duck River assailants, "the whole creek nation shall be covered with blood. fire shall consume their Towns and villages: and their lands will be divided among the whites."[58] Jackson then intimated if the Chickasaw did not assist in the capture of the Creeks responsible, it was likely "our people in pursuit of them may kill the Chickasaw through mistake."[59]

Through June and July, Jackson led a press campaign in Nashville and Knoxville newspapers stoking white paranoia and calling for the invasion of Creek territory. In the *Knoxville Gazette*, Jackson claimed "for the spirit of the whole people is on fire. They burn to carry fire and sword to the heart of the Creek Nation, and to learn these wretches in their own Towns and villages what it is to massacre Women and Children."[60] Jackson further incited white fervor by suggesting individuals and families were still in jeopardy, politicized the brutality against the Manley and Crawley families, and challenged the loyalty of white men to stand against Native southerners. In a Nashville paper, Jackson argued that if the Tennessee militia did not act immediately, the state risked being drawn into "an Indian war, protracted through several years, and kept alive by the murder of peaceful families in the dead of the night."[61]

The following month Jackson detailed the violence of the Duck River attack, portraying the Creek as murderous savages to facilitate solidarity among white southerners. In a lengthy denunciation, Jackson cast any man who was unwilling to avenge the deaths of white settlers as lacking in masculinity and a blight upon his family. Combining both an exaggerated description of violence at the Duck River with affirmations to masculine familial obligation, Jackson wrote "woe to the man who is unwilling. . . . He that can see the infant babe of nine days old torn from the arms of its mother and beat to pieces upon the walls of the house—he that can see children of six years of age stabbed with knives, their heads split open with *Tomahawks*, and others torn to pieces, and devoured alive by dogs—he that can view in the midst of this scene a distracted mother crying in vain for pity, and receiving from the hands of savage monsters stab after stab, and arrow after arrow, into her body. . . . The wretch who can view the massacre at the mouth of Duck river, and feel not his spirit kindle within him and burn for revenge, deserves not the name of a *man*; and the mother who bore him should point the finger of scorn, and say *He is not my son*."[62] In focusing on the violation of white southerners' domestic space and familial connections, Jackson asserted settler ownership to contested territory and reinforced a patriarchal system built on obligations of mastery and deference.[63]

Despite Jackson's efforts, he was unable to spur a Tennessee-led invasion against the Creek in 1812. A plethora of factors stymied Tennesseans looking for revenge and land. In the Tennessee state legislature, the house pressed for war, but the senate hesitated due to the expense of arming ten thousand militia. Additionally, Martha Crawley, the abducted survivor of the Duck River raid, managed to escape captivity, thus removing an urgent focal point for advocates of invasion. The most decisive obstacle for Tennesseans pushing for war with the Creek came from the federal government.[64] Benjamin Hawkins proved an effective federal agent in pushing for restraint. In part thanks to Hawkins's reassurances to restore peace and bring the Duck River assailants to justice, the federal government never authorized the Tennessee militia to cross into Creek territory. As a result, the federal government and Benjamin Hawkins quickly became reviled targets for hindering white Tennesseans' revenge. Jackson castigated the federal government as "entirely absorbed in the invasion of Canada" and negligent in addressing threats of Native violence against white southerners.[65] Jackson criticized Hawkins labeling him a liar and an obstructionist bureaucrat who was only interested in the prosperity of Indigenous southerners.[66] The Tennessee Legislature even denounced Hawkins and held him partly responsible for what they described as "the most horrid and inhuman" murders committed by Indians on Tennesseans. The state government declared nothing less than Hawkins's removal could atone for his alleged "false representations."[67]

As white Tennesseans sustained their accusations of federal negligence, another Creek assault on settlers provided fodder for white southerners' call to exterminate the Creek. In February 1813 Creek men led by Little Warrior attacked a settler homestead near the confluence of the Ohio and Cache Rivers along Kentucky's western border. The Creek party was returning south after spending the summer fighting against the US alongside Tecumseh and the Shawnee in the Raisin River Battles during the War of 1812. Hearing rumors suggesting that the war expanded between Indians and the southern states, Little Warrior and his party struck against the Cache River homesteads of the Clark and Phillips families while on their return to Tuckabatchee. A neighbor of the settlers, known as Shaver, managed to escape the melee and relayed his account of the raid. According to Shaver, approximately ten Creek men known to the Clarks, entered the Clark home for a meal. After eating together the Creek men blocked the door and attacked Thomas Clark, his wife, and Shaver. The Creek men then attacked the Phillips house, where Mrs. Phillips was home with her children and a neighbor named Kennedy. The Creek men shot Kennedy as he walked out into the yard. In total, the Creek left seven dead as they resumed their journey to

Creek country.[68] News of the raid spread quickly, and in similar fashion to the Lott, Meredith, and Duck River incidents, white southerners were aghast at the violence, vilified the Creeks collectively, and called for reprisals.

As described in the contemporary sources, the raid against the Cache River settlers was particularly violent. Chickasaw agent Gen. James Robertson described the raid as "showing all the savage barbarity that could be invented."[69] Eyewitnesses and the press quickly disseminated news of the settlers' suffering and undignified deaths, which included sensational descriptions of a grotesque and macabre tableau. At the Cache River site, local militia "found the bodies of Kennedy and Clark" in the yards where they fell. They also reported "the situation of Mrs. [Phillips] was shocking beyond description." According to a personal letter published in the press, the pregnant Mrs. Phillips was found "entirely naked, cut open and the child taken out and hung up on a peg in the chimney." Additionally, "Her entrails were scattered all about the door and the hogs were eating them."[70] Historian Honor Sachs writes that such gruesome descriptions tapped into a familiar narrative for early American audiences "that equated attacks against the home with a distinctly Indian form of savagery." Native violence against the household portrayed Native peoples' supposed lack of humanity.[71]

Newspapers perpetuated the spectacle, providing descriptions of the raid's aftermath in horrific details. One of the earliest notices appeared in St. Louis's *Missouri Gazette*. A pair of travelers moving down the Mississippi River from Cincinnati to New Orleans relayed the broad details of the attack as they happened upon men heading to bury the deceased.[72] The Cache River raid made national news April 20 in Washington, DC's, *National Intelligencer*.[73] Just days later, the *Niles Weekly Register* provided the most salacious account of events from a reprinted personal letter. The published letter described the innocence of the white southerners, a betrayal by the Creeks, the wounds suffered by the settlers, and finally a landscape of mutilated bodies littering the homestead.[74] As historian Peter Silver points out, "sights that had filled rural people with helpless fear could be discussed with confident outrage once they were reduced to newsprint."[75] Dissemination through the press, provided white southerners a common point of reference to affirm their preconceived notions of their Native neighbors.

Like the Duck River raid, the destruction of the Cache River settlement provided white southerners justification to destroy the Creek. A petition from Franklin County, Tennessee, asked the governor to raise the militia because "the lives of our own wives, children, brothers, sisters . . . [are] exposed to the savage barbarity of the ruthless murderers." The petitioners claimed dependents were crippled by fear of imminent death, writing that "innocent wives & helpless children" were terrorized "in the midnight hours, [as] they dread each moment the tomahawk of the unrelenting savage."[76] The death of settlers in their homes, and especially those of women and children, enraged the sensibilities of white men of the South bound to an honor ethic. The murder and mutilation of white women challenged the patriarchal mastery of white men to provide for and defend dependents within their household. The destruction of settler homesteads, particularly when Native southerners violated domestic space, publicly undermined the gendered and racial hierarchy of the white South's ordered society.[77]

Consecrating Dispossession

The settler memory of victimization from violent incidents prior to the 1813 Creek War served to indigenize white southerners in Native lands. In immediate reactions to Native violence, settlers called for reprisals through public calls to arms, demanded the extermination of the Creek people, and petitioned governments for protection. Settler accounts of Native violence spread across the region through various mediums, including person-to-person conversations, correspondence, and most broadly through newspapers. The proliferation of settler accounts facilitated a memorialization of white sufferings that remade Native land as sacred ground for settlers and their descendants. Through personal reminiscences, local folklore, memorialized sites of trauma, and regional histories, white southerners reconstituted Native land by commemorating the landscape and memory of Native aggression and settler sufferings to consecrate the dispossession of Native peoples.

The roadways through Creek country functioned as arteries of communication, and white southerners spread accounts of fear and Native aggression east and west. Initially, news of the death of white settlers traveled by word of mouth, passing from traveler to traveler. Early nineteenth-century settlers moving across the region frequently encountered fellow travelers and conversed with one another, seeking out news and rumors, often with an eye to any dangers that may lie along their way. Travelers convened at taverns, campsites, and river crossings, all sharing information about their trials and tribulations.[78] In the instance of Thomas Meredith's death, news moved quickly among government officials and travelers along Creek roads.[79] In the case of Arthur Lott's death, the Moravian missionary Johann Christian Burckard documented how the rumor of Native aggression spread quickly. In a personal journal, Burckard recorded hearing rumors of the murder repeatedly while traveling from the Chattahoochee River to "the residence of Alexander Cornells' near Tucabatchie." Burckard first heard stories of the murder of a white man by a Creek from passersby about fifty miles from his destination and then again from five travelers who repeated the story about twenty-five miles farther into his journey. Eventually, Burckard ran into Lott's son, who recounted the event in full. The surviving members of Lott's party eventually completed their approximately hundred-mile trip west, likely spreading the details of the murder east and west along the roadway among fellow travelers.[80]

White southerners who never traversed Native space themselves learned of violence against travelers through personal networks of communication, and the news of imperiled loved ones weighed heavily on the minds of those at a safe distance.[81] Edmund Bacon, a planter and lawyer of Georgia and South Carolina, communicated with family members in Natchez, Mississippi, about the tumultuous nature of Creek country. In September 1811 and July 1812, Bacon expressed concerns about the threat of Native violence against white travelers. He noted how Indian hostilities prevented reliable communication with his family in his letters. More importantly for Bacon, he feared for the safety of family members, such as his nephew traveling through Creek country. Writing his sister in July 1812, Bacon was alarmed by the "hostile disposition of our red Neighbors" as news of the recent murders of white travelers reached him back east.[82]

White southerners who traveled through Native territory came to narrate and memorialize tangible reminders of Native violence on the land. Recollecting fears of Native violence after the expulsion of the Creek, one traveler reminisced that the "savages [were] more wild and fierce than" the wolves of the region.[83] The memorialization and physical remnants of settler deaths along the roadways narrated an ominous landscape. Hastily dug graves, informal cemeteries close to taverns and homesteads, and memorialized locales conveyed an aura of foreboding and disquieting metamorphosis of the natural landscape as white southerners moved across Native territory. Tending to the dead become a practical necessity and, likely, an emotionally complicated endeavor for white travelers. Settlers were faced with burying loved ones under circumstances more closely associated with a violent battlefield death than a peaceful passing in the company of family and the comfort of their own bed.[84] White southerners who died along the roadways required burials en route, usually in the vicinity in which they met a violent end.

One account of a death along the Federal Road noted the utilitarian circumstances required to bury a lost loved one. A traveler who described the death of a settler in Creek country around 1811 noted "a few hours before we got there, he had closed his eyes in death; they [the deceased's family] had laid him out, and expected to bury him that evening; but they could not get anything to make a coffin of, only split stuff to make a kind of box, and so put him in the ground."[85] Such circumstances challenged white southerners' ability to achieve a "good death" in the company of close friends and family and pass in a stoic and comfortable calm.[86] The spartan mortuary practices were more akin to the interring of low-ranking soldiers who died on the battlefield.[87] During the 1836 campaign to expel the Florida Indians, volunteers killed in action were buried in a strikingly similar manner. Tennessee volunteer Henry Hollingsworth described burying two of his compatriots in Florida near the Withlacoochee River. After returning to camp with the deceased, Hollingsworth described, "Graves are dug and a little before dusk the melancholy duty of consigning their bodies to their last earthly home in a strange land is performed." He continued, "Our two Tennesseans are laid side and side on some split boards in one grave, wrapped up in their blankets, and then covered with earth."[88] Those who died along the Federal Road in Creek country as a result of violent exchanges with Native southerners might later be valorized in family lore, but white travelers, like low-ranking volunteer soldiers, faced entering the afterlife under less than glorified conditions.

Impromptu burials necessitated improvised funeral services and truncated ceremonies. Examining the importance of funerals in late colonial Lowcountry South Carolina, historian Peter N. Moore notes that funerals were "very much a public event where a family's reputation, status, religious identity, and neighborhood loyalties were on display."[89] The idealized death in the early American republic consisted of tolling church or courthouse bells, a wake in the deceased's home, and up to six months of ritualized mourning.[90] For men like Arthur Lott or Thomas Meredith, the transitory setting of their deaths precluded such social recognition. The travelers' burial impeded the performance of the deceased's value to their community and failed to provide opportunity for the family to properly mourn the loss of a loved one. The condensed service offered families little time to grieve and no opportunity to inter the deceased in a family plot cared for by extended family or descendants. The bodies of the dead were left behind, and their surviving caravan moved on. Settlers passing by the raw gravesites confronted the fact that to die in Creek country meant to be buried in potential obscurity and anonymity.

White southerners also memorialized a landscape of suffering in Native territory by reconstituting the natural environment. White travelers moving along the Federal Road through modern-day Conecuh County in southern Alabama crossed over a tributary of the Conecuh River locally known as "Murder Creek." The name alone alluded to violence, tragedy, and death. According to the reminiscences of three white southern merchant-traders who sold goods to the Creek, white southerners did not refer to the waterway as Murder Creek until sometime after 1788. Recorded in a nineteenth-century history of Alabama, the creek earned its local lore after three outlaws killed a party of British loyalists led by Colonel Kirkland. While a notorious Creek known as "Man-slayer" was part of the murderous party, the other two members included a white fugitive called "the Cat" who fled to Creek country to avoid murder charges in another state, and a runaway slave named Bob. The multiracial assortment of outlaws encountered Kirkland's party along a trading path that crossed the creek. Both parties encamped on opposite sides of the shallow waterway for the night, but at midnight the outlaws "cautiously came over, and, seizing the guns of Kirkland and his men, killed every one of them, except three negroes."[91] In response the Creek leader Alexander McGillivray requested a close advisor in Creek country, the Frenchman Louis Le Clerc Milfort, to lead a company to bring the outlaws to justice. Milfort and his men captured the Cat. Upon returning him to the site of his crime, the Cat was "suspended to the limb of a tree" and while "dangling in the air, and kicking in the last agonies [was] shot by Milfort."[92] The episode, as relayed through local oral tradition and recorded by nineteenth-century Alabama chronicler Albert J. Pickett, explains "such is the origin of the name 'Murder Creek.'"[93]

During the early nineteenth century, rumors of the creek's etiology and a memorial marker defined the landscape for white travelers in the early 1800s as a site of Native violence. Along the banks of the creek, an informal memorial marked the location. Passing travelers observed a "black stump" and its blood-stained roots in a garden as commemorating the "unfortunate colonel and his companions" who died at the site.[94] The name itself piqued the anxieties of white travelers moving through unfamiliar land. Around 1811 Peggy Dow described her arrival at "a creek, called Murder creek," recording "it got this name in consequence of a man having been murdered there." Dow continued, "This circumstance made it appear very gloomy to me." The timing of her arrival made it necessary that her party camp for the night along the creek bank. She described her disposition that evening as "so much afraid" that only because of extreme fatigue she was able to sleep.[95] Another traveler, Adam Hodgson, camped at Murder Creek in 1820 and recorded a similar unsettling disposition, noting the creek's name "sounded rather [terrifying]."[96] Thanks to the security afforded by his traveling party and "with the aid of the glimmering of our wood fire," Hodgson was able "to dispel any fearful visions of the night" and get some rest.[97] Eager to leave Murder Creek behind, the travelers left by moonlight at four in the morning on their trek to Mobile.

Dow provided little context for her paranoia other than the name itself and a place-based memory of an unknown murder, but Hodgson linked the creek's name and his anxieties directly to memories of Native violence against white settlers. Rumors and hearsay collected along Hodgson's travels and retold through his published account reframe the creek's past as a site of violence perpetrated exclusively by Native southerners upon whites. In his

1824 travel journal, Hodgson believed "this little creek and valley derive their name from the murder of 18 or 20 Whites by the Indians, 15 years since. They were camping out when the Indians fell upon them."[98]

Some elements in Hodgson's account remain consistent with the more complete history provided by Pickett, specifically the location, the deaths of whites, and the surprise nature of the assault. However, Hodgson's reminiscence of Murder Creek's origins exaggerated the scale of death and erased the interracial complexities of those involved. Hodgson's account perpetuated a myth in which Native southerners were altogether responsible for the murder of unsuspecting white travelers along Murder Creek. Whereas the attack on Kirkland's party most likely left only five or so white men dead, Hodgson's account testifies to the power of rumor bending the memory of the incident. Hodgson's recollection also omits that the party responsible for the assault was a multiracial band of outlaws whose white participant was wanted for murder by both white and Native communities. Finally, Hodgson's knowledge of Murder Creek's etymological origins also lacks awareness that at least one of the outlaws was held accountable. The lack of a conclusion, closure, or service of justice in the case of Hodgson's recollections leaves open to speculation that the unnamed "Indians" responsible for "the murder of 18 or 20 Whites" could still be preying upon unsuspecting travelers. The naming of the waterway, memorial markers at the site, and erasure of white culpability in the 1788 murders provided white settlers in the first quarter of the nineteenth century a place-based manifestation attesting to the collective memory of victimization and an enduring sense of vulnerability. In defining the place and public memory of Murder Creek, white settlers crafted a sense of ownership to the land where people like them had suffered and died.[99] The site, in Native territory, became part of the white South's past and a totem to the maliciousness of Native violence against defenseless and unsuspecting settlers.

In the post-Removal South, the memory of martyred settlers and Indian fighters influenced local mythologies of descendant white communities. Settlers who endured Native violence prior to the 1813 Creek War forged new homesteads, memorialized their own efforts, and came to represent a founding generation of white southerners. Those who perished because of their efforts became sacrificial martyrs who demonstrated settler assumptions of Native savagery and retroactively justified Indian Removal as unavoidable. Those who exacted violence against Native southerners provided white communities emblazoned heroes of a frontier generation and a point of origination of their own identities. In their own time, Arthur Lott, Thomas Meredith Sr., and Thomas S. Woodward not only served to displace Native southerners but also facilitated the prosperity of new white communities. After their passing, or in Lott's and Meredith's cases because of their deaths, white settlers and their descendant communities celebrated the efforts of these three men as securing the foundation of white civilization in the South.[100]

After Arthur Lott's burial in Creek country in 1812, the caravan pressed on. The Lotts and their extended family contributed to the settlement of modern-day Columbia, Mississippi, along the Pearl River, located approximately 100 miles north of New Orleans. The US acquired the territory from the Choctaw in the 1805 Treaty of Mount Dexter, and shortly thereafter members of the Lott family settled on the eastern bank of the Pearl River.[101] As documented in a late-1930s Works Project Administration initiative, the early arrival of the Lotts anointed the settlement "Lott's Bluff" before being renamed Columbia in memory of the town back in South Carolina.[102] Since the second half of the twentieth century, the Lott family and Lott's Bluff continue to serve as the point of origin for the twenty-first-century community along the east bank of the Pearl River.[103]

In the late 1960s and early 1970s, Columbia, Louisiana's local newspaper the *Caldwell Watchman* provided readers with reminiscences on the lineage of the Meredith family and connected the community's origins to Thomas Meredith Sr.'s 1812 death. While Meredith died in Creek country, his family continued their trek west. The remaining Meredith caravan, including widow Abigail Naley and their nine children, settled in Amite County south of Natchez along the Mississippi River. There the Merediths multiplied, proposed, and contributed to the creation of new settler communities in the expanding South. James Meredith, a son of Thomas and Abigail, and his wife, Mary Ann Faust, moved to Caldwell Parish, Louisiana, in 1828, where they had seven children. Descendants of James and Mary Meredith found their way into nearly every aspect of nineteenth-century settler visions of progress as doctors, farmers, planters, masons, government bureaucrats, and elected officials.[104] Looking back from 1972, the *Caldwell Watchman* anointed the Merediths the "Largest Family in Caldwell Parish" and the de facto founding family of the community. The Merediths, as described by H. Ted Woods in the newspaper, predated the county, as they had migrated to Caldwell "ten years before this parish was created." In the founder's tale of beginnings, the sacrifice of Thomas S. Meredith in 1812 was invoked prominently and frequently as the family migrated across the South.[105] Woods reminisced in the paper that "it is well conceded that all [Merediths] in this area go back to the Thomas Meredith, who was killed in Alabama in 1812 by the Indian chief, Mormouth, while en route from South Carolina to settle in Mississippi."[106] The twentieth-century reminiscences on the Merediths presented Thomas

Meredith's 1812 death as a venerated point of origin for the family and commemorated his loss as a martyred founder of Caldwell Parish.

Of the three men, Thomas S. Woodward left the most enduring mark on the American South and became a memorialized icon of settler conquest in Winn Parish, Louisiana. During his life, Woodward prospered by facilitating Native dispossession as an Indian fighter on multiple fronts across the South. In the wake of Indian Removal, he contributed to the settlement of new white communities in multiple southern states and simultaneously erased Native historic claims to the region. For his efforts as an Indian fighter and settler, white communities in the mid-twentieth century celebrated Woodward's violent delights. Local memories of Woodward's accomplishments passed from generation to generation after his death in Winn Parish in 1859, defining the community's origin. Twentieth-century, local white residents celebrated his accomplishments and eventually installed a formalized memorial and historic marker lauding Woodward as an Indian fighter, wealthy slave holder, and community founder.

During his life Woodward was at the forefront of Native dispossession across the South. He fought with Georgia and Alabama militias against the Creek and Seminole and even served under Andrew Jackson during the invasion of Florida in 1818. When the Creek attempted to oppose forced removal in 1836, Woodward received a commission from the US Army to force Creek compliance. On the heels of Creek Removal in Alabama, Woodward founded the new town of Tuskegee over the remains of a Creek settlement. In an 1858 reminiscence, he recalled that when he arrived at Tuskegee in 1833, Creeks from Tuskegee, Chunnenugee, Chehaw, and Tallasee towns had gathered to compete in "a great ball-play." The next year the US government alongside state militias began the expulsion of thousands of Creeks to Indian Territory west of the Mississippi River. Despite a prior Native presence at Woodward's settlement, he claimed to have "built the first home" along a ridge at Tuskegee.[107] In making such a claim to origination, Woodward established the denial of prior Native occupation. As of 2023 the City of Tuskegee, Alabama, frames the community's origins as "founded and laid out in 1833 by General Thomas Simpson Woodward, a Creek War Veteran under Andrew Jackson."[108]

In about 1840 Woodward moved west to Winn Parish, Louisiana. His career in military service and land speculation proved lucrative. When he relocated he took with him about a hundred slaves, likely a mix of enslaved Blacks and "Indian negroes."[109] Additionally, he purchased fifteen thousand acres of land, accumulated several thousand more over the next two decades, and, with the aid of slave labor, built the settlement's most opulent mansion.[110] When he died in 1859, he was assumed to be the wealthiest man in the county.[111] In planning for his death, Woodward ordered the construction of an elaborate mausoleum to hold his and his family's remains. Yet Woodward was not the only person invested in memorializing his conquests. Familial descendants and community members passed down reminiscences of Woodward's accolades. In the mid-1960s, H. B. Bozeman of Winn County began a newspaper campaign to celebrate and formally memorialize Woodward as the town's founder. Bozeman first learned of Woodward's legend from an "old wizened man" in 1925.[112] Through his newspaper column "Winn Parish As I Have Known It," Bozeman shared with the community his efforts to preserve Woodward's remains and install a commemorative headstone. With the aid of Louisiana congressman Speedy Long, an unapologetic Louisiana segregationist, Bozeman secured a headstone from the US Army for Woodward in 1965 in recognition of the founder's military service against the Creek in 1836.[113] Montgomery, Louisiana, whose land at one time was nearly wholly owned by Woodward, eventually placed a historical marker near the town's center along Highway 71, singling out Woodward for founding the settlement in 1840.[114]

3

"Thoroughly Aroused to Vengeance"

The Invasion of Creek Country

In 1860 John F. H. Claiborne denounced the federal government's resolve to provide for the security of white settlers in the Mississippi Territory prior to start of the 1813 Creek War. Born in Natchez in 1807, J. F. H. Claiborne descended from settlers that were closely tied and witness to the transformation of the Mississippi Territory into the settler states of Mississippi and Alabama. His father, Ferdinand Leigh Claiborne, was a militia man serving first in his native Virginia before moving to Mississippi with his young family.[1] J. F. H. Claiborne's uncle William C. C. Claiborne served as the Mississippi territorial governor under Thomas Jefferson and later as the first governor of Louisiana during the 1813 Creek War. Due to poor health throughout his life, J. F. H. Claiborne primarily stuck to politics and chronicling the history of the Mississippi Territory as it unfolded in his lifetime. In his first book, a biography of the mythologized Alabama Indian fighter Samuel Dale, Claiborne proclaimed that federal authorities "had been, and generally have been, singularly indifferent to the defense of the southern frontier." An account of their "apathy and ignorance," Claiborne wrote, "if carefully traced, would cast a deep stain on the history of our country." While never directly involved in the violence between Native and white southerners prior to Indian Removal, Claiborne portrayed himself as an inheritor of Indian victimization and placed the responsibility of violence between white settlers and Native southerners on the federal government. Saying so directly, Claiborne wrote in 1860 that the US government was "responsible for much of the blood shed on the frontiers of Georgia, Florida, Mississippi, and Texas." Negligence was key to Claiborne's indictment, as he asserted, "They paid no attention to the suspicious mission of Tecumseh, and permitted him to station in the Creek towns his emissaries and fanatics, notoriously in the pay of the British government. They allowed British and Spanish functionaries to supply the savages with arms and ammunition." As many white southerners had done prior to the 1813 Creek War, Claiborne singled out federal Indian agent Benjamin Hawkins as egregiously negligent and maliciously indifferent to the security of settlers. Claiborne wrote in 1860 that "the local agent, Colonel Hawkins, exhibited the infirmity of his employers, and was blind and deaf to what was transpiring around him."[2] White southerners reading Claiborne's work, published on the cusp of the US Civil War, saw a history of the 1813 Creek War in which their grievances had long been ignored by the Union and resulted in death and hardship for their regional compatriots. Claiborne's historical accounting effectively denounced the federal government, vilified the aggression of Native southerners, and collectivized the suffering endured by white southerners in states across the US South.

The 1813 Creek War proved to be a monumental event in the history of the antebellum South. Not only did the war cripple one of the strongest and most capable Native confederacies in the South, but it helped to secure the future prosperity of white settlers and their descendants who colonized the region. For white southerners, the conflict offered immediate opportunities relating to land acquisition and fulfillment of martial obligations of honor and vengeance. The 1813 Creek War also facilitated the coalescence of the white South through cooperative action against the Red Stick Creeks during the conflict and a collective memory in the following decades. The explosive success of the Red Sticks in the August 1813 assault on Fort Mims confirmed in the minds of many white settlers in the South their suspicions of Native malice and raised the alarm of a region-wide panic. Caught in the grip of such fear, white southerners envisioned an onslaught of Native raids rolling across Creek borders into neighboring states.

Hyperbolic and public fearmongering stirred hotbeds of settler aggression already simmering among white communities. The Red Stick success at Fort Mims renewed public condemnations of the federal government and provoked demands to exterminate the Creek people, often in apocalyptic visions. With the United States simultaneously at war with Great Britain, white southerners lambasted the federal government for neglecting to protect the American South and prioritizing defensive efforts along the Canadian border and New England coast. Federal representatives, notably Benjamin Hawkins, in the South were cast with suspicion as favoring the interests of Native peoples at the expense of white settlers. In contemporary accounts and reminiscences, white southerners put forth the federal government's failure to provide protection against the loss of white lives rather than confront how the violence of settler expansion precipitated the Creeks' desperate effort to protect themselves.

Though the 1813 Creek War started as an internal conflict among the Creek, Fort Mims provided an opening for a war of settler conquest. Southern militias and volunteers from the Mississippi Territory, Tennessee,

Georgia, and to a lesser extent the Carolinas responded in opposition to the Creek, dedicating time, money, resources, and lives to fulfill communal martial obligations. State governors collaborated on planning and executing the war effort alongside Mississippi's territorial government. While the war was ultimately an unparalleled success for white southerners, the conflict was not an easy one. The war was plagued by federal indifference, logistical nightmares, hunger, deprivation, and threats of desertion by volunteers. Even so, the southern militias who fought against a resilient opponent under less-than-glorifying acumen were celebrated in their own time and in the white South's collective memory of the conflict. Common soldiers and public officials championed the martial spirit of southern militias on display in the call to arms, execution of the war, and triumph over a stalwart opponent. The victories of southern militias on the battlefield, no matter how undisciplined or prone to personal acts of vengeance, elicited accolades for their honorable reprisals. Soldiers who reminisced on the conflict noted hardships and shortcomings but glorified their efforts and the cause at large. The events at Fort Mims and the preceding Creek violence against travelers and settler homesteads offered white volunteers from the South justification for the death, murder, mutilation, and enslavement of Native peoples during the war in their own time. With the war's conclusion, settlers claimed twenty-two million acres of Native land, displaced thousands, and celebrated how it was taken. The war was pivotal as part of the "Great conquest" of the South, as one volunteer reminisced, to secure the safety, prosperity, and progress of white southerners.[3] The legacy of the Creek War, especially the Battle of Horseshoe Bend, offered white southerners who colonized land previously occupied by the Creek a sense of legitimacy through a right of conquest. The decisive conclusion of the war provided white southerners evidence to claim their martial superiority, and the sanctification of the war dead offered justification for the suffering inflicted upon the Creek.

Federal Preoccupations

As violence escalated between the Creeks and white settlers in the South, a developing conflict with Great Britain preoccupied the US government. In June 1812 "War Hawks" in Congress helped push the federal government to declare war on the British after a series of grievances they viewed as insulting to the young nation's honor. However, the bravado of the War Hawks was not matched by the preparedness of the US military. When war began, the US started with an undersized and poorly prepared fighting force.[4] Since the end of the American Revolution, the existence of a standing army was a contentious issue that conjured memories of the British occupation in the American colonies.[5] During the two-term presidency of Thomas Jefferson, the US military underwent a reduction to its already meagerly apportioned standing forces. Jefferson did not support a large standing army and saw any overbearing centralized authority as a threat to the prosperity of the nation. In the event of a national crisis, Jefferson believed, the nation could rely on patriotic citizens to rise up in defense. If an army were needed, the US model of republican government was "the only one where every man, at the call of the law, would fly to the standard of law, and would meet invasions of the public order as his own personal concern."[6] By the start of the War of 1812, the total strength of the US military in personnel remained under ten thousand.[7] The federal government also focused military deployment and expenditures against potential European adversaries. Most federal fighting forces and resources remained along the coasts and Canadian border. Through the course of the War of 1812, the federal government prioritized protecting the Atlantic Coast. In the summer of 1814, the US War Department heavily favored positioning soldiers to defend against British naval attacks at the expense of securing interior areas against possible Indian hostilities.[8]

In the face of federal preoccupation with northern and coastal defenses, anthropologist Gregory Waselkov points out, governors in the South "stood ready to respond to attacks" to defend against what southern newspapers described as the specter of the "lawless savage."[9] In 1813 Louisiana governor William C. C. Claiborne opined on the consequences of the federal government focusing on the British and ignoring the intensifying Indian violence in the South. Claiborne feared, "There are no rumors of peace & at present no prospect of so desirable event.—The Creek Indians manifest a very unfriendly disposition towards the United States, & had in considerable numbers repaired to Pensacola, and demanded of the Spanish Governor arms & ammunition." Claiborne proved prophetic, writing, "It may be that Louisiana may remain tranquil; But I much fear in the course of next Winter, we shall have our difficulties." Seeing threats from multiple avenues, the governor intended to tour the interior parishes to aid in the organization of the militias. Claiborne suspected federal soldiers in Louisiana in July 1813 were "inadequate to our defense in case of attack." Claiborne believed it was his "sacred duty, to make such arrangement, as will enable me, in time of danger, to call speedily to the field a respectable Militia detachment."[10] With rumors of the Red Sticks, a militant faction of the Creek opposed to American expansion and assimilation, gathering supplies for war from Spanish allies in Pensacola, Mississippi territorial militia Col. James Caller struck out with a company to intercept the militant Creeks and their munitions. The resulting battle at Burnt Corn Creek in July 1813 signaled that the Red Sticks posed a resolute opponent to white settlers and demonstrated the lack of preparation by the federal government to address a blossoming Native uprising.[11]

In response to the Battle of Burnt Corn Creek, Mississippi territorial governor David Holmes mustered the militia, but federal forces still downplayed the potential of an imminent threat to settler security. Leading the Mississippi territorial militia, Brig. Gen. Ferdinand L. Claiborne began operations under the oversight of US general Thomas Flournoy, the regular army commander of the Seventh Military District, which oversaw the Mississippi Territory. Though the chain of command put Claiborne under the direction of the regular army, the Mississippi territorial government provided for the local militias. With between five hundred and six hundred men in the militia, the territory also had to arrange baggage and camp equipage in response to the developing crisis. Conditions in the South during the summer made for particularly difficult operations. Claiborne reported that on his march it "rained every day for six weeks; the waters were very high, and the roads intolerable."[12] By mid-August, illness had already struck Claiborne's men. Further exacerbating the problem were financial shortcomings. In response Claiborne authorized the commander in charge at Liberty, Mississippi, to use his personal credit to procure supplies for the ill before they ever saw combat.[13]

Concerned with having an undersized command, Claiborne requested additional soldiers from Flournoy's professionally trained forces. However, Flournoy declined, insisting on keeping his soldiers on the Gulf Coast to guard against the Spanish. Writing Governor Holmes on August 6, Flournoy felt "the best measures in his power were to guard against an attack from the Spaniards." Flournoy tried to calm what he saw as overexaggerated fears by settlers and territorial officials by forwarding on to Claiborne "a quantity of ammunition, swords, [and] pistols." If that was not enough, Flournoy expected Holmes to reach out and coordinate additional aid from Governor Blount in Tennessee. In a grossly miscalculated prediction, Flournoy further reassured the Mississippi governor that he could "scarcely think that the Creek Indians will hazard a war against the United States."[14] With little support and too few soldiers, Claiborne distributed his men among the various forts throughout Creek country. The decision proved to leave each fortified outpost isolated and exposed. Decades later, defenders of Claiborne's efforts argued that this was the only way to defend "hundreds of families forted in feeble stockades, eighty and a hundred miles apart, and threatened every day with the tomahawk" across the southern portion of Creek country.[15]

Reverberations of Fort Mims

Confined to forts and with few soldiers providing protection, settlers and local militias were ill prepared to repel a determined and well-executed raid by Red Stick Creeks and their allies. On August 30, the Red Sticks achieved their greatest military victory against an American outpost during the 1813 Creek War. Attacking Fort Mims in the Tensaw district in present-day southern Alabama, William Weatherford led the Red Sticks to a complete victory. At noon the Red Sticks charged through the gates of the fort, catching the inhabitants unprepared. By early evening the Red Sticks had complete control of the outpost. The Red Sticks spared none in regard to age or sex. The attack left more than three hundred militiamen, settlers, American-allied Indians, and enslaved Black southerners dead.[16]

The Red Stick success at Fort Mims sparked a panic that resonated across the South and scarred the memories of white settlers in the region for generations. Comparatively, settler panic went beyond the responses relative to the deaths of travelers and raids against homesteads in the prior years. White settlers abandoned the Tombigbee and Tensaw districts, fleeing for Mobile. One terrified settler, Jesse Griffin, informed his family that "our country is completely destroyed." Griffin lost his crop of corn, horses, and a good portion of his household furniture. Fearing the Indians were marauding across the entire frontier, Griffin took his family and left seeking safety.[17] In a reminiscence later in life, Margaret Ervin Austill said "the day Fort Mims fell was a sad day to all the country." When her family learned of the attack, they had already banded together with numerous others to construct a fort for protection from the Indians, because many were "expecting every moment to be scalped and tomahawked." Despite their efforts none felt safe residing in the fort after the destruction of Mims. Austill remembered that "every heart became paralyzed with fear, and our men that had been so brave became panic stricken." Margaret recalled she and others even contemplated suicide to avoid a violent death at the hands of Red Stick warriors.[18]

More than a century later, Margaret Mitchell canonized the fear felt by settlers such as Austill in her 1936 novel *Gone with the Wind*. In the region-defining literary work, heroine Scarlett O'Hara's "Grandma Fontaine" recollects her experience in "the Creek uprising, right after the Fort Mims massacre." Mitchell writes Fontaine's fear and memory of violence in vivid detail. The fictional character recalls that as a young woman she witnessed a gruesome attack on her family's homestead. As the lone survivor, she "managed to get into the bushes and hide" as she witnessed the house burn and "the Indians scalp my brothers and sisters." Fontaine continues that she "could only lie there and pray the light of the flames wouldn't show up my hiding place." In the most salacious portrayal of Native violence, Mitchell writes how Fontaine watched in horror the murder of her mother and desecration of her body. Fontaine recollected that the Creeks "dragged Mother out and killed her about twenty feet from where I was lying. And scalped her too. And ever so often one Indian would go back to her and sink his tommyhawk into her skull again . . . and I lay there and saw it all."[19]

Mitchell's portrayal of Creek violence in *Gone with the Wind* paralleled the historic chronicles produced in the antebellum period by white southern authors. In Albert Pickett's *History of Alabama*, he portrayed the Creek as indiscriminately slaughtering vulnerable settlers. Pickett reprinted one account of how "the helpless inmates [of Fort Mims] were butchered in the quickest manner, and blood and brains bespattered the whole earth." Children, Pickett wrote, "were seized by the legs, and killed by beating their heads against the stockades." Women were "scalped, and those who were pregnant were opened, while they were alive and the embryo infants let out of the womb."[20] While it is indeterminable whether Mitchell sourced her construction of Grandma Fontaine in *Gone with the Wind* from Pickett's chronicle of antebellum Alabama, the parallels are strikingly similar. The fictionalized character in the massively popular novel demonstrated the continued popular memory of Native aggression in the mind of descendant settlers and perpetuated notions of white sufferings for generations to come.

The settler hysteria after the fall of Fort Mims also sparked parallel fears of a slave rebellion. Louisiana governor Claiborne and Mississippi territorial governor David Holmes speculated enslaved southerners might make the most of the disorder resulting from the Red Stick offensive. Red Stick successes against American settlements coincided with rumors of British ships operating from bases in the Caribbean, stoking fears of an insurrection.[21] Shortly after the Mims assault, Claiborne penned a notice to his militia colonels warning that a slave revolt could be imminent and done in coordination with the Red Sticks. He asserted, "It is confidently reported that many slaves have escaped from their Masters and joined the Indians."[22] Benjamin Hawkins received information that there was some degree of collusion between Black and Native southerners in the assault on Mims, and foreign powers such as the British and Spanish were agitating for slave rebellion.[23] As it turned out, rumors of a broader slave uprising generated from within Creek country were nothing more than slaveholder paranoia.[24]

As Nathaniel H. Claiborne of Virginia wrote in 1819, "the fall of Fort Mims resounded through the Union."[25] In 1813 most Americans learned of the Red Stick victory through newspaper accounts that provided descriptions of mayhem. In Nashville, Tennessee, the local press announced "our fellow-citizens have been butchered" in "the horrid massacre at Fort Mims."[26] In Kentucky, Tennessee, Georgia, and the Carolinas, similar accounts of violence against white settlers at Fort Mims garnered the title of "Indian Massacre" in what historian Robert M. Owens describes as the initial counterstroke against the Red Sticks by the press.[27] Reporting in broad strokes, newspapers gave a familiar accounting of treacherous, violent, and barbaric Indians killing innocent whites. Most press reports did little to differentiate the division within the Creeks and referenced the Fort Mims attackers as a homogeneous "Indian" people. The generalization of Native southerners as wholly warring against settlers even influenced suspicion that the Choctaw and Cherokee were contemplating taking up arms in support of the Red Sticks.[28]

In the immediate aftermath of Fort Mims, Mississippi territorial judge Harry Toulmin leveraged the widespread exposure afforded through the press to describe a region in panic, beset by fear and expecting an imminent doom. Reprinted in multiple newspapers across the South, Toulmin's text expressed many of the fears that gripped southern settlers in the wake of the Mims attack.[29] He described a dire situation as "the Indians have broken in upon" the whites and their settlements were "overrun."[30] He continued that when news of the attack reached nearby Fort Stoddert, the white southerners seeking protection there went into a panic. The settlers fled the garrisoned stockade as "there was no longer any hesitation; and such was the hurry of a flight conducted almost at midnight, that few took any thing with them, even to support themselves on their way to Mobile." Settlers fleeing the territory "pushed off by water, others fled by land in the darkness of the night, and the whole face of the country exhibited a scene of consternation and distress." Toulmin speculated that the results of Fort Mims would be repeated across the territory. All the survivors could hope for was "that some little respite may be afforded to the straggling inhabitants, and to the town of Mobile, after the forts are demolished, and that the necessity of taking care of their wounded and carrying home their plunder may induce the Indians to delay for a few weeks an attack on the town Mobile."[31]

On a more individualized accounting of settler loss, newspapers in Raleigh, North Carolina, ran an obituary memorializing one of their "young gentlemen, who was one of those massacred by the Indians at Fort Mims." Spruce M. Osborne, claimed as "a native of North Carolina" in his obituary, died in the Fort Mims assault. The obituary described a promising and talented young man with limitless potential, educated at Chapel Hill. He had excelled at composition, literature, and was admired by his peers. In pursuit of a profession in medicine, Osborne traveled to the Mississippi Territory when he was selected as a lieutenant in the volunteer corps at the start of the "Indians breaking out in that country." The obituary described his death as regrettable yet celebrated his "heroic spirit." Alongside the others who "perished in gallantry defending their Fort," Osborne as well should be remembered for the "brave manner in which he died."[32] In the immediate aftermath of the attack on Fort Mims, memorialization of the deceased highlighted the lost potential of promising settlers and championed their steadfast martial virtue in the face of terrifying peril.

Coordinating Settler Conquest

The loss of Fort Mims accelerated calls for martial assistance across the South. In Toulmin's description of the imminent doom facing settlers in the Mississippi Territory, he pled "our only hope for aid, or rather for revenge at some distant day, rests on the energy of our fellow citizens."[33] To save the settlers of the Mississippi Territory from further annihilation, Toulmin called on his neighbors to aid in the protection of white southerners under threat of Native violence. Toulmin pleaded specifically that "should no assistance come from the Mississippi, from Tennessee and from Georgia, the whole country from the Choctaws to the sea will be desolate waste and a white man will not dare raise his head out of the limits of a military garrison." Toulmin played on the fears of his neighboring white southerners and leveraged the ties of settler networks stretching back to the communities from which they first emigrated. Challenging southern state governments, he warned that unless whites in the South stood together against the Indian threat, the entire region would descend into "one scene of desolation," with the events at Fort Mims repeated across the territory.[34]

In large part thanks to warnings from federal Indian agent Benjamin Hawkins, many state and territorial governments in the region initiated the organization of militias prior to the Fort Mims attack.[35] From beyond the Mississippi Territory, the state of Tennessee acted swiftly, and the legislature responded directly. The Tennessee Legislature passed a resolution that demanded retribution and mirrored Toulmin's concerns that if the southern states did not stand together, they were all vulnerable to Indian violence. In the opening line of the state legislature's war act, Tennessee passed a bill "to repel the invasion of the state of Tennessee by the Creek Indians."[36] With the only major Red Sticks attack having occurred in the Mississippi Territory close to the Gulf Coast, the Tennessee legislature established a broad spectrum of justifications for inserting themselves into the conflict. First, the legislature established the prospect that the Red Sticks prepared to make a war against white settlers on all borders of Creek country. This, however, was unlikely. The Red Sticks were too ill supplied and undermanned to conduct such a broad campaign. Second, the state legislature made ambiguous claims on the bounds of Tennessee's territory and where Red Stick attacks were targeting white Tennesseans. The ambiguity in the legislation crafted a vague and broadly applicable justification for reprisals against the Creek in the name of defense. Finally, for Tennessee, the act to "repel the invasion" of the Creek Indians connected the state to the prior raids made by Creek

Indians against Tennessee homesteads. The memory of the Duck River raid was still fresh in the state's public consciousness, and the state legislation facilitated a connection between the loss of white Tennesseans in the spring of 1812 and those killed at Fort Mims in the summer of 1813. Connecting the various raids, Tennesseans imagined a larger coordinated effort against white settlers by Native southerners emanating out of Creek country. The state of Tennessee effectively declared war on the "Creek nation" and allowed the governor to direct the militia to "any place" in Creek country, "or in the Mississippi territory, where said troops may give relief." While publicly declaring its intentions to invade Creek country, Tennessee continued to deride federal efforts and imply negligence in protecting the white South. Tennessee proclaimed that "the number of troops called for by the general government, to repel and subdue this savage enemy, is insufficient to answer the contemplated purpose."[37] Therefore, Tennessee authorized the mobilization of up to 3,500 men and provided the governor substantial authority to direct the invasion of Creek country as deemed necessary.

In Georgia, settlers on the western edge of the state kept a close eye on rumors of Creek hostilities in the early summer of 1813. Prior to the Fort Mims attack, the *Augusta Chronicle* reported that "the inhabitants of the frontier are greatly alarmed, and are removing families [many of them] to a place of safety." Such a decision was not made without serious consideration. The paper described that for most of the "frontier settlers" the only means of subsistence was derived from their farms. Abandoning crops meant risking the fall harvest.[38] Alongside the settler exodus, Georgia militia general John Floyd began preparing between two thousand and three thousand volunteers called into service. As rumors of an impending Creek attack spread, citizens in Milledgeville read how the Creek represented a collective threat to the white South. According to reports coming from Creeks at Coweta, the intentions of the Red Sticks were to "attack this State, Tennessee and the settlements on Tombigbee at the same time."[39] Georgia settlers feared the potential of an impending Indian attack on par with prior conflicts such as the Oconee War. In early July, papers in Savannah and Augusta printed a Milledgeville editorial anticipating that "some speedy and efficient measures must now be adopted to stop the destructive career of the warring party, or the frontier settlements of Georgia will add another list to the catalogue of savage massacre and desolation, which has blackened the page of humanity, and elicited the tear of silent agony for our butchered brethren."[40]

When reports on Fort Mims reached Georgia, presses in Savannah, Milledgeville, and Augusta described an "Indian Massacre" at "Sam Mims' Fort at Tensaw" where "1000 Indians" killed settler men, women, and children, seemingly confirming suspicions.[41] Pledging assistance and convinced of complicit Spanish agents operating in Florida, the *Georgia Journal* asserted "the arm of protection . . . will be speedily extended to all the weak and exposed parts of our frontier—the deaths of our butchered countrymen avenged—and that destruction which Spain has long meditated against us, rolled back upon herself." Georgia governor David B. Mitchell announced he would travel to Fort Hawkins himself "to complete the organization of the troops."[42] Georgia militia anticipated coordinating with "volunteers from Tennessee" against the Red Sticks, "their only ambition [. . .] to die or conquer in its defence."[43]

Alongside its adulation of the state's martial spirit, the *Georgia Journal* noted the prosperity resulting from a settler "expedition into the Creek Nation." The potential for a land grab was already at the forefront should the war "terminate as it ought" with the defeat of the Creek. The *Georgia Journal* specifically pointed to the commercial advantages for the South's sugar trade should the Alabama River basin be seized. The paper wrote that control of the river would afford "the planter on the Mississippi (River) . . . a new and extensive market for his Sugar, whilst to the citizens of Georgia and Carolina, it will, *especially in a time of war*, be the only safe reliance for obtaining this article."[44] The paper prophesied, thanks to the destruction of the Creek Nation, that white southerners could look forward to land and sweets at a discount rate.

In Tennessee a martial sprit also rallied young men to action and directed a covetous eye toward Creek land. Richard Keith Call recollected in 1861 that "the indiscriminate slaughter of men, women, and children" at the hands of the Creek motivated men to arms.[45] At the age of twenty in 1813, Call was one of numerous young men consumed with the war spirit while enrolled as a student at the Mount Pleasant Academy near Nashville, Tennessee. Looking back from 1861 on his participation in the 1813 Creek war, Call characterized his motivation as derived from a quest for retribution and martial glory. Other volunteers recollected similar sentiments. Volunteering in 1813, a young David Crockett stated, "When I heard of the mischief which was done at the fort [Mims], I instantly felt like going, and I had none of the dread of dying that I expected to feel."[46]

At the Mount Pleasant Academy, Call described his fellow classmates during the summer of 1813 as "thoroughly aroused to vengeance." The assault on Mims compounded by the preceding Creek raids unleashed a torrent of white rage against the Creek. According to Call's reminiscences, the desire for retribution manifested in the ability to enlist "almost every student in the Academy for Military service." Call took it upon himself "to lead them to join any regiment or body of soldiers ready for the field." After a conversation with the academy president, however, Call conceded to procure parental consent for the academy's proposed field trip of settler conquest. Leading "quite a number" of students, as Call remembered, he managed to attach his company to Gen. Andrew Jackson's division heading against the Creek.[47] Less explicit in Call's recollections were his interests in land acquisitions. Limited historical evidence suggests that Call worked as a land surveyor near Augusta, Georgia, prior to enrolling in the Mount Pleasant Academy.[48] Additionally, his family had been involved in southern land speculation for decades. Call's father, William, had purchased considerable acreage in several Georgia counties prior to his death in 1795.[49]

As militias prepared in the Mississippi Territory, Georgia, and Tennessee, governors in the South continued to collaborate on their war against the Creek. As early as the Red Stick excursion to Pensacola and the following engagement at Burnt Corn Creek, Governor Mitchell of Georgia and Governor Willie Blount of Tennessee discussed cooperative plans. In consultation with the secretary of war, the two governors discussed the best approach for protecting their borders and defeating the Red Sticks. Outlining his options, Blount considered operations of state militias and the number of troops needed in the event Georgia and Tennessee worked in concert to defeat the Red Sticks. Blount asked Mitchell's "opinion on the ideas . . . of acting separately in different quarters of the [Creek] Nation until they could form a junction . . . at the Hickory Ground." Blount asserted that the Tennesseans were "willing and anxious to go against the Creeks," and the governor already considered supply routes to benefit both states' volunteers. Georgia and Tennessee militias endeavored to cooperate utilizing the plan laid out in the governor's early correspondences.[50] The operation called for four armies to penetrate Creek country from different directions and converge at the confluence of the Coosa and Tallapoosa Rivers. US Army soldiers assisted the Mississippi Territorial Militia, while Tennessee supplied two militia armies and Georgia supplied the fourth.[51]

Much and Just Complaint Has Arisen

The settler war against the Creek in 1813 and 1814 was an inglorious undertaking despite the opening enthusiasm and romanticized recollections of the conflict. One volunteer plainly described the endeavor, noting "we had hard times during the whole campaign."[52] Georgia, Tennessee, and the Mississippi Territory militias struggled throughout the duration of the conflict to adequately supply their soldiers, keep men in the field, and locate Red Stick encampments. The lack of supplies created friction between the federal government and southern governors. Volunteers endured hunger and sickness. Disputes over enlistment terms created dissension within the ranks. Some volunteers simply deserted. When southern armies engaged the Red Sticks, volunteers did little to restrain violence against Native Americans. Volunteer soldiers killed Native women and children, destroyed towns, mutilated corpses, and some even collected Native body parts as souvenirs of a malicious conquest.

From the outset wartime expenses proved to be a point of concern among southern states and the Mississippi Territory, and a contentious issue with the federal government. Volunteer armies in the South lacked both available funds and the stockpile of supplies necessary to follow through on their citizenry's martial enthusiasm. Mississippi territorial governor David Holmes reached out to the secretary of war at the end of August 1813 over his concerns about the territory's ability to pay for the campaign's launch. Holmes wrote that the territorial government simply did not have "the funds requisite to furnish camp equipage, forage, and transportation" for their militias mustering to combat the Creek. Tennessee and Georgia likewise faced the dilemma of how to pay volunteers and provide supplies necessary to conduct campaigns beyond their states' border. Without an extension of credit or federal monies, Governor Holmes felt the "troops cannot be marched to a distant part of the Country" to take the war to the Red Sticks.[53] Throughout the conflict the acquisition of supplies often fell to commanders in the field purchasing necessities on their own credit.

A dearth of provisions and inadequate supply networks compounded the settlers' war effort on all fronts. From Georgia, Gen. John Floyd's campaign to cut across the middle of Creek country began slowly. Floyd's fighting force included nearly 1,500 men, but the primary obstacle for Floyd was securing enough rations and logistical support to begin his campaign. Floyd began assembling his army at Fort Hawkins in September but was still waiting on supplies more than a month later.[54] Though the delay gave Floyd an opportunity to train his troops, morale dipped before the fighting ever started. Georgia produced eager soldiers but sheer enthusiasm could not fuel a campaign. With determination beginning to wane, Floyd decided to forgo waiting on federal supplies and requisitioned them himself through Georgia contractors.[55] From Tennessee, Jackson's army of volunteers navigated parallel circumstances. Subcontractors came up short even before the Tennesseans marched south.[56] At a staging ground north of modern-day Huntsville, Alabama, Jackson expressed dismay to a subordinate that he "did not find either so many men as I had expected, or them so well equipped."[57] When the Tennessee volunteers marched into the Mississippi Territory and established Fort Deposit along the bank of the Tennessee River, Jackson reported they did so encountering "every difficulty that can possibly arise from the want of Supplies."[58] At Fort Deposit, the Tennesseans' provisions were so low that "scarcely two rations in succession have been regularly drawn."[59]

Jackson contacted US general Thomas Flournoy, reporting, "No service you could render . . . would be so important" as to "procure . . . supplies of bread stuff."[60] However, Flournoy informed the Tennessee volunteers that it was not possible to send "a supply of provisions immediately," due to the great distance and danger to Flournoy's own force.[61] From Georgia, Governor Mitchell offered assistance, informing the Tennesseans "that a sufficiency (of provisions) can be had in his state." However, logistical impediments clouded how Georgia would deliver the supplies.[62] Scrambling to acquire provisions in the field, Jackson pieced together supplies from subcontractors along the Tennessee-Mississippi Territory line.[63]

After the Tennesseans' first major engagement against the Red Sticks at Talladega in November 1813, volunteers continued to endure shortages. The lack of food proved particularly demoralizing to the volunteers. When regrouping after the battle, provisions were so scarce that "there was not one mouthful to give the wounded or well." Only a late arrival from a contactor offered some respite in the form of a "a small quantity of meat & meal." Otherwise, the volunteers had been trying to get by on helpings of "parched corn," while others healthy enough simply fasted.[64] Reminiscing about his experience during the campaign, Call recollected the men "were in want of everything" and only "received something to relieve hunger every day, though not enough to satisfy appetite."[65] Volunteer Ebenezer Hearn was more direct in describing the privations facing the Tennesseans. Hearn recollected after the campaign that "for nearly one month [the men] lived on anything we could get from meat and Bread down to Acorns nutts herbs & some dry cowhide when almost starved."[66] One of the bleakest accounts came from Sam Bains recorded during the 1813 campaign. Bains wrote his wife informing her the "scarcity of Provisions" forced the men to stretch three and a half days' worth of rations over ten days. Prior to that, volunteers were forced to get by on half-rations for a seventeen-day stretch. Bains described himself as "in tolerable good health tho much weakned by want of provisions." Others were not so lucky. Bains noted, "There is much sickness in camps and one or more dies everyday."[67]

Through late 1813 Tennesseans in the field grew restless and openly discontent. After the battle at Talladega, Tennessee volunteers were keen on returning home. Among the men, Call remembered that the volunteers discussed mutiny and challenged orders to stay in the field. As Jackson hoped to launch another assault in December, Colonel Martin, commanding the Second Regiment of Tennessee Volunteer Infantry, informed Jackson that on December 10 their enlistment would expire. The expiration of enlistments was the result of confounding jurisdiction between state and federal governments during the War of 1812. The Tennessee militiamen under

Jackson's command were one-year volunteers who had originally enlisted on December 10, 1812, in response to war with the British. Their original task was to maintain security along the Mississippi River by marching to Natchez. However, the volunteers had an uneventful operation, and on February 3, 1813, the secretary of war, Gen. John Armstrong, ordered the regiment to disband.[68] When the Tennessee governor called up the state militia in response to the Fort Mims attack, some argued they were no longer under contract but ultimately mustered for service.[69] As the December 10 deadline approached, Tennessee governor Blount informed Jackson that there was little he could do to override the expiring terms of enlistment. Blount advised Jackson to postpone his campaign until spring and muster new volunteers.[70]

The Georgians' struggle paralleled the Tennesseans' efforts against the Red Sticks. General John Floyd oversaw the execution of the Georgians' planned thrust into the heart of Creek country from the east. From the outset logistical shortcomings, wavering morale, illness, and a lack of supplies characterized Georgians' wartime experience. In early September, Georgia volunteer James A. Tait described a lackluster scene at Floyd's staging ground near Fort Hawkins. Tait noted that "much and just complaint has arisen" from the men and that "matters are not yet well organized."[71] The most immediate concern was a lack of food and the poor quality of rations. Tait complained that "this little army has been badly provisioned with victuals since it encamped."[72] By mid-September he recorded the first desertions among the volunteers.[73] Under pressure to provide supplies for the men, Floyd set to requisitioning provisions himself rather than rely on federal assistance.[74] By the end of September, men began to fall ill, allegedly due to poor camp conditions and lack of food. Tait first reported 250 men incapacitated before ever seeing combat. He described the men's sickness as "bad colds" that resulted in "violent headaches, fevers, debility, and death."[75]

Disease continued to follow the Georgians as they marched into Creek country. Pushing to the banks of the Chattahoochee River in November, Floyd ordered the construction of Fort Mitchell with the intention to eventually link up with the Tennesseans. Bolstered by US-allied Creeks, the Georgians managed to inflict a major defeat upon the Red Sticks at Autossee but could not advance on their success. In early December two hundred men were on the sick list, and camp conditions, according to Tait, contributed to the persistent illness among the volunteers. Unsanitary conditions, loss of sleep, and dealing with Georgia's cold winter rains, Tait wrote in December 1813, "are the causes of the sickness which prevailed."[76] The Georgians regrouped at Fort Mitchell, where they endured a month-long delay due to lack of supplies. Fort Mitchell's stores were further taxed due to the wartime displacement of American-allied Natives. Throughout the war, Red

Stick and American armies burned crops they were unable to carry with them, leaving many Creek towns destitute. Creeks friendly to the US arrived at Fort Mitchell looking for provisions, and Floyd dared not turn them away, fearing it might bolster the ranks of the Red Sticks.[77] With the volunteers still depleted from illness, the Georgians mounted one last offensive against the Red Sticks at the Battle of Calabee Creek in January 1814.[78] The engagement was disastrous for Floyd and the Georgians. The Red Sticks attacked at night, catching the Georgians unprepared. The Georgians fired into the dark until daybreak, when they were able to utilize cannon fire to stem the Red Stick attack. The Georgians returned to Fort Mitchell to effectively hold the line until reinforced by volunteers from the Carolinas. Despite the Georgians' mediocre campaign, Georgia newspapers celebrated "the bravery of our militia" and hyperbolically compared the engagement at Calabee Creek with William Henry Harrison's 1811 victory over Tecumseh's confederacy at Tippecanoe.[79]

Conquest, Celebration, and Commemoration

In early 1814 a renewed effort by the Tennesseans spearheaded the conclusion of the Creek War. At its peak the army encompassed approximately three thousand soldiers primarily made up of Tennessee volunteers, bolstered by about five hundred Cherokee and Creek warriors. Andrew Jackson revived the original plan of battle by marching south through the Coosa River valley heading for the heart of the Red Stick towns. In late January the Tennesseans and their allies engaged the Red Sticks at Emuckfau and Enitachopco. While the engagements were inconclusive at best, the battles were celebrated as victories, with ample praise bestowed upon the volunteers.[80] Through February the Tennesseans reorganized and stabilized supply routes between a chain of fortifications in the northern Mississippi Territory. In March, Jackson commenced an advance toward the confluence of the Coosa and Tallapoosa Rivers, targeting the largest known Red Stick stronghold at Tohopeka. On March 27 Tennesseans, alongside allied Creek and Cherokee warriors, annihilated the Red Sticks. The battle effectively ended Red Stick opposition in Creek country, and white southerners declared the 1813 Creek War won.[81]

The Battle of Horseshoe Bend at Tohopeka encapsulated the settler violence of the 1813 Creek War and represented a fulfillment of white promises to cripple the Creek Nation in the South. In 1812 Jackson publicly swore to the Tennessee governor that he would "penetrate the creek Towns, . . . and think [himself] Justifiable, in laying waste their villages, burning their houses, and killing their warriors and leading into Captivity their wives and children."[82] With similar vitriol in a letter to George Colbert, Jackson foretold that "the whole creek nation shall be covered with blood. fire shall consume their Towns and villages: and their lands will be divided among the whites."[83] Throughout the conflict, Tennessee and Georgia armies destroyed Creek towns, killed noncombatants, and took women and children prisoner. In November 1813 a Georgia volunteer recorded in a journal the delight the army took in leveling the village of Autossee and slaying unarmed Creeks. When the Georgians deployed artillery cannons against the Red Sticks, James Tait described "there were 18 rounds of canon fire shattering their miserable huts to pieces." As the Georgians advanced into the wreckage, the volunteers found "several" Red Sticks who had "remained in their houses quite passive during the battle." None were taken prisoner, as the Georgians slayed the Indians "without resistance."[84]

Figure 2. Battle of Autossee. The November 1813 Battle of Autossee was one of several militia-led assaults that took the war into Creek towns and homes. Image courtesy the Historic New Orleans Collection, The William C. Cook War of 1812 in the South Collection.

At Horseshoe Bend the Red Sticks suffered catastrophic losses. Of the estimated thousand Red Stick warriors at the battle, only three were taken captive. The Tennesseans counted 557 dead Red Stick warriors on the fortified peninsula.[85] John Coffee, who covered the riverbank along with Cherokee allies, reported killing another 250 to 300 Red Sticks in the river as they attempted to flee.[86] In the final stages of the battle, the violence turned from a martial endeavor to a quest for vengeance. Across the field militia soldiers took trophies from the bodies of the deceased and ruthlessly dispatched defeated opponents. One participant from Noxubee County, Mississippi, recalled that "many of the Tennessee soldiers cut long strips of skin from the bodies of the dead Indians and with these made bridle reins." Another militia soldier reportedly killed a Creek child of five or six, rationalizing that "the boy would have become an Indian some day" and therefore a threat to white settlers.[87] Trophies from deceased bodies asserted martial domination over a people and confirmed a fulfillment of masculine duties for white southerners.

Personally following through on his promise to lead "into Captivity [Red Sticks] wives and children," Jackson seized a Creek infant found at Tallushatchee during the war.[88] Jackson named the token of conquest Lyncoya and sent the infant to his Nashville plantation, the Hermitage, as a plaything for his white, eight-year-old adopted son, Andrew Jackson Jr.[89] Lyncoya lived a short life under the oversight of his parents' killers. When Lyncoya died at the age of sixteen, his obituary in the Tennessee press read as a paternalistic devotional of a slaveholder. Reportedly, Andrew and Rachel Jackson held a ceremony at the Hermitage where they interred Lyncoya's "remains to a decent grave, and shed a tear as the earth closed over him forever." Yet the obituary also noted that Lyncoya had "expired under the roof of the hero who conquered his nation."[90] As with a favored enslaved Black southerner, Lyncoya's captors publicly grieved over a prized possession.[91] While Jackson apologists have professed Lyncoya to be an adopted son of the family, Lyncoya was buried beyond the gates of the family cemetery like Jackson's other human property. Lyncoya's final resting place, along with upward of 150 enslaved Black southerners, remains unknown at the historic home in the early twenty-first century.[92] In justifying settler atrocities, one early twentieth-century historian invoked the power of community memory to motivate horrendous acts of violence. Historian John Bassett speculated in 1911 that even if "to some gentle spirits it seemed unnecessary to kill so many Indians; . . . to the people of Tennessee, who remembered fifty years of border warfare, it seemed just and appropriate."[93]

The settlement ending the 1813 Creek War defined a conqueror's victory and directly memorialized Creek violence against white settlers as the catalyst for the conflict. The Treaty of Fort Jackson invoked the memory of "numberless aggressions" committed against settlers and specifically referenced Creek attacks "at the mouth of the Duck River [and] Fort Mims."[94] As retribution, the Treaty of Fort Jackson demanded nearly everything white settlers could hope for with the settlement. The US acquired expanded guarantees to construct new roads and access to waterways through Creek land. The US secured the rights to further militarize settler occupation of Creek country with the construction of additional forts. The treaty also sought to monopolize the Creek trade with the expansion of US-operated trading houses and promises by the Creek to cut off commerce with Spain and other foreign powers.[95] Most important for white settlers was land. Decades after the war, Richard K. Call recollected that the punitive measures of the Treaty of Fort Jackson designed to "take from the conquered enemy territory enough to defray all the expenses" of the conflict.[96] The terms imposed upon the Creek did more than cover the cost of the war. In total the Creek lost twenty-two million acres of land spanning modern-day Georgia and Alabama.[97]

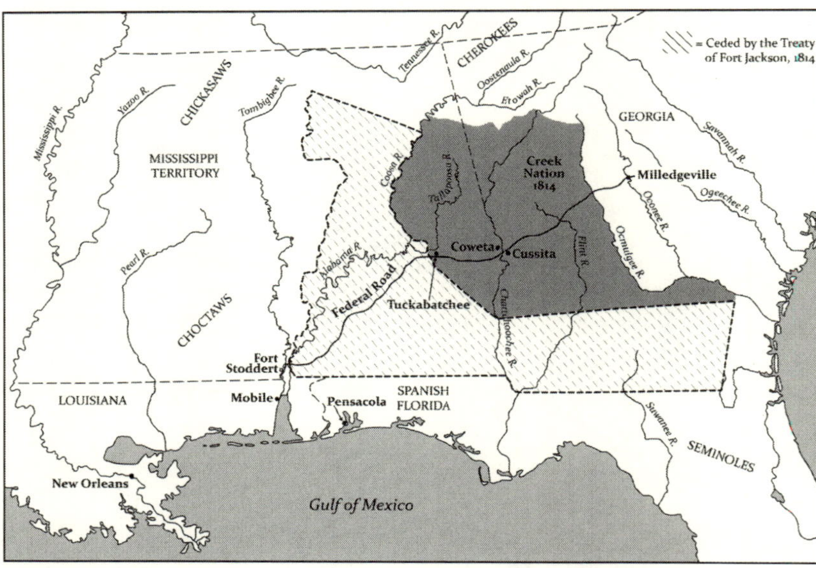

Figure 3. Map of the Treaty of Fort Jackson and Creek Land Loss. Native land seizures in the 1814 Treaty of Fort Jackson. Map by Sarah Mattics. From *Tohopeka: Rethinking the Creek War and the War of 1812*, edited by Kathryn E. Holland Braund. Tuscaloosa: University of Alabama Press.

American celebrations of the Creek War's conclusion memorialized the conflict as justified retribution for Native aggression and praised the collective marital spirit of white participants from the South. Public declarations of the war's commencement and conclusion fell in line with the Treaty of Fort Jackson. The war's cause was simplified as a response to Creek violence against settlers and frequently invoked Fort Mims as the catalytic event. Settler assessments of the war pointed to the "massacre at Fort Mims" as sufficient justification for the Creek's resulting suffering.[98] At a May 1814 dinner in Huntsville, toasts reprinted in the Natchez press lauded "the militia of Tennessee" and celebrated the contributions of "Gen. Floyd and the army of Georgia—their services tho' eclipsed in the blaze of superior and more brilliant victories out not be forgotten." Another toast championed Andrew Jackson as "the hero of Tohopeka" and "avenger of fort Mims."[99] At a celebration in Robertson County, Tennessee, attendees praised the collective martial efforts of white southerners by toasting to "the army of the south—Its late achievements prove that the militia is the bulwark and safety of a free government."[100]

In Georgia the city of Augusta celebrated returning volunteers with a festival attended by "fellow citizens, from different parts of this state and S. Carolina."[101] The *Athens Gazette* heralded the men as defenders who "placed themselves as a bulwark, between our wives, our children, and our peaceful homes and the scalping knife, the tomahawk, and the horrid barbarities of an invading savage enemy." The Georgia militias, according to the paper, had "protected a large, and otherwise defenseless population on our frontier, and prevented there the exhibition of scenes similar to that experienced at Fort Mims."[102] The Georgia press likewise acknowledged the collaborative efforts of white southerners in crushing the Red Sticks. Newspapers in Savannah and Milledgeville bestowed praise and gratitude upon the Tennesseans for the "Great Victory over the Creek Indians" at the Battle of Horseshoe Bend.[103]

In one of the earliest historical accounts of the Creek War, Virginia politician and historian Nathaniel H. Claiborne celebrated the collective martial accomplishments of the southern volunteers during the 1813 Creek War. Published in 1819, Claiborne's *Notes on the War in the South* describes how the conquest of the Creek, framed as a defense of white settlers, garnered white southerners collective praise. Claiborne writes, "The conduct of the citizens of Tennessee, Mississippi Territory and Georgia, in this war, has been such that when they visit other states in the Union, they every where not only experience all the rights of hospitality, but the ardent patriot through the whole nation extends the right arm of fellowship, and in the language of the heart exclaims, 'you too are my brethren.'"[104] As the US basked in a wave of patriotism in the conclusion of the War of 1812, white southerners from

Tennessee, Georgia, and the Mississippi Territory, as pointed out by Claiborne, found adulation in their victory over the Creek. In the white South's celebratory glow of the Creek War's conclusion, accounts of ineffective logistical support, lack of supplies, hunger, illness, and desertions became momentarily cast to the side. Georgians, Tennesseans, and settlers in the Mississippi Territory graciously thanked each other for providing mutual defense against a common enemy, and the nation recognized the collective martial spirit of the white South.

With the war's conclusion, the consecration of Indigenous dispossession and commemoration of the settlers' conquest facilitated the reconstruction of Native land for settlement by white southerners and their descendants. The deaths of settlers and volunteer militia during the 1813 Creek War continued the process of transforming Native space into settler territory. The destruction of Fort Mims offered settlers a seminal moment in the consecration of the Mississippi Territory as white space, and those killed in the summer of 1813 were memorialized as martyrs. Volunteers who died during the war, either in combat or more likely due to disease, were remembered as romanticized heroes who gave their lives in a noble cause. The remembrances of volunteers interred on the campaign trail constructed a sentimentalized link between the sites of their deaths and the communities memorializing their sacrifice. In the field, companies attempted to afford the deceased as much honor and respect as possible. The burial of war dead left a lasting impression among soldiers. Nearly fifty years afterward, Richard K. Call vividly recollected the burial of fellow Tennesseans in the rolling hills of the Tallapoosa River Valley in early 1814. In his 1861 reminiscences, Call described the burial taking place on "a gloomy night, made so by the sad task of burying our dead, which work we did by torches, the flickering and uncertain light of which added to the funeral gloom of the scene, increased by the doleful sound from the tree tops, as the winters wind swept over them, making a fitting requiem over the graves of the lamented dead." Call looked back upon the war believing it his "sacred duty" to remember the dead who were buried in unmarked graves in Alabama.[105]

As Creek War volunteers marched home to Georgia and Tennessee, white communities in the South valorized those who did not return. At the Huntsville dinner celebrating the end of the conflict, one attendee toasted the memory of the war dead, declaring that the men "who have fallen by the bullet and the tomahawk of the hostile Muskogee—they sleep 'the sleep of dead' in the bed of honor, but shall live in the fine and grateful recollection of their fellow citizens."[106] In Nashville a Fourth of July celebration in 1814 toasted "the fallen heroes of the Creek campaign" amid parades and "a sumptuous dinner . . . for a numerous and respectable company."[107] In Georgia newspapers memorialized those who were left behind, and they bristled at a lack of respect shown to the dead nationwide.[108] A Savannah paper lamented in March 1814 that "our northern brethren" had not extended the praise entitled to "the brave free men of the South and West." The column continued, "We have said before and we again repeat that the bravery of the Georgia and Tennessee militia has been, in many instances, most conspicuous—and that acts of heroism have been performed by individuals among them not surpassed by any in the annals of authentic history." The editorialist believed the war dead insultingly had not been adequately lionized. The column in the Savannah paper bemoaned "The memory of some who have fallen, however revered by their compatriots in arms" had yet to be adequately honored by the nation.[109] In their sacrifices and the perceived slight by an ill-defined North, the commemoration of the Creek War dead drew the states of Tennessee and Georgia closer together in their loss.

In sanctifying the death of Creek War volunteers, the dead served to redefine the land seized from the Creek and to connect white southerners across newly forged borders. Lemuel P. Montgomery was one of the thousands of volunteers who served in the Creek War but one of the comparatively few who died in combat. At Tohopeka in 1814, Montgomery was reported as the first soldier to breach the Red Stick's fortifications but was quickly killed by a single rifle shot to the head. In descriptions of the battle, Jackson glorified the bravery and sacrifice demonstrated by the young volunteer from East Tennessee.[110] Recollections from others at the battle suggest Montgomery was the only soldier buried with military honors, whereas the remaining killed in action were sunk in the Tallapoosa River. According to affidavits provided by two veterans, Montgomery's body was interred at the battle site and his grave left unmarked to "conceal it from the keen eyes of the savages."[111] After the Battle of Horseshoe Bend, Montgomery became a canonized hero of the Creek War and revered in the white South's memory of the conflict. One early memorialization of Montgomery took place at a dinner in June 1814. An attendee toasted "the memory of the gallant Montgomery and other patriots in arms who have fallen."[112] In 1817 the Tennessee State Legislature established the new town of Montgomery in Morgan County to "perpetuate the memory of Major Lemuel P. Montgomery, who fell on the Indian breastworks at the battle of the Horse Shoe."[113]

While Montgomery remained a revered son of Tennessee, he became a deified founder for white Alabamians. Before Alabama was even organized into a territory, the Mississippi Territorial Legislature created Montgomery County out of land seized from the Creeks in the Treaty of Fort Jackson. Formalized in December 1816, Montgomery County was named for Maj. Lemuel P. Montgomery to commemorate his death at the Battle of

Horseshoe Bend.[114] Not long after, the bones of Montgomery became sacred relics in new foundings. In 1839 the new settlement of Dudleyville, Alabama, sought to use Montgomery's corporeal remains to sanctify the town's founding. In an elaborate community event, the white citizens of Dudleyville commissioned their militia to retrieve the bones of Montgomery from his unmarked grave at Tohopeka and reinter them at the town. As reported in the local press, "accompanied by a soldier who fought in the battle, and a negro who had acted as drummer at the funeral of the unfortunate young officer," the citizens of Dudleyville located the buried remains of Montgomery two feet below the surface. The body was in a considerable state of decay after twenty-five years in the damp southern soil. Only the larger bones of the corpse remained, but the amateur forensic scientists were convinced the grave belonged to Montgomery based on "the indication of a bullet hole through the skull." Montgomery's relics were placed in a box and transported to Dudleyville in a martial procession. The local militia general and field officers, two volunteer companies, and a large concourse of citizens accompanied the parade into town. The militia oversaw the ceremonial reburial of Montgomery's remains in "a neat coffin" and provided several addresses and saluting gunfire. Montgomery's remains were deposited in a grave "dug within a few feet of the main street," where it retained a prominent place on the community's landscape.[115]

Figure 4. Lemuel P. Montgomery statue. Statue of Lemuel P. Montgomery by Clydetta Fulmer near the entrance to the Montgomery County Courthouse in Montgomery, Alabama. Photo by F. Evan Nooe.

In May 1987 Montgomery County, Alabama, publicly resanctified the suffering of Lemuel P. Montgomery and memorialized the aggression of the Creek Indians.[116] The city council commissioned Montgomery native Clydetta Fulmer to create a $28,000 life-size statue of Montgomery to stand sentinel outside a new courthouse. The artist sought to capture a realistic rendition of the twenty-eight-year-old Tennessean.[117] Without a known portrait of Montgomery, Fulmer "used an authentic uniform from Andrew Jackson's Hermitage and written descriptions of Maj. Montgomery to model the statue."[118] She molded Montgomery's facial features such as his "aquiline nose" based on his Irish descent.[119] The statue's placard described Montgomery as a "Brilliant Lawyer, Valiant Soldier, in Whose Honor Montgomery County, Alabama Was Named." The commemoration of Montgomery defines a point of origin for the settler state of Alabama gained through sacrifice and loss. As a statute of a Tennessean, it links the histories of Alabama and Tennessee in a shared memory of cooperative conquest against Native southerners. The installation provides a selective memorialization of the state's founding and representation of violence at Horseshoe Bend. In deifying Lemuel Montgomery, the statue facilitates the erasure of the skewed realities of the 1814 battle at Tohopeka. The art piece commemorates the loss of a white founder with no acknowledgment of the slaughter of Creek Indians that ensued throughout and after the battle. The annihilation of more than eight hundred Red Stick Creeks and the seizure of twenty-two million acres of Native land become silently justified acts through the remembrance and glorification of Montgomery's celebrated sacrifice.

4

"Half Peace, Half War"

Perpetual Violence on the Southern Border

While the result of the 1813 Creek War reconstructed the political geography of the American South, the Battle of Horseshoe Bend and the Treaty of Fort Jackson did not conclude Native opposition to settler expansion in the region.[1] The shockwaves of the conflict in the Mississippi Territory resonated east and south into Georgia, the Florida Panhandle, and down the interior of the peninsula over nearly a decade, connecting a multitude of events, places, and peoples across the American South in a nexus of violence between white and Native southerners. After the Treaty of Fort Jackson, displaced Red Sticks and their allies continued to oppose white expansion and settlement in the South. In a strikingly similar pattern to the violence preceding the 1813 Creek War, the US-Spanish border became a focal point of conflict. White southerners laying claim to the land in Georgia and the Mississippi Territory seized through the Treaty of Fort Jackson pressured, intimidated, and violently expelled Native southerners unwilling to acquiesce to white settlement.

In response a faction of Red Sticks and their allies rejected the Treaty of Fort Jackson. Refusing to accept the reconstruction of Creek country, stalwart Red Sticks continued to employ opportunistic strikes against exposed targets. Initial violence between Native and white southerners often took on an interpersonal form prior to escalation. Raids against vulnerable homesteads and travelers still proved to be some of the most opportunistic methods for Native southerners to challenge white expansion. In the aftermath of Native raids against settlers, white southerners leveraged the deaths of women and children to call for the militarization of the southern border. Settlers first called on local militias, yet most were poorly equipped to provide long-term protection. In fear of perpetual violence, white communities called for federal intervention and were heavily critical when the US government was not quick to act. Rather than serve as a stabilizing force, the martial build-up along the Florida border escalated violence. Consequently, settler pleas for security on the southern border drew the US into conflicts beyond American territory that directly advanced the converging interests of the white South's plantation economy.

White southerners' demands for protection against Native opposition drew the US military and thousands of volunteer militia from Tennessee, Georgia, Kentucky, and South Carolina into the violent expansion of the US South. Commonly referred to as the First Seminole War, the 1818 Florida Invasion intending to subdue Native opposition culminated in the leveraged US acquisition of Florida from Spain.[2] Almost immediately the invasion and acquisition of Florida became a contested matter in US politics. To justify the 1818 Florida Invasion, proponents pointed to the memory of Native violence against settlers and the concurrent attacks against white households. The personal experiences and memories of volunteer soldiers motivated them to action, and after the invasion they became celebrated exemplars of southern militarism. By the end of the nineteenth century, the descendants of white settlers commemorated the spoils of their conquest and defined their community's genesis through the violent subjugation of Florida's Indigenous peoples.

Migrations

The Treaty of Fort Jackson facilitated the movement of thousands of people throughout the South. For white southerners, the end of the Creek War and subsequent treaty meant the opportunity to establish a more prosperous future for their descendants. While serving in the 1813 and 1814 campaigns against the Creek, soldiers from southern states took note of land for future settlement, describing potential sites in journals and letters home.[3] Almost immediately after the Treaty of Fort Jackson, topographical engineer Howell Tatum made a detailed survey of the land, resources, and sites for future white settlements in the Mississippi Territory focusing on the Coosa and Alabama river valleys. In August 1814 Tatum recorded multiple abandoned sites or "old Indian town(s)" that looked promising for white colonization. Near "Red Bluffs," Tatum described "the site of some old town or village" as "the handsomest situation for a town of any to be found on the river." The prospective site was protected against flooding, offered easy navigation to Mobile, and already had improvements along the riverbank constructed by the location's former Native inhabitants. Tatum reported Red Bluffs benefited from "a large improvement and corn field" along with "100 to 150 acres of cleared land."[4]

White settlers claimed the former Creek land in Georgia and the Mississippi Territory with haste. White settlers from southern states purchased land, entered their names in state lotteries, or simply squatted without land titles.[5] In the Mississippi Territory, the population of white and Black southerners doubled between 1810 and 1820, indicating the concurrent expansion of slavery. Decades later 1813 Creek War veteran and two-time Florida territorial governor Richard K. Call recollected the speed with which white settlers moved into southern Georgia. In 1861 Call reminisced that within "four years after making the treaty the whole region was densely populated."[6] The surge of relocating white southerners primarily from Virginia, the Carolinas, and Tennessee onto dispossessed Native land resulted in the division of the Mississippi Territory in 1817 and formation of two new states by the end of 1819.[7]

For the Creek and Cherokee, the Treaty of Fort Jackson meant expulsion from lands they had occupied for generations.[8] Most displaced Native southerners resettled within the reduced confines of their respective nations. Yet not all were willing to relocate on US terms, nor were they necessarily welcome back into Indigenous communities. The 1813 Creek War began as an internal conflict among the Creek, and its conclusion under the direction of invading American armies did little to resolve the precipitating issues. Red Stick leaders and their sympathizers were expected to acquiesce to an increasingly powerful Creek National Council and increasing American influence in Creek affairs. The grievances that motivated them to arms in 1813 remained salient. Supporters of the Red Stick faction were expected to accept the outcome of the war not through compromise or negotiation but because of military defeat and coercion under the threat of continued persecution. Either unwelcome or unwilling to reintegrate into the reconstructed Creek country in 1814, many Red Sticks and their allies fled south.

In the aftermath of the Battle of Horseshoe Bend, US reports circulated that "hostile Indians" were heading toward Pensacola and St. Marks in the Florida Panhandle under the direction of Red Stick leader Peter McQueen.[9] Initial speculation in Tennessee, Georgia, and South Carolina assumed McQueen was joined by "five hundred followers" who established a temporary encampment along the Escambia River by late April.[10] Through the early summer, the number of "hostile Creek Indians," as described in the southern press, seeking refuge in Spanish Florida swelled. By mid-June newspapers in Georgia and the Carolinas relayed information from American spies who estimated 1,500 Creeks encamped near Pensacola.[11] Another report to Benjamin Hawkins recounted that Peter McQueen had claimed his Red Stick army at "a few more than a thousand warriors."[12] Throughout the region, rumors amplified the number of renegade Creeks threatening the South's southern border. Newspapers in Kentucky, Tennessee, and Georgia circulated accounts that upwards of "2,500 hostile Creek Indians were at Pensacola" and supposedly receiving aid and munitions from the Spanish government.[13]

The concentration of refugee Red Sticks and their allies in Pensacola led a Nashville newspaper and others in the South to declare, "The Creek War Not Over," and speculated the Indians were regrouping for an offensive campaign.[14] Most likely, refugee Native southerners were more interested in a sanctuary to recover and seek respite from encroaching white southerners.

The 1813 Creek War was just one factor in a decades-long process of Native southerners migrating to Florida because of colonial expansion in the US South. The peninsula provided displaced Native southerners in the late eighteenth and early nineteenth centuries an opportunity to start anew in a less densely populated location managed by a languishing imperial power. Throughout the eighteenth century, Florida's Native population endured the full force of colonialism in terms of slave-raiding, disease, and war. While not depopulated, the worst aspects of colonial expansion significantly reduced the Native presence in peninsular Florida.[15] The void provided an opportunity for Native people forced from their homelands and created the circumstances for the eventual coalescence of new Indigenous identities.[16] Native migrations accelerated in the 1750s and 1760s as ethnic Creeks formed separate towns; notably in northern Central Florida. During this period, Spanish officials began referring to their new neighbors as *cimarrones*, meaning "runaway" or "wild men." In 1765 English colonists started using the label "Seminole" to reference Indians in Florida, most frequently referring to the Alachua Indians near present-day Gainesville.[17] While the term "Seminole" was convenient and commonly used by colonists, Native people in Florida did not identify as a single cohesive group throughout the eighteenth and much of the nineteenth century. Native people in Florida predominantly identified with their towns and as late as 1823 did not refer to themselves with a collective affiliation or identity. After 1815 as many as six thousand Creeks lived in Spanish Florida among and alongside politically autonomous Native towns that had called Florida home for centuries.[18]

Unresolved Violence

Alongside the migrations taking place after the Battle of Horseshoe Bend, violence between Native and white southerners along the US-Spanish border resembled a state of "half peace, half war."[19] Native southerners unwilling to surrender persisted in opposing settler expansion. They sought to protect their remaining towns in the ceded land in Georgia and the Mississippi Territory and their bourgeoning communities south of the US border. Native southerners were up against white settlers who attempted to take control of Native land with a sense of righteousness afforded a conqueror. The formation of local militias provided the vanguard of new white settlements. When they proved incapable, white communities petitioned for additional assistance from the state or territory and federal government. At times to the disapproval of more-established settlers and state government officials, white marauders and vagrants took matters into their own hands to secure Native property. All of this produced a churning state of violence in the region that often took on a reciprocating interpersonal frame. When white southerners forced out, assaulted, or murdered Native southerners attempting to retain their homes, Native reprisals targeted vulnerable settlers or exposed military outposts. In response, white southerners held up the victims as martyrs. Newspapers, family mythologies, and community memories sanctified those that were lost to the "tomahawk and scalping knife," a frequently used description of Native violence against whites. The US military used the deaths of individuals and families to justify its intervention as done on behalf of protecting white families. With the presentation of such a noble cause, US military and volunteer militia from southern states waged multiple excursions into Spanish Florida in the name of national security. In the wake of these conflicts, white communities in the South remembered these acts of colonial aggression not as offensive campaigns against a reeling opponent but as retribution for personal grievances.

As complete a victory as the Battle of Horseshoe Bend may have been for the white Tennesseans, it did not compel all Red Sticks to lay down their arms. Conflict persisted in tandem with the ongoing War of 1812, and the Red Sticks made the most of vulnerable targets. Within months after the Battle of Horseshoe Bend, Red Sticks took the offensive by targeting a plantation near the site of their greatest success during the Creek War. Though militia armies from the Mississippi Territory, Tennessee, Georgia, and the Carolinas had established fortified outposts across Creek land, the Tensaw district still proved dangerous for white settlers. The nearby border with Spain offered the opportunity to travel the Florida Panhandle beyond the easy reach of US armies and militias. In one of several sporadic raids taking place, Indians attacked the Byrne plantation in the Tensaw district near Blakeley, Alabama, in late April 1814. The Byrne family presented a typical story of settler prosperity. Arriving in Savannah from Ireland, Gerald Byrne moved to the Tensaw district after stays in Pensacola and Mobile. Byrne married a young widow named Ann Palmer Allman, and the couple had three boys while residing in Mobile. By the early 1800s, Byrne established a plantation, cattle ranch, and sawmill along the Tensaw River. When war broke out between settlers and the Red Sticks, Byrne and his family took refuge in Mobile. After the Battle of Horseshoe Bend, Gerald returned to his plantation intending to prepare his fields for summer planting and resume his lumber operation.[20] As recollected by Gerald Byrne's son several years later, Byrne quickly found himself in danger. Within a few days of returning,

"Indians," according to family lore, attacked the house "about sunrise." The assailants entered the home and killed two visitors and one of Gerald's enslaved Black southerners. Gerald fled into the yard but was chased down by one or more raiders, who "killed and scalped" him. The attacking Indians looted the house, took horses, and abducted another enslaved Black southerner claimed by the Byrne family.[21]

The death of Gerald Byrne sheds light not only on the contemporary dedication of the Red Sticks to continue the war but also on how the Byrne family and his descendants mythologized their slain patriarch. Gerald Byrne's family learned of his death after boatman traveling the Tensaw River discovered the bodies at the family's plantation. Another settler who had departed the plantation prior to the attack also helped to fill out the account of Byrne's murder for the surviving family. The primary documentation of the Byrne attack comes from Alabama settler Albert J. Pickett, who wrote one of the first chronicles of the state. Working in the early nineteenth century, Pickett regularly relied on interviews of settler families and their reminiscences to reconstruct past events. While Pickett did not include extensive details of the Byrne attack in his chronicle of Alabama, he referenced the event as part of Indian "depredations in Baldwin County."[22] The Byrnes and their extended family, however, appear to have kept the memory of Gerald's violent 1814 death in their memory over nearly the next century and a half. As late as 1941, Byrne's great-granddaughters Mary Feminear and W. G. Hall, who resided in Tensaw County, shared the inherited memoires of the Byrne family's victimization for the local newspaper. According to their family lore, Gerald "was hated and feared by the Indians." They cited the point of conflict as personal rather than in the context of Native opposition to settler expansion or the preceding war. Feminear and Hall attributed the dispute to Native southerners displeasure with Gerald Byrne's mistreatment of the natural environment. The great-granddaughters shared family accounts that the Creek felt Gerald had "cut too much forest homeland" for his sawmill. In their memories this was enough to cause "a band of Indians" to murder and scalp Gerald in 1814.[23]

Crossing Boundaries

As Native violence against white settlers persisted through the 1810s, rumors of cooperation among foreign powers and Black southerners spread panic among whites in the South and became a useful justification for escalating colonial violence. In the first half of the decade, the War of 1812 between the US and Britain complicated US attempts at regional stability and subduing Native opposition. Spain's claims to Florida became a regularly invoked threat to regional and national security by white southerners.

Though officially remaining neutral throughout the War of 1812, Spain allowed Great Britain to utilize Florida as both a staging area and a medium to funnel supplies to British-allied Indians. American officials feared the consequences of Britain and possibly Spain actively supporting hostile Indians in the region as detrimental to American expansion and the South's plantation economy.[24]

Whereas in 1813 and early 1814, similar rumors were largely unfounded, Americans in the South now had demonstratable cause for concern. In July 1814 Benjamin Hawkins passed along intelligence to Secretary of War John Armstrong reporting that three British officers had invited Indians to a British merchant house in Spanish Florida. Reportedly, any Indian could receive "arms and ammunition . . . not for war, but to kill squirrels, crows, and turkeys," though Hawkins suspected the stipulation prohibiting the use of supplies for warfare a charade. Hawkins learned that several Indians residing in Florida had already benefited from the "abundant supply" of arms. Confirming his suspicions, a headman had traveled from Florida "to invite the remains of the hostile Indians from Konacau to Apalachicola." According to reports, many were already on their way. One rumor of British aid suggested as many as "10,000 brigands" arriving from Cuba.[25] As "daily rumors of hostile appearances at Apalachicola and Pensacola" persisted, Hawkins understood the British to be "unquestionably" supplying the "Indians and some negroes" with munitions.[26]

Taking advantage of foreign aid, some Red Stick parties continued to oppose settlers in southern Georgia through the summer of 1814. In mid-August rumors circulated among settlers that Red Sticks planned to attack Hartford, Georgia. Warnings first came from a resident of Baldwin County in the Mississippi Territory. The letter eventually made its way into the Georgia press, suggesting dire circumstances for any exposed settlers on Georgia's southern border. Preempting the letter, the editor of the *Augusta Chronicle* introduced the information as "of the highest importance to Georgia; because, it destroys at once, all hope of peace with the hostile Indians, and that a renewal of the war is morally certain." The unnamed Baldwin County resident warned that a British vessel had arrived at Pensacola with intentions to arm upward of six thousand Seminoles, Upper Creeks, and possibly Choctaws.[27]

While such a formidable force of Native soldiers never materialized, the subsequent raid against Hartford gave the rumors credence for white settlers. Though Hawkins did not share specifics, he described to the Georgia governor that four Indians "committed a violent outrage" against settlers.[28] Georgia newspapers described the assailants as British-inspired "Banditti" who used Spanish Florida as a haven.[29] Afterward, Lt. Allen Tooke portrayed settlers in a state of apprehensive militarism. Tooke informed Governor Early of persistent rumors that Indians in Florida intended to "make an attack" in Georgia. The mere possibility, according to Tooke, infused "great alarm among the Citizens," instilling paranoia in the elite and common citizenry alike.[30] Through the rest of the year, the Georgia press continued to print correspondences reporting on rumors of Indian raids against Hartford originating out of Spanish Florida.[31] One rumor even suggested that the British were offering the Miccosukee 100 dollars "for every trader captured or other American found in their country."[32] Responding to pleas from worried settlers, Hawkins encouraged Generals Pinckney and Jackson "to crush the mischief makers" and to "ready our friendly [Indian] warriors, of the Four Nations" in assistance.[33] By early November, US-allied Indians mustered at Fort Mitchell "for the protection of this frontier" under the request of Hawkins.[34]

Instead of acting as a defensive force, the US-allied Indians and southern state militias took the offensive. Prior to his nationally renowned defense of New Orleans against the British, Andrew Jackson orchestrated an invasion of Spanish Florida in the fall of 1814. While Jackson was receiving intelligence reports from the federal government on an imminent British invasion, Jackson prioritized wiping out Native opposition along the southern border. In doing so, Jackson hoped to capture Red Stick leaders Josiah Francis and Peter McQueen. Suspecting they were in Pensacola, Jackson set his sights on the Spanish colonial capital. Even if the federal government did not agree with his priorities, Jackson found "consolation of having done the only thing" that he believed "would give security to the country by putting down a savage war."[35] Of a similar mind-set, a solider fighting alongside the Tennesseans in the November 1814 invasion of Spanish Florida justified the action as necessary because "a certain proportion of the Creeks having refused to participate in [the Treaty of Fort Jackson], remained still at war with the United States." Reflecting on the Florida invasion after the War of 1812, he wrote that the hostile Indians were continuing to commit "depredations on . . . settlements on the Alabama, the Tombigbee, and Mobile bay." Jackson determined "to take possession of Pensacola, thereby to deprive the Indians and their British allies of a place of shelter and refuge, after their aggressions."[36] On November 7, 1814, the invading Tennesseans and Choctaw allies occupied Pensacola and temporarily displaced Spanish authority. The invasion of a neutral power's provincial capital was anticlimactic, as most of the Indians opposing the US fled east. With orders to prepare for the defense of New Orleans, Jackson headed west but ordered Maj. Uriah Blue to pursue and destroy the Indians assumed responsible for the raids against white southerners in the Mississippi Territory and Georgia.[37]

Major Blue's month-long expedition across the Florida Panhandle was reminiscent of Jackson's early tribulations of the 1813 Creek War. Heading east from Pensacola on December 1, Blue and his 1,500 soldiers intended to dislodge Red Sticks congregating at the Fort on Prospect Bluff along the Apalachicola River. Blue's expeditionary force had only one major encounter, at Miller's Landing, resulting in the death of twenty Creek men and 150 captives.[38] Blue's failed attempt to eliminate the displaced Red Sticks at Prospect Bluff represented intersecting threats to settler expansion in the South. The river landing started as a British trading outpost in the early 1800s, but the British transformed the site into a military staging ground to attract Native and Black allies during the War of 1812. As early as August 1814, British commander Edward Nicolls encamped at Pensacola and actively sought to enlist and train Native and runaway Black southerners.[39] Enlisting Native southerners as allies not only bolstered British forces against the US but also leveraged white fear of Indian violence as a tool of war. With the conclusion of the War of 1812, the British abandoned Prospect Bluff along with their former Native and Black allies.

With no prospect of assistance from the British, the Indians at Prospect Bluff were in dire straits. Reports indicated that provisions were so scarce that "Indians in the Country [were] living altogether on Alligators," and one American spy "learned for a certainty an Indian woman [ate] her own child."[40] Prospect Bluff proved untenable, causing the Red Sticks to take up residence elsewhere in Spanish Florida. However, Prospect Bluff's proximity to the US border and defensible fortifications offered an opportunity for enslaved Black southerners. Upon abandonment by the Red Sticks, former enslaved Black southerners transformed Prospect Bluff into a maroon colony. As the notoriety of the reconfigured Prospect Bluff spread across the American South, white southerners increasingly referred to the community as the "Negro Fort," which represented an affront to the racial order of the white South.[41]

After the War of 1812, white expansion along the Spanish colonial border quickly ensnared the maroon colony along the Apalachicola River. The withdrawal of federal troops from the region provided Native southerners more favorable circumstances to oppose white expansion, and settlers expressed their dismay over the lack of federal protection. In May 1815 Georgia governor Peter Early complained to the governor of East Florida, Sebastian Kindelán, about Natives in Florida threating white southerners. Early intimated that the existence of the Fort at Prospect Bluff was inspiring opposition.[42] In June a Georgian living in St. Mary's reported to Governor Early on a recent attack against his homestead. According to the correspondence, two unidentified Indians raided Mr. Tullos's settlement located "on the Frontier of [the] county" in southern Georgia. Tullos and the Indians exchanged gunfire before Tullos fled, seeking aid from his neighbors. Upon his return Tullos found the Indians "entered and plundered" the home and destroyed his property that "they could not carry off."[43] In an effort to appease white settlers, the US military stepped in, pledging to reoccupy or construct new fortifications along the Chattahoochee and Apalachicola Rivers in southwestern Georgia. As described by US Army Maj. Gen. Edmund P. Gaines, the intention of the forts was "to keep in check the Seminole Indians."[44]

In May 1816 the US military began construction of a new fort within US territory on the Apalachicola designated Fort Gaines under the command of Lt. Col. Duncan L. Clinch. The construction of Fort Gaines was not without Native opposition. By mid-May, Lt. William Bee reported that Indians were "menacing the Frontiers of Georgia" in the vicinity of Fort Hawkins.[45] In addition, Gaines reported two Georgians were killed by "Indians below the lines." White southerners claimed to witness Indians engaged in "the war-dance, and drinking of war-physic," suggesting a larger planned offensive. Shortly after, unnamed Indians killed two privates near Fort Gaines. The sporadic attacks raised logistical concerns for the US Army. Gaines reported "the distance from the [closest] settlement of Georgia [was] near 150 miles," and he feared that in a time of war, their location would prove too remote.[46] To ameliorate the outpost's isolated locale, Gaines insisted on unrestricted access to the Apalachicola River from the Gulf of Mexico through Spanish Florida. He suggested that river access would serve the dual purpose to "keep an eye upon the Seminoles, and the Negro Fort."[47] Gaines commenced "an experiment by water" to outfit Fort Gaines by shipping supplies from New Orleans via the Apalachicola River entering through the Gulf of Mexico. Georgia newspapers promptly reported on the maneuver, intimating the offensive nature of the operation. The *Savannah Republican* reported that along with the supplies, "a sufficient number of . . . gun boats, with order to destroy any force that might attempt to oppose them" departed New Orleans for Fort Gaines. As indicative of local sentiment, the paper added "this we hope will effectually destroy the . . . negro fort on the Apalachicola."[48]

There was little coincidence in what happened next along the Apalachicola River. The US military engineered the supply of Fort Gaines with the intention to destroy the maroon colony at Prospect Bluff and intimidate Native southerners. In concordance with the supply ship's departure, Gaines informed Clinch that should he meet "opposition, at what is called the Negro Fort, arrangements will immediately be made for its destruction" and preemptively provided "two 18 pounders, and one howitzer."[49] In mid-July, Clinch led about a hundred soldiers alongside 150 US-allied Creeks to take up a position north of the fortification in anticipation of the supply ships and demanded the maroons surrender. Upon their refusal, American vessels drew within range of the fort, drew fire, and promptly responded.[50] Reports from the US military described a swift and complete destruction of the maroon colony and the deaths of the fort's three hundred inhabitants.[51] Navy gunfire led to an explosion of the fortification's powder supply and reportedly "blew the whole of the battery . . . destroying all of the men, and several of the women and children" inside.[52] One eyewitness reported, "You cannot conceive, nor I describe the horrors of the scene. In an instant, hundreds of lifeless bodies were stretched upon the plain, buried in sand and rubbish, or suspended from the tops of the surrounding pines. Here lay an innocent babe, there a helpless mother; on the one side a sturdy warrior, on the other a bleeding squaw."[53]

Newspapers in the South announced the destruction of the maroon colony and praised the impact it would likely have on stamping out Native opposition. From Nashville the *National Banner and Nashville Whig* described the fort's destruction as "a happy thing for the adjacent American as well as the Spanish territories." The ruination of the fort eliminated a refuge for enslaved Black southerners seeking freedom. A shelter for "this band of brigands," the paper explained, it "had long been a receptacle for runaway negroes of Georgia, for Tennessee, the Mississippi Territory, and Pensacola." In addition, the fort had provided respite, according to the press, "for all the hostile and out-cast Indians of the Creek and Seminole Indians."[54] The success led papers in Savannah and Milledgeville to "congratulate readers upon the annihilation" of the fort and sincerely hoped that "proper steps may be taken for the acquisition of the two Floridas" to ensure the prolonged security of white settlers.[55] While the US military had not made a direct assault against Native peoples in the South, the federal government leveraged the engagement to demonstrate a concerted effort at protecting white southerners from Native violence. Shortly after the fort's destruction, Secretary of War William Crawford wrote the Georgia governor that he expected the outcome "may have a tendency to intimidate" the neighboring Indians into submission.[56] As news of the fort's destruction spread, it became clear that Americans had few qualms about making offensive campaigns against their opponents in foreign territories with exterminating fervor.

The 1818 Florida Invasion

US military intervention along the Florida border proved impermanent. By the early winter of 1816, Clinch and US soldiers withdrew from southwest Georgia, leaving local whites to feel abandoned. Within months the *Georgia Journal* described "the Indians in that quarter" as emboldened, "as if they contemplated further mischief," and the paper insinuated that the removal of federal soldiers endangered settlers. Shortly after Clinch's departure, Native southerners seized abandoned supplies and reportedly razed the remaining structures left by the US military.[57] While white southerners feared Native violence, Native southerners struggled to defend themselves against white marauders. In October 1816 Mr. Harding of Tattnall County, Georgia, pleaded with the governor to find a way to stop renegade Georgians from assaulting and antagonizing Native southerners, for fear of reprisals. Harding reported that disreputable Georgians were moving into "the Indian land adjacent to the Ocmulgee and the Altamaha [Rivers] to an alarming degree." Harding feared that if these Georgian "Vagrants" and "fugitives from Justice" were not restrained, it was only a matter of time before "the Shedding of Blood."[58] In December, Native leaders from Chehaw requested that Governor Mitchell address white violence against Natives along the Florida-Georgia border near the St. Marys River. The headmen complained that in the prior months "a party of red people were hunting near the St. Marys" when "a party of white people rushed on their camp and took one red man prisoner," along with their belongings and horses. In a similar incident, a heavily armed group of white Georgians robbed a Creek hunting party of ten horses near the Okefenokee Swamp. The Chehaw informed Mitchell that if he did not act, they would seek out retribution on their own terms as white Georgians had feared.[59]

Through early 1817 Georgia's failure to restrain settler aggression set off a sequence of reciprocating violence that escalated to another US invasion of Florida in 1818. In February, Camden County Court justices wrote the governor, concerned over the recent murder of an Indian by white men in East Florida. According to their account, Stephen Vinzant and his riding party robbed and killed an Indian man near Alachua. The Camden County petitioners, "much alarmed for themselves, their children and neighbors," anticipated that the "act of aggression . . . on the body of an Indian . . . may bring upon the defenseless inhabitants . . . the revenge of some of his nation."[60] Near the end of February, an Indian party, identified as "lower Creek Indians" by a resident of St. Marys, raided the Garrett homestead in Camden County in retaliation for Vinzant's actions. The raid resulted in the deaths of Mrs. Garrett and her two children and destruction of the homestead.[61]

The reprisal set off a panic among white settlers in southern Georgia. Newspapers in Savannah, Augusta, and Milledgeville reported on the Garretts' violent deaths, with each printing insinuating additional attacks were imminent.[62] Timothy Barnard, "who has resided nearly fifty years in the Indian country," claimed to see Indians engaged in a war dance after the attack on the Garretts.[63] By June, the *Savannah Republican* described chaos in Camden County. White southerners were reportedly "abandoning their homes for fear of the Indians."[64] Other southern states quickly began following news on the escalating violence along Georgia's southern border.[65]

Raleigh's *North-Carolina Star* sensationalized the anxiety of Camden's white residents, reporting, "Its inhabitants expecting but not knowing how soon the Indians may come down upon them, with a powerful force, leaves them the alternative of the prospect of being murdered with their families, or of abandoning their homes and plantations." Following such a dire predicament, the paper printed correspondence from a St. Marys resident sharing gruesome rumors on the Garretts' deaths. The correspondent claimed the youngest child was likely no older than three and noted the child "had not hair enough on its little head to afford a grasp to tear off its scalp, which evidently was attempted" by one assailant in the raiding party.[66]

The alarmist reports set off another round of public criticism on federal apathy. Despite a public consensus that the recent raids were in retaliation for white aggression, one settler living along the Flint River specifically pointed to the removal of Clinch's federal soldiers at Camp Crawford and the abandonment of Fort Gaines as enabling Native hostility. Likewise, former Georgia governor David B. Mitchell led much of the criticism directed at the federal government. Appointed as Benjamin Hawkins's successor by President James Madison in 1817, Mitchell wrote the US secretary of war to request "a moderate force stationed at Camp Crawford," fearing that without it "some serious mischief will result."[67] In following up with Georgia's current governor, William Rabun, Mitchell more directly asserted that "if a battalion of regular troops were stationed at Camp Crawford, that way these hostilities on the part of these Florida or Seminole Indians would vanish."[68]

Similar critiques appeared in the major newspapers across the South. Under the heading "Indian Outrage," papers in Savannah and Augusta printed correspondence from St. Marys requesting to "have a small force of one company stationed on this river, for the protection of the frontier." If not, the resident feared the settlement would "be broke up" by Native aggression.[69] Commentary from Milledgeville's *Georgia Journal* offered more specific instructions, requesting the establishment of "a small military force at Trader's Hill [to] . . . secure the peaceful citizens against violence from red or white savages."[70] Beyond Georgia accusations of federal negligence and the need for redeployment of federal troops echoed in major cities such as Charleston, Raleigh, and Baltimore. One North Carolina paper editorialized that "had only a part of the regular troops been removed from Camp Crawford, as should have been the case, there is no doubt the Indians would have remained quiet and peaceable."[71]

With immediate federal assistance uncertain, white Georgians acted of their own accord. By the end of March, private citizens in Georgia requested authorization from the governor to take the fight across the border to the Indians in Florida. In Savannah, Edward F. Tattnall wrote Governor Rabun to signify his "disposition to assist in the raising of a force in the vicinity of the St. Mary's River." Tattnall stated he had "every reason to believe that a sufficient number of volunteers could be immediately procured." Once mustered, he expected, they could aid in "reducing the Indians, . . . to a peaceable and submissive state."[72] Alongside the martial impatience of men like Tattnall, Governor Rabun likewise favored swift reprisals. According to the *Georgia Journal*, Rabun became "unwilling to rely any longer on the promised assistance of the national government."[73] By April, Rabun tasked Creek War veteran John Floyd to organize a defense of the settlements in "those parts that are menaced, and most likely to be attacked." According to a report in the *Augusta Chronicle*, Floyd was given discretion "to adopt such measures as he may deem necessary" to protect Georgia's southern border. Floyd and a brigade of militia focused on Wayne and Camden County and over the next two months launched raids against any suspicious Indian camp in the vicinity of St. Mary's.[74] By June, Rabun reported that "our people" had commenced attacks "on the Indians and have killed and wounded a number of them."[75]

With violence escalating in Georgia and spreading into the Mississippi Territory, General Gaines redeployed federal forces along the southern border, reoccupying the remnants of Camp Crawford and renaming it Fort Scott.[76] One of the first targets of the US military was Fowl Town along the Flint River near the convergence of the Chattahoochee. Though located within territory seized in the Treaty of Fort Jackson, the Fowl Town Indians led by Neamathla professed independence from Creek political authority and refused to relocate. The US military moved against the town under the pretense it was harboring Red Sticks responsible for recent murders and made an assault led by Maj. David E. Twiggs in November 1817. Largely outnumbered, the warriors set up a defensive retreat against Twiggs and fled south into Florida.[77] In reprisal for the destruction of Fowl Town, Neamathla orchestrated an ambush against an American vessel under the command of Lt. R. W. Scott sailing on the Apalachicola River. On November 30 the displaced residents of Fowl Town attacked the boat, killing forty men and six women on board and taking one woman captive. Six escaped and made their way on foot to Fort Scott to inform Clinch of the engagement.[78]

Within months news of Neamathla's ambush spread across the South and grew more sensational. Preliminary reporting focused on correspondence from Gaines likely leaked to the Milledgeville press by Governor Rabun.[79] Multiple publications in North Carolina reprinted Gaines's letters, and New Bern's *Carolina Federal Republican* deduced the act of aggression indicative of a new "Indian War."[80] The press in Tennessee, South Carolina, Louisiana, Mississippi, and Alabama likewise spread equally alarming accounts.[81] In December southern papers began to speculate that Neamathla's ambush also involved violence against white children aboard Scott's vessel. The first reports came from correspondence cited by the *Savannah Republican.* The editors of the paper claimed they had "seen a letter from Hartford [Georgia]" indicating "more lives were lost than were mentioned in the [prior] account . . . 44 men, 10 women, and three children, were killed making in all 59."[82] Within a week the same report including the murder of children in the Scott ambush appeared in a Charleston, South Carolina, paper.[83] Before long the speculation on the death of white children spread to a national audience and quickly provided political leverage for supporters of war against the Florida Indians.[84]

The escalation of conflict along the Florida-Georgia border in tandem with increasingly sensational accounts of violence against whites drew in a wider swath of participants from the US South. In late 1817 Secretary of War John C. Calhoun instructed Andrew Jackson to "assume immediate command of the forces in that section of the southern division" in response to "the increasing display of hostile intentions, by the . . . Indians." Calhoun authorized Jackson to "call on the Executives of adjacent States for such an additional militia force" as needed.[85] The bulk of the soldiers mustered from Georgia and Tennessee, with an unsolicited contingent from Kentucky joining the campaign.[86] While never called into service, a South Carolina militia company from Camden mustered as well. Militia captain Chapman Levy addressed the mustered men with urgency and internalized the violence afflicting settlers in southern Georgia as their own. In orders to the men, Levy wrote, "Our Georgia brethren are in arms to repel the ruthless savages from our borders and to take vengeance for the murder of our citizens." In motivating the volunteers, Levy invoked the South Carolinians' participation in the "late war" alongside the Georgians in reference to the cooperation during the prior Creek conflict. In appreciation of such a devoted offering of martial collaboration, the *Savannah Republican* applauded their spirit and expressed gratitude for their willingness to "assist their brethren in a neighboring state" even though they were never deployed.[87]

With similar sentiments Jackson's call to the Tennesseans made an appeal to the men's martial spirit through mutual fears of Native violence, a shared obligation of protection for white southerners, and the recent memory of the 1813 Creek War. Jackson portrayed the Native southerners resisting settler expansion as "savages on your borders," characterizing Indigenous peoples as foreigners threatening white colonized space. Though the Indians did not directly threaten Tennessee, like the South Carolinian call to muster, Jackson impressed that Georgia's southern border was their responsibility to defend. The Indians, Jackson wrote, had "raised the tomahawk to shed the blood of our citizens, and already they are assembled in considerable force to carry [out] their murderous schemes." The call challenged white Tennesseans to match the ferocity of their enemy and justified their campaign as a reprisal. Settlers along the Florida border, according to Jackson, were "peaceable and unoffending citizens" victimized by Native violence. Finally, Jackson presented the upcoming Florida campaign as a continuation of the 1813 Creek War and an opportunity to vanquish an elusive foe.[88] Jackson stated "the enemy you are going to contend with, you have heretofore met and fought."[89] When organizing militia companies, Jackson reached out to veterans of the 1813 Creek War to "accompany him to the heart of the Seminole Towns, and there aid in giving peace and safety to the Southern Frontier." Jackson reminded his former subordinates of their prior victories "on the plains of Talladega, Emuckfau, and Tohopeka."[90] Publicly, Jackson rallied volunteers to remind the Indians of their conquered status. He wrote that the Indians residing in Florida had "forgotten too soon the streams of blood their ill-fated policy heretofore cost them," and it was "but a short time since [the Red Sticks were] conquered and almost destroyed."[91] Jackson's proclamation garnered wide notoriety. Presses in Georgia and North Carolina reprinted Jackson's celebration of Tennesseans' martial ardor.[92] Beyond the South, the *National Intelligencer*, the *Niles Weekly Register*, and the *National Register* supplied readers across the country with Jackson's declaration of Tennesseans' willingness to take up arms yet again against Native southerners in defense of their suffering brethren.[93] The tactic of rallying martial support through a shared historical experience in response to Native violence became a staple in future calls to arms among southern volunteers.[94]

At the end of March 1818, an army of more than five thousand including two thousand white southern militiamen, invaded Spanish Florida. The force marched down the Apalachicola River valley and established a new outpost christened Fort Gadsden over the remains of the former maroon colony at Prospect Bluff. Over the next month and a half, the American expeditionary force tied up any loose ends stemming from the 1813 Creek War. The army struck first against Miccosukee on April 1 and destroyed three hundred homes.[95] Through the end of the month, the conglomeration of US soldiers, Tennessee, Georgia, and Kentucky militia alongside allied Creeks pushed as far south as modern-day Gainesville, razing Indian towns along the way. With few large battles to celebrate, Jackson described that "the Indians have been divided and scattered . . . they have not the power . . . of annoying our frontier."[96] Returning north from the Florida interior, Jackson set his sights for a second time on the Spanish capital of West Florida. Jackson invaded and occupied Pensacola under the justification that the Spanish had incited and supplied Indians in opposition to American settlers.[97] Though the invading American army returned Pensacola, the effort to stifle reciprocating violence between Americans on the southern border and Native southerners set in motion a permanent transition of colonial stewardship. On February 22, 1819, the Adams-Onís treaty began the transfer of the Florida peninsula to the United States.[98]

Memories of Florida Conquest

Upon the conclusion of what contemporaries labeled the "Seminole War," the US Congress debated the legality of an American army invading and occupying a foreign colony. Proponents of the 1818 Florida Invasion cited Spain's negligence in pacifying the Native inhabitants of the colony and invoked the most salacious examples of Native violence while conveniently omitting settler expansion as the catalyst. Proponents seized on the rumors of the displaced Fowl Town Indians killing children during the 1817 Scott Massacre. As part of the congressional investigation into the Florida invasion, congressmen pointed to information provided from a British agent in Florida on the rumors of Neamathla's warriors killing white children aboard R. W. Scott's vessel. Documents acquired from an agent working for Alexander Arbuthnot in Florida seemingly confirmed the worst. Writing to an acquaintance in Nassau, Peter B. Cook described that "there was a boat that was taken by the Indians, that had in [it] . . . four small children." Cook detailed the children's violent deaths, writing they "were taken by the heels, and their brains dashed out against the boat."[99] The damning account was included in the Congressional Record on the debates of the Seminole War. Advocates of the 1818 Florida Invasion saw the document as confirming an atrocity against innocent Americans and sufficient provocation to excuse any unauthorized invasion of a foreign colony. After the war newspapers across the American South printed the congressional speeches that regularly pointed to the violent deaths of white children aboard Scott's vessel in conjunction with the deaths of settler families such as the Garretts as justifying the Florida campaign.[100] In evaluating the transfer of Florida to the US, one of the first chroniclers of Territorial Florida rationalized the invasion and acquisition as necessary to stifle the aggression of the Native southerners. In his 1827 *A View of West Florida*, John Lee Williams wrote the acquisition "at once, cut from the root a thousand fruitful sources of contention and war. Our enemies can no longer . . . excite the savages on our frontier."[101]

For militia soldiers, the decision to volunteer in the 1818 Florida Invasion was often more personal. The family history of Isaac Brown Jr. in conjunction with the contemporary violence against settler households influenced his decision to join the campaign. From Twiggs County, Georgia, Brown was one of a thousand white Georgians serving in the Florida Invasion. Brown's most significant action took place at Miccosukee near present-day Tallahassee.

The engagement resulted in thirty-seven Indians dead and more than a hundred captured. In one exceptional moment, Brown helped secure the sole female survivor of the attack on Scott's vessel, Elizabeth Stuart.[102] Born prior to 1797, Isaac Brown Jr. was raised in southern Georgia by a single mother. His father had met a violent end in an Indian raid against their home at the end of the eighteenth century that left the family destitute. As a witness to the aftermath of the 1813 Creek War, Brown likely read about or heard the various accounts of Indian raids against settler families. While the violent deaths of the Garretts in February 1817 garnered the most press coverage and became a quintessential example for settler justification of the Florida Invasion, Native opposition to settler expansion targeted several other white families in southern Georgia. Through the early months of 1818, Georgia newspapers reported on the deaths of three additional families and often detailed sensational acts of violence echoing tales of Brown's childhood. In early January, correspondence in the *Savannah Republican* described an attack against the Holloway household in Camden County. According to the letter, twenty-five to thirty "Florida Indians" attacked the Holloway home on the St. Mary's River. The raiding party killed Mrs. Holloway, captured an enslaved Black southerner and her child, and pillaged the home.[103] The next month a Milledgeville paper reported on the deaths of the Grantham family near Hartford. The press printed an account telling how "the father and son . . . on returning [home] found their residence surrounded by Indians, who after plundering the house, burnt it, with the three youngest children [inside], and then cut to pieces the rest of the family." Reportedly, nine members of the Grantham family died in the attack.[104] In late February, Georgia papers reported on another attack in Wayne County. Georgia presses described the deaths of the Dykes family as a "massacre by the savages."[105] Such accounts proliferated in the major papers of Georgia before spreading to outlets in Knoxville, Charleston, and Raleigh.[106]

Native attacks against white families in 1817 and 1818 both evoked settler memories of prior conflicts and offered opportunity for the continued creation of selective memorials of white suffering. The family of Isaac Brown Jr. described his motivation to join the 1818 Florida Invasion as a quest for vengeance in response to the death of his father in 1797. Brown's participation and family lore also became memorialized and widely shared across the South. Through a series of reminiscences printed in the Georgia press in 1858 and a separate 1859 chronicle of the region titled *Reminiscences of the Creek, or Muscogee Indians*, fellow volunteer Thomas S. Woodward reinforced the memory of intergenerational Native aggression and settler suffering for a post-Removal audience. Residing in Louisiana in the final years of his life, Woodward had his "Indian Reminiscences" published in Thomasville and Columbus, Georgia, newspapers, and a later monograph offered a sense of legitimacy to the memory of the 1818 Florida Invasion.[107] Woodward enthralled readers with the tale of the widowed mother calling on her son to avenge the death of his father. Woodward reminisced that the Browns' memory of such trauma accounted for Isaac being a soldier, specifically stating, "It's in the blood," comparing Isaac's desire to fight the Seminole in 1818 as akin to the inherited pedigree of a champion racehorse.[108] The impulse to fight Indians passed from father to son as it did from sire to colt. Isaac Brown Jr.'s actions were, according to Woodward, the product of an inherited victimization passed to him by his father and the imparted memories kept alive by his mother. As presented by Woodward in 1858 and 1859, the invocation of Mary's call to avenge the family's losses justified Isaac's actions and provided an individualized sense of justice within a larger imperial system. Rather than a dubiously legal American invasion of a foreign colony, Woodward's deployment of Brown's memory shifts the focus from an act of colonizing aggression to emphasize the war as a noble quest to avenge a murdered father.

While Brown was commemorated for volunteering during the Florida Invasion in Woodward's writing, others who participated were commemorated in the southern soil. Upon the death of lifelong Georgian Thomas Glascock, his peers celebrated his martial contributions to the state and championed his zeal against Native southerners. Glascock had a long career in the Georgia militia, participating in the American Revolution, the War of 1812, and the 1818 Invasion of Florida. His militia career contributed to his notoriety, and he eventually served as a member of the US House of Representatives. When he died in 1841, a close friend, Judge Longstreet, authored the inscription upon Glascock's monument cherishing his service to the state of Georgia. As part of the inscription, Longstreet memorialized Glascock's service "in the Seminole War of 1817 under General Jackson." Glascock's efforts in the campaign, according to Longstreet, demonstrated his "unchanging kindness," his character as "a protector and a friend," and lastly "charity to his species."[109] Inscribed on his tomb in the post-Removal South, Glascock's memorialization functions as an example of the omission of violence against Native peoples that allowed for the white occupation of the region and the exclusion of Indigenous peoples as of the same species deserving charity. Over the nineteenth century, white Georgians continued to celebrate and publicly memorialize others for their contributions in various conflicts against Native southerners.[110]

At the start of the twentieth century, the descendants of white settlers living on land seized from the Creek in Georgia sought to memorialize their community's origins in connection with the 1818 Florida Invasion. White settlers established the town of Herod, located south of modern-day Dawson, after the removal of the Creek Indians in the 1840s. According to the memory of late nineteenth-century residents, Herod was originally established by Creek Indians sometime prior to 1818. The community was "named in honor of their chief, Herrod," by white southerners upon settler occupation.[111] With little direct documentation regarding the Creek town, the known history of the chief and the community was "handed down" through generations of white southerners.[112] By the late 1880s, the town was waning, with many of the buildings described as in a state of "decay."[113] In an effort to exhibit the regional heritage of the town, the Dorothy Walton Chapter of the Daughters of the American Revolution (DAR) sought to establish a commemorative monument attesting to the historic importance of the community. For the women of the DAR, Herod represented the reconstruction of the South in antebellum America from a Native South to a white South. Herod was memorialized as the last Indian village in South Georgia, and the town, according to the DAR, the "moving away of the Indian marks an epoch in Georgia history which will never be forgotten."[114]

Figure 5. Herod Boulder. Unveiling of the Herod Boulder near Dawson, Georgia, in 1913 memorializing Andrew Jackson's 1818 occupation of "the Indian village of Herodtown" and subsequent invasion of Spanish Florida. Courtesy, Georgia Archives, Vanishing Georgia Collection.

The DAR focused on celebrating Andrew Jackson's march to Florida as a definitive turning point in the region's history. According to the chapter's historian Mrs. M. C. Edwards, it was "historical fact that General Andrew Jackson at the head of nine hundred Georgia militia, together with friendly Indians, reached this spot in the year 1818, in his march through Georgia to subdue the hostile Indians." According to local legend perpetuated by the DAR, his arrival and the Georgia militia were welcomed by Chief Herod and "his friendly braves" who proceeded to join the expedition.[115]

To narrate the landscape, the DAR chapter purchased land in the town to establish a monument. Conceiving of the project in 1912, the chapter desired "to keep alive in the public memory and knowledge of colonial traditions and of matters and places of interest connected with the stirring time of the hardy forefathers in this section." At a christening ceremony in November of the next year, the DAR unveiled "a large boulder" made of local granite and inscribed with a historical narrative of Jackson's 1818 arrival.[116] According to the inscription, Jackson and nine hundred Georgia militia "occupied the village of Herodtown, located on this site March 12, 1818." The purpose of his occupation, the inscription continues, was en route "from Fort Early, Georgia to Saint Marks, Florida, in the war with the hostile Indians of Georgia."[117] As part of the unveiling, sister chapters of the DAR attended the ceremony along with "many distinguished guests" and local government officials. After his attendance, Lucian L. Knight reflected that "the magnificent pile of granite will be a constant reminder to youth who pass there, that this section is not barren of tradition and memories, and its erection by the victor to the conquered has been one of the most delightful events yet to occur in this section."[118] The 1913 ceremony and monument provided white southerners in the early twentieth century confirmation of a laudatory past with admirable forefathers, romanticized and historicized Indians, and gave affirmation to white conquest over vanquished Native southerners.

The US acquisition of the Florida peninsula initiated a temporary lull in the state of "half peace, half war" that had persisted in the South after the 1813 Creek War.[119] The Treaty of Fort Jackson had proved to be far from unanimous among the Red Sticks and their allies, yet white southerners expanded their colonization of the region through a right of conquest. Reciprocating violence characterized the region amid white settler expansion, and the escalating conflict came to envelop a broader scope of actors. As white communities expanded, the demand for security in the colonization of the American South ensnared a myriad of local and national issues. White southerners attempting to reoccupy their homesteads or establish new communities after the Treaty of Fort Jackson risked persistent Native opposition. Violent resistance by Native southerners sparked settler accusations of federal neglect and calls for assistance from the US military. Efforts to stamp out any perceived Native threat offered justification for multiple incursions into a foreign colony. Attempts to bolster the security of white settlers contributed to the destruction of one of the American South's most dynamic maroon colonies. The escalation of Native resistance in response to white violence offered yet another opportunity for white southerners to join in arms on the battlefield and celebrate the cooperative destruction of Indigenous communities. Whereas Georgians and Tennesseans only fought in coordination across the Mississippi Territory in 1813 and 1814, the invasion of Spanish Florida in 1818 gave two thousand militiamen the opportunity to fight side by side in the cooperative resolution of the unfinished Creek War. As the Treaty of Fort Jackson had opened millions of acres to white settlement at the expense of Native southerners across Georgia and the Mississippi Territory, the acquisition of Florida set up similar circumstances. Not surprisingly, a similar pattern emerged in the white settlement of the Florida peninsula. When Native southerners opposed the encroachment of settlers, white southerners criticized the federal government and called for assistance. As in the Creek War and the 1818 Florida Invasion, neighboring states came to the assistance of their suffering brethren. White southerners across the region begin to clamor en masse for the complete removal of the Eastern Indians to lands west of the Mississippi River. By 1830 decades of violent conflict and historical memories of unrest pushed many across the nation to conclude it was impossible for Native and white southerners to live side by side under any circumstances.

5

"Gallant Sons of the South"

Native Expulsion and Civic Militarism

In late 1835 Native southerners in Central Florida stood at a dire crossroads. Since 1823 Indigenous peoples of various ethnicities in Florida had been residing within a four-million-acre reservation that stretched from approximately modern-day Alachua County to the northern banks of Lake Okeechobee. The US federal government had recognized the borders of the Florida Territory's Indian country not long after acquisition of the peninsula from Spain. According to the deal, the US agreed to recognize the boundaries of Indian land, provide supplies for those towns relocating to the reservation, and even guaranteed an annuity of five thousand dollars until 1843. Despite assurances made in the agreement, white settlers, the Florida territorial government, and the federal government did little to support the sustainability of Florida's Indigenous communities. Throughout the 1820s white settlers from southern states such as the Carolinas, Georgia, and Alabama pushed into the Florida Panhandle and down the peninsula, encroaching on Native land and resources. The ensuing conflicts over property and land frequently offered white southerners the opportunity to make violent reprisals against Natives and demand federal intervention in the form of money, munitions, and soldier deployments.

When the US federal government passed the 1830 Indian Removal Act with extensive support from southern states, federally appointed treaty commissioners set out to obtain signatures for the relocation of Native Americans east of the Mississippi River to a federally managed territory in the west.[1] Treaty commissioners negotiated with any Indigenous party who could be deemed marginally representative of the various Native communities across the South. In 1832 Secretary of War Lewis Cass appointed James Gadsden as a commissioner to the Florida Indians with the intent to secure a removal treaty and the acquisition of all Native land claims in the Florida Territory. At Payne's Landing near modern-day Gainesville, Gadsden acquired the marks of seven headmen and eight of their subordinates, purportedly representative of the "Seminole Indians" with the authority to negotiate the cessions of all lands claimed in "the Territory of Florida" by Native southerners.[2] According to the treaty's stipulations, the US government would allow an exploratory expedition at the direction of the signatories to a proposed site in Arkansas prior to finalizing the forfeiture of their Florida lands. Not long after the treaty and a preliminary excursion by a party of Florida Indians to the Arkansas Territory, rumors of strong-arm tactics and fraud on behalf of the US military and treaty commissioners undermined the legitimacy of the relocation agreement. Further casting a shadow upon the negotiations was the diffuse autonomy among the various bands of Indigenous and Black occupants of the Florida Territory, some of whom had called the peninsula home since time immemorial and held no allegiances to the fifteen Native men who signed the land cession.[3] Regardless of the arrangement's dealings, the US Senate approved the treaty with a unanimous vote in April 1834 sanctioning the federal government to pursue the expulsion of Native people from Florida.[4]

Despite the veneer of validity built around the Treaty of Payne's Landing and other relocation treaties sanctioned by the US Congress, thousands of Native southerners across the region had no intention of submitting to the ethnic cleansing of the South without protest. The Cherokee famously waged their battle in US courts. The Creek fought a short-lived resistance in 1836 in Georgia.[5] In late 1835 a faction of Florida Indians initiated a martial opposition to their forced removal against the United States that lasted into the 1840s. Near the end of November, a party of Florida Indians executed Charley Emathla, one of the leading Native advocates of migrating to the Arkansas Territory. Newspaper reports described Osceola and a band of Miccosukee "waylaying" Charley Emathla outside his home not far from the Fort King Indian Agency near modern-day Ocala, Florida. The Miccosukee men, according to the report, shot Emathla almost a dozen times and left his body in the street. White Floridians recoiled at the violent manner of Emathla's execution, memorializing the pro-removal Native leader and vilifying his slayers. At his death, the *Florida Herald* commemorated Emathla and his pro-removal stance as a virtuous embodiment to white aspirations, describing him as "one of the most intelligent and enterprising of the emigrating party, and in fact of the whole nation." Such action indicated to white readers a clear opposition to removal among the Florida Indians and their willingness to fight for their right to remain in the South. Alongside news of Emathla's lamented execution, newspapers across the region reprinted a warning that Florida settlers should "consult their safety" in anticipation "against Indian depredations."[6] While Emathla's execution made significant waves in southern papers, the death of Indian agent Wiley Thompson and the defeat of Maj. Francis L. Dade's command of 110 soldiers in December 1835 produced a white panic that sparked a martial zealotry not seen in the South since the 1813 Red Stick success against Fort Mims.

As bands of Florida Indians militarily opposed forced removal in 1835, white communities throughout the South leveraged Native resistance to expulsion as justification for a mass call to arms. Across the region, a swell of civic militarism rallied a broad range of white southerners to collaborate in the ethnic cleansing of the Florida peninsula. White southerners outside of the Florida Territory championed a communal martial obligation to defend fellow settlers referred to in familial terms as their "Florida brethren."[7] The threat of Native violence against white settlers in Florida prompted a renewed outpouring of criticisms by white southerners against the federal government for negligence, lack of preparation, and general endangerment of white households. Individual white southerners from the Carolinas to Louisiana rallied local militias and called for decisive action against the Florida Indians. White communities throughout the South invoked memories of their own conflicts with Native southerners and believed it a shared duty to protect their neighboring white countrymen. City, county, and state governments organized relief efforts for white Floridians and raised militias to subdue the Florida Indians. In southern cities, public meetings led by common citizens and local municipal officials initiated and directed efforts to wage a war of expulsion. The collective martial fervor among whites prompted coordinated action across state lines that facilitated local and national fundraising, the transportation of militia companies to Florida, and even collaborative strategy on how best to defend white settlers in the territory. Major cities along the southern coast gave the appearance of military staging grounds as white volunteers prepared for their excursions to Florida.[8] The collective white exuberance to purge Indigenous peoples from the South contributed to the cooperation and coalescence of white communities across the region. White southerners rallied in opposition to a common racialized enemy, lambasted the federal government, and celebrated a shared tradition of honor and self-sufficient militarism. By 1836 one volunteer from South Carolina went so far as to claim that the cooperative dispossession of Native southerners from Florida forged a coalescence of the white South as a people "emanating from one family" in the collective defense of their suffering brethren.[9]

Native Resistance and White Panic

Native resistance to forced removal sparked a panic among white southerners beginning in December 1835. At Fort King a party of Miccosukee reported to be led by Osceola ambushed and killed Indian agent Wiley Thompson while he and a compatriot walked beyond the fortification's walls on the evening of the December 28. As Indian agent, Wiley Thompson was the leading federal government official tasked with overseeing the removal of Florida's Native peoples in the territory. His death conveyed to the federal government and white settlers that a portion of Florida's Indigenous peoples had no intention of leaving their homeland and raised an alarm of further hostilities.[10] On the same day to the west, Native southerners led by Micanopy, Jumper, and Halpatter Tustenuggee surprised Maj. Francis L. Dade and his men as they attempted to march from Fort Brooke near Tampa to Fort King. The Native attack was a resounding victory, and only 3 of Dade's 110 soldiers survived the ambush. The nearly unprecedented success of a Native force against trained US regulars spread fear across the white South reminiscent of the panic in the wake of Fort Mims.[11] A veteran of the conflict, John T. Sprague, recalled in his 1848 account of "The Florida War" that these early military victories by the Florida Indians "created a panic throughout the territory" and inspired settlers to flee "for their lives, leaving behind the common necessaries of life."[12]

In January 1836 Florida Indians expanded their resistance to expulsion by targeting white homesteads and plantations along northeast Florida's St. Johns River. Alongside terrorizing their opponent, the strategy had practical goals to draw US forces away from Native towns in the peninsula's interior and seize vulnerable war stuffs such as guns and powder.[13] Yet, for white observers, the terror of Native violence defined the campaign. According to Sprague, Florida Indians destroyed sixteen plantations between Jacksonville and modern-day Port Orange.[14] In one raid Florida Indians set fire to the Bulow Plantation, near modern-day Ormond Beach, after it was hastily abandoned by Charles W. Bulow. Established shortly after the US acquisition of Florida in 1823, the plantation was locally referred to as "Bulowville" due to its size and economic diversity. When volunteer militia reoccupied the plantation in February 1836, eyewitness accounts lamented the destruction of the property that had formerly included a large two-story home, multiple out buildings, forty slave dwellings, and a sugar mill.[15]

Within the Florida Territory, fear and paranoia among whites spread as Natives scored early victories. The seemingly random attacks and destruction of white homesteads, Sprague wrote, left settlers feeling "none could tell at what moment or in what manner, they would be assailed, and subjected to the most cruel and brutal death." By the time Sprague began documenting his chronicle of the Florida War, he noted that especially gruesome acts of Native violence marked settler recollections of early 1836. Some settlers, Sprague said, believed Natives had used acts of violence to terrorize white communities. In one instance Sprague recorded that settlers believed "in some instances, the lives of mothers were spared that they might see their children cut in pieces, and their limbs used as weapons to assail the living."[16] In contemporary accounts, Florida newspapers across the territory described the peninsula on the precipice of ruin. In December 1835 the *Jacksonville Courier* characterized settlers around Alachua in a panic. Native attacks against plantations and homesteads left whites "very much alarmed." According to one Alachua settler, "most of the families have abandoned their homes and assembled at different places where the inhabitants have erected, or are erecting forts for protection." Residents of Newnansville, south of modern-day Gainesville, turned the county courthouse into a fort and the local jail into a blockhouse for their own protection.[17] By the following January, the *Pensacola Gazette* shared, "Report says the Indians are a thousand strong, and that they are bent on war."[18] Even as far as Key West, white settlers looked suspiciously upon Natives whom they had been trading with for years and readied for a potential assault.[19]

Beyond the Florida Territory, reports of Native violence against white settlers and US military outposts spread hysteria across the South. With the initial engagements taking place in isolated areas of the Florida interior, southern cities received inconclusive and, at times, contradictory information about the fate of white victims and the broader objectives of the Florida Indians. Generally, the southern press painted a bleak picture for white Floridians relying on information provided from personal correspondence sent out of the Florida Territory or accounts sourced from Florida newspapers. Private correspondence printed in a Greensboro, North Carolina, paper relayed information that Indian raids left several plantations "entirely destroyed" and that Native warriors threatened the city of St. Augustine.[20] Also out of St. Augustine, *The Herald* gave a dire description of East Florida, printing "the whole country south of St. Augustine has been laid waste . . . there is not a single house remaining . . . [for] a distance of 250 miles." The account of East Florida's destruction proliferated through newspapers across the South. In February and March 1836, presses in Georgia, the Carolinas, Tennessee, and Virginia shared the identical report that first appeared in the St. Augustine press. Residents of major southern cities such as Milledgeville, Charleston, Raleigh, Nashville, and Richmond read how Native southerners set plantations ablaze, whites feared venturing beyond the protection of armed patrols, and Natives wreaked havoc unimpeded across Florida's northeast Atlantic coast.[21] Building from the circulation of such reports, papers in southern cities described Florida as a sacrificial altar supplied with white settlers. The *Georgia Messenger* in Macon reported that "the whole of Florida east of the Suwannee River was crying for help, and without immediate aid, the lives of a large portion of our fellow citizens, men, women, and children, were to be sacrificed by the ruthless savage."[22] In Charleston a city paper reported

"INDIAN HOSTILITIES!!" announcing to readers the "Latest Intelligence from the Theatre of War." South Carolinians were informed that hostile Indians made surprise attacks against white settlers without regard to age or sex. As relayed by the *Charleston Mercury*, in areas around Lake George and Fort King, Florida Indians "had burned all the houses and destroyed property" as well as setting a store ablaze in Palatka.[23]

Native strategy in December 1835 and January 1836 effectively cut cross-peninsula communications. As a result the South's Gulf and Atlantic coasts received news reports on Wiley Thompson and Dade's Command at different points and in different sequence. While news of Thompson's death initially provoked white southerners on the Atlantic coast, the Gulf Coast learned of Dade's annihilation first. For information to disperse across the region, correspondence and newspapers had to travel from Florida port cities northwest via oceangoing vessels. The *Mobile Daily Commercial Register and Patriot* first reported on Dade's defeat in Mobile, Alabama, on the morning of January 11, 1836. The initial account was concise but portrayed Dade and his men as noble martyrs who valiantly fought to their fated demise. The accounts from the southern press presaged rhetoric of the "Lost Cause" that would come to ease the fragile egos of vanquished Confederates in the conquest of the Confederate States of America. In Alabama, Mobilians read that "an overwhelming number of Indians" attacked Dade's detachment as they marched to Fort King unsuspecting of their imminent doom. Celebrating the martial valor of the deceased, the newspaper depicted Native Floridians launching a dishonorable ambush as the assailants shot and killed Major Dade in their opening salvo. According to the paper, Dade's subordinate Captain Frances gallantly rode forward but was likewise swiftly cut down. Such a catastrophic defeat led the Mobile paper to immediately label the demise of Dade and his company an "INDIAN MASSACRE."[24] Reporting in Mobile established a precedent that other southern communities relied on to relay information about the battle in Florida. Presses in Georgia, South Carolina, North Carolina, and Virginia relied on papers from Mobile to inform their communities on the events encompassing Dade's defeat. In each case the presses reiterated or summarized the same depiction of events provided by the *Mobile Register*. As a result, the Mobile paper constructed the initial narrative that came to inform white southerners across the region.

Alongside the depictions of glorious soldiers ambushed on the battlefield, the southern press perpetuated the label of "Massacre" when describing the deaths of Dade and his company. Following the lead of the *Mobile Register*, presses reprinting or summarizing from the Alabama paper characterized the Native victory in Florida most commonly as "Indian Massacre," "Horrid Massacre," or simply "The Massacre."[25] The incendiary description of the battle as a massacre sensationalized Dade's defeat for white readers in the South and erased the intentions of Dade's command to purge Florida of Indigenous people. By describing the defeat of Dade and his men as a massacre, the southern press and those who perpetuated the characterization framed an invading military force on Native land as innocent and unsuspecting victims murdered outside the honorable norms of civilized warfare. In addition, the label of massacre drew associations to settler memories of prior violence by Native Americans against whites such as the 1813 Red Stick attack against Fort Mims, popularly remembered as "The Fort Mims Massacre." As anthropologist Gregory Waselkov notes about the mythology of the "Fort Mims Massacre," the presentation and memory of helpless whites slaughtered by inhumane savages fueled calls for swift and morally just reprisals.[26] In the aftermath of the Florida Indians' attempt to oppose dispossession, white southerners called for what they conceived as justified retribution.

The startling success of Native southerners in Florida elicited criticisms against the federal government. White southerners and regional governments added to prior critiques claiming the federal government lacked sufficient measures to protect white settlers. Many of the accusations fell in line with well-worn claims of federal negligence that settlers had invoked over the prior decade in Alabama, Georgia, and the Mississippi Territory. Florida settlers now added that the federal government failed to adequately prepare for the relocation of the territory's Native peoples. Despite being an appointee of the US president and lifelong friend to Andrew Jackson, Florida territorial governor Richard K. Call often criticized the inadequate assistance provided by the federal government.[27]

At least a few US military leaders in Florida gave merit to settlers' complaints. In November 1835 the commanding officer at Fort King, Lt. Col. Alexander C. W. Fanning, feared the military was poorly prepared for what was about to come, speculating "there appears to be a general disaffection of the Indians, and, no doubt, War is determined." Fanning wrote Gen. Duncan L. Clinch, who now commanded the federal forces in Florida, lamenting they were undermanned should the Florida Indians resist their impending expulsion. Fanning confided, "We have fallen into the error committed at the commencement of every Indian War: The display of too little force—The attempt to do too much with inadequate men."[28] General Clinch was aware of the potential for disaster and over the previous year had made attempts to impress upon his superiors the need for a stronger military presence in Florida. Throughout 1835 Clinch wrote to both the US Army Adj. Gen. Roger Jones and Secretary Cass requesting additional support for Fort King and Fort Marion in St. Augustine. Clinch stated "that if it is the intention of the government to remove the Seminole Indians . . . whether the Nation consented or not," it was necessary to add four additional companies of US soldiers to Fort King and two additional companies to Fort Brooke. Anticipating militant Native opposition to dispossession, Clinch also requested heavier munitions. He wanted "two six pounders (field cannons) completely equipped for the field [be] sent to each of the above named Posts with as little delay as possible." Clinch foresaw a strong and imposing US military force as a possible deterrent to the rumored resistance of the Florida Indians, and, if war could not be avoided, the United States would be ready and equipped to "prevent the shedding of blood."[29]

Clinch's apprehension about the federal government's state of preparedness became a salient rumor circulating among white southerners. Upon arriving in St. Augustine in February 1836, South Carolinian Henry Summer recorded in a private diary on Clinch's efforts to bolster US forces and armaments in preparation of the removal campaigns. Summer wrote that he "was informed that Gen Clinch had said in 1835 about six or eight months previous to the breaking out of hostilities with the Seminoles, that he was afraid, there would be some difficulty with them." Rumors spread among the volunteers, according to Summer, that Clinch "had informed the government that a strong force ought to be kept there ready to be brought in to action wherever they should be needed."[30] As Clinch and Fanning had suspected, and the volunteers soon discovered, the US military was unprepared for Native opposition to forced removal in Florida.

White southerners came to see lack of adequate preparation by the federal government as indifference to their safety, in line with Washington's broader disregard of settler pleas for security. For decades white communities in Georgia, Florida, and Alabama had made appeals for protection to various levels of government for fear of Indian attacks. In 1818 inhabitants of Tuscaloosa County, Alabama, petitioned Gov. William Bibb after the deaths of three white children and a "negro woman" left the community "in great distress." Reportedly, large parties of "Hostile Indians" were passing through the vicinity unopposed, and the petitioners hoped the governor could secure "aid in men & as many arms as [it] may be" in his power to provide.[31] In 1824 Florida governor William P. DuVal contacted Secretary Calhoun directly concerning "some difficulty with the Indians." In July, Indians refusing to leave their homes in the Panhandle "threatened to drive the people out of the country and to make war" upon the territorial government. DuVal criticized the federal government's lack of support and inability to utilize federal soldiers to intimidate the Florida Indians into relocating to the reservation established by the Treaty of Moultrie Creek.[32] At times white southerners petitioned the president directly. In March 1826 residents of St. Johns County, Florida, petitioned President John Quincy Adams to intervene, as the Indians were reportedly "roaming at large over the county" and doing "serious mischief to the inhabitants."[33]

With similar feelings at the end of 1835, white southerners openly criticized the federal government as incompetent and failing to provide for the safety of Florida settlers. Through the press, white southerners blamed Washington for the Native uprising in Florida and the violence against white communities. From Apalachicola, Florida, white residents criticized the federal government for failing to provide sufficient fortifications after the death of a farm boy.[34] In North Carolina, Salisbury's *Western Carolinian* summarized recent reports on the violence in Florida and condemned the federal government. In February 1836 the paper reported, "The force in Florida at the commencement of hostilities were entirely inadequate." The lack of federal action, the paper printed, left white settlers exposed, and it rhetorically asked, "Must all the inhabitants—the wives, mothers, daughters, and helpless infants—of Florida be sacrificed to the tomahawk and scalping knife of the ruthless savage before that protection which the Government is in duty bound to give will be extended?"[35] In the same month, Macon's *Georgia Messenger* chastised the War Department for its lethargy and "negligence . . . by which hundreds of lives have been lost."[36] In March the paper continued to give a voice to those displeased with the federal government's response to the dispossession of Native Floridians. One recirculated commentary declared, "We shall ever consider it a stain on the War Department that they have suffered the defenseless inhabitants and our brave soldiers to be murdered by the Indians in Florida." The unnamed commentator believed "the government knew well that the Seminole Indians were determined not to go West of the Mississippi." Therefore, the federal government was bound "by every principle to have a portion of the United States troops on the spot to protect the scattered inhabitants of the Territory."[37]

Criticism continued from South Carolina. A Charleston paper printed correspondence from a resident of St. Augustine in January 1836 that equally condemned the federal government's lack of preparation. The letter, attributed to the pen name "Amicus Floridae" declared, "It is a melancholy and mortifying fact, that all these injuries and losses have been occasioned by the bad policy of our Government." Critical of the lack of federal troops deployed to Florida, the correspondence feared, "If the Government of the United States continue to act in this way, Florida, at least the Eastern District, in a years time, will be completely ruined."[38] Just a few days later, the paper provided community organizers in Charleston a venue to disseminate critiques of the federal government. In a notice for a public meeting regarding the Florida Indian uprising, Charlestonians read an editorial that indicted Congress and the federal government for their inaction. The author believed that "this Indian War, is no sudden incursion," sharing, "It was apprehended, and the Secretary of War informed Congress that he had taken measures to meet it." However, the essay continued, "We see that the inhabitants of this unfortunate Territory have been given up to the Tomahawk and Scalping Knife, without even an effort to protect them."[39] One attendee of the Charleston meeting echoed his doubts about the federal government's resolve to quickly extinguish Native resistance. He wrote "after the war had been raging nearly two months . . . only $80,000 had been appropriated" to combat the Florida Indians and protect white communities.[40]

The Atlantic South Coordination

Native resistance to dispossession in Florida sparked a martial zeal among white southerners across the South. White communities prepared volunteer companies on their own accord and pressured the US military to act with haste. While modern historians have typically looked to the US military as guiding the onset of the Second Seminole War, civilian organizers in southern cities played a critical role.[41] In at least one instance, white southerners' impatience became a point of contention with the US military. In December 1835 white Charlestonians attempted to muster and deploy volunteers to Florida but were turned away by Gen. Abraham Eustis, the local liaison for the War Department.[42] As violence in Florida persisted in late 1835 into 1836, white southerners rose to march to the Florida Territory against the Native southerners. Using city-based public meetings, white men in the South rallied local communities to action. Meeting organizers vilified Native opposition to removal as a war against innocent white settlers. Their calls to arms leveraged well-worn grievances and rhetoric against Native southerners to inspire men, women, businesses, and local municipalities to support volunteers. In addition to the vilification of Native southerners, Indigenous opposition to expulsion facilitated continued criticisms against the federal government by whites for failing to protect settlers against Native violence. Through the public meetings, white communities coordinated across state lines to protect settlers referred to as their "Florida brethren." From Charleston to New Orleans, white men celebrated their mutual martial spirit and characterized the collaborative expulsion of Native Floridians as noble retribution and a defense of their victimized compatriots.

From South Carolina, the city of Charleston led a fervent and expeditious effort for a campaign against the Florida Indians.[43] In December 1835 the self-proclaimed honorable and noble men of Charleston organized a local town meeting "in accordance with the popular will" of the community to accelerate the deployment of volunteer companies to Florida.[44] White men in the city professed it their duty to find a way to diminish the suffering of white settlers in distress and an obligation of their martial honor to act with urgency. The attendees at the public meeting professed a consensus to prepare volunteers for a campaign to Florida. The local paper printed an account of the initial meeting and congratulated their determined spirit despite the cold and rainy weather of the season.[45]

On New Year's Day 1836, the participants held a follow-up gathering and unanimously passed six resolutions by the "numerous and respectable" attendees. They recognized "with great anxiety" that "their countrymen in Florida [were] exposed to the rage of a ruthless and savage enemy." The committee chairman and mayor of Charleston, Gen. Robert Y. Hayne, offered to provide an advance for volunteers who were in need of arms and necessary supplies.[46] Other wealthy men of South Carolina, such as Wade Hampton II, would later follow suit by extending their personal credit to outfit volunteer companies.[47] As part of the January public meeting, Charlestonians looked to local municipal officials to request that the city council provide the funds to transport men and purchase provisions for the volunteers' Florida campaign.[48] By requesting that the Charleston city council fund the volunteers' expedition, they invited their local government to sanction the undertaking and bore responsibility for the expulsion of Florida's Native peoples. In concluding the public meeting, the community organizers resolved to announce their proceedings in "all the papers of this city" and make a call to arms for volunteers either in full companies or as individuals. The proclamation printed in Charleston papers declared that volunteers were needed "for the defense of the Inhabitants of Florida from the attacks of the Seminole Indians."[49]

By the end of January, community organizers held a second meeting at city hall in an appeal to the "patriotism of the community" in preparation "to vote for the adoption of the most active and energetic measures for the relief of our suffering fellow citizens" in Florida.[50] The meeting attendees professed a desire to provide the "suffering inhabitants of Florida" with both money and men. The organizing committee convened the session by reading a report reiterating their belief in the prevalence of Native violence against white settlers, federal lethargy in deploying sufficient forces, and the need to act immediately, fearing that additional white Floridians faced an impending doom. The public declaration also invoked familial kinship connections between Charlestonians and the Florida settlers. The committee's report publicly announced that "such is the tragedy now acting upon a Territory," the residents were "but a few degrees removed from us." The report made a direct connection between Charlestonians and the Florida settlers asserting the peninsula was "a Territory inhabited by numbers who have gone out from our own families and our own hearths."[51] At the meeting nearly one hundred men enrolled to serve in Florida, and the committee anticipated another hundred volunteers the following day.[52]

On January 17 Secretary of War Lewis Cass authorized General Eustis in Charleston to begin receiving volunteer companies for deployment to Florida. Cass directed Eustis to "gather all the troops that could be spared and lead them to St. Augustine."[53] While it is unclear what day Eustis received the order at his station in Charleston, local organizers were already well under way in readying companies for departure. Eustis quickly discovered that South Carolinians' martial enthusiasm exceeded the US military's capacity. Perhaps underestimating the state's zeal for conquest, Eustis was unable to accommodate "all the troops that could be spared," as Secretary Cass had instructed. Because of the outpouring of interest, Eustis declined the services of at least two Charleston militia companies due the enlistment of a full complement of volunteers. Not to be discouraged, the *Charleston Courier* reported "some of the men of the companies [were] determined to proceed to the scene of action, under any circumstances."[54] In support, local Charlestonian Captain Magrath offered the services of his steamboat to transport excess volunteers to Florida free of charge. In a demonstration of commercial benevolence, Magrath also offered to provide women and children in St. Augustine free passage to Charleston on his return voyage for the safety and comfort of displaced refugees.[55]

The South Carolina volunteers came from a cross-section of the state's white residents. From the Piedmont, Midlands, and Low Country, South Carolina counties sent an overwhelming number of volunteers at the start of the conflict. Between 1835 and 1839, more than two thousand served in Florida, with many responding to the initial call to arms.[56] Kershaw County in the South Carolina Midlands mustered three companies after their own series of public meetings and collected horses to provide for the Florida volunteers.[57] From the South Carolina Piedmont region, Lancaster County contributed another company in "much larger numbers than was requested."[58]

While a modest number of soldiers' accounts still exist today, historians know few specifics about most of the individuals that participated in the initial public meetings and 1836 Florida campaign. In one instance participant Myer M. Cohen detailed his involvement in Charleston's public meetings as the committee's secretary and a volunteer in East Florida. Cohen was by no means a professional soldier. Born in 1804, Cohen worked as a school headmaster, then a lawyer. In 1824 he established an English and Classical Seminary in Charleston that he operated until his admission to the bar in 1829. Cohen was well entrenched in Charleston society. He was an active member of Charleston's Literary and Philosophical Society of South Carolina and the Hebrew Benevolent Society. He was also active in civic life in the city. Cohen was a member of the Washington's Birthday Committee and a member of the Washington Volunteers.[59] In 1836 Native resistance to expulsion in Florida provided Cohen an opportunity for excitement and a chance to demonstrate his masculine honor. Cohen described his motivation to volunteer his service in the "military operations, namely, [for] a wild wish for adventure, and a humble hope to be useful!"[60] Cohen generalized the Charleston citizenry as similarly inspired by the honor of aiding their fellow southerners. He portrayed the conflict as a democratic struggle, with a diverse group of men volunteering for the campaign.

In Charleston a broad range of ethnicities and professions rallied to the cause as well. A German descendant and opponent of South Carolina's 1832 Nullifiers, William Henry Timrod, led the city's "German and United German Fusiliers" Company. The volunteer corps of Charleston Germans and men of German descent garrisoned at St. Augustine and served alongside the city's volunteers in Eustis's Left Wing.[61] In describing those enlisted, Cohen extolled the sacrifices of militiamen coming from an array of lifestyles. Volunteers left their peaceful occupations, according to Cohen, "to give up the student's pen for the soldier's sword, and his book for a shield, and to exchange the hammer of the worthy mechanic, for the musket of a militia man."[62] Charleston's Irish Volunteers mustered and offered their services but were initially turned away by the US Army due to lack of transportation. Discouraged but not deterred, the Irish Volunteers gathered at Charleston's Washington Hotel to plan a course of action. The men resolved that the whole force would stand in readiness should their services be needed.[63] As Cohen described, the plight of white Floridians appealed to young and old, rich and poor. Among the ranks of the Hamburg militia, a fourteen-year-old boy who "could not be restrained from joining the expedition, by the most earnest entreaties," enlisted to volunteer.[64] Southern students, artisans, and financiers all saw it as their responsibility to put down the tools of their trade and grasp the "musket of a militia man" in service of their Florida brethren. After his Florida campaign, Cohen presented the ongoing effort to remove the Florida Indians not as one in which Native southerners were defending their homeland but one where savages were hiding away and striking at innocent white victims. Cohen stated that "the cause of Florida was a good cause, and that hers was no manly enemy waging equal battle, in the broad face of day, in behalf of violated rights; but an ambushed foe, in mockery of the most solemn treaties, striking, like a cowardly assassin."[65]

In a similar fashion, South Carolina women celebrated the volunteers headed to Florida and described the endeavor as one of just retribution through poetry and promotional literature. In the literary magazine the *Southern Rose*, Mary Elizabeth Lee of Charleston wrote that although "a voice from the South tells a sad mournful story, of ruin and carnage" in reference to Dade's defeat, "brave volunteers" from South Carolina were certain to avenge the dead.[66] Thespian Charlotte Barnes authored and likely performed a recruitment broadside inspiring and venerating volunteers from Columbia headed to Florida.[67] In poetic prose titled "An Address to the Florida Volunteers," Barnes described the Columbia volunteers as common family men risking their lives to defend their fellow countrymen against an invading enemy. In romantic tones Barnes portrayed the common volunteer as a son, brother, husband, and father casting aside "all private gain" in their honorable venture to the Florida peninsula. With settlers in Florida under attack, Barnes described how "a sister land sends forth a wailing cry, And to that call those gallant hearts reply!" In "tearing themselves from those they love," Barnes continued, the volunteers committed to defending "our native land," against invading "stranger foes." The structure of her prose and performance turned recent white settlers into natives, and Natives into outsiders. Never identifying the Seminole or any Indigenous people of Florida, Barnes portrays Florida Indians as a nebulous enemy engaged in a dishonorable campaign of terror and violence desecrating a feminized colonial possession in need of protection. "The ills of savage war," Barnes penned, threatened the South Carolina volunteers as they faced "savage, ruthless foes." In Barnes's admiration of the Columbia volunteers, she depicts the men as noble defenders of violated homes against outsiders threatening the domestic tranquility of kinsmen. For their efforts in "arms against a common foe," Barnes assured that "when that land revives in peace, its people, far and near, Will join in thanks and gratitude to the generous Volunteer!"[68]

As part of the resolutions unanimously adopted by the Charleston public meeting on January 21, organizers opened "an immediate correspondence with the public authorities of Savannah, suggesting to the expediency of their succoring with men, munitions and provisions."[69] Charlestonians sought to encourage Georgians to organize their militia companies and collaborate on the Florida campaign. However, white communities in Georgia were already well on their way in preparing and deploying volunteers. By the end of January 1836, South Carolinians received news that volunteers in Augusta, Georgia, had mustered in preparation to head to Florida. The *Charleston Courier* congratulated the efforts of Augusta's citizens, stating, "That little city furnished one hundred and sixty volunteers . . . and her city council liberally made an appropriation for their equipment and support." In addition, businesses in Augusta guaranteed the pay of volunteers for the duration of their absence and promised their positions upon return. In describing the spirited conduct of Augusta, the Charleston paper declared that "the whole populace became zealous in the cause," against the Florida Indians.[70]

Figure 6. Charlotte Barnes broadside. "An Address to the Volunteers" performed by Charlotte Barnes rallied white South Carolinians and vilified Native Floridians opposing forced removal. From the South Caroliniana Library, University of South Carolina, Columbia, South Carolina.

In Savannah, Georgia, white community leaders had likewise been quick to organize a detachment in response to Native opposition to removal. In December 1835 white residents in the city held a similar public meeting in which some of the "most respectable citizens" volunteered to serve in a campaign against the Florida Indians. The committee appointed twelve men who canvassed the city for donations to equip and provide for the transportation of volunteers. On December 29, 1835, the first contingent of Georgia militias departed for Picolata along the St. Johns River via steamboat. Presses in Georgia and North Carolina reported the men went forth to render aid for their "fellow-citizens of Florida . . . exposed to the depredations of the Seminole Indians," all without federal assistance.[71]

When the Charlestonians reached out to the city of Savannah in January 1836, they found white Georgians in the city had a similar mind-set to collaborate across state lines. The Charleston Public Committee sent an open letter to the city of Savannah that was printed in the local press. The letter proclaimed Savannah's prompt assistance was necessary to "protect the women and children from the tomahawk and scalping knife" of marauding Native Floridians.[72] The Charleston Public Committee encouraged Savannah to send volunteers and supplies to Picolata and Jacksonville along the St. Johns River in East Florida. In tandem the Charleston committee vowed to keep up a constant communication with St. Augustine and to dedicate resources for the safety, provisioning, and defense of that post, until the "General Government should afford the requisite assistance."[73] With preparations already well under way, white residents of Savannah responded quickly. On January 23 the city of Savannah's Public Committee held a meeting with Mayor William Gordon in attendance and unanimously resolved that the Savannah volunteers would cooperate with the Charlestonians.[74]

Community leaders in Charleston and Savannah even went so far as to contemplate tactical advances against the Florida Indians along the northeast coast of the territory. Charleston volunteers anticipated that they would focus their men and materials on St. Augustine, while the volunteers of Savannah should proceed to Picolata and Jacksonville.[75] Assuming the Savannah volunteers could reach these locations unimpeded, the coordinated effort could form a defensive front in one of Florida's densest areas of white settlement. Picolata would form the forward position approximately twenty miles west of St. Augustine and thirty miles south of Jacksonville on the eastern bank of the St. Johns River. Jacksonville and St. Augustine could then form the northern and southern anchors of a defensive triangle. If volunteers formed a defensive patrol from Jacksonville to Picolata to St. Augustine, then a safe zone could theoretically be established encompassing the northeast tip of Florida while maintaining ocean-accessible transport in these three towns. If successful, the deployment set up for the secure transportation of more volunteers and munitions along with an evacuation route for settlers and wounded soldiers. With their success Picolata served as the main depot for the US regular and volunteer forces on the east coast through 1836.[76]

In addition to a mutual interest in the protection of Florida settlers and expulsion of Native Floridians, family ties facilitated the collaboration between the cities of Charleston and Savannah. The appointed secretaries for each city's Public Committee working to organize the muster of volunteers were kin. In Savannah, Octavus Cohen acted as secretary for the Public Committee, and in Charleston his cousin Myer M. Cohen functioned in the same role and was instrumental in opening a correspondence between the two cities. Although not directly related through their family name, Octavus's mother, Belle Moses, was the sister of Myer M. Cohen's mother,

Figure 7. Soldiers in camp outside fortified houses, Picolata, Florida. Settler homesteads fortified with assistance from the US Army and southern militias at Picolata, Florida, against potential Native reprisals during the removal campaigns ca. 1837. From *Views of Florida*, Soldiers in camp outside the fortified houses, Picolata. Florida, 1837, Library of Congress.

Eleanor Moses.[77] Octavus and Myer were presumably descendants from the Jewish Cohen family that emigrated from Europe prior to the American Revolution. By most accounts these men retained their Judaism while embracing the culture of the white South. In Charleston, Jews were numerous and prospered in an environment amenable to their faith. In Savannah, Jews were able to integrate into southern culture, most importantly by their adoption of the South's honor ethic and willingness to meet social adversaries on the city's dueling grounds.[78]

The citizens of Savannah were also motivated to action for many of the same reasons as their counterparts in Charleston. News in Savannah portrayed an increasingly grim story for Florida settlers. On January 19 Savannah newspapers reported on the defeat of Dade's command. The account was the same sensational excerpt received in Charleston from the *Mobile Chronicle*. The paper described the "surprise and massacre" of Dade's troops by anywhere from eight hundred to a thousand Indians.[79] By the time of publication, Secretary Cass had notified Georgia governor William Schley to prepare the state militia for potential deployment. In his letter to the governor, Cass took a cautious tone, failing to provide a specific number the governor should call to muster and speculated that "there was just reason to believe that the regular and militia forces employed [in Florida] were sufficient to subdue the Indians."[80] Matching the enthusiasm of South Carolina, residents of Georgia sent more than two thousand volunteers to join in the Florida campaign by the end of 1839.[81]

Coordinating Colonization from the Gulf South

Along the Gulf Coast, news of the Charleston public meetings reached Alabama, and the city of Mobile stood at the ready. According to the *Mobile Register*, the city's residents looked to Charleston to make the first move in the campaign to expel the Florida Indians. The Mobile newspaper openly praised the city of Charleston for its prompt response, declaring that if there was occasion for "volunteers, arms, or supplies to be forwarded to Florida," then Mobile promised to follow South Carolina's lead.[82] Farther inland a Tuscaloosa paper echoed similar sentiments on the importance of a collaborative campaign against the Florida Indians. Tuscaloosa's *Flag of the Union* informed readers that "under these alarming circumstances, it is the duty of the citizens of the adjoining States to aid their suffering brethren."[83] Like the residents of Charleston and Savannah, the residents of Mobile were spurred to action in response to reports of violence against whites in Florida. Mobile's initial notice of Dade's defeat rallied the community in the same manner the death of Wiley Thompson had on the Atlantic coast. In Mobile, public meetings mirrored events in Charleston and Savannah, and the participants adopted similar measures "without a dissenting voice."[84] The day after notice of Dade's defeat reached Alabama, citizens organized a meeting to "prepare resolutions suited to the exciting emergency" and issued a public notice the same evening.[85]

In reporting on the public meeting, the *Mobile Register* described one of the most passionate responses to Native resistance in Florida. According to the press, "measures are in progress to provide arms, ammunition, equipments and provisions, so that the volunteers may be enabled to march at the moment their services may be required." The report lamented the loss of white lives and offered an affirmation of the martial enthusiasm of white men in Mobile, writing, "The deep regret for the massacre of so many of our brave citizen soldiers, has awakened a spirit of retributive vengeance against their remorseless destroyers in the bosom of every man in this community." According to the newspaper, the passion for vengeance among white men in Mobile advocated for genocide, reporting "all are ready and anxious to aid in the extermination of a foe, whom nothing short of extermination can subdue."[86] Not only were the citizens of Mobile eager to go to Florida to protect white settlers, but Native resistance to expulsion now justified the elimination of an ethnicity. While not facing any imminent danger, white citizens in Alabama exhibited an impassioned response to protect Florida as white space, defend their neighboring citizens, and subdue Indigenous resistance to colonization. The fervor was such that they declared to only be satisfied with the eradication of every Native American in the Florida Territory.

The preparation of the Alabama volunteers followed the pattern seen in South Carolina and Georgia. On January 27 the *Mobile Register* announced a call for volunteers to prepare "for the protection of the defenseless Women and Children of Florida."[87] Mobile's Public Committee appointed twenty men to organize volunteers into companies. These companies were then to wait in readiness until commanders could coordinate with the federal army for deployment. They also expected the city, state, and federal officials to cover expenses for the impending expedition.[88] By the middle of February, the federal army was ready to deploy the Alabama volunteers. Gen. Winfield Scott sent Colonel Lindsay of the US Army to Mobile, granting him authorization to muster a full regiment from the state.[89] On February 20 Alabama governor Clement C. Clay issued a public notice that the War Department "made a requisition . . . of the militia of the state of Alabama." The War Department requested "one regiment of infantry or infantry and riflemen," not to exceed five companies.[90]

While Colonel Lindsay arrived in Mobile with authorization to draft men, if necessary, papers in Mobile and Tuscaloosa scoffed at such an idea. For white Alabamians, a draft at the time was seen as preposterous and insulting to the state's honor. The militant exuberance exuded through the press anticipated an excess of volunteers as had been the case in South Carolina. One paper assured it was "undoubtedly creditable to the public spirit and patriotism, [that] volunteers . . . come forward."[91] Another Alabama paper expected and encouraged residents to "immediately volunteer . . . protecting the people of Florida . . . and thereby honor themselves and the State."[92] Men from Tuscaloosa, Pickens, Fayette, Montgomery, and Wilcox Counties volunteered and surpassed the sum requested from the US Military.[93] According to a Tuscaloosa paper, "the patriotic and high-minded citizens of Tuscaloosa would not stand a draft and proudly and immediately came forward and volunteered their services . . . in number, more than double the number wanted."[94] Similar to militia enrollment in Charleston, the US military was overburdened with a surplus of men from across the state wishing to join the Florida campaign.

In Alabama volunteer musters became spectacles of civic militarism where individuals and municipalities celebrated their shared desire to eradicate the

Florida Indians. County musters turned into municipal festivals, and communities praised the martial pride of their volunteers. In Tuscaloosa County, the martial spirit of the community was audible in public spaces. By February the town was "the scene of much military parade and bustle," according to the local paper. The press described the fife and drum of militia parades echoing through the streets in preparation for the "proud and patriotic purpose of rendering assistance to our bleeding fellow citizens of Florida."[95] From Tuscaloosa, Alexander B. Meek joined the "State Guard" and descended the Black Warrior River headed for Mobile. Traveling aboard the steamboat *Courier*, the men sailed south, with the air behind them ringing "with the shouts and plaudits of the citizens on shore, and the farewell huzzas of the volunteers." On board the vessel, Meek described that "much sport and hilarity took place among the men." The abundance of volunteers required men to sleep on the open deck, on the cabin floor, and atop cotton bales; however, Meek said "every means was resorted to to produce laughter and gayety." As volunteers congregated in Mobile for deployment to Florida, the martial spectacle continued. Upon his arrival Meek recorded that in the bay before them "the many masts rose like a forest of pine saplings in the harbor." In the city the volunteers marched through Mobile to crowds of citizens displaying banners and playing music. Men with money to spend and time to kill attended the local theater and Shakespeare Coffee House with their compatriots and forged new bonds with volunteers passing through from Louisiana and other parts of Alabama.[96]

Mobile residents expressed gratitude for the volunteers' determination to defend the Florida settlers. On St. Joseph Street, Mrs. B. L. Barnes held a reception for the volunteers in the city at her residence on March 1. In the front lawn of her mansion, Mrs. Barnes presented Colonel Chisolm's regiment with a "beautiful banner," and a personal acquaintance made a "short and spirited address" to the volunteers in attendance. A similar engagement took place in front of the Mobile Court House, where "Messrs. H. Goldthwaite and J. F. Ross" presented a banner to the militia company the Montgomery Blues.[97] As volunteers continued to arrive in the city, the *Mobile Register* chronicled the fanfare the companies received along the way. From Dallas County, west of Montgomery, the Mobile paper noted that a company of volunteers "were peculiarly favored by the sex, whose favor is the strongest incentive to heroic actions." As they passed through Selma they received the complement of a flag "presented by the patriotic fair" of the city. The "Ladies of Cahawba," a local women's social group, granted the men another banner, described as "splendid in workmanship and taste." The adulation and offerings, the paper reported, were sure to make the men "invincible" with "these flags streaming over them" as they undertook their Florida campaign.[98]

Mobile also served as the staging ground for the deployment of volunteers from New Orleans, Louisiana. On January 11, 1836, citizens in New Orleans held a public meeting "upon the subject of the late Indian Massacre in Florida," with Mayor Denis Prieur serving as one of seven men directing the gathering. The New Orleanians expressed their "deepest indignation [at] the merciless and savage warfare now being raged by the Seminole Indians of Florida, against the unoffending inhabitants of that territory" and pledged to "receive subscriptions for the relief of the widows and orphans of those who fell victims in the late massacre of the troops on their march from Tampa Bay to Fort King." As in public meetings in South Carolina, Georgia, and Alabama, the New Orleans participants resolved to collect funds for the deployment of volunteers willing to march to "the defence of Florida" and made an appeal to "the citizens of New Orleans, and the state, to cooperate."[99] By the end of the month, the Louisiana State Legislature authorized the governor to raise volunteers and provided funds to offer a thirty-dollar bounty to those who enlisted. The *New Orleans Bee* described the men who responded to call for volunteers as from "all classes in favor of the citizens of Florida."[100]

In early February seven hundred Louisiana volunteers alongside three hundred US Army regulars departed New Orleans for Mobile. But as in other southern states, the zeal of white men exceeded the capacity for volunteers afforded by the US military. An additional three hundred Louisiana volunteers were unable to depart with their compatriots due to a lack of sufficient transportation.[101] To accommodate the excess Louisiana volunteers, the Louisiana governor authorized the enlistment of the men into the state militia, and the city council of New Orleans appropriated $5,000 for the volunteers headed for Florida.[102] The arrival of the additional Louisiana volunteers in Mobile caught the US military liaison, Colonel Lindsay, off guard. Initially, Lindsay turned the volunteers away, again due to lack of transportation. According to the *Mobile Register*, it was "with much regret that [Lindsay] was compelled to decline the service of the corps, which, by zeal it had already manifested, has given a pledge for its gallantry and good conduct."[103] As a result the city of Mobile stepped in to ensure 107 excess Louisiana volunteers could join in the Florida campaign. The Mobile Guards supplied the men with additional arms and ammunition, and the city raised money to provide for their supplies and transportation. Though they did not travel with the US Army contingent, the citizens of Mobile ensured that the determination of the Louisianans would "not be defeated in their wish for the want of pecuniary means."[104]

Volunteers from South Carolina, Georgia, Alabama, Tennessee, and Louisiana numbered into the thousands fighting alongside Florida settlers. Between

1835 and 1839, more than sixteen thousand militiamen left the safety and security of their own homes to travel hundreds of miles to aid in the expulsion of the Florida Indians from the peninsula.[105] The opening swarm of volunteers from across the South invading the Florida Territory facilitated the construction of an exclusionary and regionally bound white identity. Their participation in the conflict aspired to purge the region of Native southerners and produced a fissure between the southern states and the federal government. The participants in the Florida removal campaigns and their supporting communities provided a means for the mutual adulation of white southerners' martial traditions and honor culture. White southerners' cooperative experience in Florida helped solidify a shared vision for the white South's future.

As the volunteers of 1836 returned home, some began to reflect on their Florida campaign as a coalescing experience for the white South bound in reciprocity and a common enemy. Their assessments mirrored the civic militarism in the initial call to arms and support from municipal leaders across the South. Volunteers celebrated the honor of one another and their common cause in protecting their Florida brethren as their predecessors had done after the Battle of Horseshoe Bend. After his service in the 1836 Florida campaigns, Charlestonian Myer M. Cohen praised white southerners serving in Florida collectively as "gallant sons of the South" all made from "the same sterling material." These volunteers from Louisiana to South Carolina not only united against a common enemy; Cohen wrote they were also "gallant volunteers . . . emanating from one family, all sons of the South."[106] They were, in his estimation a region-based family bound together to protect their suffering kin in a time of need. Another South Carolina volunteer, Woodburne Potter, made a similar declaration. Potter praised the "hundreds of the bravest sons" of Georgia, South Carolina, and Alabama who rallied to aid the Florida settlers. Potter celebrated that "meetings were organized in Augusta, Savannah, Darien and Charleston [with] the most enthusiastic feeling."[107] White communities of the South fighting against the Florida Indians were not just brothers-in-arms but also children to a metaphorical father embodied in a collective regional personification of the very land in which they lived.

Native resistance to expulsion from the US South gave white communities across the region an opportunity to secure the Florida Territory through violence and build a shared sense of belonging. While the US military eventually directed the effort to remove the Florida Indians that dragged on into the 1840s, community organizers in southern cities such as Charleston, Savannah, Mobile, and New Orleans led the charge in 1836. Civic meetings and local governments provided white southerners the initial vehicle to enact their celebrated desire to exterminate the Florida Indians. Enthusiasm for a call to arms cut across class and political affiliation in the white South. Men from various trades and walks of life volunteered to serve. Wealthy families made donations. City councils diverted municipal funds to provide for the relief of Florida settlers and equip volunteer companies. Women organized celebrations and endorsed the white South's efforts to eradicate Florida's Native southerners. Civic collaboration across state lines facilitated by family connections and a shared martial spirit rallied white men against a common foe.

The effort by the Florida Indians to retain their homelands catalyzed a regional awareness among white southerners. Native violence against settlers and their households gave white communities cause to portray their efforts as a war of defense. In doing so they extended a shared sense of suffering alongside the Florida settlers. Volunteers from South Carolina, Georgia, Alabama, and Louisiana were not just joining the fight in another Indian campaign. Southern communities celebrated their efforts as protecting their "Florida brethren" in a "sister land" that called for help in protecting the white South's "native land." The perceived indifference of the federal government and assumed violent disposition of all Indians provided a distinctive "other" white southerners could define themselves against. The Florida Indian uprising showed white southerners a common interest and demonstrated they had the capability for collective and cooperative action. In 1836 to be a southerner was not simply to be from a geographical place but also to harbor honor-bound obligations shaped through a shared experience in response to Native opposition to colonialism.

6

"Suffering Seldom Equaled"

Sharing Memories of White Victimization

In 1851 Milton A. Haynes, a lawyer and local chronicler from Cornersville, Tennessee, determined to document "the experiences, the sufferings, and conduct of a single individual" with the hope that the record "may better illustrate the condition, progress, or character of the people" of Tennessee. Through a series of interviews, Haynes recorded the family history of Joseph Brown as provided to him through Brown's personal recollections. Brown shared that in 1788 his family of eleven set out from North Carolina to claim a land grant in Tennessee awarded to his father, James, for service in the Revolutionary War. While traveling down the Tennessee River, Chickamauga warriors boarded their riverboat as they passed a series of Cherokee towns near modern-day Chattanooga. Since the American Revolution, the Chickamauga were an ethnically similar but politically separatist faction of the Cherokee residing along the Tennessee River. In 1776 the Chickamauga had been a driving force among the Cherokee to resist American settler expansion, and they continued their opposition into the 1780s.[1] According to Brown's memories, the Chickamauga forced Joseph and his family to stand by as they pilfered the settlers' supplies and cargo. When a Chickamauga man decided to take Joseph captive, his father attempted to intercede. As Brown recalled more than fifty years after the event, "the Indian seized a sword which was lying on the boat, and while [his father's] back was turned to him, struck him on the back of the neck, almost severing his head from his body." Brown described how his father "turned in the agony of death and seized the Indian, and in the struggle was thrown overboard into the river, where he sank to rise no more." The Chickamauga kidnapped the fifteen-year-old Joseph and took him to Nickajack. For more than a year, Joseph served his captors, carrying water, collecting firewood, and tending livestock. In 1789 "an exchange of prisoners" between Tennessee and the Cherokee resulted in his release. Joseph and two of his sisters were sent to relatives in South Carolina. Eventually returning to Tennessee, Joseph served as a scout for the Tennesseans' 1794 Nickajack Expedition against the Chickamauga towns. Guiding a detachment of militia, Joseph participated in the annihilation of the Chickamauga. Brown recalled in one instance he "killed an Indian warrior in single combat, and carried away his scalp." Documenting these recollections in 1851, Haynes summarized that "the history of events connected with the family . . . possess all the attraction of a romance; yet it is but a plain, sad story of trials and sufferings incident to the period."[2]

Brown's tale of multigenerational suffering, captivity, and revenge spread among the early settlers of Tennessee and resonated throughout the nineteenth century. A multitude of chronicles, including a state history developed for children, retold the graphic violence against the Browns.[3] The reminiscences of Native violence and subsequent historical chronicles documenting the Brown episode emphasized a cruel and unexpected aggression against settlers, rather than contextualizing the events with the ongoing war at the time or the violence of colonial dispossession.[4]

In 1853 one of the most prominent chroniclers of the state, James Ramsey, immortalized Brown's reminiscences as a part of the state's recorded past in *The Annals of Tennessee*. Ramsey included a lengthy account of Joseph Brown's reminiscences sourced from their mutual acquaintance Felix Zollicoffer.[5] As introduced by Ramsey, the account was "given in the words . . . of Joseph Brown" and described "a horrid recital of Indian cruelty and barbarism." Ramsey assured readers of the account's authenticity as "so truthful and minute in its details" as to defy any doubt. Ramsey's printed version of Brown's reminiscence in 1853 closely mirrored the rendition given directly to Haynes in 1851.[6] As a tangible and static text, Ramsey's work served as a widely read interpretation of the state's past for the remainder of the nineteenth century. With the publication's prominence, white settlers and their descendants looked to Ramsey's chronicle of the state as an accurate representation of Tennessee history. Future nineteenth-century chroniclers came to rely on Ramsey's work and assessment of Native southerners in Tennessee's late eighteenth century. More than twenty years after the publication of Ramsey's *Annals of Tennessee*, the inclusion of Brown's reminiscence offered historian Richard Beard a point of reference for reconstructing the history of the Presbyterian Church in Middle Tennessee, perpetuating Brown's recollections of settler victimization.[7] What was once the oral history of a Tennessee frontier family had become a vetted account of the state's past of Native violence and settler victimization in the memory of white settlers.

In the mid-nineteenth century, white southerners continued to embrace and perpetuate a notion of Native violence against settlers as a hallmark of the region's past. The memory of suffering at the hands of Native Americans afforded white southerners and their descendants the opportunity to construct and propagate romanticized tales of colonizers as innocent victims in the conquest of the US South. To successfully perpetuate narratives of violence and intergenerational victimization, settlers relied on the erasure of their own culpability and homogenized the wide variety of Native ethnicities in the region. As historian Elizabeth Perkins explains, such a process allowed nineteenth-century historians and popular authors to simplify the "messy complexities of remembered experience" as the "politically inconvenient details dropped out."[8] Reminiscences venerated suffering forebearers who endured Native violence, and celebrated those who strove for retribution.[9] Constructing a regional memory of white victimization took many forms, including contemporary reporting on Native violence, the private and public adulation of the dead, monumentation of the southern landscape, intergenerational family reminiscences, and printed chronicles of the region's past. The various mediums came to function as self-referencing loops reaffirming settler assumptions of Native aggression and white sufferings, celebrating white southerners and vilifying Native Americans.[10]

Subsequent generations of white settlers could look to a corroborating historical record of their own making as validation of their community's victimization and justified conquest of the region. The intergenerational transmission of family memories of Native violence fostered the "vicarious traumatization" of subsequent generations, whereas descendants came to internalize the violence against their ancestors as their own.[11] Collectively, these totems of settler memory produced a mythology of settler innocence and Native aggression that went largely unchallenged among white southerners into the late twentieth century. Far from giving a benign retelling of past events and ancestors, settlers deployed this mythology to sanctify anti-Indian violence and Native dispossession of ancestral lands, and to construct origins stories for their nascent communities across the South. Passed from one generation to the next, the selective memory of the white South functioned to absolve current generations of responsibility in Native-settler conflict and conceptualize complex and deeply rooted imperial trends of Indigenous dispossession as personal, local, and justified.[12] Native resistance to dispossession in Florida offered white southerners another opportunity to portray themselves as victims and add to the manufactured canon of Native aggression across centuries. The shared sense of white suffering spread across the region and echoed for generations to come.

The Suffering Summer Brothers

Though white communities across the South celebrated the volunteers heading off to the Florida Territory in 1836, the conflict was far from glorious. Reports on the suffering of the volunteers began the process of memorializing white victimization and connected white communities with the Florida peninsula. In August 1836 the *Charleston Daily Courier* announced the deaths of Nicholas and John Summer from Newberry, South Carolina. The paper reported the pair died at Tampa Bay on June 13 and 16 respectively while serving in Florida as volunteers with "Hargrove's Company of Mounted Volunteers."[13] Nicholas and John were two of the thousands of white men that volunteered to make themselves useful in the expulsion of the Florida Indians. News of their passing provided a startling reminder of the risks so many white southern men enthusiastically took on and began a memorialization process that tied together their deaths, the Newberry community, and the Florida Territory. While the obituary gave a succinct notice of the men's deaths, private correspondence detailed the horrific suffering endured by the two men prior to their passing. The personal letters shared with their family the full extent of their ordeal. The Summer family, and eventually the Newberry community, came to hear accounts of how both men perished in agony. In remembrances of Nicholas's and John's demises, white southerners in the nineteenth century valorized white men who perished in the expulsion of the Florida Indians and forged a sense unity in opposition to a common enemy.

The Summer brothers served in Gen. Winfield Scott's three-pronged offensive into Florida as part of the "Left Wing" alongside other South Carolina volunteers. Under the command of Gen. Abraham Eustis, the Left Wing departed from St. Augustine to ascend the St. Johns River but quickly encountered difficulties. South Carolina volunteer C. B. Stewart noted that they "traveled over some of the worst roads" for days once beyond St. Augustine. The advancing volunteers hastily improved upon some paths, though rainy weather worked to negate the modest enhancements.[14] Once arriving at Camp Volusia near modern-day Deltona, Florida, the Left Wing expected to pursue and engage the Florida Indians into an entrapment in the middle of the peninsula.[15] On March 30 the South Carolina Volunteers were "fired upon by Indians who crossed the road" in front of them.[16] Columbia, South Carolina's Richland Rifles charged ahead into what one volunteer described as a chaotic skirmish with the enemy dashing "from behind trees and leaping from one to another like . . . squirrels."[17] South Carolinian Solomon C. Hargrove noted that while the men kept up a brisk fire, "the marsh was so thick and boggy that we could not get in on horseback."[18]

Through the foliage a bullet struck Nicholas Summer. The shot pierced his thigh and threw him from his horse. A fellow volunteer remembered the incident years later describing how Nicholas hit the ground immobilized and shouting "Don't let them scalp me!" as he prepared his bayonet. Fellow Newberry volunteer Jacob King shielded the injured Nicholas with his horse until reinforcements pushed the Seminole back.[19] Summer survived the initial wound and continued with the army to Fort Brooke, where post surgeons noted the bullet struck Nicholas about four inches above the knee and passed "through the left thigh and broke [the] bone wholly." Over the next two months, Nicholas's condition deteriorated as his brother John watched at his bedside. In a failed attempt to send Nicholas home to South Carolina, "a rupture of one of the blood vessels" in his leg further reduced his condition. US Army surgeons contemplated amputating the leg, though Nicholas was in too poor condition. John stayed by his brother's bedside watching Nicolas deteriorate as the wound festered, producing what John described as a "very offensive" discharge.

Writing home to South Carolina, John expected the worst for his brother Nicholas. On May 13 John reported Nicholas's "appetite has somewhat failed him. He is very feeble. His arms are somewhat paralyzed from his being forced to lie in the same position." Expecting to die in Florida, Nicholas was "fully sensible of the nature of his wound and has settled his concerns with this world and has given up every hope of ever more seeing Home." On June 13, two and a half months after being shot, Nicholas Summer died at Fort Brooke. Though a volunteer, Nicholas received military honors when he was buried "not far south of the Redout nearest the river" in the Florida sands.[20]

Nicholas's death was not the end of what became a South Carolina family tragedy. Volunteers proved susceptible to various ailments such as measles, fevers, and digestive disorders. Florida's natural environment exacerbated problems, as one South Carolinian noted rains and Florida's high-water table forced him to sleep on brush piles "to keep out of the water."[21] While at Fort Brooke tending to his brother, John contracted a disease that "put on the bilious typhoid appearance." On the day of Nicholas's funeral, John was visibly depressed and so ill he could not even bring himself to look out the window to watch the procession for his deceased sibling. Three days later the disease took his life, and a military guard buried John alongside his brother Nicholas.[22] The Summer brothers' former attendant wrote their family regarding the siblings' demises. Robert Pratt described how he "set to with a hearty good will and with patience and perseverance succeeded in making Sir Nicholas as comfortable as the nature of his situation would allow." Due to "rheumatism in his arms, and general weakness," Pratt was obliged to wash Nicholas and feed "him like an infant," but "worse than all [Nicholas] could not use a bed pan." In consequence of Nicholas's "invariable position an extensive abscess formed at the lower part of his back gradually extending upwards . . . and finally terminated a life of suffering seldom equaled." Pratt continued, "John for several days previous had been suffering much from diarrhea so that his weakness and being obliged to witness the ongoing sufferings of his brother Nicholas became delirious." Before he passed, John requested Pratt "cut a lock from his brother's hair; and to take a memorandum of the exact time of his brother's death." John gave special instructions to inform his father of their condition and after "he had relapsed again into a state of mental derangement, death at last put a period to [John's] sufferings."[23]

The loss of the Summer brothers and the community's sense of civic militarism connected Florida to the history of South Carolina. In the wake of their deaths, a family friend of the Summers memorialized their sacrifice, writing "with honor they fell Far away, in the land of the stranger But death cannot sever the bonds of our love." Interred in graves far from their place of birth, the memoirists continued, their deaths could not "efface the record of their story."[24] Coincidentally, within days of the Summer brothers' deaths, community leaders in nearby Camden, South Carolina, held a celebratory dinner in honor of the state's volunteers. The Summers had served alongside the Camden volunteers with the Left Wing, in the summer of 1836. As part of the dinner's celebration, men in attendance offered a round of toasts honoring the state of South Carolina, the volunteers, and the expected subjugation of the Florida Indians. In a toast presented by Mr. Matheson to "The Creek and the Seminole," he spoke to the crowd in attendance: "May they soon be made as quiet and harmless as the Indian upon the Camden Market House." Matheson's toast referenced the iron weathervane cut into a silhouette effigy of the mid-eighteenth-century Catawba war captain King Haiglar atop Camden's public market.[25] Matheson's comparison served twofold, as a preferable foil to the warring Creek and Seminole and as a tokenized memorial to a long-since-deceased Indian. In one toast put forth by the event's organizers, attendees celebrated the volunteers' willingness to die and suffer in the defense of Florida's white settlers. The dinner's organizers toasted, "If the blood of Carolina has not enriched the soil, it has been freely periled to protect the hearth stones, of Florida."[26] With the toast taking place just the day after the death of the second Summer brother, the sacrifices of men like Nicholas and John constituted an anointing of the land. Their deaths and burials in Florida bound these distant places, and their memorialization facilitated the connection across succeeding generations.

Along the coast, the Charleston City Council likewise sought to memorialize those who died in the city after serving in the 1836 campaign. As a major rallying hub for volunteers, once the campaigns were under way, Charleston, South Carolina, served as a port of respite for wounded and ill volunteers extracted from Jacksonville and St. Augustine. While likely to receive superior care there, compared to the US Army outposts in Florida, not all who made it to Charleston survived their ailments. Those who perished

Figure 8. Main Street and view of King Haigler, Camden, South Carolina, ca. 1930. Early twentieth-century postcard depicting Main Street in Camden, South Carolina, including a century-old rooftop iron effigy of mid-eighteenth-century Catawba leader King Haiglar. From the South Caroliniana Library, University of South Carolina, Columbia, South Carolina.

in Charleston were interred in the city's cemeteries and graveyards. In July 1836 the *Charleston Mercury* announced preliminary plans to "erect a Monument to the memory of the Florida Volunteers, who died and were buried in our City." There was a preference that "a plain Marble Column be put up," rather than a horizontal memorial or simple headstone.[27] The proposed column would assure the memorial's visibility on the landscape to any who passed by the gravesites.

By September the city council installed the recommended monument "over the remains of the gallant Volunteers, who died . . . after their return from the Florida Campaign." The local press described the memorial as a "handsome obelisk of white marble, ten feet high." The obelisk marked the graves of one South Carolinian from Fairfield County in the Midlands, one from Anderson County in the Upstate, and two Georgian volunteers, both from Hancock County. The monument's inscription praised "the Gallant Volunteers who left their homes to encounter a savage foe, laying waste the territory of Florida."[28] News of the monument's installation reached as far Vicksburg, Mississippi, where the local newspaper praised the Charlestonians for honoring "the gallant volunteers" from the South.[29] The memorial testified to a settler memory of Native aggression and collective suffering of the white South. These militiamen from Georgia and various parts of South Carolina volunteered to travel to Florida under the pretense of subduing a "savage foe," only to be interred side by side and memorialized in the city of Charleston. Installed while violence in Florida was expanding, the monument provided a tangible reminder in Charleston to the deaths of white southerners in Florida. It reinforced the place-based affiliation and memorialized the deaths of white southerners as sacrifices in the defense of Florida settlers considered to be a part of a fictive regional family.

Volunteers Making History

As southern volunteers returned home after their participation in the Florida removal campaigns, veterans began to chronicle their experiences and drew connections to the southern past. Arriving back in Charleston, South Carolina, volunteers Myer M. Cohen and William W. Smith each authored expositions on the "Florida War." Cohen authored *Notices of Florida and the Campaigns*, and Smith wrote *Sketch of the Seminole War and Sketches during the Campaign, by a Lieutenant of the Left Wing*, both released in 1836.[30] Cohen and Smith detailed their experiences during the 1836 campaign and interpreted the historic causes of the contemporary hostilities. After serving with the Alabama volunteers, Alexander B. Meek produced historical and poetic prose chronicling the region's past. Meek published his most notable work in 1857, *Romantic Passages in Southwestern History*.[31] At times directly drawing on their experience in the Florida campaign, Cohen, Smith, and Meek emphasized broad themes of white victimization, Native aggression, and the white South's historical creation through violence. The former volunteers looked to the region's past and drew parallels between the glory of the first European colonizers of the American South and their own circumstances of the 1830s. In describing the historical South, they looked upon early European explorers as celebrated forebears scarified to the violent defiance of the region's Native residents. Cohen, Smith, and Meek connected the violence of the colonial past with the violence of their own day as evidence of a long-continued course of aggression by Native southerners against the Spanish, French, English, and now white southerners of the United States. Their works contributed to the white South's historical affirmation of colonizers as victims and Native southerners as aggressors in white southerners' ethnic cleansing of the region.

Writing after their time in Florida, Cohen, Smith, and Meek celebrated the South's Spanish past, vilified Native Americans, and glorified the parallels to their contemporary experiences. At the time the volunteers produced and published their work, Anglo-Americans had portrayed the Spanish colonizers' conduct toward Native Americans as unusually cruel, corrupt, and authoritarian for more than a century. Modern historians have described this interpretation as the "Black Legend" and have pointed out that portrayals of Spanish colonialism by American writers as late as the nineteenth century were embedded in imperial rivalries. American criticism of Spain's colonial past was often contingent upon the degree to which Spain presented an obstacle to English and, later, US expansion.[32] After American acquisition of Florida, the utility of the Black Legend began to fade for the US. As modern historian David Weber points out, "in the absence of bitter contention with racially mixed Hispanics . . . Anglo American writers merely repeated the conventional wisdom of the Black Legend."[33] Within the context of the forced removal of the Florida Indians in 1836, the depiction of the Spanish past shifted even further from repetition of the Black Legend to outright glorification of early colonial explorers and the men who joined the expeditions. The 1836 volunteers Cohen, Smith, and Meek connected the struggles of the sixteenth-century Spanish colonizers with the efforts of white southern volunteers facilitating the expulsion of the Florida Indians.

In *Notices of Florida and the Campaigns*, Myer M. Cohen directly connected Native aggression in the 1830s with sixteenth-century precedents against Spanish explorers. In considering the colonization endeavors of Juan Ponce de Leon, Panfilo de Narvaez, and Hernando de Soto, Cohen romanticized the South's Spanish past and presented their deaths at the hands of Native southerners as progenitors of settler sufferings in contemporary Florida. Cohen began by distilling Juan Ponce de Leon's failed attempt to colonize Florida in the first quarter of the 1500s into a simple account of Native hostility and settler death. After landing on shore, Cohen wrote, Ponce de Leon "was mortally wounded in a conflict with the natives." Cohen frames the encounter as a precursor for settler-Native interactions over the next three hundred years: "Such was the fate of the first adventurer into the wild regions of Florida, and he really seems to have bequeathed his ill fortune to his successors."[34]

Moving on to Panfilo de Narvaez, Cohen misrepresents the 1528 expedition to colonize Florida's west coast. As one of several Spaniards looking for gold and glory in the early sixteenth century, Narvaez intended to establish colonies along Florida's Gulf Coast. However, his expedition was troubled from the start. Modern historical accounts assert that poor weather both disrupted the start of Narvaez's expedition and led to his death at sea. Storms forced Narvaez to land at Tampa Bay short on supplies. Once he was ashore, Florida Indians provided food and guidance for the Spaniards, who marched north hoping to reconvene with their ship. Unsuccessful in connecting with his vessel, Narvaez attempted to reach Mexico on a crudely built raft. A storm pulled Narvaez out to sea, where he drowned in the Gulf off the coast of Texas. While some Native southerners proved hostile to the Narvaez expedition, others offered aid.[35] In sharp contrast, Cohen informs readers of his 1836 *Notices of Florida and the Campaigns* that Narvaez was "decoyed into the heart of the country in search of gold" and then "encompassed by hostile enemies, who making a desperate attack, soon routed his forces with great slaughter." Cohen insisted that Narvaez "died fighting" and his surviving men were eventually "reduced to the necessity of eating their companions, for want of other food."[36]

Hernando de Soto's 1539 expedition provided Cohen the most glamorous sacrificial adventurer in the South's Spanish past. As a veteran of Francisco Pizarro's 1533 conquest of the Inca, De Soto had his own aspirations for riches and fame. De Soto's imperial incursion into the American South between 1539 and 1542 brought death upon an untold number of Indigenous peoples and shattered Native communities. De Soto's violence and its legacy contributed to the reorganization of scores of Indigenous towns and communities.[37] Long vilified as an archetypal figure of the Black Legend, De Soto was canonized by Myer M. Cohen for his violence and sacrifice. Cohen described the conquistador's rampage across the region as "poetry put in action" and largely ignored the enslavement, violence, and destruction that De Soto wrought on the Native South. Cohen regaled readers with descriptions of De Soto as "the knight [errant] of the old world carried into the depths of the American wilderness." In opposition to an uncivilized South, Cohen portrayed De Soto as an exemplar of "the feats of individual prowess, the picturesque descriptions of steel clad cavaliers, with lance and helm and prancing steed, glittering through the wilderness of Florida."[38] When chronicling the eventual destruction of De Soto's army, Cohen suggested Florida had become traumatized space for contemporary white settlers. He wrote that the survivors of De Soto's entrada "[shrank] from revisiting a country where they had suffered such hardships, which reluctance prevails in 1836."[39]

The veterans of the 1836 campaigns also expressed a shared kinship between the volunteers and their sixteenth-century Spanish predecessors. Forging a connection with Spanish colonials afforded Cohen, Smith, and Meek the opportunity to heap praise upon their peers and portray white settlers in the nineteenth century as continuing the seemingly endless effort to tame a wild Florida. In Meek's *Romantic Passages*, he celebrated the six hundred men who joined De Soto as "gallant and proud a band of soldiers, as have ever been collected together" whose zeal exhibited all "the enthusiasm of their leader."[40] In *Notices of Florida and the Campaigns*, Cohen emphasized the concordant volunteerism between the men of 1836 and their Spanish predecessor. Cohen drew a direct comparison, noting De Soto "had been joined by many volunteers and recruits in Cuba (volunteering being then, as now, the order of the day)."[41] In *Sketch of the Seminole War*, Smith professed that the 1836 volunteers held the memory of their Spanish forerunners close while preparing for orders to take the field. Smith wrote that "the assemblage on the mild shore of Florida of these gallant and select troops, reminded of the turning out of the Spanish Hidalgos, under De Soto, for the conquest of this territory." He continued, "Many a Carolinian indulged in a similar lavish personal expense, though the Spaniards may have excelled in magnificence." But while the Spaniards left their homes for the spoils of conquest, Smith assured that the South Carolinians "left their homes at the single instigation of patriotism, and looked forward to the approbation of their countrymen as the only guerdon for their toils and dangers."[42] In comparison to the civic adulation for the 1836 volunteers, Smith wrote that the sixteenth-century Spanish volunteers were celebrated when they left Santiago, Cuba, "with all manner of festivities . . . and masquerades." He related that the South Carolina volunteers who departed from St. Augustine enjoyed similar public adulation, and that the 1836 volunteers enjoyed instances of "private hospitality . . . and much real regard and interest expressed for those who had voluntarily left the bosom of their homes, to risk their lives in dreadful savage warfare for strangers."[43]

For Meek, the parallels extended to the timeless natural environment De Soto and the 1836 volunteers explored during their kindred campaigns. In *Romantic Passages*, Meek explained how De Soto's men marched "very nearly parallel with the present road from Tampa to Fort King," the same route made infamous when Dade and his men walked into an ambush in December 1835. In March 1836 Meek traveled the same route he came to describe in his chronicle. His personal journal, kept while serving with the Alabama State Guard, suggests he drew on his own observations to describe the natural environment confronting De Soto, stating the peninsula was "intersected by innumerable and extensive morasses and hammock." Meek's 1857 *Romantic Passages* referenced De Soto's trek across the "Hillsboro, the Withlacoochee, and the Suwannee" rivers; waterways he traversed in 1836.[44] Likewise, Meek amalgamated Florida's Native Americans into a singular and unchanging people between the time of De Soto and his own. Meek portrayed the violent disposition of Florida Indians as a point of uninterrupted continuity endured by the sixteenth-century Spanish explorer and still "found them true to the spirit they exhibit to this day."[45] Regardless of the ethnic diversity and political transformations of Native Floridians from the sixteenth century through the mid-nineteenth century, Meek suggested the peninsula home to an unchanging and homogeneous people inherently hostile to whites over the course of three hundred years.[46]

Cohen, Smith, and Meek also invoked the challenges faced by the French and their English colonial forefathers in the South to applaud the volunteers of 1836 and vilify Native Floridians. In explaining Florida's French past, South Carolinian William W. Smith bent the memory of the ill-fated 1565 French campaign led by Jean Ribault against the Spanish. In the mid-1560s Spain and France were grappling for control over the Florida peninsula, and each set up opposing fortifications near modern-day St. Augustine and Jacksonville, respectively. When Smith and his company marched in 1836 toward the Bulow Sugar Mill near modern-day Ormond Beach, Florida, they crossed an infamous site of the sixteenth-century imperial rivalry along the Matanzas River. Matanzas, which translated from Spanish means "slaughter," was given its name, according to Smith, "in consequence of 300 Frenchmen who took refuge there once after being wrecked on the Reef." Smith described how the Frenchmen were "massacred by the Calusa Indians, the original inhabitants of Florida."[47] However, Smith's claim that the Calusa massacred the Frenchmen is refuted by his contemporaries and modern historians. Chroniclers of Smith's own time had long attributed the murder of the three hundred sixteenth-century French colonists to Spanish soldiers under the command of Pedro Menendez de Aviles operating out of St. Augustine.[48] Smith's misattribution, printed in his 1836 *Sketches of the Florida War*, and likely told around the campfires to his volunteer company, served to perpetuate a memory of Native aggression against white settlers in Florida. Furthermore, Smith's Matanzas River mythology absolved the Spanish of responsibility for such an unseemly act at a time when volunteers from across the US South professed a kindred spirit with the first conquistadores.

The 1836 volunteers likewise invoked the memory of their English ancestors to justify and glorify nineteenth-century settler violence against Native southerners. In what was likely aided by the living memory of the American Revolution in the South, Smith directly compared his experiences fighting against the Seminole in 1836 with his revolutionary counterparts who fought the Cherokee in 1776.[49] More prominently, the early eighteenth-century Yamasee War provided nineteenth-century white southerners an opportunity to connect the past to their present. Both Cohen and Smith employed the memory of violence between the Yamasee Indians and the South Carolina colony to portray an unyielding hostility of Native southerners toward whites. Cohen professed that the Yamasee frequently engaged in wars with the Carolina colony, and the 1715 Yamasee War had even jeopardized the permanence of the English colony.[50]

Past settler conquests and forced relocations offered the 1836 volunteers further opportunity to justify the contemporary violence against and expulsion of Florida's Native people. In addition to historical violence between the Yamasee and the English colonists, Cohen and Smith professed, the Florida Indians, specifically the Seminole, shared a biological link with the Yamasee that mandated militant reprisal by white southerners in the nineteenth century. In an explanation of the interconnected past of the Yamasee and the Seminole, Cohen suggested the former were a "powerful people" in the early eighteenth century who spread across Florida, Georgia, and South Carolina. Cohen proposed the Seminole looked upon the Yamasee as their own ancient ancestors, and his explanation of Seminole ethnogenesis connected "the wars between the first settlers and the Yamasee" with Seminole resistance of the 1830s.[51] Smith echoed similar sentiments regarding the Yamasee-Carolina colony rivalry. While Smith also proposed a prominent connection between the Seminole and a Creek ancestry, he suggested that "one cannot help being struck with the remarkable coincidence in some respects between the present Seminole war in Florida with that which occurred in Carolina with the Yamasees, 120 years ago."[52]

Such pseudo-scientific postulations on Native ancestry and coalescence were not unique to the volunteers. Joseph M. White, Florida's territorial delegate to the US House of Representatives, made similar claims regarding the Florida Indians as descendants of a violent and conquered race. In a May 1836 speech to the US House, White suggested the Florida Indians were "the remains of the ancient and warlike tribe known under the designation of the Natchez . . . [from] along the Mississippi." After "being almost extirpated by the French," White said, the Natchez retreated, making their way to the Florida peninsula.[53] Not long after this speech, the southern press extracted his musings on the coalescence of the Florida Indians, thus further perpetuating misgivings about Seminole ethnogenesis and their indigeneity.[54]

In evaluating Seminole ethnogenesis from a twenty-first-century perspective, historians and anthropologists disregard the explicit continuity of Yamasee or Natchez heritage in favor of a more direct link with the Creek and Native occupants of the peninsula dating back centuries.[55] Yet the generalizations put forth by Cohen and Smith offered nineteenth-century volunteers justification for the contemporary ethnic cleansing of the peninsula. Characterizing the Florida Indians as the descendants of the Yamasee framed the violence of 1836 as a continuation of their ancestors' battles against a people with little historic claim to Florida. Cohen and Smith contended that when the Yamasee retreated into Florida after their defeat at the hands of their Carolinian ancestors, the Yamasee passed on to the Florida Indians an inherent hostility toward white southerners. Smith stressed the historical continuity in evaluating the character of the Seminole and their historical equivalent, the Yamasee, by professing to readers that a "fierce and warlike spirit . . . seems to have sprung up from" the graves of the defeated eighteenth-century enemy. Smith even declared that "some few drops of their [Yamasee] blood yet exist in the veins of the Seminole."[56] As Smith explained to readers in 1836, the violence of the Yamasee spanned the historical chasm, presenting immutable inherited traits that threatened settlers in his own time. Therefore, it was the obligation of white South Carolinians to continue the campaign against what Cohen called the "descendants of a conquered race."[57]

SHARING JANE JOHNS'S SUFFERINGS

As chronicles from veterans of the 1836 Florida campaigns contributed to a public memory of settler suffering, white families in the South and their descendants perpetuated reminiscences of their ancestors as innocent victims in the region's violent colonization. In 1836 Jane Johns lived with her husband, Clement, on a rented homestead south of Jacksonville, Florida.[58] As part of the Florida Indians' opposition to removal, they struck against a series of settler homesteads and plantations in East Florida. In the Seminole's campaign, Jane and Clement were largely caught by surprise. A raiding party led by Coacoochee (also known as Wild Cat) managed to mortally wound Clement in an opening volley of gunfire.[59] The couple made it inside their home, where Clement soon succumbed to his wounds. Jane managed a determined defense, but the Seminole forced their way into the home. They shot and scalped Jane and then set the homestead ablaze, leaving her for dead.[60] Local militia and extended family soon after discovered Jane still alive; concealed in a nearby marsh. Within days the local press in East Florida detailed an account of the violence against her, and newspapers across the South reprinted accounts and updates on the sufferings of Jane Johns. While under the care of a Jacksonville physician, Jane's notoriety led to a speaking tour in major southern cities along the Atlantic Coast and a published monograph that chronicled her family's multigenerational violence.[61]

As future generations of white Floridians came to learn of Jane's ordeal, newspapers and her written history informed her family's own published reminiscences. In the post-Removal South, family recollections of the attack against the Johns household provided Jane's extended family and descendants validation of Native expulsion and confirmation of their indigeneity to the Florida peninsula. The community memory of Jane Johns's victimization exemplified the process by which white remembrances of Native-settler conflict produced a self-referencing memorialization of intergenerational settler victimhood. Individual accounts, newspapers, published chronicles, and family reminiscences collaborated across generations to construct a collective memory of white victimization stemming from the Florida Indians' opposition to expulsion. When Jane died in 1874, her memory, written past, and gravesite conveyed white southerners' intergenerational memorialization of white suffering into the twenty-first century.

In the aftermath of the September 1836 raid on the Johns homestead, Jane's father-in-law and two compatriots, Lowder and Sparkman, were the first to discover the scene. These observers functioned as the initial vectors of settler victimization, passing retellings of the event through word-of-mouth networks.[62] They discovered Clement dead and Jane, while still alive, described as "butchered, bloody, and almost lifeless."[63] The four headed to Lowder's nearby home, where Jane recounted the ordeal to an additional three men, two women, and several children. From Lowder's homestead, the expanding party moved to Sparkman's home before setting out in pursuit of the assailants. Eventually involving twenty "Townsmen," the pursuit party traveled for two days across East Florida. In addition, Maj. Benjamin K. Pierce stationed at Jacksonville received notice of the attack on the Johns homestead and sent out a company of fifty men to search "in the direction of Santa Fe, and New River" for the Seminole party.[64] Presumably, the twenty townsmen and fifty members of the militia detachment inquired with passersby and settlers as they searched, resulting in further word-of-mouth dissemination of Jane Johns' assault.[65] To provide for the recovery of Jane, "a committee . . . of the most respectable inhabitants" of Jacksonville requested Andrew Welch, the surgeon for the city's US Army outpost, attend to her at Sparkman's homestead. As documented in Welch's journal, he traveled two days to assess Jane. Upon his arrival he was aghast at the sight of Jane, recording he had never seen anything so horrible in his career. In his initial assessment, which became widely shared, Welch catalogued extensive injuries in need of medical attention. In her fragile state, Jane returned with Welch to Jacksonville, where he could provide Jane with "every necessary for her" recovery and safety.[66]

Once under Welch's care in Jacksonville, Jane became a local curio and exhibition of Native violence. Newspapers played an extensive role in the rapid dissemination and early construction of the historical memory of the Jane Johns's assault. The *Jacksonville Courier* printed the first broadly circulated retelling of Jane's ordeal. News of her suffering quickly traveled beyond East Florida with people and newspapers along the major transportation networks of the American South's Atlantic Coast at the same time volunteers from across the South flooded into the Florida Territory. The movement of information ensured that distant communities would either learn of Jane's ordeal or confirm what they had already heard through conversation and personal correspondence.[67] Over the next few months, newspapers connected disparate southern communities through the proliferation of accounts of widening Native violence against white households in Florida, and updates on Jane Johns.[68] Papers in Charleston, South Carolina, printed retellings of the Johns raid the same month it took place.[69] The *Daily Georgian* in Savannah likewise printed news of the raid by the end of September.[70] The next month, the *Daily Georgian* again discussed Jane Johns, this time in tandem with news of a Seminole raid against another white family.[71] In November, papers in Macon and Columbus, Georgia published news of the raid on the Johns homestead.[72] News soon reached North Carolina as well. Papers in Raleigh, Newbern, and Charlotte printed the same column on the Johns raid that had appeared in the *Columbus Enquirer* and the *Macon Georgia Telegraph* alongside news of the expanding war racking East Florida.[73] Eventually, presses in Virginia and the Washington, DC, area picked up the story of Jane Johns, characterizing the Florida Indians' war against forced removal as a war against white families.[74]

Jane's celebrity as a victim of Native violence elicited requests for visits from nearby cities. In early 1837 Welch accompanied her on a tour to Savannah, Georgia, and Charleston, South Carolina, two cities that had seen thousands of volunteers depart for Florida in 1836. Her arrival in both cities was preceded by newspaper accounts of her misfortune and simultaneous reporting on the expanding violence in Florida. While on tour Jane received public visitors and "detailed in her own language" the events of the raid that left her disfigured.[75] Visitors gathered to see Jane's wounds, gawk at her destitute status, and hear her firsthand account of her disfigurement and the death of her husband. Johns's exhibition provided a personal and tangible representation of white victimization to a predisposed audience. In addition to regular news describing Native violence against white families, popular literature of the prior twenty years primed Jane's visitors for the sufferings of white settlers. In 1818 the publication of the *Narrative of the Tragical Death of Mr. Darius Barber* offered a fictional depiction of Native violence in Florida against a white settler family. The ability to visit with Jane Johns in 1837 likely reinforced the 1818 work's proposed authenticity.[76] Seeing Jane Johns in person gave visitors the opportunity to convey their own vicarious experience of Native violence to family and acquaintances.

The multicity tour also coincided with Andrew Welch's efforts to publish an account of Jane's tribulations as a fundraising effort to ameliorate her hardships.[77] After her return to Florida, papers in Charleston and Savannah began advertising in March 1837 the availability of a monograph titled *A Narrative of the Life and Sufferings of Mrs. Jane Johns, Who Was Barbarously Wounded and Scalped by Seminole Indians, in East Florida*.[78] In Charleston ads ran through May 1 enticing consumers to purchase the full account of Jane's reminiscences as written by Welch from local bookseller S. Babcock & Co. at

290 King Street in the heart of modern-day Charleston's historic district.[79] The publication provided a tangible reassurance to the white South's memory of Native violence that buyers could keep in their homes, share with acquaintances, and bequeath to future generations. The multitude of sources, including newspaper reports, personal visits with Jane, secondhand retellings, and a historical chronicle, functioned to corroborate a self-referencing settler perspective of white suffering and Native aggression as the United States attempted to annihilate and purge the Indigenous inhabitants of the Florida Territory.

As historians have noted, Welch's *A Narrative of the Life and Sufferings of Mrs. Jane Johns* sensationalized the attack against Jane using contemporary newspaper reports, his own personal experience, and Jane's family reminiscences.[80] In his publication Welch included an extract from the *Jacksonville Courier* describing the initial public accounting of the September 1836 attack. The newspaper extract offered a widely known predisposing source from the prior year to reintroduce readers to the destruction of the Johns homestead, the death of Clement, and the violence against Jane Johns.[81] From his own writings, Welch detailed an inventory of violence against Jane in gruesome detail. Welch included portions of his personal journal describing the "revolting character" of Jane's wounds. Welch wrote how the attack left Jane "with one arm deeply lacerated, so much so that the muscles absolutely gaped open nearly to the bone." The gunshot wound that pierced her arm also "passed through her neck." In addition, Jane's "legs were considerably burned." Worse still, Welch recorded that it was near impossible to "depict in colors sufficiently powerful to convey to the imagination the appalling spectacle of her head." As reported throughout the press, and gawked at by visitors, Jane was scalped during the 1836 attack. Welch described Jane's head as entirely "divested of the scalp to the bare bone, in two places of which it was not only denuded and scraped, but portions absolutely cut out by the knife." He continued that the injury spanned "from the upper part of the forehead . . . to the occiput, nine inches and a half-from above one ear to the opposite, nine inches-on the right side of the head it appeared . . . that the knife had slipped, a cut had been made obliquely, otherwise the circumcision of the scalp was tolerably regular."[82] Such fixations both provided a method for white settlers to differentiate their industriousness from the destruction wrought by Native southerners and offered propaganda confirming the need for Native expulsion.[83]

While the September 1836 raid inspired Welch's *The Suffering of Jane Johns*, the publication begins with recollections from Jane describing her family's multigenerational endurance of Native violence in Florida. As recorded by Welch, Jane's parents, Mr. and Mrs. Hall, resided in East Florida along a tributary of the St. Johns River. In 1813 "savage sons of the forest," as Welch described them, "commenced the first act of Indian tragedy, in which this worthy family bore a conspicuous part, and in which (although then in embryo) Jane was an unconscious participator."[84] With their settlement under attack, Jane's father and pregnant mother fled as the "wailings and lamentations of their friends and neighbors" echoed behind them. The couple managed to secure a small boat and rowed fifty miles north on the St. Johns River before landing on an uninhabited barrier island along Florida's Atlantic coast. Amidst the trauma of the escape, Mrs. Hall went into labor. As described by Welch, "the unfortunate subject of this narrative," Jane Johns, was "ushered into a world of trial and trouble on August 23d, 1813."

Despite barely escaping with their lives, Jane's family resettled in East Florida. However, by 1821 Native-settler violence spiked, and as Welch described, the "persecuted family were again startled from their tranquile" homestead. This time the Halls did not escape unscathed. Jane's brother "fell by the hands of the merciless savage," and her uncle was shot three times as the family fled. The Hall family was forced to again abandon the Florida frontier and took up residence near the St. Marys River along the Florida-Georgia border. Welch wrote when "peace was once more arranged between the red and white man," Jane and her parents returned to Florida. Jane's parents settled in the Alachua district of northern Central Florida; however, the recently married Jane did not join them. Instead, Jane and her husband Clement settled in a rented farm southwest of Jacksonville. That same year, as described by Welch, the newlyweds "were in the way of obtaining a comfortable maintenance, when they were suddenly and unexpectedly surrounded by Indians," resulting in the death of Clement and the assault and mutilation of Jane.[85] As a result of the attack, Welch confirmed prior accounts from Georgia newspapers noting Jane "gave birth to a still-born" child in the aftermath of her assault.[86]

By expanding the narrative beyond the 1836 attack on the Johns homestead, Welch portrayed a multigenerational victimization of white families in Florida. Welch's account conveys how Native-settler violence impacted three generations of the Johns family and afflicted individuals without agency, specifically children. Readers of Welch's *Life and Sufferings* read Jane, her parents, and her stillborn child as destined victims of Native aggression. While Jane's parents acted on their own volition as agents of colonialism, Welch's depiction of violence against Jane in her youth presented a victim whose only complicit act was being born. Later in Jane's life, the loss of her firstborn evoked parallels to her own birth and the inheritability of settler victimization and lack of agency. Jane's mother, Mrs. Hall, made a harrowing escape from an Indian raid in 1813 and went into labor giving birth to Jane under tumultuous circumstances. Jane's progeny was not so fortunate, stillborn in 1836 under similar circumstances. For white southerners, the parallel incidents demonstrated the continuity and apparent inevitability of Native violence against white settlers across generations. Conception seemingly destined the unborn white southerner to Indian depredations and even in a state of pure innocence, surviving to birth appeared uncertain under the threat of Native violence.

Settler Reassurances

The multigenerational remembrances such as the account of Jane Johns, written chronicles by the 1836 volunteers, and family letters of the Summer brothers facilitated a settler mythology of Native aggression and settler sufferings in the colonization of the American South. To successfully do so, white southerners relied on the erasure of their own culpability and collectivized Native identities in the South.[87] One of the most glaring complexities dropped from the memory and written chronicles of the southern past was the violence of Native dispossession and Indigenous sufferings. As scholars have demonstrated, the actions of settler families often precipitated and perpetuated the resistance by Native Americans that settlers proceeded to demonize as unjustified violence. In short, settlers were often either unconscious of or unwilling to acknowledge their family's own intergenerational agency and aggression in their remembrances of victimization. Instead, white southerners looked to the region's past of settler violence as a point of coalescence and evidence of their own native origins. To establish their own historical legacy in the region, white southerners looked to self-reinforcing sources that created a feedback loop reassuring settlers of their status as victims and casting white aggression as justifiable retribution. In addition to glorifying deceased and victimized relations, intergenerational reminiscences justified settler claims to recently colonized land. Stories of intergenerational violence disseminated throughout the region via word-of-mouth communication networks, state government records, and newspapers. The proliferation of settler accounts through various channels functioned as predisposing sources to confirm recirculating biases on the savagery of Native southerners and the cruelties suffered by past and present generations of whites. Eventually, the public and printed narratives of family tragedies came to reinforce the reminiscences of descendants looking to confirm inherited family oral histories.

In Newberry, South Carolina, the memory of the Summer brothers' anguish-inducing deaths during their participation in the 1836 campaign to expel the Florida Indians resonated within the community as a tale of unification. In 1892 the publication of *The Annals of Newberry* chronicled an account of Nicholas Summer's service in the Newberry militia alongside a local rival. While the nature of the dispute is unspecified, the "grave difficulty" between Nicholas Summer and Jacob H. King had on at least one occasion required intervention from mutual friends to avoid hostility. While the pair served side by side in Florida, King was instrumental in protecting Summer after he was wounded. According to community lore, King cast aside their rivalry, risking his own life to protect Summer from the Native ambush. After the skirmish passed, King "dismounted and placed Summer in as comfortable a position as possible." According to oral tradition, King "enjoyed a luxury of feeling [he] had never before experienced, when during the mutual pressure of our hands, [Summer] said to [him]: 'I can never forget your kindness.'" After securing Summer with the company medics, King never again saw Summer alive, and reportedly it was his "great regret."[88] The mythology handed down across generations and codified in a local chronicle of the town celebrated how fighting side by side against Native southerners mended disputes between white men and forged bonds that were celebrated for generations to come.

Into the twentieth century, family mythologies continue to influence the memory and memorialization of Native aggression and white sufferings. The availability of printed historical accounts offered descendants of white southerners killed or assaulted in the colonization of the region recirculated confirmations of inherited memories. Relations of Jane Johns could look to Welch's 1837 *A Narrative of the Life and Sufferings of Mrs. Jane Johns* to confirm family memory and intertwine succeeding generations' claims to indigeneity. While there is no indication Jane ever raised children, she did remarry, only to lose her second husband to a violent death as well. Keeping the name of her second husband, Jane (Johns) Matthews relocated to Florida's southwest frontier to live with her brother-in-law Francis Calvin Morgan Boggess. In 1900 Boggess published an autobiography affirming his own claims to southwest Florida's Peace River Valley and invoked the suffering of his destitute sister-in-law as part of his justification for his right of conquest. Just prior to the US Civil War, Boggess moved to Ft. Ogden in southwest Florida, and Jane Johns later joined him.[89] According to Boggess's memoir, Jane was tortured by the memory of her attack and "could not endure the looks of an Indian." In one incident, Boggess wrote, a few "old warriors" once visited the homestead to "point at her and make signs as if scalping a person."[90]

The descendants of Boggess also claimed ownership of the memory of Jane's victimization. In 1926 or 1929, Mary Gilbert of Enid, Oklahoma, publicized her familial tie to Jane Johns through her mother, Nancy McCullough, who settled in Florida prior to the Civil War.[91] Additionally,

Boggess's daughter Georgia Falany, who lived her entire life in Ft. Ogden, professed that her father spoke of Jane's sufferings among the family. In 1950 Falany even provided a corrective to a Tampa newspaper that misidentified Jane Matthews as "Sarah Mathis," testifying to her own memories of her father's stories. While her father was long deceased, others not privy to the family lore could confirm her retelling of her family's Florida heritage, because, as Falany pointed out, "The story is told in detail in my father's book," drawing direct reference to Boggess's memoir.[92]

In the late twentieth century, descendant-settler reminiscences of Jane Johns continued to propagate community memories of white victimization and Native savagery. In 1985 the Peace River Valley Historical Society in DeSoto County anointed Johns's gravesite at the Fort Ogden Cemetery near Arcadia, Florida, as a memorial to Native aggression and white sufferings. As published in the local newspaper the *DeSoto County Times*, members of the historical society "gathered . . . to pay homage" to the scalping of Jane Johns that took place nearly a century and a half ago. Members in attendance, including State Representative Vernon Peeples, forewent installing a traditional headstone on the unmarked grave and instead commissioned "a small granite stone" with an inscription reading "Mrs. Jane Matthews, Scalped September 16, 1836." As reported in the press, Peace River Valley Historical Society president Dr. Calvin Martin christened the installation by recounting the events of Jane's life "reading from the autobiography of captain F. C. M. Boggess."[93] This singular act of violence became the defining memory of Jane Johns's existence and a chiseled memorialization of Native violence against white settlers. In consecrating the land in 1985, settler memories of Native aggression continued to perpetuate self-referencing reassurances of white victimhood fashioned across the Southeast dating back to the late eighteenth century. Since the grave marker's installation, twenty-first-century reminiscences of Jane continue to obfuscate the colonizing agency of white families in the antebellum South as instigators of Native removal and impart the memorialization of white victimization to current generations.[94] In 2011 a Naples, Florida, newspaper again reiterated the memory of violence against Jane and directly invoked the account of F. C. M. Boggess. As confirmation to the certainty of white victimhood, the reporter bluntly wrote, "At Fort Ogden, a single stone announces the prominent fact in a woman's life: 'Mrs. Jane Matthews, scalped Sept. 16, 1836.'"[95] Through community memory, a century-old autobiography, and an enshrined gravesite, the modern benefactors of dispossession reassured themselves of their inherited victimhood and justifiable occupation of the South.

Figure 9. Jane Hall Johns Matthews gravesite placard, Fort Ogden, Florida. The Peace River Valley Historical Society installed a placard in 1985 on Jane Johns's gravesite inscribed with the date she was scalped in 1836. Jane died at the age of sixty in 1874. Photo by F. Evan Nooe.

7

"Result of This Great Conquest"

Sectionalism and Southern Coalescence

Reports of Native violence against white southerners in Florida during the 1830s and 1840s did not halt settler expansion or slow white southerners from pushing to the banks of the Mississippi River. Receding Native borders and affordable land proved too enticing for white settlers of various financial means. Wealthy white men and their families flocked to northern Florida, expanding the footprint of the plantation South. Less affluent white settlers squatted on federal land clearing tracts through their own labor much like white southerners had done in South Carolina after the American Revolution and on Georgia's western border after the Battle of Horseshoe Bend. In Florida the territorial government offered settlers incentive to migrate to the peninsula's interior beyond the security of federal military outposts and offered generous preemption laws. White southerners who built new homesteads upon the land seized from Native southerners could eventually obtain legal title to their initially illegal land claims.[1]

In northern Central Florida, Alachua County continued to appeal to a mix of well-financed aspiring planters and common white settlers. White settlement in modern-day Alachua County predated the Florida Indians' violent opposition to expulsion in 1836 and was witness to violence early in the conflict that became known as the Second Seminole War. By 1840 US military intervention and federal aid helped to prop up flagging settler communities. Federal dollars for infrastructure improvements, supplies for the territorial militia, and the deployment of the US Army offered protection, stability, and prosperity for white southerners eager to claim land recently occupied by Native Floridians.[2] A recent arrival to Alachua County, Theodor D. Maltby, was one of many who looked to exploit the receding borders of Native Floridians in the wake of white encroachment, settler violence, and Indigenous expulsion. In a letter to his brother George in New Haven, Connecticut, in 1841, Theodor outlined his grand designs to establish a plantation. Theodor sought to leverage Florida's tropical climate in his pursuit of financial wealth. He looked to his brother to help him secure a supply of oranges, pomegranates, plantains, bananas, figs, and coconuts to plant. Theodor wrote he "was determined to have a variety" of cash crops at his burgeoning homestead, in search of the next big revenue stream that could be extracted from the Florida soil. However, even in writing about such pressing and promising business affairs, Theodor prefaced his letter with a rebuke to his brother's sympathies for Florida's Native inhabitants.[3]

With news of the conflict in Florida covered throughout the nation, Theodor's brother George believed that white southerners "were fighting the Indians all the time." While Theodor acknowledged that was not the case, it was not due to lack of enthusiasm for martial service among white southerners. Theodor defended the seemingly impulsive and unrelenting nature with which many white southerners took up arms against the Seminole. He explained to his northern brother that by the 1840s, while every man was not in the field continuously, "When we do fight it is done voluntarily and no doubt every man considers it is his duty." Theodor, though suffering from a ravaging fever at the time, attested to his own willingness to volunteer and chided his brother by asking "who would not volunteer to fight" the Seminole. Theodor openly dismissed the suggestion that an able-bodied man would not volunteer, and only those who were "so dead, so lost to every sense of feeling" would not spring to answer a call to arms. Repeating long-standing justifications for settler violence in the South, Theodor questioned what man "would not grasp the rifle and hazard life" when "he saw [that] Father, Mother, Brother, Sister, or friend lay murdered horribly mutilated" at the hands of an Indian attack.

On the issue of white southerners and the federal government's treatment of Native southerners, George and Theodor had grown apart, living under different circumstances with different fears. George had developed "a great deal of sympathy for the Seminoles," more than Theodor thought "they deserved." Theodor attributed his brother's affection for the Florida Indians to not "being aquiuantinced with their character" and his safety living far from Native southerners who were desperately fighting to hold off their expulsion from the South. If he were, Theodor speculated, George would see that the Seminole "pay no respect to treaties, flags of truce [and] will murder men, women, and children with the white flag in their hands." Theodor went on to invoke the regional disparities of his and his brother's circumstances in the mid-nineteenth century. Theodor specifically pointed to the short memories of northern men like his brother in their ancestors' temperament toward Native peoples. Theodore wrote, "This country I mean Florida, Georgia, and in fact the whole South . . . no more belong to the Indians than the town in which you live." Theodore surmised that if the

Seminole "should come there and commence plundering; your sympathies would not last long."[4]

The Maltby brothers' rift demonstrated a familial testimonial to the increasingly sectional politics of white-Native violence, Indian Removal, and southern militarism. Theodor rebuked the aloof comfort and security that George enjoyed and alluded to New England's overlooked legacy of Indigenous dispossession. While white northeasterners chastised white southerners on the violent expulsion of Indians from the South in the 1830s and 1840s, white northeasterners did so from upon a soapbox built on the graves of Native Americans from generations past. For the Maltby brothers, sectional discord over Native American affairs in the South became a divisive family matter, and white-Native violence in the South created a point of regionally defining tension. Becoming southern was a consequence of experience, not necessarily an innate product of geographical birth. Like so many other white southerners, Theodor Maltby took advantage of the recently fleeced Indian land to pursue a path to riches through race-based chattel slavery. Established and aspiring slaveholders rapidly clamored for the newly available land on the heels of Indigenous expulsion, and many white families made their riches as a result.

Defending Conquest & Dispossession

Likely to the disappointment of Theodor Maltby, within a year of his fraternal dispute, the federal government initiated a major draw-down of men and supplies in Florida. The exuberance of white southerners' willingness to volunteer for service in Florida was unsustainable. While volunteers from the South served in the Florida expulsion campaigns for the duration of the conflict, most men committed to only one tour and returned home satisfied they had performed their honor-bound obligation to aid their suffering brethren. The Florida Indians' strategy to outlast their opponents portended success, though at a high cost. As critics of the removal campaigns and returning veterans exposed the full contours of colonialism against a resolute opponent, the nature of violence in Florida inspired fewer and fewer men to fill the ranks. Stories of ambushes, inhospitable terrain, and contagious diseases began to outweigh desires to kill Indians or the honor of postmortem memorializations by loved ones. With each passing year, the conflict became more inglorious. When Gen. Thomas S. Jesup ordered the capture of Osceola near St. Augustine in 1836 during peace discussions, any glory associated with volunteering in Florida took a precipitous decline in national esteem. Jesup's attempt to hasten the end of the war by seizing an influential Native leader proved to be a contentious gambit that exposed a sectional fissure. While the white inhabitants of Florida widely celebrated the imprisonment of Osceola and southern politicians such as Georgia congressman Thomas Glascock applauded, critics of the Florida removal campaigns jumped on the opportunity to condemn Jesup and the conduct of the war.[5] As the campaigns to expel the Florida Indians dragged into the 1840s, the honor of serving in the conflict lost its luster. The US military cycled through numerous commanders, with most ending their assignment with less admiration than when they began.[6] Still, approximately thirty thousand militia served between 1835 and 1842, with the bulk of the volunteers coming from southern states such as Florida, Georgia, Tennessee, Louisiana, South Carolina, and Alabama.[7]

Even though the white South's willingness to travel to Florida waned, the successes of the Florida Indians gave cause to continue criticizing the federal government. At the farthest reaches of the Florida Territory, a Key West newspaper described lamentable circumstances facing recently enlisted volunteers. In May 1836 a volunteer detachment arrived at Key West in no condition to provide support. The volunteers lacked tents and were starved from "not having provisions." Reportedly, men were eating dog with a quarter of the animal costing as much as five dollars in camp. The *Key West Inquirer* reported the volunteers were possibly willfully misled by the US Army despite "gallantly march[ing]" to the defense of their Florida brethren. When embarking from South Carolina and Georgia, the men were induced by the US Army "to leave their clothing, under the assurance that they would soon return, or that should be forwarded to them." Months passed before the men knew "the luxury of a change of clothing." The South Carolina and Georgia volunteers "were brought to the brink of the grave by exposure, hardship, and starvation" while under the direction of the US military. The *Inquirer* concluded the federal government had "miserably disappointed" the volunteers who risked their lives for the protection of their fellow southerners.[8]

From Tallahassee, Florida governor Richard K. Call consistently and repeatedly questioned the commitment and support of the federal government to expel the Florida Indians. Within months of Dade's defeat, the Florida Territory was going into debt to provide supplies for the volunteer militia. In late April 1836, Call challenged Secretary of War Lewis Cass on the dedication of the federal government in putting down the Indian uprising and protecting the white citizens of Florida. Call believed "that the whole Regular force now in Florida" was far too "inadequate to the defense of our frontier during the summer."[9] When US soldiers and volunteers began to settle into forts to wait out Florida's sickly summer season, Call feared there was no hope of a "suspension of the war during the summer." The Florida Indians managed to procure additional armaments from Spanish traders on the Gulf Coast by trading or selling captured enslaved Black southerners to Cuban merchants. Through the summer the Florida Indians continued to conduct raids ranging from south of Tampa to within just miles of the territorial capital. All the while, Call frequently took it upon himself to critique and advise the regular army as to its objectives in protecting white Floridians.[10] Eventually Call led an expedition bolstered by new volunteers from Tennessee; however, his summer campaign amounted to little more than a stalemate.[11] Eventually, Call's outspoken needling of the federal government contributed to President Martin Van Buren's decision to remove Call as territorial governor in 1839.[12]

Growing increasingly exasperated, Call considered alternative means to subdue Native resistance. In a conversation with a Tallahassee acquaintance in 1838, Call broached a proposal to facilitate the militarized settlement of white families to subjugate the Florida Indians. Call contemplated a plan in which the "government should invite people to settle in the territory and let them occupy the forsaken plantation free of rent or tax and also pay them monthly wages to furnish them with arms and ammunition to defend themselves and others." Call continued, "In this way there would be a gradual advance upon the Indian which would soon cause them to give up the contest."[13] Call's proposal for the militarized settlement of the Florida peninsula was not alone. From Jefferson County, Tennessee, Thomas A. Anderson wrote the secretary of war encouraging a similar plan, in 1840. Anderson believed there was enough interest to entice one thousand settlers from eastern Tennessee alone to relocate to Florida to act as an armed bulwark against Native resistance to white settlement.[14]

In the same year, Thomas H. Benton from Missouri introduced the Armed Occupation Bill in the US Senate as "the true way of settling and holding a conquered country." While more tactful than Call in critiquing the federal government, Benton declared by 1840 that the US Army had "done all that military can do; they have broken, dispersed, and scattered the enemy." It was now time, according to Benton, for "settlers and cultivators to retain possession of the country, and to defend their possessions . . . and the armed cultivator is the man for that." Benton outlined the proposed establishment of new settlements on the Florida peninsula organized into four-square mile tracts. Each community would be bordered by blockhouses set one hundred yards apart enclosing "a good field" offering "safe habitations . . . for families." Guarding against the Florida Indians that "lurk about," Benton envisioned that a "few trusty rifles in the brave hands" of settlers alongside "the faithful mastiff" would make all safe. Benton believed "the heart of the Indian sickens when he hears the crowing of the cock, the barking of the dog, the sound of the axe, and the crack of the rifle." Benton asserted "cultivation and defense then goes hand in hand." It was "the settler alone, the armed settler," Benton argued, "whose presence announces the dominion—the permanent dominion—of the white man."

Benton concluded his proposal by drawing comparisons between Florida and the South and invoking comparable histories of violence between whites and Native Americans. Benton summarized "that it was difficult to see how any one that has read history; or has heard how this new world was settled; or how Kentucky and Tennessee were settled, can doubt" the effectiveness of armed settlement. As had been done in Kentucky and Tennessee, "the armed settlers went forth to fight, and to cultivate. They lived in stations first . . . and emerged to separate settlements afterwards; and in every instance, an interest in the soil—an inheritance in the land—was the reward of their enterprise, toil, and danger." "Florida," Benton declared, "is now prepared for this armed settlement."[15]

While it was popular among white southerners, an unexpected alliance of interests coordinated to thwart Benton's Armed Occupation bill in 1840. Leading the charge against the proposal, northern Whigs and abolitionists painted the plan as a con aimed at advancing the interests of slaveholders. An editorial in St. Johnsbury, Vermont's *Caledonian* described "Mr Benton's plan of armed occupation" as a ploy "for dividing Florida, so as to create two new slave states on that peninsula."[16] With Iowa and Wisconsin rumored to be soon admitted as Free States, the paper portrayed Benton's proposal as nothing more than a scheme to preserve "the ascendancy of the south in the Senate."[17] From North Carolina, Sen. Robert Strange was the only southern Democrat to object to the bill. While his goal aligned with Whigs and abolitionists, his justifications likely left his provisional allies aghast. Strange viewed the proposal as "neither economical nor efficient" in bringing hostilities to a conclusion.[18] To best facilitate the settlement of the Florida peninsula, Strange advocated for a brutal war to either completely expel the Indians or exterminate those who remained. Comparing the conflict in Florida to the Maroon Wars of Jamaica's eighteenth century, Strange believed it necessary to rely on "bush fighting volunteers" to launch "constant and ceaseless pursuit; giving [the Indians] neither time for rest nor for gathering of food, while, at the same time, . . . deprive them of opportunity for rapine and destruction."[19] Rather than use mastiffs for defense as proposed by Benton, Strange supported using Cuban bloodhounds for offensive campaigns, as the British had done in Jamaica in the 1790s. Strange suggested one final opportunity for any Florida Indian to surrender for deportation, but all those "taken afterwards should be hung upon the gibbet." "This threat," Strange emphasized, "should be executed."[20] While passing in the Senate, the 1840 Armed Occupation Bill stalled in the House.

In 1842 Congress passed a modified version of Benton's Armed Occupation bill with significant support from the South. The act offered any head of a family or single man able to bear arms title to 160 acres in Florida free of charge if they remained a minimum of five years, built a home and cleared five acres, and did not settle within two miles of a military post. By the summer of 1843, half the applicants applying for land at the Newnansville Land Office came from the Carolinas, Georgia, and Alabama, states that were critical in supplying volunteers to expel the Florida Indians.[21]

While the 1842 version of the bill sacrificed federal grants of arms and ammunition to settlers, the spirit of the legislation remained focused on facilitating the militant settlement of the peninsula. When Jeremiah Dodson migrated from North Carolina to land south of Gainesville, he petitioned the Land Office, proclaiming, "I have come . . . with two good guns and several hundred pounds of ammunition. I pitched my tent and started to work to make land worth defending."[22] The law emphasized the need for settlers to fend for themselves and encouraged a reliance on armed individualism. Requiring that settlers establish homesteads a minimum of two miles from a military outpost signaled not just a priority to expand white settlement but also the potential vulnerability of settlers. For the last seven years, white communities across the South read of white Floridians cowering behind city walls or at army blockhouses for fear of slaughter by unpredictable Native raids. To settle beyond the purview of established communities and fortifications meant accepting the prospects of defending oneself and family, no matter how crippled the expulsion campaigns left Native Floridians. In the law's first year, the federal government issued only 43 permits, but that number increased to 1,274 in 1843.[23] In this manner the onus of defense would no longer be on an inconsistent, temporary fighting force, but on a vigilant armed populace benefiting from the financial support of the federal government and reaping the benefits of Native dispossession.

While the prospect of pacifying the Florida Indians through the deployment of armed families across the territory appeased most white southerners, some firebrands disdained any drawdown by the US Army in the Florida Territory. In Congress, Florida territorial delegate David Levy rejected any reduction of the US Army in Florida and condemned northern congressmen who had criticized the removal campaigns since 1835. In the summer of 1842, Levy took to the floor of the House to deliver an impassioned denunciation of the proposed peace with the Florida Indians. Levy refused to settle for anything less than the complete expulsion or extermination of Native southerners across the peninsula. Levy defended the past seven years of removal campaigns as a necessary act of defense. He criticized the United States for extending a "criminal kindness, moderation, and forbearance" to the Florida Indians since the acquisition of the peninsula, and Florida's settlers had paid the cost in lives lost. In a wide-ranging address, he dismissed the indigeneity of the Florida Indians and invoked the recent deaths of white settlers in condemning the federal government and northern congressmen who supported the termination of removal efforts.

Levy commenced his speech by dismissing Seminole claims to the land, arguing that "no part of the Indians found in Florida at the time [of US acquisition] were aborigines of that peninsula." Instead, he argued that the first Floridians were the Caloosa and Yamasees but had been "exterminated long ago." The Indians residing in Florida by 1830, according to Levy, were migrants from various towns in Georgia and Alabama, such as the "Mickasukies, Cowetas, Chickasaw, Uchees, Choctaws, and other refugees from the Upper Creeks," whose occupancy of the country dated back no more than fifty years. To assert his position, Levy pointed to a minimal documentary record produced by white settlers who had a limited window into Indigenous ancestry. While conceding that some small faction of the Seminole had "traceable blood of the Yemassees," Levy noted that they were clearly discernible from the Creek "by their darker color." However, Levy claimed, this limited number of ancestral Floridians "were the first to emigrate, and composed the treaty or peace-party" who had voluntarily migrated to Indian Territory in 1836. Simultaneously, Levy denied the Seminoles' ancestral claims to Florida and asserted the true Florida Indians had signed over the peninsula to the United States.[24]

Not yet finished, the most incendiary moments of Levy's performance brought the spectacle of white victimization to the House floor. Near the end of his tirade, he held above his head a blood-stained spear he claimed had been taken from the body of a five-year-old white child in Central Florida. The prior month, southern newspapers had circulated reports of an Indian attack against the Snowden family in Alachua County. According to the presses, Absolom Snowden and his three young children were killed, and his wife left horribly injured. The incident was quickly dubbed the "Alachua Massacre" as news spread from Florida to Georgia and the Carolinas.[25] Levy read from an eyewitness account that mirrored the newspapers' reports detailing a horrific scene reminiscent of numerous Indian raids against settler homesteads. Levy reported that around ten at night on May 14, Indians sacked the Snowden home near Newnansville, Florida. According to a witness responding to the attack, the only survivor was "Mrs. Snowden," who sustained multiple injuries and watched the death of her husband, Absolom, and executions of their three children. As Levy read to Congress, he described that after the Indians killed Absolom at the home, they set fire to the house and carried Mrs. Snowden and the children two hundred yards away. Levy continued that in the distant light of the blazing homestead, the

Indians "fell to shooting [Mrs. Snowden's] children with arrows, pointed with spears . . . before they molested her; they then gave her seven fatal wounds, and [left] her for dead." Not long after the assailants fled, a local militia company discovered Mrs. Snowden "stripped of her apparel to the under dress, and that stained and soaked in her own blood of the deepest hue." Levy recounted that upon further investigation, the militiamen "found her three children all together, enveloped in their own gore, massacred with arrows—two daughters and one son . . . the whole family thus mutilated."[26]

After reading the letter, Levy singled out Rep. Joshua Giddings from Ohio for both his advocacy to terminate the removal campaigns and longstanding denunciations of Indian policy in the South. Levy called on Giddings, and by extension a cadre of aligned northern congressmen who supported peace with the Florida Indians, to look upon the arrow he held above his head. Levy challenged Giddings "whether, after the recitals of the letter . . . and the view of this instrument, at once of torture and of death, one sentiment of sympathy with these monsters can rest in his bosom." Levy insisted that if the Florida Indians were permitted to be "left where they are," it would only give opportunity to "repeat their enormities." He concluded in no uncertain terms that if the Florida Indians "cannot be emigrated, they should be exterminated."[27] Levy's admonishment of federal policy and congressional endorsement fell in line with a long-held course by white southerners to frame Native resistance to settler colonialism as unprovoked violence. The nearly immediate politicization of the "Alachua Massacre" echoed the start of the removal campaigns in 1835 and similarly canonized victims of Native resistance such as Jane Johns. By focusing on Native violence against white families, Levy presented a conflict in which white southerners were suffering victims of Native aggression, and the racially distinct people could not coexist in the same region. As Levy argued before Congress, and newspapers across the South retold accounts of Native opposition to forced removal in terms of the massacre of settler children, white southerners memorialized the conflict as undertaken in defense rather than as provoked in resistance to the region's ethnic cleansing.

Expulsion, however, offered Native southerners little respite. As Native southerners moved west, white southerners did so as well, carrying with them their anti-Indian prejudices. In Texas white southerners found new grounds to collaborate in their vilification, expulsion, and extermination of both Native southerners who were expelled from the American South and long-established Indigenous peoples in the area. Men such as Georgian Mirabeau B. Lamar, Tennessean John H. Moore, and North Carolinian Edward Burleson were instrumental in the militant expulsion of Native Americans from the Republic of Texas in the late 1830s.[28] As the second president of the Texas Republic, Lamar prioritized purging Native Americans from within the new country's land claims. In his first presidential address, Lamar invoked well-worn strategies used by white southerners to vilify Native Americans and call white settlers to action. Lamar focused on the amorphous threat "native tribes of Indians" posed to settlers and their families. He emphasized "the importance of chastising these savage offenders, and extending protection to our exposed and suffering fellow-citizens . . . whose sequestered cabin is reared on our remote frontier." According to Lamar, the continued presence of Indigenous peoples in Texas offered up "the wife and the infant . . . as rich a trophy to the scalping knife, as the warrior who falls in the vigor of manhood." If not expelled or exterminated, Lamar predicted "oceans of blood; the blood of our wives and children" would be the only thing to satiate the "voracious appetite" of the "sanguinary savage."[29]

With encouragement from Lamar, the Texas government brought about an exterminating war upon Native Americans residing within the claims of their new settler state. In February 1839, former Tennessean John H. Moore led a campaign against a Comanche camp near modern-day Austin that left few survivors. Leading a cadre of volunteers, Moore annihilated the Comanche, encircling Indigenous women and children in the assault. Fellow Tennessee migrant and participant Henderson Yoakum described a massacre taking place as the white Texans "opened the doors of the wigwams . . . slaughtering the enemy in their beds." Along the border of Texas and Indian Territory to the north, white Texans targeted a band of Cherokee that had resided in the area since 1819, predating the establishment of the Republic of Texas by more than fifteen years. The Texas Cherokees had migrated from the east to Mexican-controlled Texas hoping to escape the encroaching onslaught and violence of white southerners prior to the Indian Removal Act. By the time white settlers from the United States overthrew the Mexican government, the Texas Cherokees had well-established homesteads and farms between the Angelina and Neches Rivers.[30] Despite the longevity of their residence, Lamar sent an envoy in the summer of 1839 demanding the Texas Cherokees leave. When the Cherokee rebuffed the Texans' demands, a militia of 450 returned and routed the Cherokee defenders along the Neches River. The Texas Cherokee splintered in different groups as some headed to Indian Territory to the north and others pushed farther west. White Texans proceeded to canvass the countryside, purging any remnants of Native occupation and seizing property. By the end of the year, former North Carolinian Edward Burleson and two hundred men tracked down the small band of Cherokee who headed into western Texas. The conflict was short with the remaining few Texas Cherokees suffering another devastating loss.[31]

When the secession crisis hit the US South in 1861 over the expansion of slavery, white southerners had a strong base of regional cohesion. Some of the most ardent Unionists could not bring themselves to abandon the South, even when they feared secession a terrible blunder. Former Florida governor Richard K. Call, veteran of the 1813 Creek War, and leader of the Florida militia during the removal campaigns of 1836, found himself caught between his belief in the Union and his loyalty to the South. Although Call had little faith in Lincoln and a heavy interest in slavery, he did not see secession as the best path forward for white Floridians. He sought to offer counsel to the state of Florida and encouraged white southerners to keep the nation whole.[32] On December 1, 1860, Call made a final mass appeal, marking his adamant opposition to secession, warning that if the southern states proceeded, they would be committing high treason.[33] Much to his dismay, Call's plea fell on deaf ears. On January 10, 1861, a special convention in Tallahassee voted to leave the Union, making Florida the third state to secede, preceded only by South Carolina and Mississippi. Shortly after, Call penned a letter to a friend in Pennsylvania forewarning, "We are in the midst of the most extraordinary revolution, and the most stupendous ruin is now in rapid progress that the world has ever known." His eldest daughter, Ellen, remembered him taking the news of secession hard. In 1883 Ellen reflected her father was "sad beyond expression and presented for the first time the bowed figure of an old man."[34]

Despite his fervent disapproval of secession, Call threw his full support behind Florida and the Confederate South. Despite earlier assurances to the contrary, he proclaimed a willingness to fight for the Confederacy and encouraged other white southerners to do the same. When Thomas Perkins doubted the old governor's dedication, Call replied that he took offense from any suspicion in which his "loyalty to the South was called in question." He vehemently denounced any man that would do such a thing, labeling them "a fool, or a willfully malicious lying scoundrel." Despite his age, Call declared he "was desirous of entering the military service . . . and of obtaining the command of the Troops employed in the defense of Florida."[35] Call had already fought for the white South against the Creeks in 1813 and against the Seminoles in 1836, and he refused to shirk the martial expectations of his peers in 1861.

In writing to his grandson, also named Richard, Call stressed that there was no other choice than to fight for the South. Though his grandson was not yet of age, Call demanded that if he were to "come to manhood before [the war] ends," young Richard should "espouse the cause of your own people, be it right or wrong—you must join the army of the South, and devote all your energies to the vindication of her liberty and independence." Call implored his grandson to "prefer death to dishonor—die gloriously on the battlefield, in her defense, sooner than live to see the South, the land of your birth overrun and conquered by the invading foe."[36] Even if his state and region had taken a disastrous turn, they were both his home and part of who he was as a southerner.

Call's devotion to the South was deeply intertwined with his earlier involvement in the white South's violence against Native southerners and his recollections of that experience. In the same appeal that his grandson join the Confederate Army, he regaled the young boy with the reminiscence of how he once fought for vengeance after the Red Stick Creeks destroyed Fort Mims. It was now his grandson's obligation to protect the spoils of war that white southerners had spent the first half of the nineteenth century taking from the region's Native southerners. Call championed the transformation of the region as afforded through war and conquest. The land wrestled from the Indians, he described, was now "teeming [with] millions of intelligent prosperous people with their high civilization; productive cotton and grain fields, and villages, and cities with their colleges and churches." Despite success, Call realized the prosperous expansion had come at a cost. In his aged years, Call saw "the American people divided into two hostile nations, contending for mastery on the field of battle," lands once controlled by Native southerners. For Call, the division of the United States in the early 1860s was a consequence of the white South's dismemberment of the Native South, and as a "result of this great conquest," the United States stood at the precipice of self-destruction.[37]

What's more is that Call's proclamation for the defense of the newly forged Confederacy echoed the calls to action from Indian conflicts across the prior half century. Call's letter to his grandson paralleled the language Andrew Jackson used in the wake of the Red Stick attack on Fort Mims when the elder Call had joined the Tennessee militia. In September of 1813, Jackson called upon the martial honor of white men in Tennessee to protect their frontier that was "threatened with invasion by the savage foe."[38] In demanding martial action over pacifism, Call perpetuated intergenerational martial standards that white families in the South had invoked to spur on young men of new generations. In similar fashion to the volunteers of the region's Indian wars, Call expected his grandson to uphold the same dedication to the white South's martial tradition regardless of the potential outcome. Death was preferable to dishonor.

In the wake of Confederate defeat after the Civil War, the white South's legacy of Indian fighters and martial tradition proved to be a point of continuity and pride. Prior to the Civil War, lawyer and historian John Haywood encapsulated a common sentiment among white southerners in his 1823 *The Civil and Political History of Tennessee*. When commenting on a 1792 incident between white and Native southerners in the Cumberland Mountains,

Haywood wrote that "such was the irreconcilable hatred which the Indians and whites had contracted for each other, by a long continued course of aggression and sufferings, that it was almost as impossible for the government of the United States to restrain some of their citizens from acts of enmity, as it was for the Indian chiefs to restrain and keep within bounds, all those who were of their nations."[39] In sum, Haywood's *The Civil and Political History of Tennessee* reads as an accounting of white victimization, rarely diving into the violence perpetrated and perpetuated by white settlers against Native southerners.

Haywood's work was less motivated by a desire to record the interconnected past of the South than it was intent on establishing the legitimacy of white ownership of Tennessee and giving future generations of white southerners heroic forefathers who suffered, fought, and conquered. Pointing out unsavory traits of colonial violence would undermine Haywood's glorification of the "memorable achievements of the eminent men of Tennessee," as he described the white settlers who ventured into the wilderness from Carolina and Virginia. Haywood expressed that his motivation to record the remembered past of white Tennesseans was due to concern "that already the time has come when to many of our inhabitants, their names are but just known, while in the memories of others their actions are fading away." The recency in which white southerners laid claims to much of the American South generated anxiety about their own legitimacy as masters of their domain. For Haywood, the preservation of the memory of Tennessee's white founders was predicated upon the erasure of the state's Native inhabitants. Enshrining the undertakings of white southerners provided the opportunity, Haywood described, to perpetuate the "illustrious deeds" of white settlers and guard against losing the recently forged past "from the recollections of succeeding generations" of white Tennesseans.[40]

At the end of the nineteenth century, Haywood's work was reprinted at the behest of his great-grandson William H. Haywood and included an introduction provided by Arthur St. Clair Colyar. The 1891 edition of Haywood's *The Civil and Political History of Tennessee* perpetuated the original intent of the 1823 publication as a testament to white southerners' dominion of Tennessee and a romanticization of white victimization at the hands of violent Native Americans. In the context of the post–Civil War South, the new edition offered white southerners reassurance of their past triumphs. In a concise preface, William Haywood poignantly saw it necessary to reprint the 1823 chronicle out of "patriotism and a natural love for the memory of the author." As John Haywood designed in a pre–Civil War Tennessee, William desired to ensure that the "illustrious deeds of our ancestors might not be forgotten." In the wake of Confederate defeat, William could point to the successes of Tennesseans' white progenitors on battlefields and homesteads as reflections of a glorious martial tradition. In directly invoking the Civil War, William encouraged white Tennesseans to reflect upon their early history, so as "the sons and daughters of the 'Volunteer State' may know from whence sprung that indomitable race who poured their blood as a libation upon the altar of their country and left their bones to bleach upon every battle-field in the war between the States."[41] The colonial violence of the late eighteenth century provided the wellspring of their martial character and offered a point of pride at a time when the white South was still navigating the mental anguish of its own conquest.

Arthur St. Clair Colyar's introduction to the reprinted volume similarly offered post–Civil War Tennesseans reassurances of a time of sacrifice and triumph. Colyar, a Confederate congressman during the Civil War and a New South booster from Middle Tennessee, framed *The Civil and Political History of Tennessee* as a personal, intimate, and family-bound recounting of Tennessee's early days of white settlement. He described Haywood's chronicle as offering "a diary of our ancestors of deepest interest which would have been [otherwise] lost."[42] Colyar wrote that Haywood's history provided a "diary of events, and there is scarcely an old family in the State that may not find in this diary some incident of deepest interest connected with its ancestry."[43] Like John and William Haywood, Colyar glorified the achievement of Tennessee's white settlers at the end of the eighteenth century for their stalwart persistence in the face of unrelenting Native resistance.

Colyar summarized the white settlement of Tennessee as set against the backdrop of "twenty-six years" in which "an Indian war raged" against settlers. Colyar described the early history of Tennessee as intimately personal, a history defined by white families willing to risk their lives under the threat of Indian attack. He lavished praise upon notable political and militia leaders such as John Sevier, Andrew Jackson, and John Robertson as meritorious Indian fighters but also glorified common white settlers for their efforts. Colyar equated the martial prowess of men like Jackson with "the citizens generally" who made their way to Tennessee at the end of the eighteenth century, writing "some of whom had felt the blows of the tomahawk, and all of who had shared in the dangers and hardships of the long struggle with savage foes." In characterizing Haywood's work as a diary, Colyar surmised that the history of Tennessee "is not so much a history of the great men of the time as it is of the people in general." As evidence of the contributions of the common white settler, Colyar praised Haywood's efforts to detail "more than four hundred tragedies, giving the family, the name of the member killed or scalped or taken into the Indian Nation, together with the pursuit, when pursuit was made, and the result."[44] Looking back from 1891, the conquest of Middle Tennessee and expulsion of Native southerners offered white Tennesseans in a post–Civil War South an opportunity to connect with their ancestors' past glory and depict themselves as descendants of conquerors whose forefathers likewise once made sacrifices but ultimately found prosperity and honor.

Memories and Monuments

The 1876 election cycle offered white southerners the opportunity to return to home rule and end federal Reconstruction. In South Carolina, post–Civil War remembrances of the 1776 Hampton raid in modern-day Greer continued to resonate with descendants of the family and white residents of the state. In South Carolina's 1876 gubernatorial race, great-grandson of Anthony Hampton, Wade Hampton III, leveraged the suffering of his ancestors at the hands of the Cherokee to connect with voters along the campaign trail. After the conclusion of the 1776 Cherokee War and the American Revolution, intergenerational wealth helped secure Wade Hampton III's influence in South Carolina politics. His grandfather Wade Hampton I, son to the slain Anthony Hampton, was anointed by *Nile's Weekly Register* in 1823 as "the richest planter in the South." Born in Charleston in 1818, Wade Hampton III had a privileged upbringing as a member of a wealthy and socially well-connected family far removed from his great-grandfather's rural homestead.[45] During the Civil War, Hampton and his self-financed unit of South Carolinians known as "Hampton's Legion" fought alongside the pantheon of Lost Cause heroes Robert E. Lee, Thomas "Stonewall" Jackson, and J. E. B. Stuart. As a former slaveholder and celebrated Confederate veteran, Hampton personified the ideal gubernatorial candidate for the Democratic Party. White conservatives in South Carolina saw him as an honorable patriarch capable of redeeming the state and ordering a racial hierarchy privileging white supremacy.

In early September 1876, Hampton kicked off his campaign in the South Carolina Upstate.[46] Hampton's ancestry and simple demeanor endeared him to the white electorate of the Upstate despite his aristocratic birth, Charleston connections, and Columbia residence.[47] In his campaign speeches, he professed the importance of ending Reconstruction and returning to home rule. The location of Wade Hampton's first major campaign speech intertwined and renewed the memory of Native resistance during the 1776 Cherokee War. It took place at the Spartanburg County courthouse not far from his great-grandparents' former homestead, where his ancestors were buried along the Tyger River one hundred years earlier. Hampton's speech attracted an estimated six thousand attendees, who likely passed by the roadside Hampton family cemetery.[48] It is hard to imagine that Hampton did not take a moment to visit his ancestors' graves and the site of the Hampton raid, though no confirming evidence directly indicates such a personal moment for Wade III.

As for the content of Hampton's Spartanburg speech, there are conflicting recollections as to whether he directly invoked the memory of his family's victimization to connect with voters. According to the memories of Alfred B. Williams, a reporter following Hampton's campaign trail, Wade III did not speak directly to the personal tragedy of his ancestors. Recalling the events several decades later, Williams reported that though "Spartanburg county was the original South Carolina home of the Hamptons . . . [Wade Hampton III] did not allude to this in his Spartanburg speeches, as far as can be recalled. He was too intent on 1876 to think of 1776."[49] Yet Hampton was known to invoke memories of the American Revolution in political rhetoric. When nominated for the gubernatorial ticket, Hampton invoked the memory of South Carolina's heroic ancestors and the glory of the state's contributions at Cowpens, Eutaw, and King's Mountain during the American Revolution.[50] While on the campaign trail in York, South Carolina, just fifty miles from Spartanburg, contemporary records of Hampton's speech note he likewise praised the attendees as descended from the heroes of the Revolutionary War battle at King's Mountain.[51]

Directly conflicting with Williams's remembered inferences, Mary Earle Lyles invoked the memory of Hampton's 1876 campaign speech in an 1896 student essay contest hosted by the Daughters of the Revolution in Columbia, South Carolina. In a short historical sketch of South Carolina and the American Revolution, Lyles wrote how Wade Hampton III "so eloquently referred" to the notable "massacre . . . of the Hampton family" in his 1876 Spartanburg County courthouse speech. From her 1896 perspective, Hampton spoke of the massacre that befell his ancestors and the retaliation brought against the Cherokee that secured the lands that now made up Pickens, Oconee, Anderson, and Greenville Counties. In effect, Lyles framed her version of Hampton's speech in 1876 as an appeal made by a vicarious inheritor of Native violence and a descendant of justified conquerors who secured prosperity for contemporary white South Carolinians. Lyles was eighteen years old at the time she wrote her essay, meaning she was not yet born when Hampton ran for governor, indicating she learned of Hampton's speech and the Hampton raid indirectly, likely from family or acquaintances.[52] At the time she crafted her essay, both the memory of the 1776 raid and Wade III's rallies in the Upstate were prominent local folklore.[53] In whatever manner Lyles came to such a conclusion, her assertions were well received and awarded. For her efforts the Daughters of the Revolution honored her with the gold medal prize for her essay and the submission was published in multiple South Carolina newspapers.[54] The Daughters of the Revolution's adulation of the essay gave newspaper readers reassurance of local folklore that had likely been passed down for generations.

At the start of the twentieth century, the memory of Cherokee efforts to thwart settler expansion in 1776 became a hallmark of white South Carolina's history and memory of the state's genesis, Confederate nostalgia, and vilification and erasure of Native southerners. The deification of Wade Hampton III as a romanticized Confederate general and redeemer of the white South fueled public interest in the Hampton raid throughout the first half of the twentieth century. In the fall of 1901, Walhalla, South Carolina's local newspaper, the *Keowee Courier*, named for the former Cherokee town destroyed and seized at the conclusion of the 1776 Cherokee War, reprinted an 1843 account of the Hampton raid sourced from oral histories of Upstate residents in the early nineteenth century originally produced by Revolutionary War chronicler and former South Carolina governor Benjamin F. Perry. The paper added a brief introduction stating that the republication of Perry's "Revolutionary Incidents," now retitled "Massacre of the Hampton Family" was a result of "numerous requests for information" about the family of Wade Hampton III. Across the Upstate, other papers carried the column, with some adding the more salacious title "The Fiendish Massacre of the Hampton Family." As a result, the communities of Walhalla, Lancaster, Union, Anderson, and Manning were reintroduced to the Hampton family's remembrances of Native aggression and settler sufferings and facilitated a broader memory of Native violence against white ancestors among South Carolinians.[55]

As twentieth-century newspapers provided a vehicle for the perpetuation of South Carolina's public memory of settler victimhood, white residents of the Upstate formalized a commemorative landscape upon Anthony and Elizabeth's eighteenth-century homestead.[56] By the late 1920s, white women in Greer involved with the Confederate heritage group the United Daughters of the Confederacy (UDC) began organizing an effort to place a memorial on the Hampton gravesite.[57] As reported in the local newspaper, the UDC women desired to establish "a monument to the graves of Anthony Hampton and family, who were massacred by the Cherokee Indians in July 1776."[58] On September 19, 1933, Greer's two UDC chapters, the Stonewall Chapter and Hampton-Lee Chapter, gathered on the property of William B. Bailey to mark the Hampton graves with a stone cairn memorial. The dedication ceremony provided participants an opportunity to affirm their belonging to the region and the origins of the State of South Carolina. Attendees consecrated the ground as a site of settler victimization, consumed the locality through its waters, and imposed their historical narrative onto the landscape. As reported by the *Greenville News*, participants attending the Hampton memorial dedication ceremony listened to a paper on the history of the Hampton family provided by the UDC historical committee, ceremoniously "partook of a glass of the water from the Hampton spring," and "reverently stood before the monument which marks this last resting place of the Hamptons, early settlers of Spartanburg county who were massacred by the Cherokee Indians." The monument, as described by the newspaper, was constructed of "native rocks" featuring a marble slab with the engraving:

Antony Hampton
Feb. 3, 1715–July 1776
with
wife, son, Preston and grandson.
massacred by Cherokee Indians,
Tyger river. Spartanburg District,
S.C.
Maj-Gen. Wade Hampton
1751–1835
Col. Wade Hampton,
1791–1858
Lieut-Gen. Wade Hampton,
1818–1902
Erected by Stonewall chapter
U.D.C.
Greer, S. C. 1933[59]

Figure 10. Hampton Massacre monument. In 1933 members of the United Daughters of the Confederacy installed a monument marking the 1776 Cherokee raid against the Hampton homestead in Greer, South Carolina. Photo by F. Evan Nooe.

Although three generations of Wade Hamptons are listed in the inscription, none of them are buried beneath the memorial. The inclusion of Anthony and Elizabeth's descendants on the memorial connects the family across South Carolina's past and geographically across the state. While the monument's installment marked the graves of those who died in 1776, the memorial affirmed the Upstate's connection to a deified Confederate veteran in Wade Hampton III. At the same time, white South Carolinians across the state memorialized the former slaveholder, secessionist, and segregationist with named roadways, public schools, a county bearing the family name, and monuments in Columbia and Charleston. For UDC members in Greer, the memorial to the Hampton raid connected the Upstate to South Carolina through the notoriety of the Hampton family and binding white South Carolinians through a remembrance of Native violence.

Into the twenty-first century, the landscape of Upstate South Carolina still perpetuates a public memory of victimized white settlers suffering the aggression of Native Americans. In 2009 the state granted a petition by descendants of Jacob Hite to place a historical marker memorializing a late eighteenth-century "Early White Settlement" established by the Hite family. In addition to creating a memorial to the Hite family's homestead, the reverse side of the historical marker commemorated "The Massacre of Jacob Hite" that took place in June 1776.[60] Jacob's experience parallels Anthony Hampton's death in many respects. Hite was a settler from Virginia taking advantage of land secured by the English after the French and Indian War.[61] He and his family established a homestead on land that was not legally open to white settlers. One report even suggested the Hite family settled within Cherokee territory, and at least once in 1774 Jacob was forced to flee the homestead in fear for his safety when the Cherokee sought to push out squatters.[62] Like the initial Hampton settlers, Jacob's son was involved in the Indian trade. In the summer of 1776, when the Cherokee struck against white colonists to defend their homeland, Jacob Hite was killed at his settlement, and his wife and daughter taken captive.

Among several elements omitted from the 2009 historical marker, the Hite family was exceptionally wealthy and owned a considerable number of enslaved Black southerners in the late eighteenth century. Contemporary reports of Hite's death note when he relocated from Virginia to South Carolina, "a large parcel of negroes" accompanied him on his move.[63] Hite's violence and inhumanity toward enslaved Blacks, likely unseemly or potentially inconsequential to his twenty-first century celebrants, is absent in the public recollection of his settlement and death in modern-day Upstate South Carolina. At the historical marker's dedication in 2009, one of the organizers in attendance similarly erased the agency imbedded in the Cherokee's war to defend their homes against the colonists. Mary Bird, a descendant of Jacob Hite, suggested that the Cherokee's action against the Hite family was nothing more than a consequence of British manipulations to deter upstart revolutionaries. "The Indians [went] against the Hites," Bird claims, "because they [the Hites] were Patriots." In a few short statements to the local press, Bird dismisses the colonizing agency of the Hite settlers and positions the Cherokee as outsiders in their own land. By describing the Hites as patriots, rather than invasive colonists or traitors to the British Empire, Bird frames the Hites as defenders of their home and country and simultaneously occludes the Cherokee's right to defend their sovereignty and territory. She specifically points to the Loyalist Richard Pearis as the British agent responsible for pushing the Cherokee to attack the South Carolina settlements.[64] Bird's suggestion dismisses any potential of the Cherokee acting of their own rational accord, because to do so would force the uncomfortable consideration that the actions of settlers such as the Hites threatened Cherokee communities. Blaming the British as instigators of Cherokee aggression, a centuries-old strawman, cleanses settlers of their own culpability in the violence toward Indigenous peoples.

As of 2022 the Hampton monument remains not far from the Tyger River in Greer just off the south shoulder of US Highway 29, locally known as Wade Hampton Boulevard in honor of Wade Hampton III. Yet the monument no longer serves as a grave marker for Anthony, Elizabeth, Preston, and the unnamed child of James and Elizabeth Harrison. Sometime in the 1970s, the widening of Highway 29 required the relocation of the monument. In the process the monument and the graves became detached. While the monument remains standing in its new location intact, the gravesite of the slain eighteenth-century Hamptons is lost. The separation of the monument from the graves and the loss of the Hampton burial site has proven to be a source of anxiety for the descendants of white settlers in the twenty-first century. Locals interested in the settler history of the Upstate, including elected government officials, state agencies, and descendants of the Hampton family have attempted to rediscover the graves of the Hamptons but without success.[65] Most likely the roadworks project meant to facilitate commerce and transportation between Greenville and Spartanburg Counties did not account for or was not aware of the need to relocate the interred remains of the Hampton family along with the monument. If the UDC monument's original installment did in fact mark the "last resting place of the Hamptons," as reported in 1933, then the graves of the deceased are now located under some portion of the highway that bears the name of Anthony Hampton's great-grandson.

While the Hampton family gravesite offers a symbolic point of origin for the state of South Carolina's settler history, it also embodies the violent dispossession of the Cherokee's homeland. When South Carolina settlers retaliated for the 1776 Cherokee attacks, they began their effort to cleanse the Cherokee people from the land and memory of a developing settler state. As of one of the militia's first targets, South Carolina revolutionaries burned Keowee to the ground, and the Cherokee would never occupy the land again. The next year the Treaty of Dewitt's Corner solidified settler conquest of Keowee and most of modern Upstate South Carolina, including Pickens, Anderson, and Oconee Counties. After the American Revolution, white Americans quickly pushed west, filling in the borders of the state. For the next two centuries, settler descendants occupied Keowee as the Cherokee endured southern states' increasing hostility toward their existence, the Trail of Tears, and a decades-long fight with North Carolina and the federal government to recognize their political autonomy in western North Carolina.

Though the Cherokee were forced to leave Keowee after 1776, they left behind remnants of their occupation and monuments in the town attesting to thousands of years of Indigenous occupation. When famed naturalist William Bartram visited Keowee in 1775, he recorded evidence of Cherokee and precontact Native occupation that defined the landscape. Writing in his journal, Bartram recorded "several Indian mounts or tumuli, and terraces, monuments of the ancients, at the old site of Keowee."[66] After conversation with the Cherokee, Bartram described that construction of the mounds dated to a time immemorial. According to Bartram, the Cherokee passed down a legend of the mounds in the area serving "some religious purpose, as great altars and temples."[67]

Yet by the early nineteenth century, white southerners challenged the idea that the ancestors of contemporary Native southerners constructed such monuments. In his *Notes on the State of Virginia*, Thomas Jefferson categorically denied the Indigenous origins of the nation's earthen mounds, writing "I know of no such thing existing as an Indian Monument."[68] Jefferson became instrumental in facilitating a theory that a mythical race of Mound Builders, ancestrally distinct from contemporary Native Americans, constructed the earthworks across eastern North America.[69] The plantocracy's antebellum poet and novelist William Gilmore Simms likewise aimed to dissociate Native southerners of his own time with the Indian mounds found across the American South. Simms's poem "The Mountain Tramp," completed in 1852, chronicled a fictional narrative of two travelers making a trek through the South Carolina Upstate. When passing through Keowee, the poem's protagonist identifies "ancient mounds," describing them as "For which no builder yet is found." The observer continues to "muse upon the vanish'd race, That left, without a name, a trace."[70] Producing "The Mountain

Tramp" in the post-Removal South, Simms reinforced the physical expulsion of Native southerners by dismissing their continued presence on the southern landscape.

Scattered across much of the eastern United States, Indian mounds offer physical testimonials to Indigenous occupation and community dating back centuries. In Cherokee country platform mounds often included an apex structure and provided a site for large gatherings of community members and religious leaders. Through the antebellum era, the Cherokee continued to utilize mound sites as both memorials to their ancestors and religious sites that connected the living to protective spirits. According to Cherokee oral tradition, ancestors who were buried in the mounds could enter the afterlife and transcend into protective beings. Even after forced removal in the 1830s, mounds provided Native Americans pilgrimage sites to reconnect with their ancestors and origins.[71]

In the late 1960s, archaeological surveys of Keowee and mounds in the vicinity attest to both the long-term occupation by Native Americans and the desecration of Indigenous memorials by white settlers. As part of a 1967 excavation, anthropologist Roger Grange documented a ceremonial mound, the presence of a smaller contiguous mound, and a third burial mound at the town center. Grange's team confirmed the presence of fifteen burials, skeletal remains including those of a child, and evidence of additional cremations.[72] The archaeological findings indicate that the town and burial mound likely date to between 1300 and 1450 CE, predating the Anglo-America seizure of Keowee by more than three hundred years.[73] Once white South Carolinians moved in, settlers began the process of erasing the memorials and burials of the locale's Native forebears. In his assessment, Grange reported that the site was extensively damaged. Local relic hunters had dug into the central area of the mound, pilfering keepsakes of conquest. Additionally, intensive agricultural work over decades damaged the mound and churned Native artifacts as settlers farmed the land. When Grange and his team began cataloging Keowee, he described the site's most prominent feature diminished to "a low, circular mound."[74] As a result of increasing demand on public utilities in the Upstate, the final erasure of Keowee and the Indian mounds took place when Duke Power flooded the Keowee River basin in preparation to build a nuclear power plant.[75] When South Carolina's Oconee Nuclear Station began service in 1973, it was the largest nuclear power plant ever created. Keowee and any memorial to Cherokee or Indigenous occupation of the town now lay underneath an 1,800-acre reservoir.[76]

Epilogue

In the twenty-first century, the American South is still remaking public memories of the past that glorify white southerners for facilitating Native dispossession while concurrently erasing Indigenous peoples and the violence inflicted against them. On November 22, 2000, school children, county commissioners, and the local press gathered on a cool fall morning in eastern Alabama to "make history come alive in Calhoun County."[1] The throng of onlookers in attendance waited eagerly to witness the unveiling of a new historical monument dedicated to the Creek child Lyncoya who was orphaned and abducted in the 1813 Battle of Tallushatchee.

The engagement wasn't so much a battle as it was the annihilation of a Creek village by Tennessee militia. One participant reminisced years after the assault that the action took a swift and decidedly brutal turn. As a volunteer with the Tennesseans, Richard K. Call described witnessing "a horrible and revolting scene." After an initial engagement along a nearby ridge, the Creek warriors retreated to the town, and the Tennessee militia followed close on their heels. In describing the ensuing events, Call recollected, "The battle had ended in the village, the warriors fighting in their board homes, which gave little protection against rifle bullets or musket ball." No one was safe from the invading militiamen. Call described how the Creek men "fought in the midst of their wives and children, who frequently shared their bloody fate." What was left after the killing stopped was a tangle of fire, blood, and gore. Call and the Tennesseans "found as many as eight or ten bodies in a single cabin, sometimes the dead mother clasped the dead child to her breast, and to add another appalling horror to the bloody catalogue—some of the cabins had taken fire, and half consumed human bodies were seen amidst the smoking ruins."[2] As a participant in the assault, legendary Indian fighter and Tennessean David Crockett corroborated Call's assessment, writing that the militia men "shot [the Creeks] like dogs." In a testimonial of settler violence rarely revealed by white participants, Crockett shared in his autobiography "seeing a boy who was shot down . . . His arm and thigh was broken, and he was so near the burning house that the grease was stewing out of him . . . he was only about twelve years old."[3] In sum, nearly two hundred Creek men, women, and children died in the assault against Tallushatchee. The Tennessee militia suffered five casualties.

The installation of the monument in 2000 by Calhoun County remakes the past, erasing how it was remembered by its participants, and narrates the landscape to remove the heinous acts of violence against Native people described by Call and Crockett. The twenty-first-century memorial sidesteps any acknowledgment of violence against the Tallushatchee Creek and prioritizes myths of a benevolent white caretaker as saving Lyncoya. Some 187 years after the annihilation of Tallushatchee, there was little mention of the circumstances that left Lyncoya orphaned in Calhoun County's commemoration of the site. Instead, the committee behind the monument's installation off Highway 144 celebrated the compassion of Andrew Jackson and his graciousness in adopting the Creek infant found alongside a murdered mother. According to the memorial's inscription, the monument "marks the site where Lincoyer was found and saved by Gen. Andrew Jackson after the Battle of Talluschatchee during the Creek Indian War." On the reverse side, the inscription elaborates, "Gen. Andrew Jackson found a dead Creek Indian woman embracing her living son. Gen. Jackson, upon hearing that the other Creek Indian women were planning to kill the infant, as was their custom when all relations were dead, became himself the protector and guardian of the child."

As the principal organizer for the monument's installation, Calhoun County Commission chairman Eli Henderson shared with the press the importance of the monument to representing the past. The local *Anniston Star* quoted Henderson advocating, "I don't want us to forget our history." He elaborated, "By telling the story of Lyncoyer, we can show the brutality of war during that time while showing the humanity of one of America's great leaders." While the monument marks the site of a historic event, the inscription removes the massacre of nearly two hundred Creek men, women, and children to praise the man responsible and frame his behavior as a selfless act worthy of adulation. The monument provides comfort for the descendants of settlers in the present, casting aside the location as a site of trauma, and conveys a celebratory version of the past to future generations in Calhoun County.

How future generations would remember the site was explicitly in the minds of the committee responsible for the monument's installation. At the dedication ceremony, Henderson and the co-organizers emphasized the importance of the monument as a tangible expression of the past to imprint upon the next generation of Calhoun County residents. While in attendance at the opening ceremony, county school superintendent Jacky Sparks noted

Figure 11. Battle of Tallushatchee and Lyncoya Memorial. In 2000, Calhoun County, Alabama, installed a historical marker on the 1813 Battle of Tallushatchee site memorializing Andrew Jackson's "compassion" in abducting Lyncoya after militia killed the child's mother. Lyncoya died on Jackson's Nashville plantation in 1828. The location of his burial is unknown. Photo by F. Evan Nooe.

that she expected fifty to sixty local elementary and high school students to attend the dedication ceremony. Sparks shared she felt the monument was "part of our heritage." Henderson likewise expressed the importance of conveying their inscribed story of Jackson as Lyncoya's savior to school children. He stated to the press in attendance, "I want elementary kids and high school students to be able to go to the site where it actually happened." He elaborated that the goal of the monument was "to help make history real and exciting for our students both locally and from other states."[4] One high school student in attendance affirmed how the monument reinforced the interpretation of the past provided in their prior fourth-grade Alabama history lessons. From within the halls of Alabama public schools to municipally funded roadside monuments, Calhoun County perpetuated the memory of Andrew Jackson as the caretaker to an orphaned Indian child. For visitors to the monument in November 2000, the Calhoun County commission recast the site from "a horrible and revolting scene" as described by an 1813 participant into a local heritage site celebrating the memory of Jackson overseeing the annihilation of a Creek town, deaths of nearly two hundred Creek men, women, and children, and finally the abduction of an orphaned infant.

Noticeably absent from the installation of the Lyncoya memorial in Calhoun County was any indication of an Indigenous perspective. The creation of a monument to mark the site of Lyncoya's abduction serves as little more than a shrine to Andrew Jackson and a misdirection away from the historical trauma inflicted on a Creek community. Had Native perspectives and memories been considered, the monument would have likely been something entirely different.[5] When the state of Alabama invited representatives from the Muscogee Creek Nation of Oklahoma to the two hundredth anniversary of the 1813 Creek War, an uneasy tension was felt across how to remember Lyncoya and Tallushatchee. Emman Spain, the historical officer for the Muscogee (Creek) Nation, joined the ceremonies and shared a starkly different community memory of events than those written upon the Lyncoya monument. In addressing a crowd in 2013, Spain noted that Creeks rarely talked about the 1813 War or anything else before their arrival in Oklahoma. He informed a reporter, "Most Creeks don't talk about these battles, and they don't talk about removal, because it brings back bad feelings." In addressing the inherited trauma, Spain described that the Creek remembered the events preceding the 1813 Creek War as parallel to "suffering from foreign terrorism." He likewise sharply contradicted the settler memory that Jackson saved Lyncoya. In conversation with elders of the Creek Nation, Spain contends the myth was preposterous, stating, "That's why we have the clan system." Creek clan structure, as Spain pointed out, afforded the orphaned infant an extended family to go to for support.[6] Furthermore, clan affiliation did not preclude an adoption within Creek clans or across Native ethnicities in the American South. Young children were often the easiest to incorporate into Native towns and clans regardless of tribal origin.

Despite the efforts of white southerners to memorialize the conquest and purge of Indigenous peoples across the region, Native southerners remain and have voiced their memories of the violence inflicted upon them over centuries. In Florida the Seminole Tribe express their own memories of settler violence against their ancestors through their public-facing website defining the expulsion campaigns of the nineteenth century as a "profound . . . stain" on the United States that "can never be erased." "The Seminole people," the website continues, "were hunted with bloodhounds, rounded up like cattle, and forced onto ships that carried them . . . on to strange and inhospitable new lands."[7] Family memories passed from one generation to the next reveal a long-remembered trauma carried into the twenty-first century. While conducting interviews among the Seminole in the late twentieth century, Jean Chaudhuri of the Creek Nation, noted that Seminole oral histories repeatedly told of Andrew Jackson killing young Indians and even "taking an Indian child and bashing his head against rocks and trees."[8] In another recollection one Florida Seminole remembered that during the expulsion campaigns, "if an old man or child was too old to walk anymore, or to go any further, they say that the soldiers took their bayonets and killed them right on the spot."[9] Betty Mae Tiger Jumper's autobiography compiled in the third quarter of the twentieth century crystalized the depravity of settler colonial violence. Jumper's family memories attest to the seemingly commonplace sexual assault of Native women by American soldiers during the removal process.[10]

Among the Cherokee similar family memories of violence imparted a vicarious trauma across generations. Cherokee expulsion from their lands in Georgia in the 1830s began with the threat of violence as the US Army forced Native families from their homes. Historian Jeffrey Ostler has characterized the staging grounds for relocation as "Death Camps" due to federal indifference. Conditions in the camps lacked adequate shelter, food, clean water, or medicine, resulting in exposure and rampant disease. During the removal treks, a multitude of contagious illnesses plagued the Cherokee parties, and historical records indicate examples of sexual violence against young Cherokee women.[11] During the Great Depression, a host of interviews with Cherokee in Oklahoma documented family memories of settler colonial violence along the Trail of Tears. In one particularly jarring recollection, "Bettie" Perdue Woodall shared with an interviewer in 1937 how on one occasion "an officer in charge of one of the wagons . . . killed a little [Cherokee] baby because it cried all the time." While Bettie lamented such stories "were almost unbelievable," she knew they were true, as they had been passed to her from her mother.[12]

In an individual act of Indigenous memory in the American South, Tom Hendrix commemorated his Yuchi great-great-grandmother Te-lah-nay's return to northern Alabama after her forced relocation in 1839. Prior to the removal campaigns, Yuchi Indians lived in autonomous towns from modern-day Tennessee to Florida dating back to the sixteenth century. Swept up in the expulsion drives in the 1830s, the Yuchi were often subsumed under larger groups in the Native South. From Alabama, nine hundred Yuchi Indians were removed alongside Creek detachments beginning in the summer of 1836.[13] According to the family memories of Tom Hendrix, Te-lah-nay was driven into the removal camps as a result of settler violence. When white traders visited Te-lah-nay's camp along the Tennessee River, the encounter quicky turned violent. Te-lah-nay's father, Ka-we-ta, initially welcomed seven white men traveling the river appearing to be exchanging manufactured goods for animal hides. However, the traveling market was a deception. When Ka-we-ta turned away from one of the traders, a white man referred to as "Hairy Face" pushed a short sword through his back. Hiding on a rock ledge along the river, Te-lah-nay and her sister watched in horror as the traders fanned out and killed her family one by one with rifles, side arms, and swords. Te-lah-nay's grandmother put the two girls in a canoe and sent them downriver in hopes of protecting them from the traders' massacre. Eventually landing at a white settlement, the girls were soon interned at the Creek relocation camps by the US Army and prepared for deportation to Indian Territory. Te-lah-nay wouldn't return home until five years later.[14]

Beginning in the 1980s, Hendrix started construction of a stone wall on his property as a memorial to Te-lah-nay's determination. After thirty years, the one-man project resulted in the completion of an unmortared stone wall ranging from three to five feet high and six to eighteen feet wide. The wall extends over a mile in length and is constructed with more than eight million pounds of stones. Curving through his property, the wall is built in two sections representing Te-lah-nay's forced migration west and her journey back east. The individual stones represent each step Te-lah-nay took on her journey during her five-year walk back to Alabama. With the completion of her odyssey, Hendrix notes, Te-lah-nay returned with her knowledge of Yuchi medicines and memories. Collectively, the stones represent Indigenous permanence. Speaking to visitors, Hendrix stated, "We shall all pass through this earth. Only stones remain." In constructing the memorial, Hendrix added, "We honor our ancestors with stone."[15] As travelers walk the length of the site interchangeably known as the "Wichahpi Commemorative Stone Wall," "Te-lah-nay's Wall," or simply, "The Wall," they add to the memorial as well. Visitors regularly contribute stones to the wall as a show of respect and solidarity. Māori from New Zealand, Australian Aborigines, Navajos from the American Southwest, and Siouxan Peoples from the Great Plains have all placed stones on the wall, contributing to the monument and attesting to their shared experience of resilience and defiance to colonial violence.[16]

Notes

Introduction

1. Louis De Vorsey Jr., "Early Maps as a Source in the Reconstruction of Indian Landscapes," *Red, White, and Black: Symposium on Indians in the Old South*, ed. Charles M. Hudson (Athens: University of Georgia Press, 1971): 12–30, 21; James H. O'Donnell III, *Southern Indians in the American Revolution* (Knoxville: University of Tennessee Press, 1973), 6–7; Tom Hatley, *The Dividing Paths: Cherokees and South Carolinians through the Revolutionary Era* (New York: Oxford University Press, 1995), 205–8; Archie Vernon Huff Jr., *Greenville: The History of the City and County in the South Carolina Piedmont* (Columbia: University of South Carolina Press, 1995), 18–19.

2. Ronald Edward Bridwell, "The South's Wealthiest Planter: Wade Hampton I of South Carolina," PhD diss., University of South Carolina, 1980, 5–10; for Hampton genealogy, see 787.

3. Minutes of the Lower House of the North Carolina General Assembly, April 9, 1753, *CRNC*, vol. 5, p. 69; Minutes of the Upper House of the North Carolina General Assembly, April 9, 1753, *CRNC*, vol. 5, p. 48; Jethro Rumple, *History of Rowan County North Carolina* (Charlotte: Observer Printing House, 1916), 59–62.

4. Bridwell, "South's Wealthiest Planter," 15–16, 21–22.

5. Bridwell, "South's Wealthiest Planter," 39–40.

6. Bridwell, "South's Wealthiest Planter," 33–34.

7. Rod Andrew Jr., *Wade Hampton: Confederate Warrior to Southern Redeemer* (Chapel Hill: University of North Carolina Press, 2008), 4–5.

8. *South Carolina and American General Gazette*, Charleston, South Carolina, July 10, 1767.

9. On Cherokee grievances, see Hatley, *Dividing Path*, 218–19; Tyler Boulware, *Deconstructing the Cherokee Nation: Town, Region, and Nation among Eighteenth-Century Cherokees* (Gainesville: University Press of Florida, 2011), 155–58.

10. On the confluence of Indigenous opposition to colonial expansion in the American South and the start of the American Revolution, see Robert M. Owens, *Red Dreams, White Nightmares: Pan-Indian Alliances in the Anglo-American Mind, 1763–1815* (Norman: University of Oklahoma Press, 2015), 65–69.

11. Andrew Williamson to Griffith Rutherford, August 14, 1776, *CRNC*, vol. 10, 745–48; William Moore to Griffith Rutherford, November 18, 1776, Griffith Rutherford Letter #2188-z, Southern Historical Collection, The Wilson Library, University of North Carolina at Chapel Hill; D. L. Swain, "Historical Sketch of the Indian War of 1776," *North Carolina University Magazine* 1, no. 4 (May 1852): 132–36; O'Donnell, *Southern Indians in the American Revolution*, 44–45.

12. [Benjamin F. Perry], "Revolutionary Incidents," *Magnolia; or, Southern Apalachian* 2, no. 6 (June 1843).

13. *The Journal of Major John Norton, 1816*, ed. Carl F. Klinck and James J. Talman (Toronto: Champlain Society, 1970), 43; Colin G. Calloway, *The American Revolution in Indian Country: Crisis and Diversity in Native American Communities* (New York: Cambridge University Press, 1995), 198.

14. On the importance of intergeneration oral history within the Hampton family, see Andrew, *Wade Hampton: Confederate Warrior to Southern Redeemer*, 6–7.

15. Perry, "Revolutionary Incidents," *Magnolia*.

16. Mr. Huger's Recollections of The Hamptons, Draper Manuscript Collection, Ser. VV, Sumter Papers, VI, no. 193, SCDAH.

17. Swain, "Historical Sketch of the Indian War of 1776," 135.

18. William Lenoir, "Account of Expedition against the Cherokee Indians, in 1776, under Gen'l Griffith Rutherford," June 1835, Lenoir Family Papers, 1763–1940, Southern Historical Collection, The Wilson Library, University of North Carolina at Chapel Hill.

19. Wade Hampton II, "The Hampton Family," *Charleston Mercury*, Charleston, SC, Aug. 4, 1843.

20. Bridwell, "South's Wealthiest Planter," 49–50.

21. While most retellings of the 1776 Cherokee attack at the Hampton homestead derive from Perry's 1843 publication titled "Revolutionary Incidents," the more salacious titles invoking "massacre" become popularly used in various reprintings and reiterations starting in at least 1851; see *Charleston Courier*, Charleston, SC, June 14, 1851.

22. Perry, "Revolutionary Incidents," *Magnolia*; *Charleston Mercury*, Charleston, SC, August 4, 1843.

23. [Benjamin F. Perry], "The Revolutionary History of South Carolina," *Southern Quarterly Review* 11, no. 22 (1847): 468–85; Joseph Johnson, *Traditions and Reminiscences Chiefly of the American Revolution in the South* (Charleston: Walker & James, 1851), 442–43.

24. William S. Morrison to J. B. O. Landrum, July 27, 1891 in J. B. O. Landrum, *Colonial and Revolutionary History of Upper South Carolina* (Greenville: Shannon & Co Printers, 1897), 88.

25. *Charleston Courier*, Charleston, SC, June 14, 1851.

26. John Haywood, *The Civil and Political History of the State of Tennessee, from Its Earliest Settlement up to the Year 1796; Including the Boundaries of the State* (Knoxville: Heiskell & Brown, 1823), 261.

27. Charles R. Cobb, *The Archaeology of Southeastern Native American Landscapes of the Colonial Era* (Gainesville: University Press of Florida, 2019), 107–8.

28. For an overview on global applications and multiformity of coalescence, see Stephen A. Kowalewski, "Coalescent Societies," in *Light on the Path: The Anthropology and History of the Southeastern Indians*, ed. Thomas J. Pluckhahn and Robbie Ethridge, 94–122 (Tuscaloosa: University of Alabama Press, 2006).

29. On the American Plains, increasing conflict, control over trade networks, and political realignment spurred an enlargement of late prehistoric Native communities; see Susan C. Vehik, "Conflict, Trade, and Political Development on the Southern Plains," *American Antiquity* 67, no. 1 (January 2002): 37–64. Among Amazonia's Indigenous Vaupés people, communities remained fixed but reinforced alliances through organized marriage exchanges; see Jean E. Jackson, *The Fish People: Linguistic Exogamy and Tukanoan Identity in Northwest Amazonia* (Cambridge: Cambridge University Press, 1983), 124.

30. On the coalescence of specific Native communities in the American South, see Christopher B. Rodning, "Reconstructing the Coalescence of Cherokee Communities in Southern Appalachia," in *The Transformation of the Southeastern Indians, 1540–1760*, ed. Robbie Ethridge and Charles Hudson, 155–75 (Jackson: University Press of Mississippi, 2002); Brooke M. Bauer, *Becoming Catawba: Catawba Indian Women and Nation-Building, 1540–1840* (Tuscaloosa: University of Alabama Press, 2023), esp. 48–50; Robin A. Beck Jr. "Catawba Coalescence and the Shattering of the Carolina Piedmont, 1540–1675," *Mapping the Mississippian Shatter Zone: The Colonial Indian Slave Trade and Regional Instability in the American South*, ed. Robbie Ethridge and Sheri M. Shuck-Hall, 115–41 (Lincoln: University of Nebraska Press, 2009); Vernon James Knight Jr., "The Formation of the Creeks," in *The Forgotten Centuries: Indians and Europeans in the American South, 1521–1704*, ed. Charles Hudson and Carmen Chaves Tesser, 373–92 (Athens: University of Georgia Press, 1994); Brent Richards Weisman, *Unconquered People: Florida's Seminole and Miccosukee Indians* (Gainesville: University Press of Florida, 1999), esp. 5–29; Andrea P. White, "Refuge among the Spanish: Yamasee Community Coalescence in St. Augustine after 1715," in *The Yamasee Indians: From Florida to South Carolina*, ed. Denise I. Bossy, 251–80 (Lincoln: University of Nebraska Press, 2018).

31. For discussions of coalescence as a model for the transformation of Southeastern Native chieftaincies to tribes, confederacies, and nations, see Gregory D. Smithers, *Native Southerners: Indigenous History from Origins to Removal* (Norman: University Press of Oklahoma, 2019), 55–70; Robin Beck, *Chiefdoms, Collapse, and Coalescence in the Early American South* (New York: Cambridge University Press, 2013), esp. 237; Sheri M. Shuck-Hall, "Alabama and Coushatta Diaspora and Coalescence in the Mississippian Shatter Zone," in *Mapping the Mississippian Shatter Zone: The Colonial Indian Slave Trade and Regional Instability in the American South*, ed. Robbie Ethridge and Sheri M. Shuck-Hall, 250–271 (Lincoln: University of Nebraska Press, 2009).

32. C. Vann Woodward, "The Search for Southern Identity," *The Burden of Southern History*, 3rd ed. (Baton Rouge: Louisiana State University Press, 1993), 3–25, 16; originally published in *Virginia Quarterly Review* 34 (1958): 321–38.

33. David M. Potter, "The Historian's Use of Nationalism and Vice Versa," *American Historical Review* 67, no. 4 (July 1962): 924–950, 935.

34. On the concept of place as a constructed and community-based process, see John Harner, "Place Identity and Copper Mining in Sonora, Mexico," *Annals of the Association of American Geographers* 91, no. 4 (December 2001): 660–80; on place and identity, see Timothy Oakes, "Place and the Paradox of Modernity," *Annals of the Association of American Geographers* 87, no. 3 (September 1997): 509–31; and Edward Soja, *Postmodern Geographies: The Reassertion of Space in Critical Social Theory* (London: Verso, 1989).

35. The experience of white southerners in this time frame was not unique but became distinctive to settlers and their descendants in the region. The global history of settler colonialism shows that violence against Indigenous peoples was a common outgrowth of settler expansion. For a broad overview, see Lorenzo Veracini, *Settler Colonialism: A Theoretical Overview* (New York: Palgrave Macmillan, 2010).

36. Historians have previously put forth various frames to classify the binding of white society in the antebellum South. Mitchell Snay suggested "separatism" to understand a sectional consciousness and growing distinctiveness that encompasses both sectionalism and regional nationalism, see *Gospel of Disunion: Religion and Separatism*

in the Antebellum South (Chapel Hill: University of North Carolina Press, 1993). Rachel Klein considered "consolidation" as a process in which leading slaveholders in South Carolina unified the political interests of the state through an egalitarian legislative apportionment for white citizens; see *Unification of a Slave State: The Rise of the Planter Class in the South Carolina Backcountry, 1760–1808* (Chapel Hill: University of North Carolina Press, 1990).

37. On violence as a generative force for Native coalescence in the Southeast, see Robbie Ethridge, "Introduction: Mapping the Mississippian Shatter Zone," in *Mapping the Mississippian Shatter Zone: The Colonial Indian Slave Trade and Regional Instability in the American South*, ed. Robbie Ethridge and Sheri M. Shuck-Hall (Lincoln: University of Nebraska Press, 2009), 20–26, 38–40; Matthew Jennings, *New Worlds of Violence: Cultures and Conquests in the Early American Southeast* (Knoxville: University of Tennessee Press, 2011), xxxii–xxxiv, 166; Stephen Warren, *The Worlds the Shawnees Made: Migration and Violence in Early America* (Chapel Hill: University of North Carolina Press, 2014), esp. 219–23. On violence as a generative force for US imperial expansion, see Richard Slotkin, *Regeneration through Violence: The Mythology of the American Frontier, 1600–1860* (Norman: University of Oklahoma Press, 1973); Reginald Horsman, *Race and Manifest Destiny: The Origins of American Racial Anglo-Saxonism* (Cambridge: Harvard University Press, 1981); Laurel Clark Shire, *The Threshold of Manifest Destiny: Gender and National Expansion in Florida* (Philadelphia: University of Pennsylvania Press, 2016). On influential works for this project on violence as a transformative force across Native America, see Ned Blackhawk, *Violence over the Land: Indians and Empires in the Early American West* (Cambridge: Harvard University Press, 2006); Karl Jacoby, *Shadows at Dawn: A Borderlands Massacre and the Violence of History* (New York: Penguin Press, 2008); Boyd Cothran, *Remembering the Modoc War: Redemptive Violence and the Making of American Innocence* (Chapel Hill: University of North Carolina Press, 2014); and David J. Silverman, *Thundersticks: Firearms and the Violent Transformation of Native America* (Cambridge: Belknap Press of Harvard University, 2016).

38. Jennings, xxxii–xxxiii. In an examination of the Caddoan Indians, Mark van de Logt argues that supernatural beings in oral traditions represent historical traumas connected to settler colonialism; see *Monsters of Contact: Historical Trauma in Caddoan Oral Traditions* (Norman: University of Oklahoma Press, 2018).

39. Joshua S. Haynes, *Patrolling the Border: Theft and Violence on the Creek-Georgia Frontier, 1770–1796* (Athens: University of Georgia Press, 2018), 104; see also 3–5. On parallel assessments of violence as a formative component for the Cherokee and Catawba, see Cobb, *Archaeology of Southeastern Native American Landscapes of the Colonial Era*, 116, 118–119.

40. Sheldon Hackney enumerated the "various guises" of the violent white southerner taking shape in a wide range of manifestations, including duels, whites whipping enslaved Blacks, rough-and-tumble fighting, the suppression of real and imagined slave revolts, and extralegal violence; see "Southern Violence," *American Historical Review* 74, no. 3 (February 1969): 906–25, 906.

41. Bertram Wyatt-Brown, *Southern Honor: Ethics and Behavior in the Old South* (New York: Oxford University Press, 1983), 34, 61; for an earlier influential consideration, see Dickson Bruce Jr., *Violence and Culture in the Antebellum South* (Austin: University of Texas Press, 1979).

42. Wyatt-Brown, *Southern Honor*, 33.

43. For explanatory causes of distinctiveness and violence among white antebellum southerners, see Ulrich Bonnell Phillips, *Life and Labor in the Old South*, intro. John David Smith (Columbia: University of South Carolina Press, 2007); Edward L. Ayers, *Vengeance and Justice: Crime and Punishment in the 19th-Century American South* (New York: Oxford University Press, 1984), esp. 26; Elliot J. Gorn, "'Gouge and Bite, Pull Hair and Scratch': The Social Significance of Fighting in the Southern Backcountry," *American Historical Review*, 90, no. 1 (1985): 18–43; Steven M. Stowe, *Intimacy and Power in the Old South: Ritual in the Lives of the Planters* (Baltimore: Johns Hopkins University Press, 1987), esp. 5–49; Grady McWhiney, *Cracker Culture: Celtic Ways in the Old South*, prologue by Forrest McDonald (Tuscaloosa: University of Alabama Press, 1988), esp. 170; Stephanie McCurry, *Masters of Small Worlds: Yeoman Households, Gender Relations, and the Political Culture of the Antebellum South Carolina Low Country* (New York: Oxford University Press, 1995), esp. 7, 15, 59; Kenneth S. Greenberg, *Honor and Slavery: Lies, Duels, Noses, Masks, Dressing as a Woman, Gifts, Strangers, Humanitarianism, Death, Slave Rebellions, the Proslavery Argument, Baseball, Hunting, and Gambling in the Old South* (Princeton: Princeton University Press, 1996); and Harry S. Laver, *Citizens More than Soldiers: The Kentucky Militia and Society in the Early Republic* (Lincoln: University of Nebraska Press, 2007); Lorri Glover, *Southern Sons: Becoming Men in the New Nation* (Baltimore: Johns Hopkins University Press, 2007). Subsequent to the antebellum period, lynching provided white southerners a participatory spectacle of violence that reinforced and protected white solidarity in the region. For key studies, see Terence Finnegan, "Lynching and Political Power in Mississippi and South Carolina," in *Under Sentence of Death: Lynching in the South*, ed. W. Fitzhugh Brundage, 189–218 (Chapel Hill: University of North Carolina Press, 1997); Stewart E. Tolnay and E. M. Beck, *A Festival of Violence: An Analysis of Southern Lynchings, 1882–1930* (Urbana: University of Illinois Press, 1995); and Amy Louise Wood, *Lynching and Spectacle: Witnessing Racial Violence in America, 1890–1940* (Chapel Hill: University of North Carolina Press, 2009).

44. Such approaches have defined considerations of southern sectionalism for decades; for quote, see Mary A. Decredico, "Sectionalism and the Secession Crisis," in *A Companion to the American* South, ed. John B. Boles, 235–48 (Malden: Blackwell, 2002), 237; for influential examples, see John Richard Alden, *The First South* (Baton Rouge: Louisiana State University Press, 1961); William R. Taylor, *Cavalier and Yankee: The Old South and American National Character* (New York: George Braziller, 1961); Charles S. Sydnor, *The Development of Southern Sectionalism, 1819—1848* (Baton Rouge: Louisiana State University Press, 1948); Avery O. Craven, *The Growth of Southern Nationalism, 1848–1861* (Baton Rouge: Louisiana State University Press, 1953); David M. Potter, *The Impending Crisis, 1848–1861*, completed and ed. Don E. Fehrenbacher (New York: Harper & Row, 1976); Charles R. Wilson, *Baptized in Blood: The Religion of the Lost Cause, 1865–1920* (Athens: University of Georgia Press, 1980); Adam Rothman, *Slave Country: American Expansion and the Origins of the Deep South* (Cambridge: Harvard University Press, 2005); Anne Sarah Rubin, *A Shattered Nation: The Rise and Fall of the Confederacy, 1861–1868* (Chapel Hill: University of North Carolina Press, 2005); Jason Phillips, *Diehard Rebels: The Confederate Culture of Invincibility* (Athens: University of Georgia Press, 2007).

45. Edward L. Ayers noted a similar stagnation in historiographical approaches to the causes of the Civil War: "What Caused the Civil War," *What Caused the Civil*

War: Reflections on the South and Southern History (New York: W. W. Norton, 2005), 131–44.

46. Frederick Jackson Turner, "Geographic Sectionalism in American History," *Annals of the Association of American Geographers* 16, no. 2 (June 1926): 85–93, 85.

47. Franklin, *Militant South*, 122, xiii–xiv, 36; on Franklin's development of *The Militant South*, see Franklin, *Mirror to America: The Autobiography of John Hope Franklin* (New York: Farrar, Straus and Giroux, 2005), 142; John Hope Franklin, "Slavery and the Martial South," *Journal of Negro History* 37, no. 1 (January 1952): 36–53.

48. Franklin, *Militant South*, 80–95; as Franklin's career progressed, historians primarily valued *The Militant South* as a consideration of slavery's impact on the region; see Franklin, *Mirror to America*, 142; Merton E. Coulter, "Review of *The Militant South*" in *The Annals of the American Academy of Political and Social Science*," 309 (January 1957): 187–188.

49. Franklin, *Militant South*, 25.

50. John Hope Franklin, *Race and History: Selected Essays, 1938–1988* (Baton Rouge: Louisiana State University Press, 1989), 71.

51. Tiya Miles, "Uncle Tom Was an Indian: Tracing the Red in Black Slavery," *Relational Formations of Race: Theory, Method, and Practice*, ed. Natalia Molina, Daniel Martinez Hosang, and Ramon A. Gutierrez (Oakland: University of California Press, 2019): 121–44, 123.

52. John H. Peterson Jr. "The Indian in the Old South," in *Red, White, and Black: Symposium on Indians in the Old South*, ed. Charles M. Hudson, 116–33 (Athens: University of Georgia Press, 1971); James Taylor Carson, Robbie Ethridge, and Greg O'Brien, "Editor's Introduction: A Line in the Sand," *Native South* 1 (2008): ix–xvi; Theda Perdue, "The Legacy of Indian Removal," *Journal of Southern History* 78, no. 1 (February 2012): 3–36; Andrew Frank and Kristofer Ray, "Guest Editors' Introduction: Indians as Southerners; Southerners as Indians: Rethinking the History of a Region," *Native South* 10 (2017): vii–xiv; Angela Pulley Hudson, "Unsettling Histories of the South," *Southern Cultures* 25, no. 3 (Fall 2019): 30–45; Christina Snyder and Theda Perdue, "The Native South," in *Reinterpreting Southern Histories: Essays in Historiography*, ed. Craig Thompson Friend and Lorri Glover, 415–44 (Baton Rouge: Louisiana State University Press, 2020).

53. Horsman, *Race and Manifest Destiny*; Jill Lepore, *The Name of War: King Philip's War and the Origins of American Identity* (New York: Knopf, 1998); Fred Anderson, *Crucible of War: The Seven Years' War and the Fate of Empire in British North America, 1754–1766* (New York: Vintage Books, 2001); Patrick Griffin, *American Leviathan: Empire, Nation, and Revolutionary Frontier* (New York: Hill and Wang, 2007); and Peter Silver, *Our Savage Neighbors: How Indian War Transformed Early America* (New York: W. W. Norton, 2007); and Owens, *Red Dreams, White Nightmares*.

54. Silver, *Our Savage Neighbors*, xx, 83–84, 115.

55. Silver, *Our Savage Neighbors*, xx.

56. Franklin, *Militant South*, 25.

57. Franklin first suggested "frontier life" as a contributing factor to the white South's martial tradition; see *Militant South*, 24–32.

58. On the antebellum South's martial tradition as a post–Civil War revision, see Marcus Cunliff, *Soldiers and Civilians: The Martial Spirit in America, 1775–1865* (London: Macmillan, 1973), 384; and Robert E. May, "Dixie's Martial Image: A Continuing Historiographical Enigma," *The Historian* 40, no. 2 (February 1978):

213–234, 214. On the South's martial tradition as a reaction to abolitionism, see R. Don Higginbotham, "The Martial Spirit in the Antebellum South: Some Further Speculation in a National Context," *Journal of Southern History* 58, no. 1 (February 1992): 3–26, 12, 14–15.

59. On militia service, see Dickson, *Violence and Culture in the Antebellum South*, 167–69, Franklin, *Militant South*, 171–92, Laver, *Citizens More than Soldiers*; on military education, see Rod Andrew Jr., *Long Gray Lines: The Southern Military School Tradition, 1839–1915* (Chapel Hill: University of North Carolina Press, 2001), 8–25; Jennifer R. Green, *Military Education and the Emerging Middle Class in the Old South* (Cambridge: Cambridge University Press, 2008); and on slavery, see Greenberg, *Honor and Slavery*, 98–100; Sally E. Hadden, *Slave Patrols: Law and Violence in Virginia and the Carolinas* (Cambridge: Harvard University Press, 2001).

60. On settler-colonial violence perpetuating whiteness after the American Revolution, see David Andrew Nichols, *Red Gentlemen and White Savages: Indians, Federalists, and the Search for Order on the American Frontier* (Charlottesville: University of Virginia Press, 2008), esp. 65–68; Horsman, *Race and Manifest Destiny*, 204–7; Cynthia Cumfer, *Separate Peoples, One Land: The Minds of Cherokees, Blacks, and Whites on the Tennessee Frontier* (Chapel Hill: University of North Carolina Press, 2007), 70–74, 158–76. Conversely, Patrick Bottiger finds that Native-settler violence in and along the borders of the Miami homeland created multiethnic factionalism within race; see *The Borderland of Fear: Vincennes, Prophetstown, and the Invasion of the Miami Homeland* (Lincoln: University of Nebraska Press, 2016), esp. 11, 47–48, 82–84.

61. On an "ethic of reciprocity" as a cornerstone of Indigenous coalescence in the eighteenth and nineteenth centuries, see Ethridge, "Introduction: Mapping the Mississippian Shatter Zone," 39; Andrew Frank, *Creeks and Southerners: Biculturalism on the Early American Frontier* (Lincoln: University of Nebraska Press, 2005), 11–12; Smithers, *Native Southerners*, 21.

62. Gina Caison argues that the white South leveraged a fantasy of Native nations as historically static referents to bolster its own sense of place and nativism. While this work concurs with Caison's assertion that white southerners built their sentimental ownership of and to the South through the erasure of Indigenous peoples and their past; Caison's suggestion that the continued presence of Native people in the South disrupted the formation of a regionally bound white identity does not apply to the early nineteenth-century South; see *Red States: Indigeneity, Settler Colonialism, and Southern Studies* (Athens: University of Georgia Press, 2018), 3, 19.

63. Michel-Rolph Trouillot, *Silencing the Past: Power and the Production of History* (Boston: Beacon Press, 1995), 6.

64. For a valuable corrective integrating the 1813 Creek War with the War of 1812, see *Tohopeka: Rethinking the Creek War & the War of 1812*, ed. Kathryn E. Holland Braund (Tuscaloosa: University of Alabama Press, 2012). On a broader perspective, Alan Taylor places the 1813 Creek War in the context of violence and US expansion as part of "the War of the 1810s"; see *American Republics: A Continental History of the United States, 1783–1850* (New York: W. W. Norton, 2021), 136, 130–31.

65. For a broad overview of settler-colonial expansion and the violence of Native dispossession, see Walter L. Hixson, *American Settler Colonialism: A History* (New York: Palgrave Macmillan, 2013), esp. 75–85. For relevant case studies considering the centrality of settler households, see Shire, *Threshold of Manifest Destiny*; Honor

Sachs, *Home Rule: Households, Manhood, and National Expansion on the Eighteenth-Century Kentucky Frontier* (New Haven: Yale University Press, 2015).

66. "Fictive kin" essentially created familial bonds among peoples with no family ties through either blood or marriage; see Greg O'Brien, "The Conqueror Meets the Unconquered: Negotiating Cultural Boundaries on the Post-revolutionary Southern Frontier," *Journal of Southern History* 67, no. 1 (February 2001): 39–72, 57–60; Reid, *Law of Blood*, 89; Robbie Ethridge, *Creek Country: The Creek Indians and Their World* (Chapel Hill: University of North Carolina Press, 2003), 109–10. Sociologists Charles A. Ibsen and Patricia Klobus add that fictive kin identification added "public validation of a special kind of association" that is not otherwise institutionally recognized; see "Fictive Kin Term Use and Social Relationships: Alternative Interpretations," *Journal of Marriage and Family* 34, no. 4 (November 1972): 615–20, 615, 616–17.

Chapter 1

1. Wyatt-Brown, *Southern Honor*, 350–61; John Lyde Wilson, *The Code of Honor; or, Rules for the Government of Principles and Seconds in Dueling* (Charleston, SC: Thomas J. Eccles, 1838).

2. Gorn, "Gouge and Bite, Pull Hair and Scratch"; see also Bruce, *Culture and Violence in the Antebellum South*, 89–113; and Franklin, *Militant South: 1800—1861*, 33–62.

3. On the delineation of the South's tri-racial system in the last third of the eighteenth century in relation to Native Americans, see George Edward Milne, *Natchez Country: Indians, Colonists, and the Landscapes of Race in French Louisiana* (Athens: University of Georgia Press, 2015), especially 136–74; Nancy Shoemaker, *A Strange Likeness: Becoming Red and White in Eighteenth-Century North America* (Oxford: Oxford University Press, 2004); and Kathryn E. Holland Braund, "The Creek Indians, Blacks, and Slavery," *Journal of Southern History* 57, no. 4 (November 1991): 601–36.

4. For the events under consideration here, exchanges of violence represent the expression of culture and agency indicating intention and objectives. Ned Blackhawk has shown how "violence as both a subject and method" functions to assert that the shifting relations of violence between Spanish colonizers and Great Basin Indians remade the West as intrinsically violent and connected to a global colonialism; see *Violence over the Land*, 5. For examinations of the American South, see Matthew Jennings, *New Worlds of Violence*, esp. xxxii–xxxiv, 166; Wayne E. Lee, "Peace Chiefs and Blood Revenge: Patters of Restraint in Native American Warfare, 1500–1800," *Journal of Military History* 71, no. 3 (July 2007): 701–41; Christina Snyder, "Conquered Enemies, Adopted Kin, and Owned People: The Creek Indians and Their Captives," *Journal of Southern History* 73, no. 2 (May 2007): 255–88, esp. 263–67.

5. *Cherokee Phoenix*, New Echota, GA, February 18, 1829; Wayne E. Lee, *Barbarians and Brothers: Anglo-American Warfare, 1500–1865* (Oxford: Oxford University Press, 2011), 133. On blood revenge as a global practice with prehistoric origins, see Georg Heyne, "Notes on Blood Revenge among the Reindeer Evenki of Manchuria (Northeast China)," trans. Peter Knecht, *Asian Folklore Studies* 66, no. 1/2 (2007): 165–78; Shkelqim Bozgo, Xheni Sinakoli, and Emin Spahia, "Customary Law, Conflict, and Development in the Mountains of Albania," *Mountain Research and Development* 22, no. 4 (November 2002): 341–43, 341; Colin Lawson and Douglas

Saltmarshe, "Security and Economic Transition: Evidence from North Albania," *Europe-Asia Studies* 52, no. 1 (January 2000): 133–48, 138–39; Kemal Vokopola, "The Albanian Customary Law," *Quarterly Journal of the Library of Congress* 25, no. 4 (October 1968): 306–16, 313–14.

6. On blood revenge and balance, see Ethridge, *Creek Country*, 228–30. On clan obligations, see George Stiggins, *Creek Indian History*, notes and intro. William Stokes Wyman, ed. Virginia Pounds Brown (Tuscaloosa: University of Alabama Press, 1989), 66–68. On interethnic retaliation, see James Adair, *The History of the American Indians*, ed., intro, and annotations Kathryn E. Holland Braund (Tuscaloosa: University of Alabama Press, 2005), 185–86. On the legal operation of blood revenge, see John Reid, *A Law of Blood: The Primitive Law of the Cherokee Nation* (DeKalb: Northern Illinois University Press, 2006), 75; and James P. Evans, "Cherokee Characteristics, Customs, and Manners," *The Payne-Butrick Papers*, ed. and annotations William L. Anderson, Jane L. Brown, and Anne F. Rogers, 6 vols. (Lincoln: University of Nebraska Press, 2010), 6: 431–47, 432. On the persistence of blood revenge among Native southerners, see Tiya Miles, *The House on Diamond Hill: A Cherokee Plantation Story* (Chapel Hill: University of North Carolina Press, 2010), 122–29; and *Mississippi State Gazette*, Natchez, MS, November 13, 1824.

7. On the importance of clans to southern Indians, see Christina Snyder, *Slavery in Indian Country: The Changing Face of Captivity in Early America* (Cambridge: Harvard University Press, 2012), 20; Reid, *Law of Blood*, 38. On the matrilineal clans' intersection with justice and retaliatory killing, see the matriarchal prerogative of infanticide, Louis Le Clerc Milfort, *Memoirs or a Quick Glance at My Various Travels and My Sojourn in the Creek Nation*, trans. Ben C. McCary (Savannah: Beehive Press, 1972), 110; Reid, *Law of Blood*, 38; John R. Swanton, "Social Organization and Social Usages of the Indians of the Creek Confederacy," *42nd Annual Report of the Bureau of American Ethnology* (Washington, DC: Government Printing Office, 1928), 23–272, 345; *Cherokee Phoenix*: New Echota, GA, February 18, 1829.

8. James H. Merrell, *The Indians' New World: Catawbas and Their Neighbors from European Contact through the Era of Removal* (Chapel Hill: University of North Carolina Press, 1989); Colin G. Calloway, *New Worlds for All: Indians, Europeans, and the Remaking of Early America* (Baltimore: Johns Hopkins University Press, 1997); James Axtell, *The Indians' New South: Cultural Change in the Colonial Southeast* (Baton Rouge: Louisiana State University Press, 1997).

9. Adair and Braund, *History of the American Indians*, 184; Dean R. Snow, "Iroquois-Huron Warfare," in *North American Indigenous Warfare and Ritual Violence*, ed. Richard J. Chacon and Rubén G. Mendoza (Tucson: University of Arizona Press, 2007): 151–52, 149–59.

10. Adair and Braund, *American Indians*, 185.

11. Benjamin Hawkins, *CW-BH*, 75s; Reid, *Law of Blood*, 103–7.

12. Kathryn H. Braund, *Deerskins and Duffels: The Creek Indian Trade with Anglo-America, 1685–1815* (Lincoln: University of Nebraska Press, 1993), 154.

13. Steven C. Hahn, *The Invention of the Creek Nation, 1670–1763* (Lincoln: University of Nebraska Press, 2004), 72–73.

14. Hahn, *Creek Nation, 1670–1763*, 124–27.

15. Hahn, *Creek Nation, 1670–1763*, 147–48; "Tobias Fitch's Journal to the Creeks," *Travels in the American Colonies*, ed. Newton D. Mereness (New York: Macmillan, 1916): 176–212, 211.

16. George Edward Milne, *Natchez Country: Indians, Colonists, and the Landscapes of Race in French Louisiana* (Athens: University of Georgia Press, 2015), 74–76.

17. Patricia Galloway, "The Barthelemy Murders: Bienville's Establishment of the Lex Talionis as a Principle of Indian Diplomacy," in *Practicing Ethnohistory: Mining Archives, Hearing Testimony, Constructing Narrative* (Lincoln: University Press of Nebraska, 2006): 245–58, 253.

18. Braund, *Deerskins and Duffels*, 154–56.

19. Joshua Piker, *Okfuskee: A Creek Indian Town in Colonial America* (Cambridge: Harvard University Press, 2004), 59–60.

20. Thomas Nairne, *Nairne's Muskhogean Journals: The 1708 Expedition to the Mississippi River*, ed. Alexander Moore (Jackson: University Press of Mississippi, 1988), 34; for a similar incident in 1784, see Hawkins, *Sketch*, *CW-BH*, 75s, 62.

21. Joshua Piker, *The Four Deaths of Acorn Whistler: Telling Stories in Colonial America* (Cambridge: Harvard University Press, 2013), 118–21.

22. *The Colonial Records of the State of Georgia*, ed. Allen D. Candler (Atlanta, 1907), 10:696–99, hereafter *CRSGA*; and E. R. R. Green, "Queensborough Township: Scotch-Irish Emigration and the Expansion of Georgia, 1765–1776," *William and Mary Quarterly* 17 (1960): 183–99,188–90; Edward Barnard letter, October 23, and Deposition of Martin Weatherford, October 24, 1771, *CRSGA*, 12:81–84.

23. Georgia Governor and Council, October 29, 1771, *CRSGA*, 12:80–87, quote, 84.

24. Georgia Council Meeting, July 13, 1771, *CRSGA*, 11:432–34, 432–33; Habersham to Creek Nation, October 29, 1771, *CRSGA*, 12:85–87, quote, 86.

25. Habersham to the Head Men, *CRSGA*, 12:85.

26. A Talk given at the Cheehaws Square, November 2, 1771, *CRSGA*, 12:148–150, quotes, 149 and 150; David Corkan, *The Creek Frontier, 1540–1783* (Norman: University of Oklahoma Press, 1967), 279–80.

27. Habersham to Wright, March 16, 1772, *GHS:HL*, 6:169–70, 170.

28. Galphin to lower Creek, December 2, 1771, *CRSGA*, 12:150–52, quote, 150; see also Habersham to Creek Nation, December 7, 1771, *CRSGA*, 12:152–54; Habersham to Wright, March 16, 1772, *GHS:HL*, 6:169–70.

29. Habersham to Creek Nation, December 7, 1771, *CRSGA*, 12:152–54, quote, 153. On Galphin's ability to leverage his influence in Native and colonial communities to calm tensions, see Bryan C. Rindfleisch, *George Galphin's Intimate Empire: The Creek Indians, Family, and Colonialism in Early America* (Tuscaloosa: University of Alabama Press, 2019), 149–51.

30. The Cheehaws Square to Georgia Colonial Assembly, March 17, 1772, *CRSGA*, 12:316–17, quote, 317; Journal of the Upper House, April 22, 1772, *CRSGA*, 17:657; Habersham to Wright, March 28, 1772, *GHS:HL*, 6:171–74; Habersham to Earl of Hillsborough, June 15, 1772, *GHS:HL*, 6:189–90; Habersham to Galphin, October 16, 1772, *GHS:HL*, 6:213–14.

31. Claudio Saunt argues these incidents suggest that "clan-based justice remained the law of the land" however Creeks attempted to amend traditional practices to satisfy obligations imposed upon the entire nation. *A New Order of Things: Property, Power, and the Transformation of the Creek Indians, 1733–1816* (Cambridge: Cambridge University Press, 1999), 94–95.

32. Habersham to Wright, March 16, 1772, *GHS:HL*, 6:169–70, 170.

33. On origination of the civilization plan, see Reginald Horsman, *Expansion and*

American Indian Policy, 1783–1812 (Norman: University of Oklahoma Press, 1992), 57–61; Francis Paul Prucha, *The Great Father: The United States Government and the American Indians*, vols. 1–2, unabridged (Lincoln: University of Nebraska Press, 1995), 135–48. On the civilization plan and US land acquisition, see Jefferson to Hawkins, February 18, 1803, *The Writings of Thomas Jefferson*, ed. Paul L. Ford (New York: G. P. Putnam's Sons, 1897), 8:211–16, 213.

34. Theda Perdue, "George Washington and the 'Civilization' of the Southern Indians," in *George Washington's South*, ed. Tamara Harvey and Greg O'Brien (Gainesville: University Press of Florida, 2004), 313–25, quote on 314. On the civilization plan and the Creeks, see Ethridge, *Creek Country*, 13–16, 148–49, and 193–94; and Florette Henri, *The Southern Indians and Benjamin Hawkins, 1796–1816* (Norman: University of Oklahoma Press, 1986), 95–96 and 145–46.

35. On the civilization plan as an alternative to military force and the influence of Indigenous military capability, see Horsman, *Expansion and American Indian Policy*, 54–56; Tim Allan Garrison, *The Legal Ideology of Removal: The Southern Judiciary and the Sovereignty of Native American Nations* (Athens: University of Georgia Press, 2002), 18–21; and Deborah A. Rosen, *American Indians and State Law: Sovereignty, Race, and Citizenship, 1790–1880* (Lincoln: University of Nebraska Press, 2007), 12–13.

36. Anthony F. C. Wallace, *Jefferson and the Indians: The Tragic Fate of the First Americans* (Cambridge: Belknap Press of Harvard University, 1999), 166–69; Horsman, *Expansion and American Indian Policy*, 58, 62–63; Theda Perdue and Michael Green, *The Cherokee Removal: A Brief History with Documents* (Boston: Bedford/St. Martin's Press, 2004), 9–10.

37. For example, a Moravian mission in Cherokee County succeeded in educating children but had limited success in religious conversions; see Perdue and Green, *Cherokee Removal*, 11; Request of Four Cherokee Chiefs to Return J. Meigs, March 1, 1818, Southeastern Indian Papers, Mss. 2820, LSU-LLMVC.

38. Letter from Nashville, February 1, 1797, *Aurora General Advertiser*, Philadelphia, PA, April 15, 1797; on date of Gentry's death, see *Weekly Franklin Repository*, Chambersburg, PA, March 9, 1797.

39. Letter from Nashville to the Editor, February 1, 1797, *Independent Gazetteer*, Philadelphia, PA, April 21, 1797.

40. Hawkins to Barnard, July 13, 1797, *LJWBH*, 1:120–21.

41. *Vermont Gazette*, Bennington, VT, May 4, 1797.

42. *Philadelphia Inquirer*, Philadelphia, PA, May 17, 1797.

43. *Columbian Museum & Savannah Advertiser*, Savannah, GA, April 25, 1797; *Augusta Chronicle and Gazette of the State*, Augusta, GA, April 29, 1797.

44. Saunt, *New Order of Things*, 80.

45. Augustus Christian George Elholm to James Jackson, April 11, 1793, UGA-H, Keith M. Read collection, SNAD; Affidavit of Henry Carrel, September 6, 1793, UGA-H, C. Mildred Thompson collection, SNAD; Affidavit of James Dennard, March 11, 1798, TCC, SNAD.

46. Haynes, *Patrolling the Border*, 202.

47. Rey Buen Hijo, Rey Mas Distante, Perro Raviosos to Juan Nepomuceno de Quesaday, January 8, 1795, quoted in Saunt, *New Order of Things*, 100.

48. Kristofer Ray, *Middle Tennessee, 1775–1825: Progress and Popular Democracy on the Southwestern Fronter* (Knoxville: University of Tennessee Press, 2007), 24–27.

49. Petition of Tennessee County to Gen. Robertson, February 1, 1792,

"Correspondence of Gen. James Robertson," *American Historical Magazine* 1, no. 3 (July 1896): 280–91, 284–85.

50. James Seagrove to Henry Knox, May 24, 1792, *ASPIA* 1:296.

51. Haynes, *Patrolling the Border*, 13.

52. Haynes, *Patrolling the Border*, 7, 202.

53. *Kentucky Gazette*, Lexington, KY, January 25, 1797; *Maryland Gazette*, Annapolis, MD, March 2, 1797; also appearing in *Weekly Franklin Repository*, Chambersburg, PA, March 9, 1797; and *Vermont Gazette*, Bennington, VT, March 9, 1797.

54. *Independent Gazetteer*, Philadelphia, PA, April 21, 1797; *Vermont Gazette*, Bennington, VT, May 4, 1797; *Aurora General Advertiser*, Philadelphia, PA, April 15, 1797; *North Carolina Minerva and Fayetteville Advertiser*, Fayetteville, NC, June 10, 1797.

55. *Aurora General Advertiser*, Philadelphia, PA, April 15, 1797.

56. *Weekly Franklin Repository*, Chambersburg, PA, March 9, 1797.

57. *North Carolina Minerva and Fayetteville Advertiser*, Fayetteville, NC, June 10, 1797.

58. John Sevier to The Warriors and Chiefs of the Cherokee Nation, March 28, 1797, John Sevier Papers, 1796–1801, TSLA.

59. John Sevier to The Warriors and Chiefs of the Cherokee Nation, June 8, 1797, John Sevier Papers, 1796–1801, TSLA.

60. David Andrew Nichols, *Red Gentlemen and White Savages: Indians, Federalists, and the Search for Order on the American Frontier* (Charlottesville: University of Virginia Press, 2008), 188.

61. *Knoxville Gazette*, Knoxville, TN, April 24, 1795, quoted in Ray, *Middle Tennessee 1775–1825*, 27; see also 36–37; Horsman, *Expansion and American Indian Policy*, 81–82.

62. *Columbian Museum & Savannah Advertiser*, Savannah, GA, April 25, 1797; *Augusta Chronicle and Gazette of the State*, Augusta, GA, April 29, 1797.

63. *Columbian Museum & Savannah Advertiser*, Savannah, GA, May 9, 1797.

64. James Seagrove to Edward Telfair, September 17, 1793, *PWD*-RRC, accessed July 25, 2021, 3d Cong, House, Sec War Confidential Rep, RG233, National Archives and Records Administration.

65. *Columbian Museum & Savannah Advertiser*, Savannah, GA, April 25, 1797.

66. *Aurora General Advertiser*, Philadelphia, PA, May 22, 1797.

67. *Columbian Museum & Savannah Advertiser*, Savannah, GA, April 25, 1797; *Augusta Chronicle and Gazette of the State*, Augusta, GA, April 29, 1797.

68. Henry Knox to Edward Telfair, March 14, 1791, *PWD*-RRC, accessed July 25, 2021, Northwest Territory Coll., M367, Indiana Historical Society Library, Indianapolis, IN.

69. Sevier to McHenry, June 6, 1797, John Sevier Papers, 1796–1801, TSLA.

70. Hawkins to Beloved Creeks, July 13, 1797, *LJWBH*, 1:121–122, quote, 121; Hawkins to Barnard, July 13, 1797, *LJWBH*, 1:120–21; Hawkins to Richard Thomas, July 14, 1797, *LJWBH*, 1:122; Extract to Mr. Dinsmoor, May 23, 1797, *GHS:BH*, 175–76.

71. Journal, November 24 and December 28, 1797, *LJWBH*, 1:138–40 and 145–46; Creek Stipend for the Years 1796 and 1797, *GHS:BH*, 9:324.

72. Journal, May 29, 1798, *LJWBH*, 1:188–90, 189; Hawkins to Beloved Creeks, July 13, 1797, *LJWBH*, 1:121–22; Hawkins to Barnard, July 13, 1797, *LJWBH*, 1:120–21.

73. James Seagrove to Edward Telfair, September 17, 1793, *PWD*-RRC, RG233, National Archives and Records Administration.

74. Journal, May 28, 1798, *LJWBH*, 1:187; on role of the speaker, see Journal, May 26, 1798, *LJWBH*, 1:184; for overview of the National Council, see Annual Report of Benjamin Hawkins, 1801, *ASPIA*, 1:647–48; and Hawkins to Jefferson, from James F. Doster, *Creek Indians: The Creek Indians and Their Florida Lands, 1740–1823*, 2 vols. (New York: Garland, 1974), 1:216–17. Ethridge indicates "The Speaker of the Nation was actually two men"; however, by Hawkins's tenure, only one speaker acted as "voice of the nation"; see *Creek Country*, 106. For Hawkins's demarcation, see Journal, May 24, 1802, *LJWBH*, 2:430; and in *Sketch*, *CW-BH*, 80s; Hawkins to Jefferson, from Doster, *Creek Indians*, 1:216–217, quote, 217.

75. Hawkins, *Sketch*, *CW-BH*, 67s-68s; on national laws, see Hawkins to Butler, June 6, 1798, *LJWBH*, 1:198, Hawkins to Jackson, August 2, 1798, *LJWBH*, 1:212, Hawkins to Dinsmoor, August 24, 1798, *LJWBH*, 1:217.

76. Hawkins, *Sketch*, *CW-BH*, 68s; Hawkins to McHenry, December 4, 1799, *LJWBH*, 1:275–76; Hawkins to Ellicott, December 15, 1799, *LJWBH*, 1:280–81; Hawkins to Cornells, November 5, 1799, *LJWBH*, 1:267–69, Laws quote, 268; Hawkins to Choctaw Chiefs, August 26, 1800, *LJWBH*, 1:347–48.

77. Hawkins to Henley, April 15, 1799, *LJWBH*, 1:244–45, quotes, 245; Hawkins to McHenry, April 15, 1799, *LJWBH*, 1:245–46; Hawkins to Dearborn, June 1, 1801, *LJWBH*, 1:359–60.

78. Hopoie Micco became speaker in 1802; see Hawkins to Dearborn, July 15, 1802, *LJWBH*, 2:448–51, 450.

79. *Annals of Congress*, Fourth Congress, Session II, January 23, 1797, "Military Establishment," 1953–54.

80. *The Philadelphia Inquirer*, Philadelphia, PA, March 3, 1797; also in *Annals of Congress*, Fourth Congress, Session II, March 1, 1797, "Military Establishment," 2331–32.

81. *United States Statutes at Large*, "An Act to regulate trade and intercourse with the Indian tribes, and to preserve peace on the frontier," Fifth Congress, Session III, March 3, 1799. 744.

82. Sevier to McHenry, June 6, 1797, John Sevier Papers, 1796–1801, TSLA.

83. Hawkins to McHenry, September 4, 1798, *LJWBH*, 1:222–23; Petition of Mary Brown, ca. 1798.

84. Thomas S. Woodward, *Woodward's Reminiscences of the Creek, or Muscogee Indians* (Montgomery: Barrett & Wimbish, 1859), 55–56.

85. Wyatt-Brown, *Southern Honor*, 34, 122.

Chapter 2

1. Woodward, *Woodward's Reminiscences of the Creek*, 144. Prior to publication, Georgia newspapers printed extracts from Woodward's correspondence relevant to local areas; see *Wire-Grass Reporter*, Thomasville, GA, November 10, 1858.

2. Woodward, *Reminiscences of the Creek*, 35.

3. A multitude of examinations explore the causes of the 1813 Creek War as a civil war. On the historical divisions of the Upper and Lower Creek towns, see Michael D. Green, *The Politics of Indian Removal: Creek Government and Society in Crisis* (Lincoln: University of Nebraska Press, 1982), 38; on the role of Creek religious revival, see Joel W. Martin, *Sacred Revolt: The Muskogees' Struggle for a New World*

(Boston: Beacon Press, 1991), 133; and Adam Jortner, *The Gods of Prophetstown: The Battle of Tippecanoe and the Holy War for the American Frontier* (New York: Oxford University Press, 2012), 208; on the role of the war as a "nativist" versus an "accommodationist" split, see Gregory Evans Dowd, *A Spirited Resistance: The North American Indian Struggle for Unity, 1745–1815* (Baltimore: Johns Hopkins University Press, 1992), 167–71; and Andrew K. Frank, *Creeks and Southerners: Biculturalism on the Early American Frontier* (Lincoln: University of Nebraska Press, 2005), 106–7; on economic causes of the war, see Braund, *Deerskins and Duffels*, 185–86, and Claudio Saunt, *New Order of Things* (Cambridge: Cambridge University Press, 1999), 250–51; on the influence of American access and travel through Creek country, see Angela Pulley Hudson, *Creek Paths and Federal Roads: Indians, Settlers, and Slaves and the Making of the American South* (Chapel Hill: University of North Carolina Press, 2010), 91; on contests over violence and justice, see Evan Nooe, "Common Justice: Vengeance and Retribution in Creek Country," *Ethnohistory* 62, no. 2 (April 2015): 241–61; on opposition to the Creek National Council, see Kevin Kokomoor, *Of One Mind and of One Government: The Rise and Fall of the Creek Nation in the Early Republic* (Lincoln: University of Nebraska Press, 2019), 331.

4. Gregory A. Waselkov, *A Conquering Spirit: Fort Mims and the Redstick War of 1813–1814* (Tuscaloosa: University of Alabama Press, 2006), 29; also see Henri, *Southern Indians and Benjamin Hawkins, 1796–1816*, 62; Benjamin Hawkins to Henry Dearborn, February 1, 1802, *LJWBH*, 2:433.

5. See Hudson, *Creek Paths and Federal Road*, 63, 91.

6. Gary Burton has provided the most extensive examination on Meredith's death; see "Pintlala's Cold Murder Case: The Death of Thomas Meredith in 1812," *Alabama Review* 63 (2010): 163–91.

7. Hawkins to Eustis and Hawkins to Mitchell April 6, 1812, *LJWBH*, 2:605–6; on Moniac, see Hawkins to Eustis, August 21, 1810, *LJWBH*, 2:566–67; "Deposition by Sam Manac, a plantation owner in Alabama and a warrior of the Creek Nation," Samuel Manac deposition, SPR26, ADAH.

8. Hawkins to William Eustis, April 6, 1812, *LJWBH*, 2:605; various sources spell Sam Moniac as Macrae, Manacs, Macnac, and Manack.

9. Hudson, *Creek Paths and Federal Roads*, 55.

10. Kathryn H. Braund, Gregory A. Waselkov, and Raven M. Christopher, *The Old Federal Road in Alabama: An Illustrated Guide* (Tuscaloosa: University of Alabama Press, 2019), 25.

11. Margaret Ervin Austill, "Memories of Journeying through Creek Country and Childhood in Clarke County, 1811–1814," ADAH, Digital Archives, reproduced from SPR237; see also Burton, "Pintlala's Cold Murder Case," 170.

12. James Adair, *The History of the American Indians*, ed., intro, and annotations Kathryn E. Holland Braund (Tuscaloosa: University of Alabama Press, 2005), 380–81, 382, 389.

13. Hawkins to Mitchell, April 6, 1812, *LJWBH*, 2:605–6.

14. Hawkins to Eustis, October 3, 1811, *LJWBH*, 2:592.

15. Albert James Pickett, *History of Alabama, and Incidentally of Georgia and Mississippi, from the Earliest Period*, vol. 2 (Charleston: Walker and James, 1851), 248.

16. Hawkins to Eustis, May 25, 1812, *LJWBH*, 2:609; Johann Christian Burckard and Karsten Petersen, *Partners in the Lord's Work: The Diary of Two Moravian Missionaries in the Creek Indian Country, 1807–1813*, ed. and trans. Carl Mauelshagen and

Gerald H. Davis, Research Paper Number 21 (Atlanta: School of Arts and Sciences Research Papers, Georgia State College, 1969), 73.

17. Burckard and Petersen, "Partners in the Lord's Work," 72.

18. Burckard and Petersen, "Partners in the Lord's Work," 73.

19. Petition of the Inhabitants of Burke County, 1787, Oct. 18 to Governor, SNADD, TCC TCC938.

20. Petition of the inhabitants of Burke County, 1782, Mar. 2, Burke County, Georgia to John Martin, Governor of Georgia and the Executive Council," SNADD, TCC TCC269; [Letter], 1782 Aug. 11, Silver Bluff, Georgia to Govorner [*sic*] John Martin, Georgia / Patrick Carr, SNADD, TCC, TCC271.

21. Petition of the inhabitants of Burke County, [Georgia] to Samuel Elbert, Governor [of Georgia] and the Executive Council, 1785 May 5 / John Fulton [?] . . . [et al.], SNADD, TCC TCC940.

22. Petition of the inhabitants of Burke County, 1787, Oct. 18 to Governor, SNADD, TCC TCC938.

23. Haynes, *Patrolling the Border*, 138–39.

24. Haynes, *Patrolling the Border*, 145.

25. Petition of the inhabitants of Burke County, 1787, Oct. 18 to Governor, SNADD, TCC TCC938.

26. Absalom H. Chappell, *Miscellanies of Georgia, Historical, Biographical, Descriptive, Etc.* (Atlanta: James F. Meegan, 1874), 8.

27. Chappell, *Miscellanies of Georgia*, 8.

28. Chappell, *Miscellanies of Georgia*, 7.

29. "Reports from Augusta, Georgia, August 1 and 15, 1786," John Walton Caughey, *McGillivray of the Creeks*, intro. by William Bauer Jr. (Columbia: University of South Carolina Press, 2007), 121.

30. Chappell, *Miscellanies of Georgia*, 8.

31. Wilson's congressional speech received widespread republication in the Georgia press; see *The Athenian*, Athens, GA, June 29, 1830; *Washington News*, Washington, GA, July 6, 1830; *Federal Union*, Milledgeville, GA, September 29, 1831.

32. Wilson Lumpkin, *The Removal of the Cherokee Indians from Georgia* (New York: Dodd, Mead, 1907), 9. For a comparable reminiscence expressing settler fears of Native violence in the South, see Mia Taylor, "Early Recollections of Madison County," *Huntsville Historical Review* 2, no. 2 (April 1972): 20–35, 21–22.

33. Petition of the inhabitants of Burke County, 1787, Oct. 18 to Governor, SNADD, TCC TCC938.

34. George Mathews, November 15, 1787, *ASPIA*, 1:23.

35. Historian John Hope Franklin notes that in 1798 the state of Tennessee "required militia service of all free men and indented servants between eighteen and forty-five," see *Militant South*, 172.

36. Andrew Pickens to Thomas Pinckney, December 18, 1787, Andrew Pickens papers, 1780–1819, CUSC.

37. Andrew Pickens to Alexander McGillivray, December 24, 1787, Andrew Pickens papers, 1780–1819, CUSC; Rod Andrew Jr., *The Life and Times of General Andrew Pickens: Revolutionary War Hero, American Founder* (Chapel Hill: University of North Carolina Press, 2017), 210.

38. Chappell, *Miscellanies of Georgia*, 8.

39. Alexander McGillivray to Andrew Pickens, February 15, 1788, Governor's Messages, #462, SCDAH.

40. Mr. William Henry to John I. Henry, June 26, 1812, *Message from the President of the United States* (Washington, DC: Roger C. Weightman, 1812), 16–18, EAIS, 30257; the Committee of Claims, to which was presented the petition of Jesse Manley, 23rd Cong., 1st sess. (April 9, 1834), H.rp. 402. Historians have at times confused the May 1812 Duck River assault with a later 1813 Creek attack on settlers living along the Cache River, incorrectly attributing the former as precipitating the Creek civil war, see Donald R. Hickey, *The War of 1812: A Forgotten Conflict* (Urbana: University of Illinois Press, 1989), 146–47.

41. The Committee of Claims, to which was presented the petition of Jesse Manley 23rd Cong., 1st sess. (April 9, 1834), H.rp. 402.

42. "Extract of a letter from Mr. William Henry to John I. Henry, Esq. of William County, Tennessee, dated, St. Stephens, Mobile, 26th June 1812," EAIS, 30257; *Tennessee Herald*, Shelbyville, TN, n.d., reprinted in *Weekly Register*, June 13, 1812, ed. H. Niles (Baltimore: Franklin Press) 2:256.

43. The Committee of Claims, to which was presented the petition of Jesse Manley, 23rd Cong., 1st sess. (April 9, 1834), H.rp. 402.

44. In assessing the United States' war against the Red Sticks as a whole, Jeffrey Ostler states that "more than any other officially sanctioned action against Indians from 1783 to 1814, [it] revealed the contours of a war of extermination"; see *Surviving Genocide: Native Nations and the United States from the American Revolution to Bleeding Kansas* (New Haven: Yale University Press, 2019), quote on 176; see also 175–79.

45. Homes to Secretary of War, June 29, 1812, *TPUS*, 6:297.

46. Ferdinand L. Claiborne to James Caller, June 23, 1812, James Caller papers, SPR554, ADAH.

47. The Committee of Claims, to which was presented the petition of Jesse Manley 23rd Cong., 1st sess. (April 9, 1834), H.rp. 402.

48. Blount to Eustis, June 25, 1812, EAIS, 30257, 15.

49. Legislative Message, September 25, 1812, *Messages of the Governors of Tennessee, 1796–1821*, ed. Robert H. White (Nashville, 1952) 1:385–86.

50. *Nashville Clarion*, n.d. in *Weekly Register*, September 26, 1812, ed. H. Niles (Baltimore: Franklin Press), 3:53.

51. *Nashville Clarion*, n.d. in *Weekly Register*, September 26, 1812, 3:53.

52. *Tennessee Herald*, September 5, 1812, in *Weekly Register*, October 17, 1812, 3:107.

53. *Tennessee Herald*, September 5, 1812.

54. *Nashville Clarion*, May 23, 1812, quoted in Tom Kanon, "The Kidnapping of Martha Crawley and Settler-Indian Relations prior to the War of 1812," *Tennessee Historical Quarterly* 64, no. 1 (Spring 2004): 3–23, 9–10.

55. *Nashville Clarion*, n.d. in *Weekly Register*, September 26, 1812, 3:53.

56. *Nashville Democratic Clarion and Tennessee Gazette*, Nashville, TN, July 27, 1813, quoted in Tom Kanon, "Before Horseshoe: Andrew Jackson's Campaigns in the Creek War prior to Horseshoe Bend," *Tohopeka: Rethinking the Creek War and the War of 1812*, ed. Kathryn E. Holland Braund (Tuscaloosa: University of Alabama Press, 2012):105–21, 106.

57. Andrew Jackson to Willie Blount, July 3, 1812, *The Papers of Andrew Jackson*,

1804–1813, ed. Harold D. Moser and Sharon Macpherson (Knoxville: University of Tennessee Press, 1984), 2:307–8, 308.

58. Andrew Jackson to George Colbert, June 5, 1812, *Papers of Andrew Jackson*, 2:302–3, 303.

59. Andrew Jackson to George Colbert, June 5, 1812, *The Papers of Andrew Jackson*, 2:302–3, 302.

60. Andrew Jackson to Willie Blount, June 5, 1812, *Knoxville Gazette*, June 15, 1812, *Papers of Andrew Jackson*, 2:301–2, 301.

61. "The Massacre at the Mouth of Duck River," *Papers of Andrew Jackson*, 2:310–11, 311.

62. "To the 2nd Division," July 9, 1812, *Democratic Clarion*, July 14, 1812, *Papers of Andrew Jackson, 1804–1813*, 2:313–15, 314.

63. For a comparison, see Shire, *Threshold of Manifest Destiny*, 91–94.

64. Tom Kanon, *Tennesseans at War, 1812–1815: Andrew Jackson, The Creek War, and the Battle of New Orleans* (Tuscaloosa: University of Alabama Press, 2014), 64.

65. Andrew Jackson to Willie Blount, July 10, 1812, *Correspondence of Andrew Jackson*, ed. John Spencer Bassett (Washington, DC: Carnegie Institution of Washington, 1926), 1:230–32, 231.

66. Jackson to Blount, June 17, 1812, *Papers of Andrew Jackson*, 2:306; Jackson to the 2nd Division, July 9, 1812, *Papers of Andrew Jackson*, 2:314; Jackson to George Washington Campbell, October 15, 1812, 2:335.

67. "Legislative Message, September 25, 1812," *Messages of the Governors of Tennessee, 1796–1821*, ed. Robert H. White (Nashville: Tennessee Historical Commission, 1952), 1:385–86; Tennessee's denunciation of Hawkins and the federal government made its way to the national press in an excerpt from the resolutions in "Creek Indians," *Weekly Register*, November 7, 1812, 3:159–60, 160.

68. "Extract of a letter from a gentleman at Kaskaskia, dated February 27," *Weekly Register*, April 24, 1813, 4:135; Gillum Ferguson, *Illinois in the War of 1812* (Urbana: University of Illinois Press, 2012), 120; Saunt, *New Order of Things*, 250; Rothman, *Slave Country*, 125.

69. Hawkins to Upper Creeks, March 29, 1813, *ASPIA*, 1:839.

70. "Extract of a letter from a gentleman at Kaskaskia, dated February 27," *Weekly Register*, April 24, 1813, 4:135.

71. Sachs, *Home Rule*, 24; see also Lepore, *Name of War*, 74–76, Silver, *Our Savage Neighbors*, 84–85; and Shire, *Threshold of Manifest Destiny*, 84–94.

72. *Missouri Gazette*, St. Louis, MO, February 20, 1813.

73. *National Intelligencer*, April 20, 1813, in Richard C. Knopf, *Document Transcriptions of the War of 1812 in the Northwest* (Columbus: Ohio Historical Society, 1958), vol. 5, pt. 2, 84.

74. "Extract of a letter from a gentleman at Kaskaskia, dated February 27," *Weekly Register*.

75. Silver, *Our Savage Neighbors*, 79; see also Sachs, *Home Rule*, 101; and Shire, *Threshold of Manifest Destiny*, 73–80.

76. *Nashville Examiner*, Nashville, TN, September 29, 1813, published as "A Memorial, Citizens of Franklin County," *Messages of the Governors of Tennessee, 1796–1821*, ed. Robert H. White (Nashville: Tennessee Historical Commission, 1952) 1:396–97.

77. Historian Bertram Wyatt-Brown points out that "fierce retaliation was

therefore mandatory when a daughter, wife, or mother had been dishonored," and furthermore, "violence against family dependents, particularly females, was a breach not to be ignored without risk of ignominy"; see *Southern Honor*, 53; on gender and patriarchal mastery in the antebellum South, see McCurry, *Masters of Small Worlds*, 7, 15, 59.

78. Traveling through the Mississippi Territory, Peggy Dow attested to the regularity with which passersby conversed with one another and the frequency in which men, women, and children took to the roadways; see Lorenzo Dow and Peggy Dow, *History of Cosmopolite: Or the Writings of Rev. Lorenzo Dow* (Cincinnati: Anderson, Gates & Wright, 1859), 650, 651.

79. Hawkins to Eustis, May 25, 1812, *LJWBH*, 2:609.

80. Johann Christian Burckard and Karsten Petersen, *Partners in the Lord's Work*, 71, 72–73.

81. Alejandra Dubcovsky, *Informed Power: Communication in the Early American South* (Cambridge: Harvard University Press, 2016), 4.

82. Edmund Bacon to Mama, September 1, 1811, and Edmund Bacon to Agnes Pannill July 19, 1812, Bacon (Edmund) Letters, Mss. 2178, LSU-LLMVC; on Indian violence disrupting communication across the South, see also Robert Dickson to William Dickson, June 5, 1836, Dickson Family Papers, USC-SCL.

83. Dow and Dow, *History of Cosmopolite*, 652.

84. On nineteenth-century anxieties over a proper burial for white southerners, see Drew Gilpin Faust, *This Republic of Suffering: Death and the American Civil War* (New York: Alfred A. Knopf, 2008), 62–63.

85. Dow and Dow, *History of Cosmopolite*, 651.

86. Greenberg, *Honor and Slavery*, 92–93.

87. Erik R. Seeman, *Death in the New World: Cross-Cultural Encounters, 1492–1800* (Philadelphia: University of Pennsylvania Press, 2010), 272.

88. Henry Hollingsworth, "Tennessee Volunteers in the Seminole Campaign of 1836: The Diary of Henry Hollingsworth," ed. Stanley F. Horn, *Tennessee Historical Quarterly* 2, no. 1 (March 1943): 61–73, 62.

89. Peter N. Moore, "The Usable Death: Evangelicals, Anglicans, and the Politics of Dying in the Late-Colonial Lowcountry," *Death and the American South*, ed. Craig Thompson Friend and Lorri Glover, 36–57 (New York: Cambridge University Press, 2015), 48.

90. David S. Heidler and Jeanne T. Heidler, *Daily Life in the Early American Republic, 1790–1820* (Westport, CT: Greenwood Press, 2004), 47–48.

91. Pickett, *History of Alabama*, 2:81.

92. Pickett, *History of Alabama*, 2:82; for Milfort describing a similar situation, potentially the Kirkland incident, see Louis Le Clerc Milfort, *Memoirs or a Quick Glance*, 74.

93. Pickett, *History of Alabama*, 2:82.

94. Adam Hodgson, *Letters from North America, Written during a Tour of the United States and Canada*, vol. 1 (London: Hurst, Robinson; and Edinburgh; A. Constable, 1824), 143; Pickett, *History of Alabama*, 2:82.

95. Dow and Dow, *History of Cosmopolite*, 650.

96. Hodgson, *Letters from North America*, 142–43.

97. Hodgson, *Letters from North America*, 143.

98. Hodgson, *Letters from North America*, 143.

99. On colonizers renaming practices as method of acquisition, see Jean M. O'Brien, *Firsting and Lasting: Writing Indians out of Existence in New England* (Minneapolis: University of Minnesota Press, 2010), 93.

100. On white southerners commemorating Cherokee expulsion to emphasize racial difference and lay claim to the land, see Andrew Denson, *Monuments to Absence: Cherokee Removal and the Contest over Southern Memory* (Chapel Hill: University of North Carolina Press, 2017), esp. 88–95.

101. Petition to Congress by Inhabitants of the Territory, December 27, 1811, *TPUS*, 6:253–57.

102. WPA County Files, Mississippi Library Commission, Susie V. Powell, *Source Material for Mississippi History, Preliminary Manuscript: Marion County*, Works Project Administration, 1936–1939, 14.

103. As of 2023, the City of Columbia, Mississippi, points to a legacy of South Carolina settlers at Lott's Bluff and as the town's "founding," see The City of Columbia, Mississippi, web, accessed March 15, 2021. For earlier examples of the town's origins connected to the Lott family, see Woodward, *Reminiscences of the Creek*, 35; *Clarion-Ledger*, Jackson, MS, February 12, 1927; *Columbian-Progress*, Columbia, MS, February 12, 1953; *Columbian-Progress*, Columbia, MS, September 25, 1986; Brandi Perry, *Hattiesburg American*, Hattiesburg, MS, November 4, 2007.

104. H. Ted Woods, "More about the Creek Indian Wars," *Caldwell Watchman*, Columbia, LA, December 12, 1974.

105. H. Ted Woods, "Caldwell Parish in Slices: Part One," *Caldwell Watchman*, Columbia, LA, March 2, 1972. On other local accounts invoking Meredith's death and settler origins, also see *Caldwell Watchman*, Columbia, LA, April 24, 1969; *Caldwell Watchman*, Columbia, LA, January 22, 1970; *Caldwell Watchman*, Columbia, LA, November 26, 1970; *Caldwell Watchman*, Columbia, LA, December 12, 1974.

106. H. Ted Woods, "Caldwell Parish in Slices: Part One," *Caldwell Watchman*, Columbia, LA, March 9, 1972.

107. Woodward, *Woodward's Reminiscences of the Creek*, 8.

108. City of Tuskegee, "Tuskegee History," accessed January 29, 2023.

109. On potential "Indian negroes," see Woodward, *Reminiscences of the Creek*, 106; on number of slaves taken to Winn Parish by Woodward, see H. B. Bozeman, *Winn Parish Enterprise*, Winnfield, LA, January 28, 1965, H. B. Bozeman Papers, AUL.

110. H. B. Bozeman, *Winn Parish Enterprise*, Winnfield, LA, January 28, and July 22, 1965, H. B. Bozeman Papers, AUL.

111. Bozeman, *Winn Parish Enterprise*, Winnfield, LA, March 11, 1965, H. B. Bozeman Papers, AUL.

112. Bozeman, *Winn Parish Enterprise*, Winnfield, LA, January 28, 1965, H. B. Bozeman Papers, AUL.

113. Bozeman, *Winn Parish Enterprise*, Winnfield, LA, June 10 and July 8, 1965, H. B. Bozeman Papers, AUL; *Shreveport Journal*, Shreveport, LA, July 18, 1964; *St. Louis Post-Dispatch*, St. Louis, MO, July 27, 1964.

114. "Montgomery, Louisiana," Historical Marker Database, accessed March 21, 2021.

Chapter 3

1. Dunbar Rowland, *Encyclopedia of Mississippi History* (Madison: Selwyn A. Brant, 1907), 423–24.

2. J. F. H. Claiborne, *Life and Time of Gen. Sam. Dale, the Mississippi Partisan* (New York: Harper and Brothers, 1860), 83–84. On criticism of Hawkins, see also Tennessee governor Willie Blount on Hawkins over his response to the attacks on the Duck River in June 1812, *EAIS*, 30257, 16.

3. Call Journal, FHS.

4. Donald R. Hickey, *The War of 1812: A Short History* (Urbana: University of Illinois Press, 1995), 6–9.

5. For various examples of concerns over the military establishment in early US history, see Alexis de Tocqueville, *Democracy in America*, ed. Phillips Bradley (New York: Knopf, 1945), II, 270; Address to Congress by Elbridge Gerry, Representative of Massachusetts, June 2, 1784, *Journals of the Continental Congress*, XXVII, ed. Gaillard Hunt (New York: Johnson Reprint Corporation, 1968), 518–19; and Arthur A. Ekirch Jr., "The Idea of a Citizen Army," *Military Affairs* 17, no. 1 (Spring 1953): 30–36, 30.

6. Peter S. Onuf, *Jefferson's Empire: The Language of American Nationhood* (Charlottesville: University Press of Virginia, 2000), 53; quotes from "Thomas Jefferson First Inaugural Address," The Avalon Project, accessed April 5, 2021.

7. William B. Skelton argues this was primarily a result of "the deficiency of the militia's mounting offensive operations and the refusal of the New England states to support the war" against the British; see *An American Profession of Arms: The Army Officer Corps, 1784–1861* (Lawrence: University Press of Kansas, 1992), 9.

8. J. C. A. Stagg, *The War of 1812: Conflict for a Continent* (Cambridge: Cambridge University Press, 2012), 106; Requisition of Militia, War Department circular to state governors, *Weekly Register*, July 9, 1814, ed. H. Niles (Baltimore: Franklin Press): 6:321–22.

9. Waselkov, *Conquering Spirit*, 96–97; The Floridas, *Clarion*, Nashville, TN, reproduced in *Weekly Register*, September 26, 1812, 3:52–53.

10. W. C. C. Claiborne to W. L. Andrews, July 28, 1813, *OLB-WC*, 6:248–249.

11. On the formation of the Red Sticks as a faction within the Creek confederacy and their adoption of war clubs as their symbol of resistance, see Kathryn E. Holland Braund, "Red Sticks," *Tohopeka: Rethinking the Creek War and the War of 1812*, ed. Kathryn E. Holland Braund (Tuscaloosa: University of Alabama Press, 2012): 84–104.

12. F. L. Claiborne to Maj. Gen. Flournoy, July 8, 1813; J. F. H. Claiborne, *Life and Time of Gen. Sam Dale*, 90.

13. F. L. Claiborne to the Officer in command at Liberty, Mississippi Territory, August 13, 1813, in J. F. H. Claiborne, *Life and Time of Gen. Sam. Dale*, 90–91.

14. Thomas Flournoy to Governor Holmes, August 6, 1813, enclosed in Governor Holmes to the Secretary of War, August 30, 1813, *TPUS*, 6:396–98; Waselkov, *Conquering Spirit*, 105.

15. J. F. H. Claiborne, *Life and Time of Gen. Sam. Dale*, 95.

16. For the best modern assessments of the battle, see Waselkov, *Conquering Spirit*, 116–38; and Frank L. Owsley Jr., *Struggle for the Gulf Borderlands: The Creek War and the Battle of New Orleans, 1812–1815* (Gainesville: University Presses of Florida, 1981), 34–41. For contemporary accounts, see George Stiggins, *Creek Indian History: A Historical Narrative of the Genealogy, Traditions and Downfall of the Ispocoga or Creek Indian Tribe of Indians*, intro. and notes William Stokes Wyman, ed. Virginia Pounds Brown (Birmingham: Birmingham Public Library Press, 1989), 107–14; Pickett, *History of Alabama*, 267–79; J. F. H. Claiborne, *Life and Time of Gen. Sam Dale*, 99–115.

17. Jesse Griffin to parents, September 5, 1813, Jesse Griffin letter, 1813, W. S. Hoole Special Collections Library, University of Alabama Libraries Digital Collections, University of Alabama, Tuscaloosa, Alabama.

18. Margaret Ervin Austill, "Memories of Journeying through Creek Country and Childhood in Clarke County, 1811–1814," ADAH, Digital Archives, reproduced from SPR237; see also Waselkov, *Conquering Spirit*, 142–144. For news of families prepared to leave the area as early as April 1813, fearing the "hostile disposition of the Creek Indians," see Inhabitants of St. Stephens to James Wilkinson, April 17, 1813, ADAH, Digital Archive, reproduced from Creek War military records, SPR359. For a similar Alabama settler reminiscence on the anxiety over Native violence in this period, see Mia Taylor, "Early Recollections of Madison County." *Huntsville Historical Review* 2, no. 2 (April 1972): 20–35, 34.

19. Margaret Mitchell, *Gone with the Wind* (New York: Simon and Schuster, 1964), 452.

20. Pickett, *History of Alabama,* 2:275.

21. Owsley Jr., *Struggle for the Gulf Borderlands*, 39–40.

22. "Circular to Colonels of Militia," W. C. C. Claiborne, September 8, 1813, *OLB-WC*, 6:265.

23. Chiefs at Coweta to Benjamin Hawkins, September 16, 1813, and Benjamin Hawkins to Secretary of War, September 21, 1813, *ASPIA*, 1:853–54; Owsley Jr., *Struggle for the Gulf Borderlands*, 40.

24. Waselkov notes that "most Africans shared whites' fear of the Red Sticks and fled with the rest of the evacuees" in the wake of the Fort Mims assault; see *Conquering Spirit*, 148.

25. Nathaniel Herbert Claiborne, *Notes on the War in the South* (Richmond, VA: William Ramsay, 1819), 23. Claiborne assembled one of the first histories of the Creek War, primarily aimed at vindicating his late uncle Gen. Ferdinand Claiborne; see Waselkov, *Conquering Spirit*, 179–80.

26. "From the Knoxville Paper," *Carolina Gazette*, Charleston, SC, November 6, 1813.

27. Owens, *Red Dreams, White Nightmares*, 213; on southern newspapers' deployment of "Indian massacre" to describe the Red Stick attack against Fort Mims, see also *Georgia Journal*, Milledgeville, GA, September 22, 1813; *Charleston Courier*, October 1, 1813, and *The Star*, Raleigh, NC, May 13, 1814.

28. Waselkov, *Conquering Spirit*, 177–79; "Circular to Colonels of Militia," W. C. C. Claiborne, September 8, 1813, *OLB-WC*, 6:265; W. C. C. Claiborne to Judge Toulmin, September 16, 1813, *OLB-WC*, 6:267.

29. Harry Toulmin, Indian Warfare, *Weekly Register*, October 16, 1813, 5:105–7, 107; the Letter was also printed in the *Raleigh Register*, Raleigh, NC, and *Georgia Journal*, Milledgeville, GA, September 29, 1813.

30. Toulmin, Indian Warfare, *Weekly Register*, Oct. 16, 1813, 5:105–7, 105.

31. Toulmin, Indian Warfare, *Weekly Register*, Oct. 16, 1813, 5:105–7, 107.

32. Obituary, Spruce M. Osborne, printed in both *North-Carolina Star* and *Raleigh Minerva*, Raleigh, NC, December 10, 1813.

33. *Georgia Journal*, Milledgeville, GA, September 29, 1813; *Virginia Argus*, Richmond, VA, October 18, 1813; *Weekly Register*, Baltimore, MD, October 16, 1813, 5:105–7, 107, reprinted from the *Raleigh Register*, Raleigh, NC.

34. *Weekly Register*, Baltimore, MD, October 16, 1813, 105–7, 107.

35. Waselkov, *Conquering Spirit*, 154.

36. "Patriotism of Tennessee," *Weekly Register*, Baltimore, MD, October 16, 1813, 5:105.

37. "Patriotism of Tennessee," *Weekly Register*, Baltimore, MD, October 16, 1813, 5:105.

38. *Augusta Chronicle*, Augusta, GA, July 23, 1813.

39. *Augusta Chronicle*, Augusta, GA, September 3, 1813.

40. *Augusta Chronicle*, Augusta, GA, July 9, 1813; *Republican and Savannah Evening Ledger*, Savannah, GA, July 13, 1813.

41. *Georgia Journal*, Milledgeville, GA, September 22, 1813; *Mirror of the Times*, Augusta, GA, September 25, 1813; *Republican and Savannah Evening Ledger*, Savannah, GA, September 28, 1813.

42. *Georgia Journal*, Milledgeville, GA, September 29, 1813; see also *Augusta Chronicle*, Augusta, GA, October 8, 1813.

43. *Augusta Chronicle*, Augusta, GA, August 6, 1813.

44. *Georgia Journal*, Milledgeville, GA, September 29, 1813.

45. The Journal of Governor Richard K. Call, 1861, FHS.

46. David Crockett, *Narrative of the Life of David Crockett of the State of Tennessee* (Philadelphia: E. L. Carey and A. Hart, 1834), 72; for similar expression of popular sentiment in response to the attack at Fort Mims, see "A Memorial, Citizens of Franklin County," *Messages of the Governors of Tennessee, 1796–1821*, ed. Robert H. White (Nashville: Tennessee Historical Commission, 1952) 1:396–97.

47. Call Journal, FHS.

48. In a court-administrated estate sale, the Inferior Court of Richmond County, Georgia, listed "Richard Call's survey" as the southwest border of one of the late John Catlett's land tracts; see "Administrators Sales," *Augusta Chronicle*, Augusta, GA, July 31, 1812.

49. Call Journal, FHS; Richard Keith Call to unnamed Georgia lawyer, June 23, 1820, Richard K Call correspondence, Miscellaneous Manuscripts 00,733, UF-PKY; Herbert J. Doherty Jr., *Richard Keith Call: Southern Unionist* (Gainesville: University of Florida Press, 1961), 3.

50. Willie Blount to David B. Mitchell, August 8, 1813, and Willie Blount to David B. Mitchell, August 13, 1813, TCC, UGA-H, SNAD; Owsley Jr., *Struggle for the Gulf Borderlands*, 51.

51. Owsley Jr., *Struggle for the Gulf Borderlands*, 43–45.

52. Ebenezer Hearn autobiography, n.d., ADAH, Digital Archives, reproduced from Ebenezer Hearn autobiography, SPR37.

53. Governor Holmes to Secretary of War, August 30, 1813, *TPUS*, 6:396–97.

54. Benjamin Hawkins to Secretary of War, October 1813, *ASPIA*, 1:857.

55. Owsley Jr., *Struggle for the Gulf Borderlands*, 52.

56. Andrew Jackson to William Coffee, March 16, 1813, Andrew Jackson Collection, USC-SCL; Jackson to John Coffee, October 7, 1813, *Papers of Andrew Jackson*, 2:435–436, 435.

57. Jackson to Coffee, October 7, 1813, *The Papers of Andrew Jackson, 1804–1813*, ed. Harold D. Moser, Sharon Macpherson, and Charles F. Bryan Jr. (Knoxville: University of Tennessee Press, 1984), 2:435.

58. Jackson to Thomas Flournoy, October 24, 1813, *Papers of Andrew Jackson*, 2:441.

59. Jackson to Willie Blount, October 28, 1813, *Papers of Andrew Jackson*, 2:442–443, 442.

60. Jackson to Thomas Flournoy, October 24, 1813, *Papers of Andrew Jackson*, 2:441.

61. Flournoy to Jackson, November 9, 1813, Andrew Jackson papers, 1775–1874, Manuscript/Mixed Material, Library of Congress.

62. Jackson to Willie Blount, October 28, 1813, *Papers of Andrew Jackson*, 2:442–443, 442.

63. Jackson to Leroy Pope, October 31, 1813, *Papers of Andrew Jackson*, 2:443.

64. Jackson to Rachel Jackson, November 12, 1813, *Papers of Andrew Jackson*, 2:448–449, 449.

65. Call Journal, FHS.

66. Ebenezer Hearn autobiography, ADAH, Digital Archives, SPR37.

67. Sam Bains to Christina, November 25, 1813, Sam Bains letter, 1813, ADAH, Digital Archives, SPR542.

68. Secretary of War John Armstrong to Jackson, February 5, 1813, in Amos Kendall, *The Life of Andrew Jackson* (New York: Harper & Brothers, 1843), 143.

69. Call Journal, FHS.

70. See Blount to Secretary of War Armstrong, December 10, 1813 and December 24, 1813, Governor Willie Blount Papers, 1809–1815 [Microfilm], TSLA; Jackson to Willie Blount, December 15, 1813, *Papers of Andrew Jackson*, 2:487–90; and Jackson to John Armstrong December 16, 1813, *Papers of Andrew Jackson*, 2:492–93.

71. Peter A. Brannon, "Journal of James A. Tait for the Year 1813," *Georgia Historical Quarterly* 8, no. 3 (September 1924): 229–39, 230, 230, 231.

72. Brannon, "Journal of James A. Tait for the Year 1813," 230, 232.

73. Brannon, "Journal of James A. Tait for the Year 1813," 232.

74. Owsley Jr., *Struggle for the Gulf Borderlands*, 52.

75. Brannon, "Journal of James A. Tait for the Year 1813," 233.

76. Brannon, "Journal of James A. Tait for the Year 1813," 235, 238.

77. Owsley Jr., *Struggle for the Gulf Borderlands*, 54–55.

78. Dr. Williamson, January 16, 1814, *The Republican; and Savannah Evening Ledger*, Savannah, GA, February 1, 1814; on illness in camp, see also *The Republican; and Savannah Evening Ledger*, Savannah, GA, January 18, 1814.

79. *Georgia Journal*, Milledgeville, GA, February 2, 1814. Adam Jortner points out that William Henry Harrison's success at the Battle of Tippecanoe was also overblown in the US press; see *The Gods of Prophetstown: The Battle of Tippecanoe and the Holy War for the American Frontier* (New York: Oxford University Press, 2012), 195–96. On parallels between Tippecanoe and the start of the 1813 Creek War, see Owens, *Red Dreams, White Nightmares*, 230–31.

80. Owsley Jr., *Struggle for the Gulf Borderlands*, 76.

81. Daniel Dupree, *Alabama's Frontiers and the Rise of the Old South* (Bloomington: Indiana University Press, 2018), 241.

82. Jackson to Willie Blount, July 3, 1812, *Papers of Andrew Jackson,* 2:307–8, 308.

83. Jackson to George Colbert, June 5, 1812, *Papers of Andrew Jackson,* 2:302–3, 303.

84. Brannon, "Journal of James A. Tait for the Year 1813," 235.

85. Jackson to Thomas Pinckney, March 23, 1814, *Weekly Register*, April 23, 1814, 6:130–31, 130; and John Henry Eaton, *The Life of Andrew Jackson, Major-General in the Service of the United States: Comprising a History of the War in the South, from the Commencement of the Creek Campaign, to the Termination of Hostilities before New*

Orleans (Philadelphia: Samuel F. Bradford, 1824), 164; both specify 557 Red Stick deaths at the Battle of Horseshoe Bend.

86. Report from General Coffee to General Jackson, dated April 1, *Weekly Register*, April 23, 1814, 6:148; Owsley Jr., *Struggle for the Gulf Borderlands*, 81.

87. H. S. Halbert and T. S. Ball, *The Creek War of 1813 and 1814*, ed. and intro. Frank L. Owsley Jr. (Tuscaloosa: University of Alabama Press, 1995), 276–77.

88. Jackson to Blount, July 3, 1812, *Papers of Andrew Jackson*, 2:307–8, 308.

89. Jackson frames Lyncoya as a possession when inquiring if "little andrew has got his little Lyncoya—and what he thinks of him"; see Jackson to Hays, January 4, 1814, *Papers of Andrew Jackson, 1814–1815*, 3:6–10, 8; for Jackson presenting Lyncoya as a gift to Jackson Jr., also see Jackson to Rachel, January 28, 1814, February 1, 1814, February 21, 1814, and May 8, 1814, *Papers of Andrew Jackson*, 3:17–21, 23–24, 34–35, 70–71.

90. *Village Messenger*, Fayetteville, TN, June 26, 1828.

91. On paternalism and the performance of benevolent mastery by white slaveholders at a slave burial, see Jamie Warren, "To Claim One's Own: Death and the Body in the Daily Politics of Antebellum Slavery," *Death and the American South*, ed. Craig Thompson Friend and Lorri Glover (New York: Cambridge University Press, 2015):110–30, esp. 120–22; and Eugene Genovese, *Roll, Jordan, Roll: The World the Slaves Made* (New York: Vintage Books, 1976), 195.

92. "Cadaver Dogs Probe The Hermitage for Slave Remains," *Nashville Post*, July 17, 2003, web, accessed April 1, 2021; Michael Cass, "The Hermitage Honors Slaves with Memorial Event," *The Tennessean*, Nashville, TN, February 21, 2014, web, accessed April 1, 2021.

93. John Spencer Bassett, *The Life of Andrew Jackson* (Garden City: Doubleday, Page, 1911), 1:118.

94. Treaty of Fort Jackson, August 9, 1814, in Halbert and Ball, *Creek War of 1813 and 1814*, 282–84.

95. Dupree, *Alabama's Frontiers and the Rise of the Old South*, 242.

96. Call Journal, FHS.

97. Treaty of Fort Jackson, August 9, 1814, in Halbert and Ball, *Creek War of 1813 and 1814*, 282–84.

98. On Fort Mims invoked to announce the end of the war and use of "massacre at Fort Mims," see *Charleston Daily Courier*, Charleston, SC, May 9, 1814; and *Susquehanna Democrat*, Wilkes-Barre, PA, June 10, 1814; on Fort Mims as justification for settler reprisals, see *Republican; and Savannah Evening Ledger*, Savannah, GA, May 17, 1814.

99. *Mississippi Free Trader*, Natchez, MS, June 1, 1814.

100. *Clarion and Tennessee State Gazette*, Nashville, TN, July 12, 1814.

101. *Augusta Chronicle*, Augusta, GA, March 11, 1814; for other community celebrations, see *Georgia Journal*, Milledgeville, GA, March 2, 1814.

102. *Athens Gazette*, Athens, GA, March 10, 1814.

103. *Republican; and Savannah Evening Ledger*, Savannah, GA, April 9, 1814; see also *Georgia Journal*, Milledgeville, GA, April 6, 1814.

104. Claiborne, *Notes on the War in the South*, 16.

105. Call Journal, FHS.

106. *Mississippi Free Trader*, Natchez, MS, June 1, 1814.

107. *Clarion and Tennessee State Gazette*, Nashville, TN, July 12, 1814.

108. *Athens Gazette*, Athens, GA, March 10, 1814.

109. *Republican; and Savannah Evening Ledger*, Savannah, GA, March 22, 1814.

110. Jackson to Pinckney, March 28, 1814, *Papers of Andrew Jackson*, 3:52–53; and Jackson to Rachel, April 1, 1814, *Papers of Andrew Jackson*, 3:54–55.

111. Pickett, *History of Alabama*, 2:346.

112. *Mississippi Free Trader*, Natchez, MS, June 1, 1814.

113. *National Banner and Nashville Whig*, Nashville, TN, November 3, 1817.

114. Pickett, *History of Alabama*, 2:346.

115. *Wetumpka Argus*, Wetumpka, AL, June 26, 1839.

116. *Montgomery Advertiser*, Montgomery, AL, May 11, 1987.

117. Quote in *Montgomery Advertiser*, Montgomery, AL, February 12, 1985; *Alabama Journal*, Montgomery, AL, February 12, 1985.

118. *Montgomery Advertiser*, Montgomery, AL, March 17, 1997.

119. *Alabama Journal*, Montgomery, AL, May 26, 1987.

Chapter 4

1. Historians have presented the end of the 1813 Creek War as a conclusive moment in Creek history. Joel W. Martin suggested that the Battle at Horseshoe "ended Redstick military action" and left the Creeks fragmented and confused; see *Sacred Revolt*, 163. More recently Kevin Kokomoor finds as a result of the Creek War "Creek sovereignty was officially dead"; see *Of One Mind and of One Government*, 365. For similar assessments of the Creek War's conclusion, see also Kathryn Braund's assessment in *Deerskins and Duffels*, 188; and Ethridge, *Creek Country*, 241. Nineteenth-century chroniclers are even more fatalistic concerning the Creek's relevance to the South after the Battle of Horseshoe Bend; see Halbert and Ball, *Creek War of 1813 and 1814*, 275; Alexander Beaufort Meek, *Romantic Passages in Southwestern History* (Mobile, AL: S. H. Goetzel, 1857), 282–83, 289.

2. The 1818 Florida Invasion is best viewed as part of a continuous conflict between white settlers and the federal government against Native southerners opposing American expansion, with direct links to the 1813 Creek War, rather than an episodic conflict with a clear start and conclusion focused on a cohesive Seminole people. On the First Seminole War as part of the "unabated, aggressive American expansion" against Seminole, see William S. Belko, "Introduction," *America's Hundred Years War: U.S. Expansion to the Gulf Coast and the Fate of the Seminole, 1763–1858*, ed. William S. Belko (Gainesville: University Press of Florida, 2011), 8. On the 1818 Florida Invasion as an extension of the 1813 Creek War and transborder links between the Creek and the Indians of Florida, see J. Leitch Wright Jr., *Creeks and Seminoles* (Lincoln: University Nebraska Press, 1986), 202; and Rosen, *Border Law*, 109–11; and Andrew K. Frank, "Red, Black, and Seminole: Community Convergence on the Florida Borderlands, 1780–1840," *Borderland Narratives: Negotiation and Accommodation in North America's Contested Spaces, 1500–1850* (Gainesville: University Press of Florida, 2017), 46–67, esp. 49–51.

3. Hudson, *Creek Paths and Federal Roads*, 122; Thomas D. Clark and John D. W. Guice, *The Old Southwest, 1795–1830: Frontiers in Conflict* (Norman: University of Oklahoma Press, 1996), 178.

4. Howell Tatum, "Howell Tatum's Journal while Acting Topographical Engineer to Andrew Jackson Commanding the Seventh Military District," *Smith College Studies in History*, 7, no. 1–3 (October 1921 to April 1922), 26.

5. Thomas P. Abernethy notes that the "flood of humanity" arriving in the newly seized land was "almost entirely from the Southern states"; see *The South in the New Nation: 1789–1819* (Baton Rouge: Louisiana State University Press, 1989), 465; see also Hudson, *Creek Paths and Federal Roads*, 121–30; Rothman, *Slave Country*, 168–71.

6. The Journal of Governor Richard K. Call, 1861, FHS.

7. Waselkov, *Conquering Spirit*, 204.

8. On Cherokee land loss stemming from the Treaty of Fort Jackson, see William G. McLoughlin, *Cherokee Renascence in the New Republic* (Princeton: Princeton University Press, 1986), 198–205.

9. *Athens Gazette*, Athens, GA, April 28, 1814; *Republican; and Savannah Evening Ledger*, Savannah, GA, April 30, 1814.

10. *Georgia Journal*, Milledgeville, GA, May 4, 1814; *Athens Gazette*, Athens, GA, May 5, 1814; *Republican; and Savannah Evening Ledger*, Savannah, GA, May 7, 1814; *Clarion and Tennessee State Gazette*, Nashville, TN, June 7, 1814; *Charleston Daily Courier*, Charleston, SC, May 9, 1814.

11. *Republican; and Savannah Evening Ledger*, Savannah, GA, June 14, 1814; *Charleston Daily Courier*, Charleston, SC, June 20, 1814; *Raleigh Minerva*, Raleigh, NC, June 17, 1814.

12. *Georgia Journal*, Milledgeville, GA, June 22, 1814; *Republican; and Savannah Evening Ledger*, Savannah, GA, June 21, 1814.

13. *Kentucky Gazette*, Lexington, KY, June 20, 1814; *Clarion and Tennessee State Gazette*, Nashville, TN, July 12, 1814; *Athens Gazette*, July 14, 1814.

14. *Clarion and Tennessee State Gazette*, Nashville, TN, July 12, 1814; *Kentucky Gazette*, Lexington, KY, June 20, 1814; *Republican; and Savannah Evening Ledger*, Savannah, GA, June 14, 1814.

15. For the transformation of Indian the population of Florida, see Jerald T. Milanich, *The Florida Indians and the Invasion from Europe* (Gainesville: University Press of Florida, 1995); Paul Kelton, *Epidemics and Enslavement: Biological Catastrophe in the Native Southeast, 1492–1715* (Lincoln: University of Nebraska Press, 2007); and John E. Worth, "Razing Florida: The Indian Slave Trade and the Devastation of Spanish Florida, 1659–1715," *Mapping the Mississippian Shatter Zone: The Colonial Indian Slave Trade and Regional Instability in the American South*, ed. Robbie Ethridge and Sheri M. Shuck-Hall (Lincoln: University of Nebraska Press, 2009): 295–311. For a broader assessment of the colonial Indian slave trade in the South, see Alan Gallay, *The Indian Slave Trade: The Rise of the English Empire in the American South, 1670–1717* (New Haven: Yale University Press, 2002); Robbie Ethridge, *From Chicaza to Chickasaw: The European Invasion and the Transformation of the Mississippian World, 1540–1715* (Chapel Hill: University of North Carolina Press, 2010); and Eric E. Bowne, *The Westo Indians: Slave Traders of the Early Colonial South* (Tuscaloosa: University of Alabama Press, 2005).

16. On Seminole ethnogenesis, see William C. Sturtevant, "Creek into Seminole," in *North American Indians in Historical Perspective*, ed. Eleanor Burke Leacock and Nancy Oestreich Lurie (Prospect Heights, IL: Waveland Press, 1988): 92–128; James W. Covington, *The Seminoles of Florida* (Gainesville: University Press of Florida, 1993), 3–27; Brent R. Weisman, "Archeological Perspectives on Florida Seminole Ethnogenesis," *Indians of the Greater Southeast: Historical Archeology and Ethnohistory*, ed. Bonnie G. McEwan (Gainesville: University Press of Florida, 2000): 299–317, 303; and Frank, "Red, Black, and Seminole," p. 49–50.

17. Saunt, *New Order of Things*, 35.

18. For instance, 1823 Treaty of Moultrie Creek refers to "the Florida tribes of Indians," referencing a multitude of peoples; see "Treaty with the Florida Tribes of Indians, 1823," in *Indian Affairs: Laws and Treaties*, comp. and ed. Charles J. Kappler (Washington, DC: Government Printing Office, 1904), 2:203–7; Covington, *Seminoles of Florida*, 47; Sturtevant, "Creek into Seminole," 106.

19. Jackson to Gaines, April 8, 1816, *Letter from the Secretary of War, Transmitting, Pursuant to a Resolution of the House of Representatives, of the 26th Ult. Information in Relation to the Destruction of the Negro Fort, in East Florida, in the Month of July, 1816, &c. &c.*, 15th Cong., 2nd sess., (1819), H. Doc. 122, hereafter cited as 15th Cong., 2nd sess., (1819), H. Doc. 122.

20. *Baldwin Times*, Bay Minette, AL, September 4, 1941; Peter Joseph Hamilton, *Colonial Mobile: An Historical Study* (Boston: Houghton, Mifflin, 1897), 319.

21. Section 20 of A. J. Pickett's "Interesting Notes upon the History of Alabama," Albert J. Pickett papers, LPR185, Digital Archives, ADAH.

22. Pickett, *History of Alabama*, 321.

23. *Baldwin Times*, Bay Minette, AL, September 4, 1941.

24. Waselkov, *Conquering Spirit*, 325–26, fn 24; Hawkins to Peter Early, June 15, 1814, TCC, UGA-H, SNAD; *Augusta Chronicle*, Augusta, GA, August 26, 1814.

25. Hawkins to Armstrong, July 12, 1814, *ASPIA*, 1:860; *Weekly Register*, July 23, 1814, ed. H. Niles (Baltimore: Franklin Press), 6:353.

26. Hawkins to Armstrong, July 12, 1814, *ASPIA*, 1:860.

27. *Augusta Chronicle*, Augusta, GA, August 26, 1814.

28. Hawkins to Peter Early, August 23, 1814, TCC, UGA-H, SNAD.

29. *Georgia Journal*, Milledgeville, GA, August 31, 1814.

30. Tooke to Early, September 8, 1814, TCC, UGA-H, SNAD.

31. *Georgia Journal*, Milledgeville, GA, September 14 and November 2, 1814; *Augusta Chronicle*, Augusta, GA, September 22 and November 17, 1814; *Republican; and Savannah Evening Ledger*, November 8, 1814.

32. Hawkins to Early, November 15, 1814, TCC, UGA-H, SNAD; Owsley Jr., *Struggle for the Gulf Borderlands*, 20, 28 and 92.

33. Hawkins to Armstrong, August 16, 1814, *ASPIA*, 1:860.

34. Hawkins to Captain Lagueux, November 4, 1814; and Hawkins to Early, November 5, 1814, TCC, UGA-H, SNAD.

35. Andrew Jackson to Rachel Jackson, July 16, 1814, Andrew Jackson Letter, LSU-LLMVC; Robert V. Remini, *Andrew Jackson—Volume One: The Course of American Empire, 1767–1812* (Baltimore: Johns Hopkins University Press, 1998), 239; James Monroe to Willie Blount, October 10, 1814, in Arsène Lacarrière Latour, *Historical Memoir of the War in West Florida and Louisiana in 1814–15, with an Atlas*, expanded ed., ed. and intro. by Gene Allen Smith (Gainesville: University Press of Florida and The Historic New Orleans Collection, 2008), 183–84; James Monroe to Andrew Jackson, October 10, 1814, *Correspondence of Andrew Jackson*, ed. John Spencer Bassett (Washington, DC: Carnegie Institution of Washington, 1927), 2:71.

36. Latour, *Historical Memoir of the War*, 42.

37. Call Journal, FHS; Frank L. Owsley Jr., "Prophet of War: Josiah Francis and the Creek War," *American Indian Quarterly* 9, no. 3 (Summer 1985): 273–93, 285; Remini, *Andrew Jackson*, 1:245.

38. Brian R. Rucker, "In the Shadow of Jackson: Uriah Blue's Expedition into West

Florida," *Florida Historical Quarterly* 73, no. 3 (January 1995): 325–38; McIntosh to Governor Early, December 12, 1814, TCC. UGA-H, SNAD; Crockett, *Narrative of the Life*, 106, 116, and 120; Section 25 of A. J. Pickett's "Interesting Notes upon the History of Alabama," Albert J. Pickett papers, LPR185, Digital Archives, ADAH.

39. Nathaniel Millett, *The Maroons of Prospect Bluff and Their Quest for Freedom in the Atlantic World* (Gainesville: University Press of Florida, 2013), 55–56; Boyd, "Events at Prospect Bluff on the Apalachicola River, 1808–1818," *Florida Historical Quarterly* 16, no. 2 (October 1937), 55–71.

40. Edward Nicolls, "Orders of the Day for the First Colonial Battalion of the Royal Corps of Marines," Latour, *Historical Memoir of the War*, 199–200; Owsley Jr., *Struggle for the Gulf Borderlands*, 180–82; *Weekly Register*, March 15, 1817, 12:46; *Weekly Register*, June 13, 1818, 14:269; Hawkins to Early, April 21, 1815, TCC, UGA-H, SNAD.

41. Boyd, "Events at Prospect Bluff," 76; Millett, *Maroons of Prospect Bluff*, 129–30.

42. Frank Lawrence Owsley Jr. and Gene A. Smith, *Filibusters and Expansionists: Jeffersonian Manifest Destiny, 1800–1821* (Tuscaloosa: University of Alabama Press, 1997), 108.

43. John Ross to Peter Early, June 10, 1815, TCC, UGA-H, SNAD.

44. John Floyd to David B. Mitchell, April 12, 1816, TCC, UGA-H, SNAD; Gaines to Jackson, March 20, 1816, 15th Cong., 2nd sess. (1819), H. Doc. 122.

45. Lieutenant William Bee to David B. Mitchell, May 11, 1816, TCC, UGA-H, SNAD.

46. Gaines to Patterson, May 22, 1816, *Letter from the Secretary of the Navy, Transmitting in Obedience to a Resolution of the House of Representatives, of the Twenty-Sixth Ultimo, Sundry Documents Relating to the Destruction of the Negro Fort in East Florida, in the Month of July, 1816*, 15th Cong., 2nd sess. (1819), H. Doc. 119, hereafter cited as 15th Cong., 2nd sess. (1819), H. Doc. 119.

47. Gaines to Jackson, March 20, 1816, 15th Cong., 2nd sess. (1819), H. Doc. 122; Saunt, *New Order of Things*, 286; Owsley Jr. and Smith, *Filibusters and Expansionists*, 108–9.

48. Gaines to Patterson, May 22, 1816, 15th Cong., 2nd sess. (1819), H. Doc. 119; *Savannah Republican*, Savannah, GA, August 17, 1816.

49. Gaines to Clinch, May 23, 1816, 15th Cong., 2nd sess. (1819), H. Doc. 122; Patterson to Crawley, June 19, 1816, 15th Cong., 2nd sess. (1819), H. Doc. 119.

50. Marcus C. Buck, August 4, 1816, *The Army and Navy Chronicle*, ed. B. Homans (Washington, DC: B. Homans): 2:115–16, 115; Clinch to Butler, August 2, 1816, in James Grant Forbes, *Sketches Historical and Topographical of the Floridas; More Particularly of East Florida* (New York: C. S. Van Winkle, 1821): 200–205; Loomis to Patterson, August 13, 1816, 15th Cong., 2nd sess. (1819), H. Doc. 119.

51. Modern historians have challenged the US-reported casualties at Prospect Bluff, suggesting they were much lower; see Saunt, *New Order of Things*, 288; and Millet, *Maroons of Prospect Bluff*, 231.

52. For quote, see Colonel Nicolls to Sir John Barrow, September 11, 1843, *Correspondence of the Slave Trade with Foreign Powers* (London: William Clowes and Sons, 1844), 13. On the various accounts of the fort's destruction, see Duncan L. Clinch to Col. R. Butler, August 2, 1816, in Forbes, *Sketches Historical and Topographical of the Floridas*, 200–205, 203; J. Loomis to Daniel T. Patterson, August 13, 1816, 15th Cong., 2nd sess. (1819), H. Doc. 119; Millett, *Maroons of Prospect Bluff*, 227–28.

53. Marcus C. Buck to Father, August 4, 1816, *Army and Navy Chronicle*, 2:115–16, 116.

54. *National Banner and Nashville Whig*, Nashville, TN, September 3, 1816; see also *Louisiana State Gazette*, New Orleans, LA, August 21, 1816; *Charleston Daily Courier*, Charleston, SC, August 22, 1816; *Carolina Federal Republican*, New Bern, NC, September 7, 1816; and *Virginia Argus*, September 25, 1816.

55. *Savannah Republican*, Savannah, GA, August 20, 1816.

56. Crawford to Mitchell, September 24, 1816, TCC, UGA-H, SNAD.

57. *Georgia Journal*, Milledgeville, GA, February 25, 1817; R. Sands to Officer of Fort Hawkins, February 2, 1817, *ASPMA*, 1:681; Boyd, "Events at Prospect Bluff," 84.

58. M. Harding to Mitchell, October 2, 1816, TCC, UGA-H, SNAD.

59. Chehaw Chiefs to David B. Mitchell, December 27, 1816, TCC, UGA-H, SNAD. For complaints about squatters on Indian land, see also Martin Harden to David B. Mitchell, December 28, 1816, TCC, UGA-H, SNAD; "Depositions Respecting Depredations on the Indian Land," May 28, 1817, TCC, UGA-H, SNAD. On settler grievances over Native horse thefts, see Adam James to Creek "Brothers," November 29, 1813, SPR54, ADAH; Ethridge, *Creek Country*, 182–85.

60. William Gibson, Thomas H. Miller, and William Bailey to Mitchell, February 8, 1817, TCC, UGA-H, SNAD.

61. *Savannah Republican*, Savannah, GA, March 6, 1817; Sands to King, March 15, 1817, *ASPMA*, 1:683.

62. *Savannah Republican*, Savannah, GA, March 6, 1817; *Augusta Herald*, Augusta, GA, March 11, 1814; *Augusta Chronicle*, Augusta, GA, March 12, 1817; *Georgia Journal*, Milledgeville, GA, March 25, 1817.

63. Mitchell to Secretary of War, March 30, 1817, *ASPMA*, 1:683.

64. *Savannah Republican*, Savannah, GA, n.d. in *Weekly Register*, July 26, 1817, 12:347–48, 348; see also *Savannah Republican*, July 1, 1817.

65. *North Carolina Star*, Raleigh, NC, July 18, 1817; *Charleston Daily Courier*, Charleston, SC, April 2, 1817; *Weekly Raleigh Register*, Raleigh, NC, April 11, 1817.

66. *North Carolina Star*, Raleigh, NC, July 18, 1817.

67. Mitchell to Secretary of War, March 30, 1817, *ASPMA*, 1:683.

68. Mitchell to Rabun, March 31, 1817, TCC, UGA-H, SNAD.

69. *Savannah Republican*, Savannah, GA, March 6, 1817; *Augusta Herald*, Augusta, GA, March 11, 1814; *Augusta Chronicle*, Augusta, GA, March 12, 1817.

70. *Georgia Journal*, Milledgeville, GA, March 25, 1817; see April 1, 1817.

71. Quote from *Weekly Raleigh Register*, Raleigh, NC, April 11, 1817; *Charleston Daily Courier*, Charleston, SC, April 2, 1817; *Niles Weekly Register*, Baltimore, MD, July 26, 1817; *North-Carolina Star*, Raleigh, NC, April 18, 1817.

72. Edward F. Tattnall to Rabun, March 20, 1817, TCC, UGA-H, SNAD.

73. *Georgia Journal*, Milledgeville, GA, June 24, 1817.

74. *Augusta Chronicle*, Augusta, GA, April 16, 1817; *Georgia Journal*, Milledgeville, GA, June 24, 1817.

75. Rabun to Mitchell, June 18, 1817, Keith M. Read collection, UGA-H, SNAD.

76. Leftwich to Gaines, July 28, 1817, *ASPMA*, 1:684; Boyd, "Events at Prospect Bluff," 84.

77. April J. Buffington, "Creek/Seminole Archeology in the Apalachicola River Valley, Northwest Florida," MA thesis, University of South Florida, 2009, 46 and 49; John T. Ellisor, *The Second Creek War: Interethnic Conflict and Collusion on a Collapsing*

Frontier (Lincoln: University of Nebraska Press, 2010), 32; Covington, *Seminoles of Florida*, 41–42; Gaines to Jackson, November 21, 1817, *ASPMA*, 1:686.

78. James Hendry Miller Jr., "Fowltown and the First Seminole War: 'Civilization,' Centralization, and Politics in the Early American Republic," MA thesis, Florida State University, 2011, 40–41; General Gaines to the Governor of Georgia, December 24, 1817, *Georgia Journal*, Milledgeville, GA, December 16, 1817.

79. *Georgia Journal*, Milledgeville, GA, December 16, 1817; and *The Reflector*, Milledgeville, GA, December 16, 1817; *Savannah Republican*, Savannah, GA, December 16, 1817; *Augusta Herald*, Augusta, GA, Dec. 16, 1817; *Augusta Chronicle*, Augusta, GA, December 17, 1817.

80. *Carolina Federal Republican*, New Bern, NC, February 14, 1818; *Raleigh Minerva*, Raleigh, NC, December 26, 1817; *Weekly Raleigh Register*, Raleigh, NC, December 26, 1817; *North Carolina Star*, Raleigh, NC, December 26, 1817.

81. *Clarion and Tennessee State Gazette*, December 30, 1817; *National Banner and Nashville Whig*, Nashville, TN, January 5, 1818; *Charleston Daily Courier*, Charleston, SC, December 18, 1817; *Louisiana State Gazette*, New Orleans, LA, December 16, 1817; *Natchez Gazette*, Natchez, MS, January 18, 1818; *Huntsville Republican*, Huntsville, AL, January 6, 1818.

82. *Savannah Republican*, Savannah, GA, December 17, 1817.

83. *Charleston Dailey Courier*, Charleston, SC, December 20, 1817.

84. *Lancaster Intelligencer*, Lancaster, PA, January 3, 1818; *Pittsburgh Weekly*, Pittsburgh, PA, January 6, 1818; *Weekly Franklin Repository*, Chambersburg, PA, January 6, 1818.

85. Calhoun to Jackson, December 26, 1817, *ASPMA*, 1:690; John K. Mahon, "The First Seminole War, November 21, 1817–May 24, 1818," *Florida Historical Quarterly* 77, no. 1 (Summer 1998): 62–67, 64.

86. On Kentucky Volunteers, see *York Gazette*, York, PA, February 26, 1818.

87. *Savannah Republican*, Savannah, GA, February 11, 1818.

88. On Jackson's desire to seek out Red Sticks leaders, see J. M. Opal, *Avenging the People: Andrew Jackson, The Rule of Law, and the American Nation* (New York: Oxford University Press, 2017), 163.

89. *Weekly Register*, Baltimore, MD, February 28, 1818.

90. Jackson to Robert Henry Dyer et al., January 11, 1818, *Papers of Andrew Jackson, 1816–1820*, ed. Harold Moser, David R. Hoth, and George H. Hoemann (Knoxville: University of Tennessee Press, 1994): 4:168–69, quote on 168.

91. *Weekly Register*, Baltimore, MD, February 28, 1818.

92. *The Reflector*, Milledgeville, GA, March 3, 1818; *Georgia Journal*, Milledgeville, GA, March 3, 1818; *North Carolina Star*, Raleigh, NC, February 27, 1818.

93. *Weekly Register*, Baltimore, MD, February 28, 1818; *National Register*, Washington City, February 28, 1818.

94. William Wragg Smith, *Sketch of the Seminole War and Sketches during the Campaign, by a Lieutenant of the Left Wing* (Charleston: Dan J. Dowling, 1836), 25.

95. Jackson to Calhoun, April 8, 1818, *British and Foreign State Papers, 1818–1819*, (London: J. Harrison and Son, Printers to the Foreign Office, 1835), 6:409–10, 410.

96. Jackson to Calhoun, Fort St. Marks, April 20, 1818, *ASPMA*, 1:701.

97. Mahon, "The First Seminole War," 66; Remini, *Jackson and His Indian Wars*, 157; Jose Mazot to General Jackson, May 23, 1818, *British and Foreign State Papers,*

1818–1819, 6: 392; *Weekly Register*, July 11, 1818, 14:334; see also depositions from J. C. Bronaugh and Richard K. Call in Abner Lacock, *Prosecution of War against Seminole Indians, and Occupation of East Florida by United States' Troops*, 15th Cong., 2nd sess., 1819, S. Doc 100, 42–43.

98. Mahon, "First Seminole War," 67; Paul E. Hoffman, *Florida's Frontiers* (Bloomington: Indiana University Press, 2002), 279–81.

99. Peter B. Cook to Elizabeth A. Carney, January 19, 1818, *ASPFR*, 4:605.

100. Rosen, *Border Law*, 132–. For the congressional debate on the legality of Andrew Jackson's actions, see Opal, *Avenging the People*, 164–71.

101. John Lee Williams, *A View of West Florida*, a facsimile reproduction of the 1827, ed. and intro. Herbert J. Doherty, Jr. (Gainesville: University Presses of Florida, 1976), 76; for a similar assessment by a contemporary chronicler, see William Hayne Simmons, *Notices of East Florida, a Facsimile Reproduction of the 1822 Edition*, intro. and index by George E. Buker (Gainesville: University of Florida Press, 1973), 73.

102. Jackson, April 2, 1818, *ASPMA*, 1:699–700; McIntosh to Mitchell, April 13, 1818, TCC, SNAD; Woodward to John Banks, June 16, 1858, in Woodward, *Reminiscences of the Creek, or Muscogee Indians*, 51–57, 55; Joe Knetsch, *Florida's Seminole Wars: 1817–1858* (Charleston: Arcadia, 2003), 33.

103. *Savannah Republican*, Savannah, GA, January 15, 1818; *The Reflector*, Milledgeville, GA, January 20, 1818.

104. *Georgia Journal*, Milledgeville, GA, February 24 and March 3, 1818; *The Reflector*, Milledgeville, GA, February 10, 1818; *Savannah Republican*, Savannah, GA, February 26, 1818.

105. *Savannah Republican*, Savannah, GA, February 26, 1818; *Georgia Journal*, Milledgeville, GA, March 10, 1818; *The Reflector*, Milledgeville, GA, March 10, 1818.

106. *Knoxville Register*, Knoxville, TN, February 3, 1818; *Charleston Daily Courier*, Charleston, SC, March 2 and 13, 1818; *North Carolina Star*, Raleigh, NC, March 6, 1818.

107. *Daily Sun*, Columbus, GA, July 13, 1858; *Wire Grass Reporter*, Thomasville, GA, November 10, 1858.

108. Woodward, *Reminiscences of the Creek, or Muscogee Indians*, 56.

109. Lucian Lamar Knight, *Georgia's Landmarks, Memorials and Legends*, vol. 2 (Atlanta: Byrd Printing, 1914), 329.

110. For examples, see "The Nelson Monument" in Calhoun, the "Tomb of Hon. Wiley Thompson," in Elberton, and the "Herod Town Memorial," near Dawson; see Knight, *Georgia's Landmarks, Memorials and Legends*, 2: 726–27, 771, 989–91.

111. *Americus Weekly Recorder*, Americus, GA, October 19, 1888.

112. *Atlanta Constitution*, Atlanta, GA, November 16, 1913.

113. *Americus Weekly Recorder*, Americus, GA, October 19, 1888.

114. *Walker County Messenger*, LaFayette, GA, December 6, 1912.

115. Knight, *Georgia's Landmarks, Memorials and Legends*, 2: 990.

116. *Atlanta Constitution*, Atlanta, GA, November 16, 1913.

117. Herod Town Memorial, Historical Marker Database, web, accessed May 29, 2021.

118. Knight, *Georgia's Landmarks, Memorials and Legends*, 2: 991.

119. Jackson to Gaines, April 8, 1816, 15th Cong., 2nd sess. (1819), H. Doc. 122.

Chapter 5

1. US Congress, *An Act to Provide for an Exchange of Lands with the Indians Residing in Any of the States or Territories, and for Their Removal West of the River Mississippi, 21st Congress, 1st Session (May 28, 1830), Statutes at Large*, vol. 4 (1846): 411–12.

2. "Treaty with the Seminole, 1832," *Indian Affairs: Laws and Treaties*, comp. and ed. Charles J. Kappler (Washington, DC: Government Printing Office, 1904), 2: 344–45.

3. On the variety of Native ethnicities in Florida circa the Treaty of Payne's Landing, see Edwin C. McReynolds, *The Seminoles* (Norman: University of Oklahoma Press, 1957), 95–97; Wright Jr., *Creeks and Seminoles*, 217–19; Weisman, *Unconquered People*, 5–29, 80–83. On the contemporary awareness of ethnic diversity among the Florida Indians, see John T. Sprague, *The Origins, Progress and Conclusion of the Florida War* (New York: D. Appleton, 1848), reproduction by Seminole Wars Historic Foundation, intro. John K. Mahon (Tampa: University of Tampa Press, 2000), 270; and Simmons, *Notices of East Florida*, 54–59. On Black Seminoles and maroons, see Kenneth W. Porter, *The Black Seminoles: History of a Freedom-Seeking People*, rev. and ed. Alcione M. Amos and Thomas P. Senter (Gainesville: University Press of Florida, 1996); George Klos, "Blacks and the Seminole Removal Debate, 1821–1835," *Florida Historical Quarterly* 68, vol. 1 (July 1989): 55–78; Patrick Riordan, "Finding Freedom in Florida: Native Peoples, African Americans, and Colonists, 1670–1816," *Florida Historical Quarterly* 75, no. 1 (Summer 1996): 24–43; Daniel F. Littlefield, *Africans and Seminoles: From Removal to Emancipation* (Jackson: University Press of Mississippi, 2001); Kevin Mulroy, *Seminole Freedmen: A History* (Norman: University of Oklahoma Press, 2005); Jane Landers, "Blood Seminoles and Black Seminoles on the Florida Frontier," *Coastal Encounters: The Transformation of the Gulf South in the Eighteenth Century*, ed. Richard F. Brown (Lincoln: University of Nebraska Press, 2007): 99–116; Millet, *Maroons of Prospect Bluff*; C. S. Monaco, "Whose War Was It? African American Heritage Claims and the Second Seminole War," *American Indian Quarterly* 41, vol. 1 (Winter 2017): 31–66.

4. For a closer examination of Seminole removal negotiations, see John K. Mahon, *History of the Second Seminole War, 1835–1842* (Gainesville: University of Florida Press, 1985), 69–86; for accounts of fraud and bribery during the treaty negotiations, see Claudio Saunt, *Unworthy Republic: The Dispossession of Native Americans and the Road to Indian Territory* (New York: W. W. Norton, 2020), 236–37; and Ethan Allen Hitchcock, *Fifty Years in Camp and Field: Diary of Major General Ethan Allen Hitchcock, U.S.A.*, ed. W. A. Croffut (New York: G. P. Putnam's Sons, 1909), 76–81.

5. On violent resistance to dispossession in this time frame beyond Florida, see Saunt, *Unworthy Republic*, 249–54; Ellisor, *Second Creek War*; Christopher D. Haveman, *Rivers of Sand: Creek Indian Emigration, Relocation, & Ethnic Cleansing in the American South* (Lincoln: University of Nebraska Press, 2016), 180–99. For Cherokee persistence in the Native South, see Lance Greene, *Their Determination to Remain: A Cherokee Community's Resistance to the Trail of Tears in North Carolina* (Tuscaloosa: University of Alabama Press, 2022).

6. *Charleston Daily Courier*, December 9, 1835; see also *The Georgian*, Savannah, GA, December 11, 1835; *Georgia Courier*, Albany, GA, December 11, 1835; *Southern Banner*, Athens, GA, December 17, 1835; *Daily Selma Reporter*, Selma, AL, December 19, 1835; *Richmond Enquirer*, Richmond, VA, December 22, 1835; *Newbern Spectator*, New Bern, NC, December 25, 1835; *Weekly Mississippian*, Jackson, MS, December 25, 1835. Similarly, white southerners initially criticized and sensationalized

Creek leader William McIntosh's execution in 1825 for agreeing to a Native land cession in the Treaty of Indian Springs; see Frank, *Creeks and Southerners*, 97–98.

7. The phrase "Florida Brethren" becomes prominent in the press when describing assistance to settlers in Territorial Florida by early 1836; see *The Georgian*, Savannah, GA, December 15, 1835; *Federal Union*, Milledgeville, GA, December 25, 1835; *Georgia Constitutionalist*, Augusta, GA, January 26, 1836; *Georgia Messenger*, Macon, GA, January 28, 1836; *National Banner and Nashville Whig*, Nashville, TN, February 10, 1836; *Cheraw Gazette*, Cheraw, SC, February 16, 1836; *Tarboro Press*, Tarboro, NC, February 13, 1836.

8. Carol Anna Lesesne, February 9, 1836, A Journal commenced by A. C. Lesesne, 1836, SCHS.

9. Myer M. Cohen, *Notices of Florida and the Campaigns* (Charleston: Burges & Honour, 1836), 108; portions of this chapter were previously published in F. Evan Nooe, "'Zealous in the Cause': The Second Seminole War and the Southern Consciousness," *Native South* 4 (2011): 55–81.

10. Smith, *Sketch of the Seminole War*, 13–14; *Army and Navy Chronicle*, January 21, 1836, 2:43; Woodburne Potter, *The War in Florida: Being an Exposition of Its Causes, and an Accurate History of the Campaigns of Generals, Gaines and Scott* (Baltimore: Lewis and Coleman, 1836), 111.

11. Mahon, *History of the Second Seminole War*, 104–6; Frank Laumer, *Dade's Last Command* (Gainesville: University Press of Florida, 1995).

12. Sprague, *Origins, Progress and Conclusion of the Florida War*, 106.

13. On Seminole strategy in 1835 and 1836, see Silverman, *Thundersticks*, 200–216; Samuel Watson, "Seminole Strategy, 1812–1858: A Perspective for Further Research," *America's Hundred Years' War: U.S. Expansion to the Gulf Coast and the Fate of the Seminole, 1763–1858* (Gainesville: University Press of Florida, 2011), 155–80, esp. 159–63 and 167–68; Mahon, *History of the Second Seminole War*, 102–6.

14. Sprague, *Origins, Progress and Conclusion of the Florida War*, 106.

15. Charles W. Bulow obituary, *Charleston Courier*, Charleston, SC, May 23, 1823; To the Claim of the Executor of John J. Bulow, Bulow/Bucknor Papers, 1836–1896, FHS; Ruth Danenhower Wilson, "The Bulow Plantation, 1821–1835," *Florida Historical Quarterly* 23, no. 4 (April 1945): 227–40, 233–34; Cohen, *Notices of Florida* (1836), 143.

16. John T. Sprague, *The Origins, Progress and Conclusion of the Florida War*, 106.

17. *Jacksonville Courier*, Jacksonville, FL, December 24, 1835.

18. *Pensacola Gazette*, Pensacola, FL, January 2, 1836.

19. *The Key West Inquirer*, Key West, FL, January 16, 1836; *Key West Inquirer*, Key West, FL, January 23, 1836.

20. *Greensborough Patriot*, Greensboro, NC, March 15, 1836.

21. *Southern Recorder*, Milledgeville, GA, February 23, 1836; *Macon Georgia Telegraph*, Macon, GA, February 25, 1836; *Charleston Daily Courier*, Charleston, SC, February 18, 1836; *Newbern Spectator*, New Bern, NC, February 26, 1836; *North Carolina Star*, Raleigh, NC, February 25, 1836; *National Banner and Nashville Whig*, Nashville, TN, March 7, 1836; *Richmond Enquirer*, Richmond, VA, February 27, 1836.

22. *Georgia Messenger*, Macon, GA, January 14, 1836.

23. *Charleston Mercury*, Charleston, SC, December 29, 1835.

24. *Mobile Daily Commercial Register and Patriot*, Mobile, AL, January 11, 1836, hereafter cited as *Mobile Register*.

25. *Daily Savannah Republican*, Savannah, GA, January 19, 1836; *Georgia Journal*, Milledgeville, GA, January 19, 1836; *Georgia Constitutionalist*, Augusta, GA, January 19, 1836; *Augusta Chronicle*, Augusta, GA, Jan. 23, 1836; *Charleston Daily Courier*, Charleston, SC, January 20, 1836; *Charleston Mercury*, Charleston, SC, Jan. 21, 1836; *People's Press and Wilmington Advertiser*, Wilmington, NC, January 22, 1836; *Fayetteville Weekly Observer*, Fayetteville, NC, January 28, 1836; *Farmers' Reporter*, Winston-Salem, NC, January 30, 1836; *Weekly Raleigh Register*, Raleigh, NC, January 26, 1836; *Western Carolinian*, Salisbury, NC, January 30, 1836; *Richmond Enquirer*, Richmond, VA, January 28 and 30, 1836.

26. Waselkov, *Conquering Spirit*, 212.

27. Richard K. Call to Secretary of War Lewis Cass, April 20, 1836, Governor Call letterbook, SLAF.

28. Duncan L. Clinch to the Adjutant General, November 29, 1835, *TPUS: Florida Territory, 1834–1839*, 25: 199–201.

29. General Duncan L. Clinch to Adjutant General Roger Jones, January 18, 1835, Duncan Clinch Letterbook, 1824–36 and Slave List 1859 Camden County, GA, Records of Antebellum Southern Plantations from the Revolution through the Civil War, Series C, Part 2, Reel 1, ed. Kenneth M. Stampp.

30. Henry Summer journal, February 22, 1836, USC-SCL.

31. Petition to Governor Bibb by Inhabitants of Tuscaloosa County, October 7, 1818, *TPUS: The Territory of Alabama, 1817–1819*, 18: 429–30.

32. Governor DuVal to the Secretary of War, July 29, 1824, *TPUS*, 23: 22–24; James Gadsden also wrote Secretary Calhoun encouraging the placement of US soldiers at either St. Marks or Tallahassee, see Gadsden to Calhoun, July 24, 1824, Indian Affairs, Florida Seminoles Indian Collection, UF-PKY; *Florida Intelligencer*, Tallahassee, FL, December 8, 1826.

33. Petition to the President of the United States, March 6, 1826, Indian Affairs, Florida Seminoles Collection, UF-PKY.

34. *Apalachicola Gazette*, Apalachicola, FL, May 21, 1836.

35. *Western Carolinian*, Salisbury, NC, February 6, 1836.

36. *Georgia Messenger*, Macon, GA, February 18, 1836.

37. *Georgia Messenger*, Macon, GA, March 3, 1836.

38. *Charleston Mercury*, Charleston, SC, January 19, 1836.

39. *Charleston Mercury*, Charleston, SC, January 21, 1836.

40. Smith, *Sketch of the Seminole War*, 62.

41. Mahon, *History of the Second Seminole War*, 138.

42. *Charleston Mercury*, Charleston, SC, January 1, 1836.

43. James M. Denham and Canter Brown Jr. add that some South Carolinians were motivated to action as an indirect critic against the Jackson administration over lingering contempt regarding the Nullification Crisis; see James M. Denham and Canter Brown Jr., "South Carolina Volunteers in the Second Seminole War: A Nullifier Debacle as Prelude to the Palmetto State Gubernatorial Election of 1836," *America's Hundred Years' War*, 209–36.

44. Cohen, *Notices of Florida* (1836), 107.

45. *Charleston Mercury*, Charleston, SC, December 31, 1835; Anna Carol Lesesne, A Journal commenced by A. C. Lesesne, 1836, SCHS.

46. *Charleston Mercury*, Charleston, SC, January 1, 1836.

47. W. Hampton, February 10, 1836, Hampton Family papers, USC-SCL.

48. *Charleston Mercury*, Charleston, SC, January 1, 1836.

49. *Charleston Mercury*, Charleston, SC, January 1, 1836; see also *Charleston Courier*, Charleston, SC, January 1, 1836.

50. *Charleston Courier*, Charleston, SC, January 21, 1836.

51. *Charleston Courier*, Charleston, SC, January 22, 1836.

52. *Charleston Courier*, Charleston, SC, January 23, 1836.

53. Letter to General Eustis from Secretary of War Lewis Cass, January 17, 1836, quoted in Mahon, *History of the Second Seminole War*, 138.

54. *Charleston Courier*, Charleston, SC, January 25, 1836; F. Evan Nooe, "'Renders It Necessary That We Should Be Prepared': A Reexamination of the Militant South Thesis in Territorial Florida," MA thesis, Clemson University, 2008, 84–88.

55. *Charleston Courier*, Charleston, SC, January 25, 1836; *Savannah Republican*, Savannah, GA, January 26, 1836.

56. Sprague, *Florida War*, 102.

57. *Camden Weekly Journal*, Camden, SC, February 6, 1836; see also February 13, 1836, and February 27, 1836.

58. *Camden Weekly Journal*, Camden, SC, February 22, 1836.

59. *Charleston Daily Courier*, Charleston, SC, April 1, 1835; *Charleston Daily Courier*, Charleston, SC, September 22, 1835; Cohen, Patrick, and Tyler, *Notices of Florida and the Campaigns: A Facsimile Reproduction*, xxxviii–xxxix, xii.

60. Cohen, *Notices of Florida and the Campaigns*, 5.

61. Henry Timrod scrapbook, 1836–1901, USC-SCL; *Charleston Daily Courier*, January 26, 1836; Paul H. Hayne, *The Poems of Henry Timrod* (New York: E. J. Hale & Son, 1873), 16.

62. Cohen, *Notices of Florida and the Campaigns*, 107.

63. *Charleston Mercury*, Charleston, SC, January 21, 1836; *Charleston Daily Courier*, Charleston, SC, January 25, 1836; Cohen, *Notices of Florida and the Campaigns*, 107.

64. *Charleston Daily Courier*, Charleston, SC, January 25, 1836.

65. Cohen, *Notices of Florida and the Campaigns*, 106.

66. "The Brave Volunteers," Mary Elizabeth Lee, *The Poetical Remains of the Late Mary Elizabeth Lee*, ed. Samuel Gilman (Charleston: Walker & Richards, 1851), 45–46; the poem was originally published in the *Southern Rose*; see Cohen, Patrick, and Tyler, *Notices of Florida and the Campaigns: A Facsimile Reproduction*, 106; for other poetry by Lee concerning the Seminoles in Florida, see "The Burial of Dade and His Comrades," in *The Poetical Remains of the Late Mary Elizabeth Lee*, 56–61.

67. Various South Carolina newspaper advertisements identify Charlotte Barnes as an actor and a theater promoter working in Charleston ca. 1835; see *Charleston Daily Courier*, Charleston, SC, March 7, 1835; *Charleston Mercury*, Charleston, SC, February 20, 1836.

68. Charlotte Barnes, "An Address to the Florida Volunteers, by Miss Charlotte Barnes [poem] Names of the Columbia, South Carolina, Volunteers to Florida," ca. December 1835, USC-SCL.

69. *Charleston Courier*, Charleston, SC, January 22, 1836.

70. *Charleston Courier*, Charleston, SC, January 22, 1836.

71. *North Carolina Standard*, Raleigh, NC, January 7, 1836; *Daily Savannah Republican*, Savannah, GA, December 29, 1835.

72. *Savannah Republican*, Savannah, GA, January 25, 1836.

73. *Charleston Courier*, Charleston, SC, January 22, 1836.

74. *Savannah Republican*, Savannah, GA, January 25, 1836.

75. *Charleston Courier*, Charleston, SC, January 22, 1836.

76. Mahon, *History of the Second Seminole War, 1835–1824*, 151.

77. Malcolm Henry Stern, *First American Jewish Families: 600 Genealogies, 1654–1988*, 35, 39, and 205, made available by the Jacob Rader Marcus Center of the American Jewish Archives, web, accessed February 10, 2012.

78. See Charles Reznikoff, *The Jews of Charleston, a History of an American Jewish Community* (Philadelphia: Jewish Publication Society of America, 1950); and Mark I. Greenberg, "Becoming Southern: The Jews of Savannah, Georgia, 1830–70," *American Jewish History* 86, no. 1 (March 1998): 55–75.

79. *Savannah Republican*, Savannah, GA, January 19, 1836.

80. Secretary of War Lewis Cass to Georgia Governor William Schley, January 8, 1836, *Savannah Republican*, Savannah, GA, January 21, 1836.

81. Sprague, *Florida War*, 102.

82. *Mobile Register*, Mobile, AL, January 14, 1836; for the importance of the city of Charleston to southern identity, see David Moltke-Hansen, "Southern Genesis: Regional Identity and the Rise of the 'Capital of Southern Civilization,' 1760–1780," PhD diss., University of South Carolina, 2000.

83. *Flag of the Union*, Tuscaloosa, AL, January 30, 1836.

84. *Mobile Register*, Mobile, AL, March 1, 1836.

85. *Mobile Register*, Mobile, AL, January 12, 1836.

86. *Mobile Register*, Mobile, AL, January 13, 1836.

87. *Mobile Register*, Mobile, AL, January 13 and 27, 1836.

88. *Mobile Register*, Mobile, AL, January 13 and 28, 1836.

89. *Mobile Register*, Mobile, AL, February 2, 1836.

90. Open Letter from Executive Department, Governor of Alabama Clement C. Clay, February 11, 1836, *Mobile Register*, Mobile, AL, February 20, 1836.

91. *Mobile Register*, Mobile, AL, February 2, 1836.

92. Excerpt from *Flag of the Union*, Tuscaloosa, AL, in *Mobile Register*, Mobile, AL, February 22, 1836.

93. *Mobile Register*, Mobile, AL, February 27, 1836.

94. *Flag of the Union*, Tuscaloosa, AL, February 20, 1836.

95. *Flag of the Union*, Tuscaloosa, AL, February 20, 1836.

96. A. B. Meek, "The Journal of A. B. Meek and the Second Seminole War, 1836," ed. John K. Mahon, *Florida Historical Quarterly* 38, no. 4 (1960): 302–18, 303–5.

97. *Mobile Register*, Mobile, AL, March 1, 1836.

98. *Mobile Register*, Mobile, AL, March 10, 1836; *Daily Selma Reporter*, Selma, AL, March 19, 1836.

99. *New Orleans Bee*, New Orleans, LA, January 12, 1836.

100. *New Orleans Bee*, New Orleans, LA, January 29, 1836.

101. *New Orleans Bee*, New Orleans, LA, February 4, 1836.

102. *New Orleans Bee*, New Orleans, LA, February 8, 1836; *New Orleans Bee*, New Orleans, LA, February 9, 1836.

103. *Mobile Register*, Mobile, AL, February 26, 1836.

104. *Mobile Register*, Mobile, AL, March 3, 1836.

105. Volunteers between December 20, 1835, to the end of 1839 total 16,327: 6,421 from Florida, 2,124 from South Carolina, 2,381 from Georgia, 1,112 from Louisiana, 2,244 from Alabama, and 2,045 from Tennessee; see Sprague, *Florida War*, 102.

106. Cohen, *Notices of Florida* (1836), 135, 226, 108.
107. Potter, *War in Florida*, 124.

Chapter 6

1. On the Chickamauga Towns as a separatist movement from the Cherokee, see Boulware, *Deconstructing the Cherokee Nation*, 153; for Chickamauga resistance to settler expansion, see Smithers, *Native Southerners*, 121, 128–30.

2. M[ilton]. A. H[aynes]., "Historical Traditions of Tennessee: the captivity of Jane Brown and her family, 1851 December," Edward E. Ayer Digital Collection, Newberry Library.

3. Edwin Paschall, *Old Times; or, Tennessee History, for Boys and Girls* (Nashville: Southern Methodist Publishing House, 1869), 214–17; see also M.A.H., "Historical Traditions of Tennessee," *American Whig Review* 9, no. 15 (New York: John A. Gray Printer, 1852), 235–49; A. W. Putnam, *History of Middle Tennessee: or, Life and Times of Gen. James Robertson* (Nashville: Southern Methodist Publishing House, 1859), 304–9; and Elizabeth Ellet, *Pioneer Women of the West* (New York: Charles Scribner, 1856), 79–106. Into the twentieth century, Duane H. King cites at least half a dozen local histories retelling the Brown captivity narrative; see Duane H. King, "Captivity Narrative: Joseph Brown," *Journal of Cherokee Studies* 2, no. 2 (1977): 208–29, 218.

4. On Chickamauga adoption practices and the Browns' incursion into a war zone, see Natalie Inman, *Brothers and Friends: Kinship in Early America* (Athens: University of Georgia Press, 2020), 1–2, 66–67.

5. James Ramsey, *The Annals of Tennessee to the End of the Eighteenth Century* (Charleston: John Russell, 1853), 509–10. For a critique on Ramsey as romanticizing the Anglo-American colonization of Tennessee, see Kevin T. Barksdale and Kristofer Ray, "Searching for John Sevier: Myth, Memory, and the History of Early Tennessee History," *Before the Volunteer State: New Thoughts on Early Tennessee, 1540–1800*, ed. Kristofer Ray (Knoxville: University of Tennessee Press, 2015): 201–15, 205–7.

6. Ramsey, *Annals of Tennessee*, 509.

7. Richard Beard, *Brief Biographical Sketches of Some of the Early Ministers of the Cumberland Presbyterian Church*, 2nd ser. (Nashville: Cumberland Presbyterian Board of Publication, 1874), 218–20.

8. For a similar process framed as "forgetting," in the Ohio Valley, see Elizabeth Perkins, *Border Life: Experience and Memory in the Revolutionary Ohio Valley* (Chapel Hill: University of North Carolina Press, 1998), 173–75.

9. On the veneration of prior generations and traditions of family record keeping, both oral and written, in the nineteenth-century South, see Orville Vernon Burton, *In My Father's House Are Many Mansions: Family and Community in Edgefield, South Carolina* (Chapel Hill: University of North Carolina Press, 1985), 325; Bertram Wyatt-Brown, *Southern Honor*, 45; Andrew Jr., *Wade Hampton*, 6–7.

10. On narratives as tools of colonialism, see Veracini, *Settler Colonialism*, 41–43, 96–104. On settler colonialism influencing historical neglect of accounting for Native influences on the South, see Hudson, "Unsettling Histories of the South," 32–33, 35–36.

11. On "vicarious traumatization," see Doukessa Lerias and Mitchell K. Byrne, "Vicarious Traumatization: Symptoms and Predictors," *Stress and Health* 19 (2003): 129–38; on intergenerational transmission of trauma within families, see Rachel Lev-Wiesel, "Intergenerational Transmission of Trauma across Three Generations,"

Qualitative Social Work 6, no. 1 (2007): 75–94; on the agency of family memory and the transmission of trauma, see Carol A. Kidron, "Survivor Family Memory Work at Sites of Holocaust Remembrance: Institutional Enlistment of Family Agency?" *History and Memory* 27, no. 2 (2015): 45–73, esp. 65–67; on how children and grandchildren romanticize the contemporary experiences of their ancestors' shared family memories through negotiation, re-creation, bias, and selective remembrances, see Karoline Tschuggnail and Harald Welzer, "Rewriting Memories: Family Recollections of the National Socialist Past in Germany," *Culture & Psychology* 8, no. 1 (2002): 130–45, esp. 141–42.

12. On crafting intergenerational memories as a tool of colonialism during the nineteenth century, see James Joseph Buss, *Winning the West with Words: Language and Conquest in the Lower Great Lakes* (Norman: University of Oklahoma Press, 2011), 172–83; Perkins, *Border Life*, 170–73; Jacoby, *Shadows at Dawn*, 234–44. For a critique on the lack of scholarly investigation into memorialization and the Native South, see Hudson, "Unsettling Histories of the South," 34. On memory and colonialism in the Native South more generally, see James Taylor Carson, "'The Obituary of Nations': Ethnic Cleansing, Memory, and the Origins of the Old South," *Southern Cultures* 14, no. 4 (Winter 2008): 6–31. On memory and Cherokee removal, see Denson, *Monuments to Absence*.

13. *Charleston Daily Courier*, Charleston, SC, August 12, 1836.

14. C. B. Stewart Journal, 1836–1839, USC-SCL.

15. Mahon, *History of the Second Seminole War*, 143.

16. Journal of the Volunteer Company from Columbia [S.C.], Benjamin T. Elmore, Captain, February 11–May 12, 1836, Second Seminole War (1835–1842), SCDAH.

17. Smith, *Sketch of the Seminole War*, 288.

18. Solomon C. Hargrove Journal, 50th Day, Thursday, 31st March, USC-SCL; Mahon, *History of the Second Seminole War*, 156–57.

19. John Belton O'Neill and John A. Chapman, *The Annals of Newberry in Two Parts* (Newberry, SC: Aull & Houseal, 1892), 453–54.

20. John Summer to Henry Summer, April 23, 1836, John Summer to Henry Summer, May 13, 1836, Augustus Steele to Henry Summer, June 17, 1836, Henry Summer papers, USC-SCL; Henry Prince, *Amidst a Storm of Bullets: The Diary of Lt. Henry Prince in Florida, 1836–1842*, ed. Frank Laumer, foreword John K. Mahon (Tampa: University of Tampa Press, 1998), 52–53.

21. Solomon C. Hargrove Journal, USC-SCL; on the prevalence of disease, see Order No. 23, April 9, 1836, S. Doc. 224, 304–5; John Chesnut to Mrs. Chesnut, April 21, 1836, James Chesnut (1773–1866) papers, USC-SCL. On disease among soldiers during the Second Seminole War, see C. S. Monaco, "Shadows and Pestilence: Health and Medicine during the Second Seminole War," *Journal of Social History* 48, no. 3 (2015): 565–88, esp. 567–72.

22. Augustus Steele to Henry Summer, June 17, 1836, Henry Summer papers, USC-SCL; Prince, *Amidst a Storm of Bullets*, 53.

23. Sir Robert Pratt to John Summer, June 25, 1836, Henry Summer papers, USC-SCL.

24. Memorial of the Summer Brothers, Henry Summer papers, USC-SCL.

25. Thomas J. Kirkland and Robert M. Kennedy, *Historic Camden: Part One Colonial and Revolutionary* (Columbia: State Company, 1905), 20–22.

26. *Camden Weekly Journal*, Camden, SC, June 18, 1836; Augusta, GA, held a

similar event honoring the Florida volunteers; see *National Banner and Nashville Whig*, Nashville, TN, June 15, 1836.

27. *Charleston Mercury*, Charleston, SC, July 18, 1836.

28. *Charleston Daily Courier*, Charleston, SC, September 7, 1836.

29. *Vicksburg Whig*, Vicksburg, MS, October 20, 1836.

30. Cohen, *Notices of Florida and the Campaigns* (1836); Smith, *Sketch of the Seminole War*.

31. Meek, *Romantic Passages*.

32. David J. Weber, "The Spanish Legacy in North America and the Historical Imagination," *Western Historical Quarterly* 23, no. 1 (1992): 5–24, 6–8; Benjamin Keen, "The Black Legend Revisited: Assumptions and Realities," *Hispanic American Historical Review* 49, no. 4 (1969): 703–19.

33. Weber, "Spanish Legacy in North America and the Historical Imagination," 8.

34. Cohen, *Notices of Florida* (1836), 10.

35. Alvar Nunez Cabeza de Vaca, *The Narrative of Cabeza de Vaca*, ed., trans., and intro. Rolena Adorno and Patrick Charles Pautz (Lincoln: University of Nebraska Press, 2003), 103; Paul E. Hoffman, *Florida's Frontiers* (Bloomington: Indiana University Press, 2002), 29–31.

36. Cohen, *Notices of Florida* (1836), 12.

37. On Hernando De Soto's role as an agent of colonialism and contributing to the transformation of Indigenous communities in the American South, see Smithers, *Native Southerners*, 50; Charles Hudson, "Introduction," *The Transformation of the Southeastern Indians, 1540–1760*, ed. Robbie Ethridge and Charles Hudson (Jackson: University Press of Mississippi, 2002): xi–xxxix; Charles Hudson, "Hernando do Soto Expedition, 1539–1543," *The Forgotten Centuries: Indians and Europeans in the American South, 1521–1704*, ed. Charles Hudson and Carmen Chaves Tesser, 74–103 (Athens: University of Georgia Press, 1994).

38. Cohen, *Notices of Florida* (1836), 12.

39. Cohen, *Notices of Florida* (1836), 15.

40. Meek, *Romantic Passages*, 216.

41. Cohen, *Notices of Florida* (1836), 14.

42. Smith, *Sketch of the Seminole War* (1835), 117.

43. Smith, *Sketch of the Seminole War* (1835), 118.

44. Meek, *Romantic Passages*, 219; A. B. Meek, "Journal of A. B. Meek and the Second Seminole War, 1836."

45. Meek, *Romantic Passages*, 219.

46. Anthropologist Jerald T. Milanich posits that the De Soto expedition met at least three distinct Native groups while in Florida known as the Uzita, Apalachee, and Mocoso; see *Florida Indians and the Invasion from Europe* (Gainesville: University Press of Florida, 1995), 129; David Silverman finds a similar experience shaping colonial Euro-Americans' perception of New England Indians; see *Faith and Boundaries: Colonists, Christianity, and Community among the Wampanoag Indians of Martha's Vineyard, 1600–1871* (New York: Cambridge University Press, 2005), 119.

47. Smith, *Sketch of the Seminole War*, 159.

48. For contemporary historical examinations on the 1564 massacre of the French, see James Grant Forbes, *Sketches, Historical and Topographical, of the Floridas; More Particular of East Florida* (New York: C. S. Van Winkle, 1821), 12; Cohen, *Notices of Florida* (1836), 16.

49. Smith, *Sketch of the Seminole War*, 78.

50. Cohen, *Notices of Florida* (1836), 32.

51. Cohen, *Notices of Florida* (1836), 32.

52. Smith, *Sketch of the Seminole War*, 25.

53. Joseph M. White, "Removal of the Florida Indians," June 3, 1836, *Congressional Globe*, House of Representatives, 24th Congress, 1st Session, 431.

54. *National Banner and Nashville Whig*, Nashville, TN, July 6, 1836.

55. Brent R. Weisman, "Archeological Perspectives on Florida Seminole Ethnogenesis," in *Indians of the Greater Southeast: Historical Archeology and Ethnohistory*, ed. Bonnie G. McEwan (Gainesville: University Press of Florida, 2000): 299–317, 302–3; Sturtevant, "Creek into Seminole," 101.

56. Smith, *Sketch of the Seminole War*, 25.

57. Cohen, *Notices of Florida* (1836), 33.

58. Jane's husband is at times referred to as either Clement or Flemming. Most newspaper reports on Jane do not name her husband; Welch identifies him as Clement; see *A Narrative of the Life and Sufferings of Mrs. Jane Johns*, 9. Alternatively, he is referred as "Flemming Johns," by a relative; see Francis Calvin Morgan Boggess, *A Veteran of Four Wars: The Autobiography of F. C. C. Boggess. A Record of Pioneer Life and Adventure, and Heretofore Unwritten History of the Florida Seminole Indian Wars* (Arcadia: Champion Rooms, 1900), 20, FHS.

59. Captain N. S. Jarvis of the US Army claims Wild Cat boasted of his involvement in the attack against Jane Johns; see "An Army Surgeon's Notes of Frontier Service, 1833–48," *Journal of the Military Service Institution of the United States* 39, no. 143 (September–October 1906): 275–86, 277.

60. On the historiographical and cultural significance of scalping, see James Axtell and William C. Sturtevant, "The Unkindest Cut, or Who Invented Scalping," *William and Mary Quarterly* 37, no. 3 (July 1980): 451–72.

61. Andrew Welch, *A Narrative of the Life and Sufferings of Mrs. Jane Johns, Who Was Barbarously Wounded and Scalped by Seminole Indians, in East Florida* (Charleston: Burke & Giles, 1837), reprinted in *A Narrative of the Early Days and Remembrances of Oceola Nikkanochee, Prince of Econchatti, Written by His Guardian: Facsimile Reproduction of the 1841 Edition, and of the Pamphlets of 1837 and 1847*, intro. and indexes by Frank Laumer, (Gainesville: University Presses of Florida, 1977).

62. For similar examples of found homesteads raided by Native Americans and the disbursement of retellings by those making the discovery, see the 1812 Duck River raid in Tennessee, "The Committee of Claims, to which was presented the petition of Jesse Manley," 23rd Cong., 1st sess. (April 9, 1834), H.rp. 402; The Cache River raid near the confluence of the Ohio and Cache Rivers along Kentucky's western border February 1813, "Extract of a letter from the Post Master of New Madrid," *Missouri Gazette*, St. Louis, February 20, 1813; and "Extract of a letter from a gentleman at Kaskaskia, dated February 27," *Weekly Register*, April 24, 1813, 4:135; and the destruction of the Hampton homestead in May 1775, "Revolutionary Incidents," Hampton Family papers, USC-SCL.

63. Quote from *Daily Georgian*, Savannah, GA, September 27, 1836; Boggess, *Veteran of Four Wars*, 22.

64. *Daily Georgian*, Savannah, GA, September 27, 1836.

65. For an example of how accounts of Native violence against white settlers moved among travelers along roadways during the early nineteenth century, see

Burckard and Petersen, "Partners in the Lord's Work," 72–73; for a comprehensive examination of communication in the colonial South, see Dubcovsky, *Informed Power*; on the spread on rumors as a result of Indian violence, see Gregory Evans Dowd, *Groundless: Rumors, Legends, and Hoaxes on the Early American Frontier* (Baltimore: Johns Hopkins University Press, 2015), esp. 83–85.

66. Welch, *Narrative of the Life and Sufferings of Mrs. Jane Johns*, 9–11.

67. For examples of white southerners transmitting accounts of Native violence through personal correspondence, see Edmund Bacon to Mama, September 1, 1811, Edmund Bacon to Agnes Pannill, July 19, 1812, Bacon (Edmund) Letters; Theodor Maltby to George Maltby, October 14, 1841, Edward Clifton Wharton Family Papers, LSU-LLMVC; George L. Brown to Mannevillette E. D. Brown, January 7, 1843, *The Letters of George Long Brown: A Yankee Merchant on Florida's Antebellum Frontier*, ed. James M. Denham and Keith L. Huneycutt (Gainesville: University Press of Florida, 2019), 55–58; Ellen Brown to Mannevillette Brown, January 10, 1836, *Echoes from a Distant Frontier: The Brown Sisters' Correspondence from Antebellum Florida* (Columbia: University of South Carolina Press, 2004), 19–21.

68. Mary A. Favert notes on the propensity for war (and by extension violence) fought beyond the purview of individuals to increase the "desire and mass consumption of print news"; see *War at a Distance: Romanticism and the Making of Modern Wartime* (Princeton: Princeton University Press, 2010); on newspapers providing a connecting experience, see Benedict Anderson, *Imagined Communities: Reflections on the Origins and Spread of Nationalism* (New York: Verso, 2006), 35.

69. *Charleston Mercury*, Charleston, SC, September 24 and 26, 1836.

70. *Daily Georgian*, Savannah, GA, September 27, 1836.

71. *Daily Georgian*, Savannah, GA, October 3, 1836.

72. *Columbus Enquirer*, Columbus, GA, November 17, 1836; *Macon Georgia Telegraph*, November 17, 1836.

73. *Biblical Recorder*, Raleigh, NC, November 23, 1836; *Newbern Spectator*, New Bern, NC, October 14, 1836; and *Charlotte Journal*, Charlotte, NC, November 25, 1836; see also *Fayetteville Weekly Observer*, Fayetteville, NC, March 30, 1837.

74. *Richmond Enquirer*, Richmond, VA, November 18, 1836; *Alexandria Gazette*, Washington, DC, November 23, 1836; and *Niles' Weekly Register*, Baltimore, MD, October 1, 1836.

75. *Daily Georgian*, Savannah, GA, February 16, 1837; *Charleston Courier*, Charleston, SC, March 21, 1837.

76. The captivity account of Eunice Barber offers an instructive parallel. Daniel E. Williams argues Barber was likely a fabrication to justify the international, ethical, and moral lines Andrew Jackson crossed in the First Seminole War, *Liberty's Captives: Narratives of Confinement in the Print Culture of the Early Republic* (Athens: University of Georgia Press, 2006), 300; Eunice Barber, *Narrative of the Tragical Death of Mr. Darius Barber and His Seven Children Who Were Inhumanly Butchered by the Indians, in Camden County, Georgia, January 26th, 1818* (Boston: David Hazen, 1818).

77. Frank Laumer, "Introduction," in *A Narrative of the Early Days and Remembrances of Oceola Nikkanochee*, xxi.

78. *Charleston Courier*, Charleston, SC, March 28, 1837; *Daily Georgian*, Savannah, GA, March 28, 1837.

79. *Charleston Courier*, Charleston, SC, May 1, 1837.

80. Welch, *Narrative of the Life and Sufferings of Mrs. Jane Johns*, 11; Shire, *Threshold of Manifest Destiny*, 62–63, 92.

81. *Jacksonville Courier*, quoted in Welch, *Narrative of the Life and Sufferings of Mrs. Jane Johns*, 25–26.

82. Welch, *Narrative of the Life and Sufferings of Mrs. Jane Johns*, 11.

83. Eric Gary Anderson, notes the grotesque accounts against Jane aimed at depicting "local Indians as gangs of all-consuming homicidal psychopaths who need to be removed"; see "On Native Ground: Indigenous Countercolonial Strategies in Southern Narratives of Captivity, Removal, and Repossession," *Southern* Spaces, August 9, 2007; similarly, Laurel Clark Shire assesses Welch's publication as employing descriptions of wanton destruction as colonizing narratives to differentiate between whites and Native Americans in the settlement of Florida; see *Threshold of Manifest Destiny*, 84, 91–94.

84. Welch, *Narrative of the Life and Sufferings of Mrs. Jane Johns*, 7.

85. Welch, *Narrative of the Life and Sufferings of Mrs. Jane Johns*, 8, 9.

86. Welch, *Narrative of the Life and Sufferings of Mrs. Jane Johns*, 12; *Macon Georgia Telegraph*, Macon, Georgia, November 17, 1836; *Columbus Enquirer*, Columbus, Georgia, November 17, 1836.

87. Perkins, *Border Life*, 173–75.

88. O'Neill and Chapman, *Annals of Newberry*, 453–54.

89. Boggess, *Veteran of Four Wars*, 1, 38. For a similar serialized account in Lake City, Florida's *The Florida Index*, see George Gillett Keen's 1899 reminiscences, *Cracker Times and Pioneer Lives: The Florida Reminiscences of George Gillett Keen and Sarah Pamela Williams*, ed. James M. Denham and Canter Brown Jr. (Columbia: University of South Carolina Press, 2000), esp. 29–35, 37–40.

90. Boggess, *Veteran of Four Wars*, 22. On the white settlement of southwest Florida, see Canter Brown Jr. *Florida's Peace River Frontier* (Orlando: University of Central Florida Press, 1991).

91. D. B. McKay, *Tampa Tribune*, Tampa, FL, December 21, 1947; D. B. McKay, *Tampa Tribune*, Tampa, FL, October 22, 1950.

92. For "Sarah Mathis," see D. B. McKay, *Tampa Tribune*, Tampa, FL, October 22, 1950; for Georgia Falany quote, see D. B. McKay, *Tampa Tribune*, Tampa, FL, November 5, 1950.

93. Luke Wilson, *DeSoto County Times*, Arcadia, FL, February 2, 1985, DeSoto County Historical Society, Arcadia, Florida.

94. For examples, see *Herald Advocate*, Hardee County, FL, June 1, 1989; Roger Williams, *Florida Weekly*, Naples, FL, June 16, 2011; Carol Mahler, *The Arcadian*, Arcadia, FL, May 16, 2019.

95. Williams, *Florida Weekly*, June 16, 2011.

Chapter 7

1. Edward E. Baptist, *Creating an Old South: Middle Florida's Plantation Frontier before the Civil War* (Chapel Hill: University of North Carolina Press), 29, 46–48.

2. Everett W. Caudle, "Settlement Patterns in Alachua County, Florida, 1850–1860," *Florida Historical Quarterly* 67, no. 4 (April 1989): 428–40, 433–34.

3. Theodor Maltby to George Maltby, October 14, 1841, Edward Clifton Wharton Family Papers, LSU-LLMVC.

4. Theodor to George Maltby, October 14, 1841, LSU-LLMVC.

5. Charles L. Kieffer, *Maligned General: A Biography of Thomas S. Jesup* (San Rafael: Presidio Press, 1979), 185–90.

6. Mahon, *History of the Second Seminole War*, 321–22.

7. Saunt, *Unworthy Republic*, 292–93; Sprague, *Florida War*, 106.

8. *Key West Inquirer*, Key West, FL, May 7, 1836.

9. Richard K. Call to Lewis Call, April 20, 1836, Richard K. Call to Lewis Cass, April 22, 1836, Governor Call letterbook April 19, 1836–September 18, 1836, Territorial and State Governors letterbooks, 1836–1909, SLAF; for an extended account of the correspondence between Call and Cass, see 26th Cong., 1st sess. (1840), S. Doc. 278; Governor Call's First Message to the Legislative Council of Florida, R. K. Call Papers, *FHS*.

10. Silverman, *Thundersticks*, 210–11; Richard K. Call to Lewis Cass, May 4, 1836, Call to Commanding Officer at Tampa Bay, May 6, 1836, Governor Call letterbook April 19, 1836–September 18, 1836, Territorial and State Governors letterbooks, 1836–1909, SLAF; Call to Colonel Davenport, March 11, 1839, Call to George H. Griffin, March 24, 1839, Call to Colonel Davenport, July 17, 1839, William Davenport Papers, UF-PKY.

11. Mahon, *History of the Second Seminole War*, 168–89.

12. Doherty Jr., *Richard Keith Call*, 115–17.

13. Daniel H. Wiggins diary, SLAF.

14. Franklin, *Militant South*, 27.

15. Thomas Hart Benton, *Thirty Years' View* (New York: D. Appleton, 1856), 167–69.

16. *Caledonian*, St. Johnsbury, VT, February 25, 1840.

17. *Caledonian*, St. Johnsbury, VT, February 25, 1840.

18. Speech of Mr. Strange of North Carolina, January 10, 1840, *Congressional Globe*, Senate, 26th Congress, 1st Session, 78.

19. Speech of Mr. Strange, *Congressional Globe*, 79.

20. Speech of Mr. Strange, *Congressional Globe*, 79.

21. *Florida Herald and Southern Democrat*, June 15, 1843; James W. Covington, "The Armed Occupation Act of 1842," *Florida Historical Quarterly* 40, no. 1 (July 1961): 41–52, 46.

22. Letter of Jeremiah Dodson, June 14, 1843, quoted in Covington, "The Armed Occupation Act of 1842," 47.

23. Mahon, *History of the Second Seminole War*, 313–14.

24. David Levy, June 13, 1842, *Congressional Globe*, House of Representatives, 27th Congress, 2nd sess., 499.

25. *Florida Herald and Southern Democrat*, St. Augustine, FL, May 19, 1842, in *Congressional Globe*, Senate, 27th Congress, 2nd sess., 618; *Savannah Daily Republican*, Savannah, GA, June 1, 1842; *Charleston Daily Courier*, June 3, 1842; *Edgefield Advertiser*, Edgefield, SC, June 8, 1842; *Fayetteville Weekly Observer*, Fayetteville, NC, June 8, 1842; *News & Planters' Gazette*, June 9, 1842, Washington, GA.

26. Levy, June 13, 1842, *Congressional Globe*, 502–3.

27. Levy, June 13, 1842, *Congressional Globe*, 503.

28. Gary Clayton Anderson, *The Conquest of Texas: Ethnic Cleansing in the Promised Land, 1812–1875* (Norman: University of Oklahoma Press, 2005), 172–74.

29. Mirabeau B. Lamar, "Message of the President," December 21, 1838, *The*

Papers of Mirabeau B. Lamar, ed. Charles A. Gulick Jr. and Katherine Elliot (Austin: A. C. Baldwin and Sons Printers, 1922), 2:346–79, 352–53.

30. Gregory D. Smithers, *The Cherokee Diaspora: An Indigenous History of Migration, Resettlement, and Identity* (New Haven: Yale University Press, 2015), 54–55.

31. Anderson, *Conquest of Texas*, 178–79.

32. Doherty, *Richard Keith Call*, 146–61; on public recognition of Call's love for the Union, see *Floridian and Journal*, Tallahassee, FL, December 3, 1859; on Call's political identity as "an old line Whig" and "opposed to secession," see *Floridian and Journal*, Tallahassee, FL, September 1, 1860.

33. Call initially claimed under no circumstances would he fight against the Union; see Doherty, *Richard Keith Call*, 158.

34. Richard K. Call, *Union, Slavery Secession: Letter from Governor R. K. Call, of Florida, to John S. Littell, of Germantown, Pennsylvania* (Philadelphia: C. Sherman & Son, Printers, 1861), 3; Ellen Call Long, *Florida Breezes; or, Florida, New and Old*, intro. Margaret Louise Chapman, reproduction of 1883 ed. (Gainesville: University of Florida Press, 1962), 308, 311, 335; Call Journal, HS.

35. Richard Keith Call to Thomas J. Perkins, March 19, 1862, Richard K Call Correspondence, Miscellaneous Manuscript Collection, UF-PKY.

36. Call Journal, FHS.

37. Call Journal, FHS.

38. To the Tennessee Volunteers, September 24, 1813, *Democratic Clarion*, September 25, 1813, *Papers of Andrew Jackson, 1804–1813*, 2:428–29, 428.

39. Haywood, *Civil and Political History of the State of Tennessee*, 261.

40. Haywood, *Civil and Political History of the State of Tennessee*, preface.

41. William H. Haywood, "Preface to the Second Edition," *The Civil and Political History of the State of Tennessee, from Its Earliest Settlement up to the Year 1796; Including the Boundaries of the State*, John Haywood, intro. Arthur St. Clair Colyar (Nashville: Methodist Episcopal Church, 1891), 3.

42. Colyar, "Sketch of the Author," in John Haywood, *The Civil and Political History of the State of Tennessee, from Its Earliest Settlement up to the Year 1796; Including the Boundaries of the State*, intro. by Arthur St. Clair Colyar (Nashville: Methodist Episcopal Church, 1891), 13.

43. Colyar, "Sketch of the Author," 9.

44. Colyar, "Sketch of the Author," 8.

45. *Niles' Weekly Register*, Baltimore, MD, November 15, 1823.

46. For Hampton III's campaign schedule, see *The Intelligencer*, Anderson, SC, August 1, 1876; on his appeal among the majority white base in the Upstate, see *Cincinnati Enquirer*, Cincinnati, OH, October 20, 1876.

47. Alfred B. Williams, *Hampton and His Red Shirts: South Carolina's Deliverance in 1876* (Charleston: Walker, Evans, and Cogswell, 1935), 89–91.

48. *Southern Home*, Charlotte, NC, September 18, 1876; *Whig and Tribune*, Jackson, TN, September 23, 1876.

49. Williams, *Hampton and His Red Shirts*, 181.

50. *Pickens Sentinel*, Pickens, SC, July 20, 1876.

51. *Yorkville Enquirer*, York, SC, September 19, 1876.

52. *Barnwell People*, Barnwell, SC, May 28, 1896.

53. William S. Morrison to J. B. O. Landrum, July 27, 1891, in Landrum, *Colonial and Revolutionary History of Upper South Carolina*, 87–89.

54. *Barnwell People*, Barnwell, SC, May 28, 1896; *Union Times*, Union, SC, June 5, 1896; Find a Grave, database and images, memorial page for Mary Earle Lyles, web, accessed November 27, 2020.

55. *Keowee Courier*, Walhalla, SC, November 27, 1901; *Lancaster Ledger*, Lancaster, SC, November 20, 1901; *Union Times*, Union, SC, December 13, 1901; *Anderson Intelligencer*, Anderson, SC, November 27, 1901; *Manning Times*, Manning, SC, December 11, 1901.

56. William S. Morrison to J. B. O. Landrum, July 27, 1891, in Landrum, *Colonial and Revolutionary History of Upper South Carolina*, 88.

57. *Greenville News*, Greenville, SC, September 9, 1929.

58. *Greenville News*, Greenville, SC, December 6, 1929.

59. *Greenville News*, Greenville, SC, September 23, 1933.

60. Edwin C. Breeden, *A Guidebook to South Carolina Historical Markers* (Columbia: University of South Carolina Press, 2021), 211.

61. "Revolutionary Incidents: The Hite Family," *The Magnolia*, August 1842.

62. *Virginia Gazette*, Williamsburg, VA, September 30, 1775; *Virginia Gazette*, Williamsburg, VA, March 24, 1774.

63. *Pennsylvania Gazette*, Philadelphia, PA, September 11, 1776.

64. *Greenville News*, Greenville, SC, December 15, 2009.

65. *Greenville News*, Greenville, SC, April 2, 1997; *Augusta Chronicle*, Augusta, GA, May 19, 1999; *Greenville News*, Greenville, SC, July 11, 2000; *Greenville News*, Greenville, SC, April 5, 2005; *Greenville News*, Greenville, SC, April 14, 2005.

66. William Bartram, *William Bartram on the Southeastern Indians*, ed. and annotated Gregory A. Waselkov and Kathryn E. Holland Braund (Lincoln: University of Nebraska Press, 1995), 75.

67. Bartram, *William Bartram on the Southeastern Indians*, 84.

68. Thomas Jefferson, *Notes on the State of Virginia* (Richmond: J. W. Randolph, 1853), 104.

69. Nicholas A. Timmerman, "Contested Indigenous Landscapes: Indian Mounds and the Political Creation of the Mythical 'Mound Builder' Race," *Ethnohistory* 67, no. 1 (January 2020): 75–96, esp. 80; Robert Silverberg, *Mound Builders of Ancient America: The Archeology of a Myth* (Greenwich: New York Graphic Society, LTD, 1968), 42–44.

70. William Gilmore Simms, "The Mountain Tramp," *An Early and Strong Sympathy: The Indian Writings of William Gilmore Simms*, ed. John Caldwell Guilds and Charles Hudson (Columbia: University of South Carolina Press, 2003): 504–72, 520.

71. Christina Snyder, "The Once and Future Moundbuilders," *Southern Cultures* 26, no. 2 (Summer 2020): 96–116, 110–11; James Mooney, *History, Myths, and Sacred Formulas of the Cherokees*, intro. George Ellison (Asheville: Bright Mountain Books, 1992), 330–32, 335–36.

72. Roger T. Grange Jr., "The I. C. Few Site," *South Carolina Institute of Archeology and Anthropology Notebook* (January/February 1971): 19–20.

73. David G. Anderson, David J. Hally, and James L. Rudolph, "The Mississippian Occupation of the Savannah River Valley," *Southeastern Archaeology* 5, vol. 1 (Summer 1986): 32–51, 35.

74. Grange Jr., "I. C. Few Site," 19.

75. In Tennessee, similar circumstance unfolded with the creation of the Tellico dam and submergence of yet another Cherokee heritage site in 1979; see Jefferson

Chapman, *Tellico Archeology: 12,000 Years of Native American History*, 3rd ed. (Knoxville: University of Tennessee Press, 2014), 12–18, 99–122.

76. New South Associates, "Keowee-Toxaway Hydroelectric Project Historic Context," Federal Energy Regulatory Commission Project No. 2503 (February 22, 2008), 43.

Epilogue

1. *Anniston Star*, Anniston, AL, November 19, 2000.

2. Call Journal, FHS.

3. Crockett, *Narrative of the Life*, 88–89.

4. *Anniston Star*, Anniston, AL, November 18, 2000.

5. In comparison, Andrew Denson details how the Eastern Band of Cherokee were able to "repatriate" the Daughters of the American Revolution memorial at Junaluska's gravesite to insert Indigenous voices in Native history; see *Monuments to Absence*, 223–24; and Kenneth Adams (Upper Mattaponi Tribe of King William County, Virginia) on the necessity to include Native community members in the four hundredth anniversary commemoration of Jamestown in 2007; see "Jamestown 2007: A Native American Perspective," *We Will Always Be Here: Native Peoples on Living and Thriving in the South*, ed. Denise E. Bates, 78–81 (Gainesville: University Press of Florida, 2016).

6. *Anniston Star*, Anniston, AL, November 3, 2013.

7. The Seminole Tribe of Florida, "History: Indian Resistance and Removal," web, accessed April 19, 2022.

8. Jean Chaudhuri and Joyotpaul Chaudburi, *A Sacred Path: The Way of the Muscogee Creeks* (Los Angeles: UCLA American Indian Studies Center, 2001), 114.

9. Interview with unnamed Seminole by Jean Chaudhuri, 1970s, Samuel Proctor Oral History Program, University of Florida, quoted in Mikaëla M. Adams, *Who Belongs: Race, Resources, and Tribal Citizenship in the Native South* (New York: Oxford University Press, 2016), 177.

10. Betty Mae Tiger Jumper and Patsy West, *A Seminole Legend: The Life of Betty Mae Tiger Jumper* (Gainesville: University Press of Florida, 2001), 4.

11. Ostler, *Surviving Genocide*, 271–72.

12. Interview with Bettie Perdue Woodall, September 20, 1937, Western History Collection, Indian-Pioneer Papers, University of Oklahoma Libraries, Norman, Oklahoma.

13. Jason Baird Jackson, *Yuchi Folklore: Cultural Expression in a Southeastern Native American Community* (Norman: University of Oklahoma Press, 2013), 3–4, 24–27; John E. Worth, "Enigmatic Origins: On the Yuchi of the Contact Era," *Yuchi Indian Histories before the Removal Era*, ed. Jason Baird Jackson, 33–42 (Lincoln: University of Nebraska Press, 2012); Haveman, *Rivers of Sand*, 187.

14. Tom Hendrix, *If the Legends Fade* (Chapel Hill: Professional Press, 2000), 7–10.

15. Jennifer Crossley Howard, "Off Alabama's Beaten Path, Tribute to a Native American's Journey Home," *New York Times*, July 22, 2014, web, accessed April 23, 2022.

16. Tom Hendrix, "Te-lah-nay's Wall," *We Will Always Be Here*, 121–23; Rheta Grimsley Johnson, "Sitting on Top of a Magic Wall," *Knoxville News-Sentinel*, Knoxville, TN, June 26, 2016.

Bibliography

Unpublished Sources

Manuscripts

Alabama Department of Archives and History, Montgomery, Alabama

Austill, Margaret Ervin. "Memories of Journeying through Creek Country and Childhood in Clarke County, 1811–1814," SPR237.

Bains, Sam. Letter. SPR542.

Caller, James. Papers. 1795–1824, SPR554.

Carson, Joseph. Letter. 1813, SPR42.

Creek War military records, SPR359.

Hearn, Ebenezer. Autobiography. SPR37.

James, Adam. Letter. 1813, SPR542.

Manac, Samuel. Deposition. SPR26.

Pickett, Albert J. Papers. LPR185.

Auburn University Libraries, Special Collections & Archives, Auburn, Alabama

Bozeman, H. B. Papers. Record Group #0012.

Clemson University Libraries, Clemson, South Carolina

Pickens, Andrew. Papers. 1780–1819.

DeSoto County Historical Society, Arcadia, Florida

DeSoto County Times.

Florida Historical Society, Cocoa Beach, Florida

Bulow/Bucknor. Papers. 1836–1896.

Call, Governor Richard K. Journal. 1861.

Call, R. K. Papers.

Indiana Historical Society Library, Indianapolis, Indiana

Northwest Territory Collection, 1721–1802, M367.

Library of Congress, Washington, DC

Manuscript Division

Jackson, Andrew. Papers. 1775–1874.

Louisiana State University, Baton Rouge, Louisiana

Hill Memorial Library.

Bacon, Edmund. Letters. Mss. 2178, LLMVC.

Jackson, Andrew. Letter. Mss. 4694, LLMVC.
Southeastern Indian Papers. Mss. 2820, LLMVC.
Edward Clifton Wharton Family Papers. Mss. 1553, 1575, 1594, 1610, 1613, 1663, 1714, 1736, LLMVC.

Mississippi Department of Archives and History, Jackson, Mississippi
WPA County Files, Mississippi Library Commission, Susie V. Powell, *Source Material for Mississippi History, Preliminary Manuscript: Marion County*, Works Project Administration, 1936–39.

National Archives and Records Administration, Washington, DC
3d Cong., House, Sec War Confidential Rep, RG233.

The Newberry Library, Chicago, Illinois
Edward E. Ayer Collection.

Records of Antebellum Southern Plantations from the Revolution through the Civil War, ed. by Kenneth M. Stampp and Randolph Boehm
Clinch, Duncan. Letterbook. 1824–36 and Slave List 1859 Camden County GA, Series C, Part 2, Reel 1.

South Carolina Department of Archives and History, Columbia, South Carolina
Draper Manuscript Collection. Ser. VV, Sumter Papers, VI, no. 193.
Governor's Messages.
Journal of the Volunteer Company from Columbia, [S.C.] Benjamin T. Elmore, Captain Feb. 11–May 12, 1836 Second Seminole War (1835–42).

South Carolina Historical Society, Charleston, South Carolina
Lesesne, Anna Caroline, 1809–1887. A journal commenced by A. C. Lesesne, 1836, (34/38).

State Library and Archives of Florida, Tallahassee, Florida
Governor Call Letterbook. April 19, 1836–September 18, 1836, Territorial and State Governors letterbooks, 1836–1909, RG 000101, Series 32.
Wiggins, Daniel H. Diary. RG 900000, Series M89–32.

Tennessee State Library and Archives, Nashville, Tennessee
Blount, Governor Willie. Papers. 1809–1815.
Sevier, John. Papers. 1796–1801.

University of Alabama, W. S. Hoole Special Collections Library, Tuscaloosa, Alabama
Griffin, Jesse. Letter. 1813.

University of Florida, P. K. Yonge Library of Florida History, Gainesville, Florida
Call, Richard K. Correspondence. Miscellaneous Manuscripts 00,733.
Davenport, William. Papers.
Indian Affairs—Florida Seminoles Indian Collection.

University of Georgia, Hargrett Rare Book and Manuscript Library, Athens, Georgia
Keith M. Reid Collection.
Telamon Cruger Smith Cuyler Collection. 1754–1941.
C. Mildred Thompson Collection.

University of North Carolina, The Wilson Library, Chapel Hill, North Carolina

The Southern Historical Collection
Lenoir Family Papers. 1763–1940.
Rutherford, Griffith. Letter. 2188-z.

University of Oklahoma Libraries, Norman, Oklahoma
Western History Collection, Indian-Pioneer Papers.

University of South Carolina, South Caroliniana Library, Columbia, South Carolina
Barnes, Charlotte. "An address to the Florida Volunteers, by Miss Charlotte Barnes [poem] Names of the Columbia, South Carolina, Volunteers to Florida," ca. 1835.
Chesnut, James. Papers. (1773–1866).
Dickson Family Papers. 1818–60.
Hampton Family Papers.
Hargrove, Solomon C. Journal.
Henry Summer Family Papers.
Andrew Jackson Collection.
Stewart, C. B. Journal. 1836–39.
Timrod, Henry. Scrapbook. 1836–1901.

United States Congressional Documents

Calhoun, John C. *Letter from the Secretary of War, Transmitting, Pursuant to a Resolution of the House of Representatives, of the 26th Ult. Information in Relation to the Destruction of the Negro Fort, in East Florida, in the Month of July, 1816, &c. &c.*, 15th Cong., 2nd sess., 1819, H. Doc. 122.

Lacock, Abner. *Prosecution of War against Seminole Indians, and Occupation of East Florida by United States' Troops*. 15th Cong., 2nd sess., 1819, S. Doc. 100.

Thompson, Smith. *Letter from the Secretary of the Navy, Transmitting in Obedience to a Resolution of the House of Representatives, of the Twenty-Sixth Ultimo, Sundry Documents Relating to the Destruction of the Negro Fort in East Florida, in the Month of July, 1816*. 15th Cong., 2nd sess., 1819, H. Doc. 119.

US Congress. *An Act to Provide for an Exchange of Lands with the Indians Residing in any of the States or Territories, and for their Removal West of the River Mississippi*, 21st Congress, 1st Session (May 28, 1830), *Statutes at Large*, Volume 4 (1846): 411–12.

———. *The Committee of Claims, to which was presented the petition of Jesse Manley*, 23rd Cong., 1st sess. (April 9, 1834), H.rp. 402.

———. *Message from the President of the United States, communicating, in compliance with a resolution of the Senate, copied of the correspondence between the War Department and Governor Call, concerning the war in Florida*, 26th Cong., 1st sess. (1840), S. Doc. 278.

———. *Proceedings of the Military Court of Inquiry in the Case of Major General Scott and Major General Gaines*, 24th Cong., 2nd sess. (1837), S. Doc. 224.

Newspapers and Periodicals

Alabama Journal, Montgomery, AL
Alexandria Gazette, Washington, DC
Americus Weekly Recorder, Americus, GA
Anderson Intelligencer, Anderson, SC

Anniston Star, Anniston, AL
Apalachicola Gazette, Apalachicola, FL
Army and Navy Chronicle; Washington, DC
Atlanta Constitution, Atlanta, GA
Athenian, Athens, GA
Athens Gazette, Athens, GA
Augusta Chronicle, Augusta, Georgia
Augusta Chronicle and Gazette of the State, Augusta, GA
Augusta Herald, Augusta, GA
Aurora General Advertiser, Philadelphia, PA
Baldwin Times, Bay Minette, AL
Barnwell People, Barnwell, SC
Biblical Recorder, Raleigh, NC
Caldwell Watchman, Columbia, LA
The Caledonian, St. Johnsbury, VT
Camden Weekly Journal, Camden, SC
Carolina Federal Republican, New Bern, NC
Carolina Gazette, Charleston, SC
Clarion-Ledger Jackson, MS
Clarion and Tennessee State Gazette, Nashville, TN
Charleston Courier, Charleston, SC
Charleston Daily Courier, Charleston, SC
Charleston Mercury, Charleston, SC
Charlotte Journal, Charlotte, NC
Cheraw Gazette, Cheraw, SC
Cherokee Phoenix, New Echota, GA
Cincinnati Enquirer, Cincinnati, OH
Columbian Museum & Savannah Advertiser, Savannah, GA
Columbian-Progress, Columbia, MS
Columbus Enquirer, Columbus, GA
Daily Georgian, Savannah, GA
Daily Savannah Republican, Savannah, GA
Daily Selma Reporter, Selma, AL
Daily Sun, Columbus, GA
DeSoto County Times, Arcadia, FL
Edgefield Advertiser, Edgefield, SC
Farmers' Reporter, Winston-Salem, NC
Fayetteville Weekly Observer. Fayetteville, NC
Federal Union, Milledgeville, GA
Flag of the Union, Tuscaloosa, AL
Florida Herald and Southern Democrat, St. Augustine, FL
Florida Intelligencer, Tallahassee, FL
Florida Weekly, Naples, FL
Floridian and Journal, Tallahassee, FL
Georgia Constitutionalist, Augusta, GA

Georgia Courier, Albany, GA
Georgia Journal, Milledgeville, GA
Georgia Messenger, Macon, GA
The Georgian, Savannah, GA
Greensborough Patriot, Greensborough, NC
Greenville News, Greenville, SC
Hattiesburg American, Hattiesburg, MS
Herald Advocate, Hardee County, FL
Huntsville Republican, Huntsville, AL
Independent Gazetteer, Philadelphia, PA
The Intelligencer, Anderson, SC
Jacksonville Courier, Jacksonville, FL
Kentucky Gazette, Lexington, KY
Keowee Courier, Walhalla, SC
Key West Inquirer, Key West, FL
Knoxville Gazette, Knoxville, TN
Knoxville News-Sentinel, Knoxville, TN
Knoxville Register, Knoxville, TN
Lancaster Intelligencer, Lancaster, PA
Lancaster Ledger, Lancaster, SC
Louisiana State Gazette, New Orleans, LA
Macon Georgia Telegraph, Macon, GA
Manning Times, Manning, SC
Maryland Gazette, Annapolis, MD
Mirror of the Times, Augusta, GA
Mississippi Free Trader, Natchez, MS
Mississippi State Gazette, Natchez, MS
Missouri Gazette, St. Louis, MO
Mobile Daily Commercial Register and Patriot, Mobile, AL
Montgomery Advertiser, Montgomery, AL
Nashville Clarion, Nashville, TN
Nashville Democratic Clarion and Tennessee Gazette, Nashville, TN
Nashville Examiner, Nashville, TN
Nashville Post, Nashville, TN
Natchez Gazette, Natchez, MS
National Banner and Nashville Whig, Nashville, TN
National Intelligencer, Washington, DC
Newbern Spectator, New Bern, NC
New Orleans Bee, New Orleans, LA
News and Planters' Gazette, Washington, Wilkes County, GA
New York Times, New York, NY
North Carolina Minerva and Fayetteville Advertiser, Fayetteville, NC
North Carolina Standard, Raleigh, NC
North Carolina Star, Raleigh, NC
Pennsylvania Gazette, Philadelphia, PA

Pensacola Gazette, Pensacola, FL
People's Press and Wilmington Advertiser, Wilmington, NC
Philadelphia Inquirer, Philadelphia, PA
Pickens Sentinel, Pickens, SC
Pittsburgh Weekly, Pittsburgh, PA
Raleigh Minerva, Raleigh, NC
Raleigh Register, Raleigh, NC
The Reflector, Milledgeville, GA
Republican and Savannah Evening Ledger, Savannah, GA
Richmond Enquirer, Richmond, VA
Savannah Daily Republican, Savannah, GA
Savannah Republican, Savannah, GA
Shreveport Journal, Shreveport, LA
South Carolina and American General Gazette, Charleston, SC
Southern Banner, Athens, GA
Southern Home, Charlotte, NC
Southern Recorder, Milledgeville, GA
Southern Rose, Charleston, SC
St. Louis Post-Dispatch, St. Louis, MO
The Star, Raleigh, NC
Susquehanna Democrat, Wilkes-Barre, PA
Tampa Tribune, Tampa, FL
Tarboro Press, Tarboro, NC
The Tennessean, Nashville, TN
Tennessee Herald, Shelbyville, TN
Union Times, Union, SC
Vicksburg Whig, Vicksburg, MS
Village Messenger, Fayetteville, TN
Virginia Argus, Richmond, VA
Virginia Gazette, Williamsburg, VA
Vermont Gazette, Bennington, VT
Walker County Messenger, LaFayette, GA
Washington News, Washington, GA
Weekly Franklin Repository, Chambersburg, PA
Weekly Mississippian, Jackson, MS
Weekly Register, Baltimore, MD
Western Carolinian, Salisbury, NC
Wetumpka Argus, Wetumpka, AL
Whig and Tribune, Jackson, TN
Wilmington Advertiser, Wilmington, NC
Winn Parish Enterprise, Winnfield, LA
Wire-Grass Reporter, Thomasville, GA
York Gazette, York, PA
Yorkville Enquirer, York, SC
YourSun.com, Port Charlotte, FL

Digital Sources

The Avalon Project: Documents in Law, History and Diplomacy, Yale Law School, Lillian Goldman Law Library. avalon.law.yale.edu.

Biographical Directory of the United States Congress, 1774–Present, United States Library of Congress. http://bioguide.congress.gov.

A Century of Lawmaking for a New Nation: U.S. Congressional Documents and Debates, Law Library/National Digital Library Program, Library of Congress. http://memory.loc.gov/.

Colonial Williamsburg Digital Library, the Colonial Williamsburg Foundation. http://research.history.org/.

First American Jewish Families, the Jacob Rader Marcus Center of the American Jewish Archives. http://americanjewisharchives.org.

Florida Digital Newspaper Library, George A. Smathers Libraries, University of Florida Digital Collections. http://ufdc.ufl.edu/fdn11.

Georgia Historic Newspapers Archive, Digital Library of Georgia, University of Georgia Libraries. https://gahistoricnewspapers.galileo.usg.edu/.

Historical Marker Database. https://www.hmdb.org/.

Historical Newspapers of South Carolina, University of South Carolina Libraries. https://historicnewspapers.sc.edu/.

Papers of the War Department, 1784–1800, Roy Rosenzweig Center for History and New Media, George Mason University. https://wardepartmentpapers.org.

Southeastern Native American Documents, 1730–1842, Digital Library of Georgia. http://dlg.galileo.usg.edu/.

Published Sources

Abernethy, Thomas P. *The South in the New Nation: 1789–1819*. Baton Rouge: Louisiana State University Press, 1989.

Adair, James. *The History of the American Indians*. Edited and with an introduction and annotations by Kathryn E. Holland Braund. Tuscaloosa: University of Alabama Press, 2005.

Adams, Kenneth. "Jamestown 2007: A Native American Perspective." In *We Will Always Be Here: Native Peoples on Living and Thriving in the South*, edited by Denise E. Bates, 78–81. Gainesville: University Press of Florida, 2016.

Adams, Mikaëla M. *Who Belongs? Race, Resources, and Tribal Citizenship in the Native South*. New York: Oxford University Press, 2016.

Alden, John Richard. *The First South*. Baton Rouge: Louisiana State University Press, 1961.

American State Papers: Foreign Relations. 6 vols. Washington, DC: Gales and Seaton, 1833–1998.

American State Papers: Indian Affairs. 2 vols. Washington, DC: Gales and Seaton, 1832–1834.

American State Papers: Military Affairs. 7 vols. Washington, DC: Gales and Seaton, 1832–1861.

Anderson, Benedict. *Imagined Communities: Reflections on the Origins and Spread of Nationalism*. New York: Verso, 2006.

Anderson, David G., David J. Hally, and James L. Rudolph. "The Mississippian Occupation of the Savannah River Valley." *Southeastern Archaeology* 5, no. 1 (Summer 1986): 32–51.

Anderson, Eric Gary. "On Native Ground: Indigenous Countercolonial Strategies in Southern Narratives of Captivity, Removal, and Repossession." *Southern Spaces*, August 9, 2007. doi: 10.18737/M7PC8K.

Anderson, Fred. *Crucible of War: The Seven Years' War and the Fate of Empire in British North America, 1754–1766*. New York: Vintage Books, 2001.

Anderson, Gary Clayton. *The Conquest of Texas: Ethnic Cleansing in the Promised Land, 1812–1875*. Norman: University of Oklahoma Press, 2005.

Andrew, Rod Jr. *The Life and Times of General Andrew Pickens: Revolutionary War Hero, American Founder*. Chapel Hill: University of North Carolina Press, 2017.

———. *Long Gray Lines: The Southern Military School Tradition, 1839–1915*. Chapel Hill: University of North Carolina Press, 2001.

———. *Wade Hampton: Confederate Warrior to Southern Redeemer*. Chapel Hill: University of North Carolina Press, 2008.

Axtell, James. *The Indians' New South: Cultural Change in the Colonial Southeast*. Baton Rouge: Louisiana State University Press, 1997.

Axtell, James, and William C. Sturtevant. "The Unkindest Cut, or Who Invented Scalping?" *William and Mary Quarterly* 37, no. 3 (July 1980): 451–72.

Ayers, Edward L. *Vengeance and Justice: Crime and Punishment in the Nineteenth-Century American South*. New York: Oxford University Press, 1974.

———. "What Caused the Civil War." In *What Caused the Civil War: Reflections on the South and Southern History*, 131–44. New York: W. W. Norton, 2005.

Baptist, Edward. *Creating an Old South: Middle Florida's Plantation Frontier before the Civil War*. Chapel Hill: University of North Carolina Press, 2002.

———. "The Migration of Planters to Antebellum Florida: Kinship and Power." *Journal of Southern History* 62, no. 3 (August 1996): 527–54.

Barber, Eunice. *Narrative of the Tragical Death of Mr. Darius Barber and His Seven Children Who Were Inhumanly Butchered by the Indians, in Camden County, Georgia, January 26th, 1818*. Boston: David Hazen, 1818.

Barksdale, Kevin T., and Kristofer Ray. "Searching for John Sevier: Myth, Memory, and the History of Early Tennessee History." In *Before the Volunteer State: New Thoughts on Early Tennessee, 1540–1800*, edited by Kristofer Ray, 201–15. Knoxville: University of Tennessee Press, 2015.

Bartram, William. *William Bartram on the Southeastern Indians*, edited and annotated by Gregory A. Waselkov and Kathryn E. Holland Braund. Lincoln: University of Nebraska Press, 1995.

Bassett, John Spencer. *The Life of Andrew Jackson*. Vol. 1. Garden City: Doubleday, Page, 1911.

Bassett, John Spencer, ed. *Correspondence of Andrew Jackson*. Vols. I and II. Washington, DC: Carnegie Institution of Washington, 1926–27.

Bauer, Brooke M. *Becoming Catawba: Catawba Indian Women and Nation-Building, 1540–1840*. Tuscaloosa: University of Alabama Press, 2023.

Beard, Richard. *Brief Biographical Sketches of Some of the Early Ministers of the*

Cumberland Presbyterian Church. 2nd ser. Nashville: Cumberland Presbyterian Board of Publication, 1874.

Beck. Robin A. Jr. "Catawba Coalescence and the Shattering of the Carolina Piedmont, 1540–1675." In *Mapping the Mississippian Shatter Zone: The Colonial Indian Slave Trade and Regional Instability in the American South*, edited by Robbie Ethridge and Sheri M. Shuck-Hall, 115–41. Lincoln: University of Nebraska Press, 2009.

———. *Chiefdoms, Collapse, and Coalescence in the Early American South*. New York: Cambridge University Press, 2013.

Belko, William S., ed. *America's Hundred Years' War: U.S. Expansion to the Gulf Coast and the Fate of the Seminole, 1763–1858*. Gainesville: University Press of Florida, 2011.

Benton, Thomas Hart. *Thirty Years' View*. New York: D. Appleton, 1856.

Blackhawk, Ned. *Violence over the Land: Indians and Empires in the Early American West*. Cambridge: Harvard University Press, 2008.

Boggess, Francis Calvin Morgan. *A Veteran of Four Wars: The Autobiography of F. C. C. Boggess. A Record of Pioneer Life and Adventure, and Heretofore Unwritten History of the Florida Seminole Indian Wars*. Arcadia, FL: Champion Rooms, 1900.

Bottiger, Patrick. *The Borderland of Fear: Vincennes, Prophetstown, and the Invasion of the Miami Homeland*. Lincoln: University of Nebraska Press, 2016.

Boulware, Tyler. *Deconstructing the Cherokee Nation: Town, Region, and Nation among Eighteenth-Century Cherokees*. Gainesville: University Press of Florida, 2011.

Bowne, Eric E. *The Westo Indians: Slave Traders of the Early Colonial South*. Tuscaloosa: University of Alabama Press, 2005.

Boyd, Mark F. "Events at Prospect Bluff on the Apalachicola River, 1808–1818." *Florida Historical Quarterly* 16, no. 2 (October 1937): 55–96.

Bozgo, Shkelqim, Xheni Sinakoli, and Emin Spahia. "Customary Law, Conflict, and Development in the Mountains of Albania." *Mountain Research and Development* 22, no. 4 (November 2002): 341–43.

Brannon, Peter A. "Journal of James A. Tait for the Year 1813." *Georgia Historical Quarterly* 8 no. 3 (September 1924): 229–39.

Braund, Kathryn E. Holland. "The Creek Indians, Blacks, and Slavery." *Journal of Southern History* 57, no. 4 (November 1991): 601–36.

———. *Deerskins and Duffels: The Creek Indian Trade with Anglo-America, 1685–1815*. Lincoln: University of Nebraska Press, 1993.

———. "Red Sticks." In *Tohopeka: Rethinking the Creek War and the War of 1812*, edited by Kathryn E. Holland Braund, 84–104. Tuscaloosa: University of Alabama Press, 2012.

———. *Tohopeka: Rethinking the Creek War and the War of 1812*. Tuscaloosa: University of Alabama Press, 2012.

Braund, Kathryn H., Gregory A. Waselkov, and Raven M. Christopher, *The Old Federal Road in Alabama: An Illustrated Guide*. Tuscaloosa: University of Alabama Press, 2019.

Breeden, Edwin C. *A Guidebook to South Carolina Historical Markers*. Columbia: University of South Carolina Press, 2021.

Bridwell, Ronald Edward. "The South's Wealthiest Planter: Wade Hampton I of South Carolina." PhD diss, University of South Carolina, 1980.

British and Foreign State Papers, 1818–1819. Vol. 6. London: J. Harrison and Son, Printers to the Foreign Office, 1835.

Brown, Canter Jr. *Florida's Peace River Frontier*. Orlando: University of Central Florida Press, 1991.

Bruce, Dickson D. *Violence and Culture in the Antebellum South*. Austin: University of Texas Press, 1979.

Buffington, April J. "Creek/Seminole Archeology in the Apalachicola River Valley, Northwest Florida." MA thesis, University of South Florida, 2009.

Burckard, Johann Christian, and Karsten Petersen. *Partners in the Lord's Work: The Diary of Two Moravian Missionaries in the Creek Indian Country, 1807–1813*. Edited and translated by Carl Mauelshagen and Gerald H. Davis. Research Paper Number 21. Atlanta: School of Arts and Sciences Research Papers, Georgia State College, 1969.

Burton, Gary. "Pintlala's Cold Murder Case: The Death of Thomas Meredith in 1812." *Alabama Review* 63 (2010): 163–91.

Burton, Orville Vernon. *In My Father's House Are Many Mansions: Family and Community in Edgefield, South Carolina*. Chapel Hill: University of North Carolina Press, 1985.

Buss, James Joseph. *Winning the West with Words: Language and Conquest in the Lower Great Lakes*. Norman: University of Oklahoma Press, 2011.

Cabeza de Vaca, Alvar Nunez. *The Narrative of Cabeza de Vaca*. Edited and translated with an introduction by Rolena Adorno and Patrick Charles Pautz. Lincoln: University of Nebraska Press, 2003.

Caison, Gina. *Red States: Indigeneity, Settler Colonialism, and Southern Studies*. Athens: University of Georgia Press, 2018.

Call, Richard K. *Union, Slavery, Secession: Letter from Governor R. K. Call, of Florida, to John S. Littell, of Germantown, Pennsylvania*. Philadelphia: C. Sherman & Son, Printers, 1861.

Calloway, Colin G. *The American Revolution in Indian Country: Crisis and Diversity in Native American Communities*. New York: Cambridge University Press, 1995.

———. *New Worlds for All: Indians, Europeans and the Remaking of Early America*. Baltimore: Johns Hopkins University Press, 1997.

Candler, Allen D., Kenneth Coleman, and Milton Ready, eds. *The Colonial Records of the State of Georgia*. Vols 1–28. Atlanta: Franklin, 1904–16.

Carson, James Taylor. "'The Obituary of Nations': Ethnic Cleansing, Memory, and the Origins of the Old South." *Southern Cultures* 14, no. 4 (Winter 2008): 6–31.

Carson, James Taylor, Robbie Ethridge, and Greg O'Brien. "Editor's Introduction: A Line in the Sand." *Native South* 1 (2008): ix–xvi.

Carter, Clarence Edwin, ed. *The Territorial Papers of the United States: The Territory of Alabama, 1817–1819*. Vol. 18. Washington, DC: Government Printing Office, 1952.

———. *The Territorial Papers of the United States: The Territory of Florida, 1821–1824*. Vol. 22. Washington, DC: Government Printing Office, 1958.

———. *The Territorial Papers of the United States: The Territory of Florida, 1824–1828*. Vol. 23. Washington, DC: Government Printing Office, 1958.

———. *The Territorial Papers of the United States: The Territory of Florida, 1834–1839*. Vol. 25. Washington, DC: Government Printing Office, 1960.

———. *The Territorial Papers of the United States: The Territory of Mississippi, 1809–1817*. Vol. 6. Washington, DC: Government Printing Office, 1938.

Caudle, Everett W. "Settlement Patterns in Alachua County, Florida, 1850–1860." *Florida Historical Quarterly* 67, no. 4 (April 1989): 428–40.

Caughey, John Walton. *McGillivray of the Creeks*. Introduction by William Bauer Jr. Columbia: University of South Carolina Press, 2007.

Chapman, Jefferson. *Tellico Archeology: 12,000 Years of Native American History*. 3rd ed. Knoxville: University of Tennessee Press, 2014.

Chappell, Absalom H. *Miscellanies of Georgia, Historical, Biographical, Descriptive, Etc.* Atlanta: James F. Meegan, 1874.

Chaudhuri, Jean, and Joyotpaul Chaudhuri. *A Sacred Path: The Way of the Muscogee Creeks*. Los Angeles: UCLA American Indian Studies Center, 2001.

The City of Columbia, Mississippi. http://www.cityofcolumbiams.com. Accessed March 15, 2021.

City of Tuskegee. "Tuskegee History." https://www.tuskegeealabama.gov. Accessed March 19, 2021.

Claiborne, J. F. H. *Life and Time of Gen. Sam. Dale, the Mississippi Partisan*. New York: Harper and Brothers, 1860.

Claiborne, Nathaniel Herbert. *Notes on the War in the South*. Richmond, VA: William Ramsay, 1819.

Clark, Thomas D., and John D. W. Guice. *The Old Southwest, 1795–1830: Frontiers in Conflict*. Norman: University of Oklahoma Press, 1996.

Cobb, Charles R. *The Archaeology of Southeastern Native American Landscapes of the Colonial Era*. Gainesville: University Press of Florida, 2019.

Cohen, Myer M. *Notices of Florida and the Campaigns*. Charleston: Burges & Honour, 1836.

———. *Notices of Florida and the Campaigns*. Charleston: Burges & Honour, 1836. Reprinted as *Notices of Florida and the Campaigns: A Facsimile Reproduction*. Edited By Rembert W. Patrick, with an introduction by Colonel O. Z. Tyler Jr. Gainesville: University of Florida Press, 1964.

Collections of the Georgia Historical Society: The Letters of Honorable James Habersham, 1756–1775. Vol. 6. Savannah: Savannah Morning News Print, 1904.

Colonial Records of North Carolina. Edited by William L. Saunders. Vol. 5, 1752–1759. Raleigh: Josephus Daniels, Printer to the State, 1887.

Colonial Records of North Carolina. Edited by William L. Saunders. Vol. 10, 1775–1776. Raleigh: Josephus Daniels, Printer to the State, 1890.

Corkan, David H. *The Creek Frontier, 1540–1783*. Norman: University of Oklahoma Press, 1967.

Correspondence of the Slave Trade with Foreign Powers. London: William Clowes and Sons, 1844.

Cothran, Boyd. *Remembering the Modoc War: Redemptive Violence and the Making of American Innocence*. Chapel Hill: University of North Carolina Press, 2014.

Coulter, E. Merton. Review of John Hope Franklin. *The Militant South, 1800–1860*. *Annals of the American Academy of Political and Social Science* 309 (January 1957): 187–88.

Covington, James W. "The Armed Occupation Act of 1842." *Florida Historical Quarterly* 40, no. 1 (July 1961): 41–52.

———. *The Seminoles of Florida*. Gainesville: University Press of Florida, 1993.

Craven, Avery O. *The Growth of Southern Nationalism, 1848–1861*. Baton Rouge: Louisiana State University Press, 1953.

Crockett, David. *Narrative of the Life of David Crockett of the State of Tennessee*. Philadelphia: E. L. Carey and A. Hart, 1834.

Cumfer, Cynthia. *Separate Peoples, One Land: The Minds of Cherokees, Blacks, and Whites on the Tennessee Frontier*. Chapel Hill: University of North Carolina Press, 2007.

Cunliff, Marcus. *Soldiers and Civilians: The Martial Spirit in America, 1775–1865*. London: Macmillan, 1973.

Decredico, Mary A. "Sectionalism and the Secession Crisis." In *A Companion to the American South*, edited by John B. Boles, 235–48. Malden: Blackwell, 2002.

Denham, James M., and Canter Brown Jr., eds. *Cracker Times and Pioneer Lives: The Florida Reminiscences of George Gillett Keen and Sarah Pamela Williams*. Columbia: University of South Carolina Press, 2000.

———. "South Carolina Volunteers in the Second Seminole War: A Nullifier Debacle as Prelude to the Palmetto State Gubernatorial Election of 1836." In *America's Hundred Years' War: U.S. Expansion to the Gulf Coast and the Fate of the Seminole, 1763–1858*, edited by William S. Belko, 209–36. Gainesville: University Press of Florida, 2011.

Denham, James M., and Keith L. Huneycutt, eds. *Echoes from a Distant Frontier: The Brown Sisters' Correspondence from Antebellum Florida*. Columbia: University of South Carolina Press, 2004.

———. *The Letters of George Long Brown: A Yankee Merchant on Florida's Antebellum Frontier*. Gainesville: University Press of Florida, 2019.

Denson, Andrew. *Monuments to Absence: Cherokee Removal and the Contest over Southern Memory*. Chapel Hill: University of North Carolina Press, 2017.

De Vorsey, Louis J. "Early Maps as a Source in the Reconstruction of Indian Landscapes." In *Red, White, and Black: Symposium on Indians in the Old South*, edited by Charles M. Hudson, 12–30. Athens: University of Georgia Press, 1971.

Doherty, Herbert J. Jr. *Richard Keith Call: Southern Unionist*. Gainesville: University of Florida Press, 1961.

Doster, James F. *Creek Indians: The Creek Indians and Their Florida Lands, 1740–1823*. 2 vols. New York: Garland, 1974.

Dow, Lorenzo, and Peggy Dow. *History of Cosmopolite: Or the Writings of Rev. Lorenzo Dow*. Cincinnati: Anderson, Gates & Wright, 1859.

Dowd, Gregory Evans. *Groundless: Rumors, Legends, and Hoaxes on the Early American Frontier*. Baltimore: Johns Hopkins University Press, 2015.

———. *A Spirited Resistance: The North American Indian Struggle for Unity, 1745–1815*. Baltimore: Johns Hopkins University Press, 1992.

Dubcovsky, Alejandra. *Informed Power: Communication in the Early American South*. Cambridge: Harvard University Press, 2016.

Dupree, Daniel. *Alabama's Frontiers and the Rise of the Old South*. Bloomington: Indiana University Press, 2018.

Eaton, John Henry. *The Life of Andrew Jackson, Major-General in the Service of the United States: Comprising a History of the War in the South, from the Commencement of the Creek Campaign, to the Termination of Hostilities before New Orleans*. Philadelphia: Samuel F. Bradford, 1824.

Ekirch, Arthur A. Jr. "The Idea of a Citizen Army." *Military Affairs*, no. 1 (Spring 1953): 30–36.

Ellet, Elizabeth. *Pioneer Women of the West*. New York: Charles Scribner, 1856.

Ellisor, John T. *The Second Creek War: Interethnic Conflict and Collusion on a Collapsing Frontier*. Lincoln: University of Nebraska Press, 2010.

Ethridge, Robbie. *Creek Country: The Creek Indians and Their World*. Chapel Hill: University of North Carolina Press, 2003.

———. *From Chicaza to Chickasaw: The European Invasion and the Transformation of the Mississippian World, 1540–1715*. Chapel Hill: University of North Carolina Press, 2010.

Ethridge, Robbie, and Sheri M. Shuck-Hall. *Mapping the Mississippian Shatter Zone: The Colonial Indian Slave Trade and Regional Instability in the American South*. Lincoln: University of Nebraska Press, 2009.

Faust, Drew Gilpin. *This Republic of Suffering: Death and the American Civil War*. New York: Alfred A. Knopf, 2008.

Favert, Mary A. *War at a Distance: Romanticism and the Making of Modern Wartime*. Princeton: Princeton University Press, 2010.

Ferguson, Gillum. *Illinois in the War of 1812*. Urbana: University of Illinois Press, 2012.

Finnegan, Terence. "Lynching and Political Power in Mississippi and South Carolina." In *Under Sentence of Death: Lynching in the South*, edited by W. Fitzhugh Brundage, 189–218. Chapel Hill: University of North Carolina Press, 1997.

Forbes, James Grant. *Sketches, Historical and Topographical of the Floridas; More Particularly of East Florida*. New York: C. S. Van Winkle, 1821.

Ford, Paul L., ed. *The Writings of Thomas Jefferson*. 10 vols. New York: G. P. Putnam's Sons, 1892–99.

Foster, H. Thomas II, ed. *Collected Works of Benjamin Hawkins, 1796–1810*. Tuscaloosa: University of Alabama Press, 2003.

Frank, Andrew K. *Creeks and Southerners: Biculturalism on the Early American Frontier*. Nebraska: University of Nebraska Press, 2005.

———. "Red, Black, and Seminole: Community Convergence on the Florida Borderlands, 1780–1840." In *Borderland Narratives: Negotiation and Accommodation in North America's Contested Spaces, 1500–1850*, 46–67. Gainesville: University Press of Florida, 2017.

Frank, Andrew K., and Kristofer Ray. "Guest Editors' Introduction: Indians as Southerners; Southerners as Indians: Rethinking the History of a Region." *Native South* 10 (2017): vii–xiv.

Franklin, John Hope. *The Militant South 1800–1861*. Chicago: University of Illinois Press, 2002.

———. *Mirror to America: The Autobiography of John Hope Franklin*. New York: Farrar, Straus and Giroux, 2005.

———. *Race and History: Selected Essays, 1938–1988.* Baton Rouge: Louisiana State University Press, 1989.

———. "Slavery and the Martial South." *Journal of Negro History* 37, no. 1 (January 1952): 36–53.

Frost, John. *Pictorial Life of Andrew Jackson.* Hartford, CT: Belknap and Hamersley, 1847.

Gallay, Alan. *The Indian Slave Trade: The Rise of the English Empire in the American South, 1670–1717.* New Haven: Yale University Press, 2002.

Galloway, Patricia. "The Barthelemy Murders: Bienville's Establishment of the Lex Talionis as a Principle of Indian Diplomacy." In *Practicing Ethnohistory: Mining Archives, Hearing Testimony, Constructing Narrative.* Lincoln: University Press of Nebraska, 2006: 245–58.

Garrison, Tim Alan. *The Legal Ideology of Removal: The Southern Judiciary and the Sovereignty of Native American Nations.* Athens: University of Georgia Press, 2002.

Genovese, Eugene. *Roll, Jordan, Roll: The World the Slaves Made.* New York: Vintage Books, 1976.

Glover, Lorri. *Southern Sons: Becoming Men in the New Nation.* Baltimore: Johns Hopkins University Press, 2007.

Gorn, Elliot J. "'Gouge and Bite, Pull Hair and Scratch': The Social Significance of Fighting in the Southern Backcountry." *American Historical Review* 90, no. 1 (1985): 18–43.

Grange, Roger T. Jr. "The I. C. Few Site." *South Carolina Institute of Archeology and Anthropology Notebook* (January/February 1971): 19–20.

Grant, C. L. *Letters, Journals and Writings of Benjamin Hawkins.* 2 vols. Savannah: Beehive Press, 1980.

Green, E. R. R. "Queensborough Township: Scotch-Irish Emigration and the Expansion of Georgia, 1765–1776." *William and Mary Quarterly* 17, no. 2 (1960): 183–99.

Green, Jennifer R. *Military Education and the Emerging Middle Class in the Old South.* Cambridge: Cambridge University Press, 2008.

Green, Michael D. *The Politics of Indian Removal: Creek Government and Society in Crisis.* Lincoln: University of Nebraska Press, 1982.

Greenberg, Kenneth S. *Honor and Slavery: Lies, Duels, Noses, Masks, Dressing as a Woman, Gifts, Strangers, Humanitarianism, Death, Slave Rebellions, the Proslavery Argument, Baseball, Hunting, and Gambling in the Old South.* Princeton: Princeton University Press, 1996.

Greenberg, Mark I. "Becoming Southern: The Jews of Savannah, Georgia, 1830–70." *American Jewish History* 86, no. 1 (March 1998): 55–75.

Greene, Lance. *Their Determination to Remain: A Cherokee Community's Resistance to the Trail of Tears in North Carolina.* Tuscaloosa: University of Alabama Press, 2022.

Griffin, Patrick. *American Leviathan: Empire, Nation, and Revolutionary Frontier.* New York: Hill and Wang, 2007.

Hackney, Sheldon. "Southern Violence." *American Historical Review* 74, no. 3 (February 1969): 906–25.

Hadden, Sally E. *Slave Patrols: Law and Violence in Virginia and the Carolinas.* Cambridge: Harvard University Press, 2001.

Hahn, Steven C. *The Invention of the Creek Nation, 1670–1763*. Lincoln: University of Nebraska Press, 2004.

Halbert, H. S., and T. S. Ball. *The Creek War of 1813 and 1814*, edited and with an introduction by Frank L. Owsley Jr. Tuscaloosa: University of Alabama Press, 1995.

Hamilton, Peter Joseph. *Colonial Mobile: An Historical Study*. Boston: Houghton, Mifflin, 1897.

Harner, John. "Place Identity and Copper Mining in Sonora, Mexico." *Annals of the Association of American Geographers* 91, no. 4 (December 2001): 660–80.

Hatley, Tom. *The Dividing Paths: Cherokees and South Carolinians through the Revolutionary Era*. New York: Oxford University Press, 1995.

Haveman, Christopher D. *Rivers of Sand: Creek Indian Emigration, Relocation, & Ethnic Cleansing in the American South*. Lincoln: University of Nebraska Press, 2016.

Hayne, Paul H. *The Poems of Henry Timrod*. New York: E. J. Hale & Son, 1873.

Haynes, Joshua S. *Patrolling the Border: Theft and Violence on the Creek-Georgia Frontier, 1770–1796*. Athens: University of Georgia Press, 2018.

H[aynes], M[ilton] A. "Historical Traditions of Tennessee." *American Whig Review* 9, no. 15. New York: John A. Gray Printer, 1852. 235–49.

Haywood, John. *The Civil and Political History of the State of Tennessee, from Its Earliest Settlement up to the Year 1796; Including the Boundaries of the State*. Knoxville: Heiskell & Brown, 1823.

Haywood, John, William H. Haywood, and Arthur St. Clair Colyar. *The Civil and Political History of the State of Tennessee, from Its Earliest Settlement up to the Year 1796; Including the Boundaries of the State*. Nashville: Methodist Episcopal Church, 1891.

Heidler, David S., and Jeanne T. Heidler. *Daily Life in the Early American Republic, 1790–1820*. Westport, CT: Greenwood Press, 2004.

Hendrix, Tom. *If the Legends Fade*. Chapel Hill, NC: Professional Press, 2000.

———. "Te-lah-nay's Wall." In *We Will Always Be Here: Native Peoples on Living and Thriving in the South*, edited by Denise E. Bates 121–23. Gainesville: University Press of Florida, 2016.

Henri, Florette. *The Southern Indians and Benjamin Hawkins, 1796–1816*. Norman: University of Oklahoma Press, 1986.

Heyne, F. Georg. "Notes on Blood Revenge among the Reindeer Evenki of Manchuria (Northeast China)," translated by Peter Knecht. *Asian Folklore Studies* 66, no. 1–2 (2007): 165–78.

Hickey, Donald R. *The War of 1812: A Forgotten Conflict*. Urbana: University of Illinois Press, 1989.

———. *The War of 1812: A Short History*. Urbana: University of Illinois Press, 1995.

Higginbotham, R. Don. "The Martial Spirit in the Antebellum South: Some Further Speculation in a National Context." *Journal of Southern History* 58, no. 1 (February 1992): 3–26.

Hitchcock, Ethan Allen. *Fifty Years in Camp and Field: Diary of Major General Ethan Allen Hitchcock, U.S.A.* Edited by W. A. Croffut. New York: G. P. Putnam's Sons, 1909.

Hixson, Walter L. *American Settler Colonialism: A History*. New York: Palgrave Macmillan, 2013.

Hodgson, Adam. *Letters from North America, Written during a Tour of the United States and Canada*. Vol. 1. London: Hurst, Robinson; and Edinburgh; A. Constable, 1824.

Hoffman, Paul E. *Florida's Frontiers*. Bloomington: Indiana University Press, 2002.

Hollingsworth, Henry. In "Tennessee Volunteers in the Seminole Campaign of 1836: The Diary of Henry Hollingsworth," edited by Stanley F. Horn. *Tennessee Historical Quarterly* 2, no. 1 (March 1943): 61–73.

Homans, Benjamin. *The Army and Navy Chronicle*. Vol. II. January 1 to June 30, 1836. Washington, DC: B. Homans.

Horsman, Reginald. *Expansion and American Indian Policy, 1783–1812*. Norman: University of Oklahoma Press, 1992.

———. *Race and Manifest Destiny: The Origins of American Racial Anglo-Saxonism*. Cambridge: Harvard University Press, 1981.

Hudson, Angela Pulley. *Creek Paths and Federal Roads: Indians, Settlers, and Slaves and the Making of the American South*. Chapel Hill: University of North Carolina Press, 2010.

———. "Unsettling Histories of the South." *Southern Cultures* 25, no. 3 (Fall 2019): 30–45.

Hudson, Charles. "The Hernando do Soto Expedition, 1539–1543." In *The Forgotten Centuries: Indians and Europeans in the American South, 1521–1704*, edited by Charles Hudson and Carmen Chaves Tesser, 74–103. Athens: University of Georgia Press, 1994.

———. "Introduction." In *The Transformation of the Southeastern Indians, 1540–1760*, edited by Robbie Ethridge and Charles Hudson. Jackson: University Press of Mississippi, 2002, xi–xxxix.

Huff, Archie Vernon Jr. *Greenville: The History of the City and County in the South Carolina Piedmont*. Columbia: University of South Carolina Press, 1995.

Ibsen, Charles A., and Patricia Klobus. "Fictive Kin Term Use and Social Relationships: Alternative Interpretations." *Journal of Marriage and Family* 34, no. 4 (November 1972): 615–20.

Inman, Natalie. *Brothers and Friends: Kinship in Early America*. Athens: University of Georgia Press, 2020.

Jackson, Jason Baird. *Yuchi Folklore: Cultural Expression in a Southeastern Native American Community*. Norman: University of Oklahoma Press, 2013.

Jackson, Jean E. *The Fish People: Linguistic Exogamy and Tukanoan Identity in Northwest Amazonia*. Cambridge: Cambridge University Press, 1983.

Jacoby, Karl. *Shadows at Dawn: A Borderlands Massacre and the Violence of History*. New York: Penguin Press, 2008.

Jarvis, N. S. "An Army Surgeon's Notes of Frontier Service, 1833–48." *Journal of the Military Service Institution of the United States* 39, no. 143 (September–October 1906): 275–86.

Jefferson, Thomas. *Notes on the State of Virginia*. Richmond: J. W. Randolph, 1853.

Jennings, Matthew. *New Worlds of Violence: Cultures and Conquest in the Early American Southeast*. Knoxville: University of Tennessee Press, 2011.

Johnson, Joseph. *Traditions and Reminiscences Chiefly of the American Revolution in the South*. Charleston: Walker & James, 1851.

Jortner, Adam. *The Gods of Prophetstown: The Battle of Tippecanoe and the Holy War for the American Frontier*. New York: Oxford University Press, 2012.

Jumper, Betty Mae Tiger, and Patsy West. *A Seminole Legend: The Life of Betty Mae Tiger Jumper*. Gainesville: University Press of Florida, 2001.

Kanon, Tom. "Before Horseshoe: Andrew Jackson's Campaigns in the Creek War prior to Horseshoe Bend." In *Tohopeka: Rethinking the Creek War and the War of 1812*, edited by Kathryn E. Holland Braund, 105–21. Tuscaloosa: University of Alabama Press, 2012.

———. "The Kidnapping of Martha Crawley and Settler-Indian Relations prior to the War of 1812." *Tennessee Historical Quarterly* 64, no. 1 (Spring 2004): 3–23.

———. *Tennesseans at War, 1812–1815: Andrew Jackson, The Creek War, and the Battle of New Orleans*. Tuscaloosa: University of Alabama Press, 2014.

Kappler, Charles J., ed. and comp. *Indian Affairs: Laws and Treaties*. Volume II. Washington, DC: Government Printing Office, 1904.

Keen, Benjamin. "The Black Legend Revisited: Assumptions and Realities." *Hispanic American Historical Review* 49, no. 4 (1969): 703–19.

Kelton, Paul. *Epidemics and Enslavement: Biological Catastrophe in the Native Southeast, 1492–1715*. Lincoln: University of Nebraska Press, 2007.

Kendall, Amos. *The Life of Andrew Jackson*. New York: Harper & Brothers, 1843.

Kidron, Carol A. "Survivor Family Memory Work at Sites of Holocaust Remembrance: Institutional Enlistment of Family Agency?" *History and Memory* 27, no. 2 (2015): 45–73.

Kieffer, Charles L. *Maligned General: A Biography of Thomas S. Jesup*. San Rafael, CA: Presidio Press, 1979.

King, Duane H. "Captivity Narrative: Joseph Brown." *Journal of Cherokee Studies* 2, no. 2 (1977): 208–29.

Kirkland, Thomas J., and Robert M. Kennedy. *Historic Camden: Part One, Colonial and Revolutionary*. Columbia: State Company, 1905.

Klein, Rachel. *Unification of a Slave State: The Rise of the Planter Class in the South Carolina Backcountry, 1760–1808*. Chapel Hill: University of North Carolina Press, 1990.

Klos, George. "Blacks and the Seminole Removal Debate, 1821–1835." *Florida Historical Quarterly* 68, no. 1 (July 1989): 55–78.

Knetsch, Joe. *Florida's Seminole Wars: 1817–1858*. Charleston, SC: Arcadia, 2003.

Knight, Lucian Lamar. *Georgia's Landmarks, Memorials and Legends*. Vol. 2. Atlanta: Byrd Printing, 1914.

Knight, Vernon James Jr. "The Formation of the Creeks." In *The Forgotten Centuries: Indians and Europeans in the American South, 1521–1704*, edited by Charles Hudson and Carmen Chaves Tesser, 373–92. Athens: University of Georgia Press, 1994.

Knopf, Richard C., transcriber. *Document Transcriptions of the War of 1812 in the Northwest*. Vol. 5. Columbus: Ohio Historical Society, 1958.

Kokomoor, Kevin. *Of One Mind and of One Government: The Rise and Fall of the Creek Nation in the Early Republic*. Lincoln: University of Nebraska Press, 2019.

Kowalewski, Stephen A. "Coalescent Societies." In *Light on the Path: The Anthropology and History of the Southeastern Indians*, edited by Thomas J. Pluckhahn and Robbie Ethridge, 94–122. Tuscaloosa: University of Alabama Press, 2006.

Lamar, Mirabeau B. *The Papers of Mirabeau B. Lamar*. Vol. 2. Edited by Charles A. Gulick Jr. and Katherine Elliot. Austin: A. C. Baldwin and Sons Printers, 1922.

Landers, Jane. "Blood Seminoles and Black Seminoles on the Florida Frontier." In *Coastal Encounters: The Transformation of the Gulf South in the Eighteenth Century*, edited by Richard F. Brown, 99–116. Lincoln: University of Nebraska Press, 2007.

Landrum, J. B. O. *Colonial and Revolutionary History of Upper South Carolina*. Greenville, SC: Shannon Printers, 1897.

Laver, Harry S. *Citizens More than Soldiers: The Kentucky Militia and Society in the Early Republic*. Lincoln: University of Nebraska Press, 2007.

Latour, Arsène Lacarrière. *Historical Memoir of the War in West Florida and Louisiana in 1814–15, with an Atlas*. Expanded ed. Edited and with an introduction by Gene Allen Smith. Gainesville: University Press of Florida and the Historic New Orleans Collection, 2008.

Laumer, Frank. *Dade's Last Command*. Gainesville: University Press of Florida, 1995.

Lawson, Colin, and Douglas Saltmarshe. "Security and Economic Transition: Evidence from North Albania." *Europe-Asia Studies* 52, no. 1 (January 2000): 133–48.

Lee, Mary Elizabeth. *The Poetical Remains of the Late Mary Elizabeth Lee*. Edited by Samuel Gilman. Charleston: Walker & Richards, 1851.

Lee, Wayne E. *Barbarians and Brothers: Anglo-American Warfare, 1500–1865*. Oxford: Oxford University Press, 2011.

———. "Peace Chiefs and Blood Revenge: Patterns of Restraint in Native American Warfare, 1500–1800." *Journal of Military History* 71, no. 3 (July 2007): 701–41.

Lepore, Jill. *The Name of War: King Philip's War and the Origins of American Identity*. New York: Knopf, 1998.

Lerias, Doukessa, and Mitchell K. Byrne. "Vicarious Traumatization: Symptoms and Predictors." *Stress and Health* 19, no. 3 (2003): 129–38.

Lev-Wiesel, Rachel. "Intergenerational Transmission of Trauma across Three Generations." *Qualitative Social Work* 6, no. 1 (2007): 75–94.

Littlefield, Daniel F. *Africans and Seminoles: From Removal to Emancipation*. Jackson: University Press of Mississippi, 2001.

Logt, Mark van de. *Monsters of Contact: Historical Trauma in Caddoan Oral Traditions*. Norman: University of Oklahoma Press, 2018.

Long, Ellen Call. *Florida Breezes; or, Florida, New and Old*. With an introduction by Margaret Louise Chapman. Reproduction of 1883 edition. Gainesville: University of Florida Press, 1962.

Lumpkin, Wilson. *The Removal of the Cherokee Indians from Georgia*. New York: Dodd, Mead, 1907.

Mahon, John K. "The First Seminole War, November 21, 1817–May 24, 1818." *Florida Historical Quarterly* 77, no. 1 (Summer 1998): 62–67.

———. *History of the Second Seminole War, 1835–1842*. Gainesville: University of Florida Press, 1985.

Martin, Joel W. *Sacred Revolt: The Muskogees' Struggle for a New World*. Boston: Beacon Press, 1991.

May, Robert E. "Dixie's Martial Image: A Continuing Historiographical Enigma." *The Historian* 40, no. 2 (February 1978): 213–34.

McCurry, Stephanie. *Masters of Small Worlds: Yeoman Households, Gender Relations, and the Political Culture of the Antebellum South Carolina Low Country*. New York: Oxford University Press, 1995.

McLoughlin, William G. *Cherokee Renascence in the New Republic*. Princeton: Princeton University Press, 1986.

McReynolds, Edwin C. *The Seminoles*. Norman: University of Oklahoma Press, 1957.

McWhiney, Grady. *Cracker Culture: Celtic Ways in the Old South*. Prologue by Forrest McDonald. Tuscaloosa: University of Alabama Press, 1988.

Meek, A[lexander]. B[eaufort]. "The Journal of A. B. Meek and the Second Seminole War, 1836," edited by John K. Mahon. *Florida Historical Quarterly* 38, no. 4 (April 1960): 302–18.

Meek, Alexander Beaufort. *Romantic Passages in Southwestern History*. Mobile: S. H. Goetzel, 1857.

Mereness, Newton D., ed. *Travels in the American Colonies*. New York: Macmillan, 1916.

Merrell, James H. *The Indians' New World: Catawbas and Their Neighbors from European Contact through the Era of Removal*. Chapel Hill: University of North Carolina Press, 1989.

Message from the President of the United States, Transmitting a Report of the Secretary of War, Relative to Murders Committed by the Indians, in the State of Tennessee. Washington, DC: Roger C. Weightman, 1812. Early American Imprint Series, 1801–19, series no. 30257. 16–18.

Milanich, Jerald T. *The Florida Indians and the Invasion from Europe*. Gainesville: University Press of Florida, 1995.

Miles, Tiya. *The House on Diamond Hill: A Cherokee Plantation Story*. Chapel Hill: University of North Carolina Press, 2010.

———. "Uncle Tom Was an Indian: Tracing the Red in Black Slavery." In *Relational Formations of Race: Theory, Method, and Practice*, edited by Natalia Molina, Daniel Martinez Hosang, and Ramon A. Gutierrez, 121–14. Oakland: University of California Press, 2019.

Milfort, Louis Le Clerc. *Memoirs or a Quick Glance at My Various Travels and My Sojourn in the Creek Nation*. Translated by Ben C. McCary. Savannah: Beehive Press, 1972.

Miller, James Hendry Jr. "Fowltown and the First Seminole War: 'Civilization,' Centralization, and Politics in the Early American Republic." MA thesis, Florida State University, 2011.

Millett, Nathaniel. *The Maroons of Prospect Bluff and Their Quest for Freedom in the Atlantic World*. Gainesville: University Press of Florida, 2013.

Milne, George Edward. *Natchez Country: Indians, Colonists, and the Landscapes of Race in French Louisiana*. Athens: University of Georgia Press, 2015.

Mitchell, Margaret. *Gone with the Wind*. New York: Simon and Schuster, 1964.

Moltke-Hansen, David. "Southern Genesis: Regional Identity and the Rise of the 'Capital of Southern Civilization,' 1760–1780." Ph.D. diss., University of South Carolina, 2000.

Moore, Peter N. "The Usable Death: Evangelicals, Anglicans, and the Politics of

Dying in the Late-Colonial Lowcountry." In *Death and the American South*, edited by Craig Thompson Friend and Lorri Glover, 36–57. New York: Cambridge University Press, 2015.

Monaco, C. S. "Shadows and Pestilence: Health and Medicine during the Second Seminole War." *Journal of Social History* 48, no. 3 (Spring 2015): 565–88.

———. "Whose War Was It? African American Heritage Claims and the Second Seminole War." *American Indian Quarterly* 41, no. 1 (Winter 2017): 31–66.

Mooney, James. *History, Myths, and Sacred Formulas of the Cherokees*. With an introduction by George Ellison. Asheville: Bright Mountain Books, 1992.

Moser, Harold D., Sharon Macpherson, and Charles F. Bryan Jr., eds. *The Papers of Andrew Jackson, 1804–1813*. Vol. 2. Knoxville: University of Tennessee Press, 1984.

———. *The Papers of Andrew Jackson, 1814–1815*. Vol. 3. Knoxville: University of Tennessee Press, 1991.

Moser, Harold, David R. Hoth, and George H. Hoemann, eds. *The Papers of Andrew Jackson, 1816–1820*. Vol. 4. Knoxville: University of Tennessee Press, 1994.

Moser, Harold D., J Clint Clift, and Wyatt C. Wells, eds. *The Papers of Andrew Jackson, 1825–1828*. Vol. 6. Knoxville: University of Tennessee Press, 2002.

Mulroy, Kevin. *Seminole Freedmen: A History*. Norman: University of Oklahoma Press, 2005.

Nairne, Thomas. *Nairne's Muskhogean Journals: The 1708 Expedition to the Mississippi River*. Edited by Alexander Moore. Jackson: University Press of Mississippi, 1988.

New South Associates. "Keowee-Toxaway Hydroelectric Project Historic Context." Federal Energy Regulatory Commission, Project No. 2503 (February 22, 2008).

Nichols, David Andrew. *Red Gentlemen and White Savages: Indians, Federalists, and the Search for Order on the American Frontier*. Charlottesville: University of Virginia Press, 2008.

Niles, Hezekiah, ed. *The Weekly Register*, 75 vols. Baltimore: Franklin Press, 1811–1849.

Nooe, F. Evan. "Common Justice: Vengeance and Retribution in Creek Country." *Ethnohistory* 62, no. 4 (April 2015): 241–61.

———. "'Renders It Necessary That We Should Be Prepared': A Reexamination of the Militant South Thesis in Territorial Florida." MA thesis, Clemson University, 2008.

———. "'Zealous in the Cause': The Second Seminole War and the Southern Consciousness." *Native South*. 4 (2011): 55–81.

Norton, John. *The Journal of Major John Norton, 1816*. Edited by Carl F. and James J. Talman. Toronto: Champlain Society, 1970.

Oakes, Timothy. "Place and the Paradox of Modernity." *Annals of the Association of American Geographers* 87, no. 3 (September 1997): 509–31.

O'Brien, Greg. "The Conqueror Meets the Unconquered: Negotiating Cultural Boundaries on the Post-Revolutionary Southern Frontier." *Journal of Southern History* 67, no. 1 (February 2001): 39–72.

O'Brien, Jean M. *Firsting and Lasting: Writing Indians out of Existence in New England*. Minneapolis: University of Minnesota Press, 2010.

O'Donnell, James H. III. *Southern Indians in the American Revolution*. Knoxville: University of Tennessee Press, 1973.

O'Neill, John Belton, and John A. Chapman. *The Annals of Newberry in Two Parts*. Newberry, SC: Aull & Houseal, 1892.

Onuf, Peter S. *Jefferson's Empire: The Language of American Nationhood.* Charlottesville: University Press of Virginia, 2000.

Opal, J. M. *Avenging the People: Andrew Jackson, the Rule of Law, and the American Nation.* New York: Oxford University Press, 2017.

Ostler, Jeffrey. *Surviving Genocide: Native Nations and the United States from the American Revolution to Bleeding Kansas.* New Haven: Yale University Press, 2019.

Owens, Robert M. *Red Dreams, White Nightmares: Pan-Indian Alliances in the Anglo-American Mind, 1763–1815.* Norman: University of Oklahoma Press, 2015.

Owsley, Frank L., and Gene A. Smith. *Filibusters and Expansionists: Jeffersonian Manifest Destiny, 1800–1821.* Tuscaloosa: University of Alabama Press, 1997.

Owsley, Frank L. Jr. "Prophet of War: Josiah Francis and the Creek War." *American Indian Quarterly* 9, no. 3 (Summer 1985): 273–93.

———. *Struggle for the Gulf Borderlands: The Creek War and the Battle of New Orleans, 1812–1815.* Gainesville: University Presses of Florida, 1981.

Paschall, Edwin. *Old Times; or, Tennessee History, for Boys and Girls.* Nashville: Southern Methodist Publishing House, 1869.

The Payne-Butrick Papers: Volumes 4, 5, 6. Edited and annotated by William L. Anderson, Jane L. Brown, and Anne F. Rogers. Lincoln: University of Nebraska Press, 2010.

Perdue, Theda. "George Washington and the 'Civilization' of the Southern Indians." In *George Washington's South,* edited by Tamara Harvey and Greg O'Brien, 313–26. Gainesville: University Press of Florida, 2004.

———. "The Legacy of Indian Removal." *Journal of Southern History* 79, no. 1 (February 2013): 3–36.

Perdue, Theda, and Michael Green. *The Cherokee Removal: A Brief History with Documents.* Boston: Bedford/St. Martin's Press, 2004.

Perkins, Elizabeth. *Border Life: Experience and Memory in the Revolutionary Ohio Valley.* Chapel Hill: University of North Carolina Press, 1998.

[Perry, Benjamin F.]. "The Revolutionary History of South Carolina." *Southern Quarterly Review* 11, no. 22 (1847): 468–85.

———. "Revolutionary Incidents." *Magnolia; or Southern Apalachian* 2, no. 6 (June 1843).

Peterson, John H. Jr. "The Indian in the Old South." In *Red, White, and Black: Symposium on Indians in the Old South,* edited by Charles M. Hudson, 116–33. Athens: University of Georgia Press, 1971.

Phillips, Jason. *Diehard Rebels: The Confederate Culture of Invincibility.* Athens: University of Georgia Press, 2007.

Phillips, Ulrich Bonnell. *Life and Labor in the Old South.* Introduction by John David Smith. Columbia: University of South Carolina Press, 2007.

Pickett, Albert James. *History of Alabama, and Incidentally of Georgia and Mississippi, from the Earliest Period.* Vol. 2. Charleston: Walker and James, 1851.

Piker, Joshua. *The Four Deaths of Acorn Whistler: Telling Stories in Colonial America.* Cambridge: Harvard University Press, 2013.

———. *Okfuskee: A Creek Indian Town in Colonial America.* Cambridge: Harvard University Press, 2004.

Porter, Kenneth W. *The Black Seminoles: History of a Freedom-Seeking People.* Revised and edited by Alcione M. Amos and Thomas P. Senter. Gainesville: University Press of Florida, 1996.

Potter, David M. "The Historian's Use of Nationalism and Vice Versa." *American Historical Review* 67, no. 4 (July 1962): 924–50.

———. *The Impending Crisis, 1848–1861*. Completed and edited by Don E. Fehrenbacher. New York: Harper & Row, 1976.

Potter, Woodburne. *The War in Florida: Being an Exposition of Its Causes, and an Accurate History of the Campaigns of Generals, Gaines and Scott*. Baltimore: Lewis and Coleman, 1836.

Prince, Henry. *Amidst a Storm of Bullets: The Diary of Lt. Henry Prince in Florida, 1836–1842*. Edited by Frank Laumer, with a foreword by John K. Mahon. Tampa: University of Tampa Press, 1998.

Prucha, Francis Paul. *The Great Father: The United States Government and the American Indians*. Vols. 1 and 2 unabridged. Lincoln: University of Nebraska Press, 1984.

Putnam, A. W. *History of Middle Tennessee: or, Life and Times of Gen. James Robertson*. Nashville: Southern Methodist Publishing House, 1859.

Ramsey, James. *The Annals of Tennessee to the End of the Eighteenth Century*. Charleston: John Russell, 1853.

Ray, Kristofer. *Middle Tennessee: Progress and Popular Democracy on the Southwestern Frontier*. Knoxville: University of Tennessee Press, 2007.

Reid, John Phillip. *A Law of Blood: The Primitive Law of the Cherokee Nation*. DeKalb: Northern Illinois University Press, 2006.

Remini, Robert V. *Andrew Jackson—Volume One: The Course of American Empire, 1767–1812* Baltimore: Johns Hopkins University Press, 1998.

———. *Andrew Jackson and His Indian Wars*. Boston: Penguin, 2002.

Reznikoff, Charles. *The Jews of Charleston, a History of an American Jewish Community*. Philadelphia: Jewish Publication Society of America, 1950.

Rindfleisch, Bryan C. *George Galphin's Intimate Empire: The Creek Indians, Family, and Colonialism in Early America*. Tuscaloosa: University of Alabama Press, 2019.

Riordan, Patrick. "Finding Freedom in Florida: Native Peoples, African Americans, and Colonists, 1670–1816." *Florida Historical Quarterly* 75, no. 1 (Summer 1996): 24–43.

Robertson, James. "Correspondence of Gen. James Robertson." *American Historical Magazine* 1, no. 3 (1896): 280–91.

Rodning, Christopher B. "Reconstructing the Coalescence of Cherokee Communities in Southern Appalachia." In *The Transformation of the Southeastern Indians, 1540–1760*, edited by Robbie Ethridge and Charles Hudson, 155–75. Jackson: University Press of Mississippi, 2002..

Rosen, Deborah A. *American Indians and State Law: Sovereignty, Race, and Citizenship, 1790–1880*. Lincoln: University of Nebraska Press, 2007.

———. *Border Law: The First Seminole War and American Nationhood*. Cambridge: Harvard University Press, 2015.

Rothman, Adam. *Slave Country: American Expansion and the Origins of the Deep South*. Cambridge: Harvard University Press, 2005.

Rowland, Dunbar. *Encyclopedia of Mississippi History*. Madison: Selwyn A. Brant, 1907.

———. *The Official Letter Books of W. C. C. Claiborne, 1800–1816*. 6 vols. Jackson: Mississippi State Department of Archives and History, 1917.

Rubin, Anne Sarah. *A Shattered Nation: The Rise and Fall of the Confederacy, 1861–1868*. Chapel Hill: University of North Carolina Press, 2005.

Rucker, Brian R. "In the Shadow of Jackson: Uriah Blue's Expedition into West Florida." *Florida Historical Quarterly* 73, no. 3 (January 1995): 325–38.

Rumple, Jethro. *History of Rowan County North Carolina*. Charlotte: Observer Printing House, 1916.

Sachs, Honor. *Home Rule: Households, Manhood, and National Expansion on the Eighteenth-Century Kentucky Frontier*. New Haven: Yale University Press, 2015.

Saunt, Claudio. *A New Order of Things: Property, Power, and the Transformation of the Creek Indians, 1733–1816*. Cambridge: Cambridge University Press, 1999.

———. *Unworthy Republic: The Dispossession of Native Americans and the Road to Indian Territory*. New York: W. W. Norton, 2020.

Seeman, Erik R. *Death in the New World: Cross-Cultural Encounters, 1492–1800*. Philadelphia: University of Pennsylvania Press, 2010.

The Seminole Tribe of Florida. "History: Indian Resistance and Removal." www.semtribe.com. Accessed April 19, 2022.

Shire, Laurel Clark. *The Threshold of Manifest Destiny: Gender and National Expansion in Florida*. Philadelphia: University of Pennsylvania Press, 2016.

Shoemaker, Nancy. *A Strange Likeness: Becoming Red and White in Eighteenth-Century North America*. Oxford: Oxford University Press, 2004.

Shuck-Hall, Sheri Marie. "Alabama and Coushatta Diaspora and Coalescence in the Mississippian Shatter Zone." In *Mapping the Mississippian Shatter Zone: The Colonial Indian Slave Trade and Regional Instability in the American South*, edited by Robbie Ethridge and Sheri M. Shuck-Hall, 250–71. Lincoln: University of Nebraska Press, 2009.

Silver, Peter. *Our Savage Neighbors: How Indian War Transformed Early America*. New York: W. W. Norton, 2007.

Silverberg, Robert. *Mound Builders of Ancient America: The Archeology of a Myth*. Greenwich: New York Graphic Society, LTD, 1968.

Silverman, David. *Faith and Boundaries: Colonists, Christianity, and Community among the Wampanoag Indians of Martha's Vineyard, 1600–1871*. New York: Cambridge University Press, 2005.

———. *Thundersticks: Firearms and the Violent Transformation of Native America*. Cambridge: Belknap Press of Harvard University, 2016.

Simmons, William H. *Notices of East Florida, A Facsimile Reproduction of the 1822 Edition*. Introduction and index by George E. Buker. Gainesville: University of Florida Press, 1973.

Simms, William Gilmore. "The Mountain Tramp." In *An Early and Strong Sympathy: The Indian Writings of William Gilmore Simms*, edited by John Caldwell Guilds and Charles Hudson, 504–72. Columbia: University of South Carolina Press, 2003.

Skelton, William B. *An American Profession of Arms: The Army Officer Corps, 1784–1861*. Lawrence: University Press of Kansas, 1992.

Slotkin, Richard. *Regeneration through Violence: The Mythology of the American Frontier, 1600–1860*. Norman: University of Oklahoma Press, 1973.

Smith, William Wragg. *Sketch of the Seminole War and Sketches during the Campaign, by a Lieutenant of the Left Wing*. Charleston: Dan J. Dowling, 1836.

Smithers, Gregory D. *The Cherokee Diaspora: An Indigenous History of Migration, Resettlement, and Identity*. New Haven: Yale University Press, 2015.

———. *Native Southerners: Indigenous History from Origins to Removal*. Norman: University Press of Oklahoma, 2019.

Snay, Mitchell. *Gospel of Disunion: Religion and Separatism in the Antebellum South*. Chapel Hill: University of North Carolina Press, 1993.

Snow, Dean R. "Iroquois-Huron Warfare." In *North American Indigenous Warfare and Ritual Violence*, edited by Richard J. Chacon and Rubén G. Mendoza, 151–52. Tucson: University of Arizona Press, 2007.

Snyder, Christina. "Conquered Enemies, Adopted Kin, and Owned People: The Creek Indians and Their Captives." *Journal of Southern History* 73, no. 2 (May 2007): 255–88.

———. "The Once and Future Moundbuilders." *Southern Cultures* 26, no. 2 (Summer 2020): 96–116.

———. *Slavery in Indian Country: The Changing Face of Captivity in Early America*. Cambridge: Harvard University Press, 2010.

Snyder, Christina, and Theda Perdue. "The Native South." In *Reinterpreting Southern Histories: Essays in Historiography*, edited by Craig Thompson Friend and Lori Glover, 415–44. Baton Rouge: Louisiana State University Press, 2020.

Soja, Edward. *Postmodern Geographies: The Reassertion of Space in Critical Social Theory*. London: Verso, 1989.

Sprague, John T. *The Origins, Progress and Conclusion of the Florida War*. New York: D. Appleton, 1848. Reproduction by Seminole Wars Historic Foundation, with an introduction by John K. Mahon. Tampa: University of Tampa Press, 2000.

Stagg, J. C. A. *The War of 1812: Conflict for a Continent*. Cambridge: Cambridge University Press, 2012.

Stiggins, George. *Creek Indian History: A Historical Narrative of the Genealogy, Traditions and Downfall of the Ispocoga or Creek Indian Tribe of Indians*. With an introduction. and notes by William Stokes Wyman. Edited by Virginia Pounds Brown. Birmingham: University of Alabama Press, 1989.

Stowe, Steven M. *Intimacy and Power in the Old South: Ritual in the Lives of the Planters*. Baltimore: Johns Hopkins University Press, 1987.

Sturtevant, William C. "Creek into Seminole." In *North American Indians in Historical Perspective*, edited by Eleanor Burke Leacock and Nancy Oestreich Lurie, 92–128. Prospect Heights, IL: Waveland Press, 1988.

Swain, D. L. "Historical Sketch of the Indian War of 1776." *North Carolina University Magazine* 1, no. 4 (May 1852): 132–36.

Swanton, John R. "Social Organization and Social Usages of the Indians of the Creek Confederacy." *42nd Annual Report of the Bureau of American Ethnology*, 23–272 Washington, DC: Government Printing Office, 1928.

Sydnor, Charles S. *The Development of Southern Sectionalism, 1819–1848*. Baton Rouge: Louisiana State University Press, 1948.

Tatum, Howell. "Howell Tatum's Journal while Acting Topographical Engineer to Andrew Jackson Commanding the Seventh Military District," edited by John Spencer Bassett. *Smith College Studies in History* 7, no. 1–3 (October 1921 to April 1922).

Taylor, Alan. *American Republics: A Continental History of the United States, 1783–1850.* New York: W. W. Norton, 2021.

Taylor, Mia. "Early Recollections of Madison County." *Huntsville Historical Review* 2, no. 2 (April 1972): 20–35.

Taylor, William R. *Cavalier and Yankee: The Old South and American National Character.* New ed. New York: Oxford University Press, USA, 1993.

Timmerman, Nicholas A. "Contested Indigenous Landscapes: Indian Mounds and the Political Creation of the Mythical 'Mound Builder' Race." *Ethnohistory* 67, no. 1 (January 2020): 75–96.

Tocqueville, Alexis de. *Democracy in America.* Edited by Phillips Bradley. New York: Knopf, 1945.

Tolnay, Stewart E., and E. M. Beck. *A Festival of Violence: An Analysis of Southern Lynchings, 1882–1930.* Urbana: University of Illinois Press, 1995.

Trouillot, Michel-Rolph. *Silencing the Past: Power and the Production of History.* Boston: Beacon Press, 1995.

Tschuggnail, Karoline, and Harald Welzer. "Rewriting Memories: Family Recollections of the National Socialist Past in Germany." *Culture & Psychology* 8, no. 1 (2002): 130–45.

Turner, Frederick Jackson. "Geographic Sectionalism in American History." *Annals of the Association of American Geographers* 16, no. 2 (June 1926): 85–93.

Vehik, Susan C. "Conflict, Trade, and Political Development on the Southern Plains." *American Antiquity* 67, no. 1 (January 2002): 37–64.

Veracini, Lorenzo. *Settler Colonialism: A Theoretical Overview.* New York: Palgrave Macmillan, 2010.

Vokopola, Kemal. "The Albanian Customary Law." *Quarterly Journal of the Library of Congress* 25, no. 4 (October 1968): 306–16.

US Congress. *Annals of Congress, Debates and Proceedings in the Congress of the United States, 1789–1825.* Vol. 6. Washington, DC: Gales and Seaton, 1849.

———. *Congressional Globe: Sketches of the Debates and Proceedings.* 24th Congress, 1st Session. Vol. 2–3. Washington, DC: Blair & Rivers, 1836.

———. *Journals of the Continental Congress, 1774–1789.* Vol. 27. Washington, DC: Government Printing Office, 1928.

———. *United States Statutes at Large, 1789–1799.* Vol. 1. Washington, DC: Little, Brown, 1845.

Wallace, Anthony F. C. *Jefferson and the Indians: The Tragic Fate of the First Americans.* Cambridge: Belknap Press of Harvard University, 1999.

Warren, Jamie. "To Claim One's Own: Death and the Body in the Daily Politics of Antebellum Slavery." In *Death and the American South*, edited by Craig Thompson Friend and Lorri Glover, 110–30. New York: Cambridge University Press, 2015.

Warren, Stephen. *The Worlds the Shawnees Made: Migration and Violence in Early America.* Chapel Hill: University of North Carolina Press, 2014.

Waselkov, Gregory A. *A Conquering Spirit: Fort Mims and the Redstick War of 1813–1814.* Tuscaloosa: University of Alabama Press, 2009.

Watson, Samuel. "Seminole Strategy, 1812–1858: A Perspective for Further Research." *America's Hundred Years' War: U.S. Expansion to the Gulf Coast and the Fate of the Seminole, 1763–1858.* Gainesville: University Press of Florida, 2011, 155–80.

Weber, David J. "The Spanish Legacy in North America and the Historical Imagination." *Western Historical Quarterly* 23, no. 1 (1992): 5–24.

Weisman, Brent Richards. "Archeological Perspectives on Florida Seminole Ethnogenesis." In *Indians of the Greater Southeast: Historical Archeology and Ethnohistory*, edited by Bonnie G. McEwan, 299–317. Gainesville: University Press of Florida, 2000.

———. *Unconquered People: Florida's Seminole and Miccosukee Indians*. Gainesville: University Press of Florida, 1999.

Welch, Andrew. *A Narrative of the Life and Sufferings of Mrs. Jane Johns, Who Was Barbarously Wounded and Scalped by Seminole Indians, in East Florida*. Charleston: Burke & Giles, 1837. Reprinted in *A Narrative of the Early Days and Remembrances of Oceola Nikkanochee, Prince of Econchatti, Written by His Guardian: Facsimile Reproduction of the 1841 Edition, and of the Pamphlets of 1837 and 1847*. With an introduction and indexes by Frank Laumer. Gainesville: University Presses of Florida, 1977.

White, Andrea P. "Refuge among the Spanish: Yamasee Community Coalescence in St. Augustine after 1715." In *The Yamasee Indians: From Florida to South Carolina*, edited by Denise I. Bossy, 251–80. Lincoln: University of Nebraska Press, 2018.

White, Robert H., ed. Messages of the Governors of Tennessee, 1796–1821. Nashville: Tennessee Historical Commission, 1952.

Williams, Alfred B. *Hampton and His Red Shirts: South Carolina's Deliverance in 1876*. Charleston, SC: Walker, Evans, and Cogswell, 1935.

Williams, Daniel E. *Liberty's Captives: Narratives of Confinement in the Print Culture of the Early Republic*. Athens: University of Georgia Press, 2006.

Williams, John Lee. *A View of West Florida*. A Facsimile Reproduction of the 1827 ed. With an introduction by Herbert J. Doherty Jr. Gainesville: University Presses of Florida, 1976.

Wilson, Charles R. *Baptized in Blood: The Religion of the Lost Cause, 1865–1920*. Athens: University of Georgia Press, 1980.

Wilson, John Lyde. *The Code of Honor; or, Rules for the Government of Principles and Seconds in Dueling*. Charleston, SC: Thomas J. Eccles, 1838.

Wilson, Ruth Danenhower. "The Bulow Plantation, 1821–1835." *Florida Historical Quarterly* 23, no. 4 (April 1945): 227–40.

Wood, Amy Louise. *Lynching and Spectacle: Witnessing Racial Violence in America, 1890–1940*. Chapel Hill: University of North Carolina Press, 2009.

Woodward, C. Vann. "The Search for Southern Identity." *The Burden of Southern History*. 3rd ed. Baton Rouge: Louisiana State University Press, 1993, 3–25.

Woodward, Thomas S. *Woodward's Reminiscences of the Creek, or Muscogee Indians, Contained in Letters to Friends in Georgia and Alabama*. Montgomery: Barrett & Wimbish, 1859.

Worth, John E. "Enigmatic Origins: On the Yuchi of the Contact Era." In *Yuchi Indian Histories before the Removal Era*, edited by Jason Baird Jackson, 33–42. Lincoln: University of Nebraska Press, 2012.

———. "Razing Florida: The Indian Slave Trade and the Devastation of Spanish Florida, 1659–1715." In *Mapping the Mississippian Shatter Zone: The Colonial Indian*

Slave Trade and Regional Instability in the American South, edited by Robbie Ethridge and Sheri M. Shuck-Hall, 295–311. Lincoln: University of Nebraska Press, 2009.

Wyatt-Brown, Bertram. *Southern Honor: Ethics and Behavior in the Old South*. New York: Oxford University Press, 1983.

Index